The Honeymoon Ends With "I Do"

The Honeymoon Ends With "I Do"

✦

The Adverse Effect of Marriage on Lasting Love and What You Can Do About It

Rick Lannoye

iUniverse, Inc.
New York Lincoln Shanghai

The Honeymoon Ends With "I Do"

The Adverse Effect of Marriage on Lasting Love and What You Can Do About It

iUniverse books may be ordered through booksellers or by contacting:

iUniverse
2021 Pine Lake Road, Suite 100
Lincoln, NE 68512
www.iuniverse.com
1-800-Authors (1-800-288-4677)

ISBN-13: 978-0-595-43447-3 (pbk)
ISBN-13: 978-0-595-87774-4 (ebk)
ISBN-10: 0-595-43447-9 (pbk)
ISBN-10: 0-595-87774-5 (ebk)

Printed in the United States of America

"Human beings,
who are almost unique in their ability to learn from the experience of others,
are remarkable for their apparent disinclination to do so."

—Douglas Adams

Contents

Introduction

After reading the following conversations about two married couples, see if their stories sound familiar to you.

Conversation One—At the Water Cooler:

Office Worker A: "Hey, do you remember John and Susan?"
Office Worker B: "Sure do. What a happy couple! Never met any two people more in love.
Office Worker A: "Well, you're not gonna believe it … they're getting a divorce!"
Office Worker B: "What? You gotta be kidding. They've been together since college … and I thought they just got married about a year ago."
Office Worker A: "Actually, it was only six months ago."
Office Worker B: "What's up with that? It's not like they rushed things. They dated a long time … and didn't they live together, for like, five years?"
Office Worker A: "More like seven."
Office Worker B: "And the last time I saw them, they seemed happy as clams."
Office Worker A: "Yeah, I thought the same thing."
Office Worker B: (pause) "Makes ya wonder doesn't it?"
Office Worker A: "'Bout what?"
Office Worker B: "Well, what is it about that little piece of paper that just seems to do love in every time?"
Office Worker A: "I don't know. Guess that's why everyone talks about how it's all downhill once the honeymoon is over."

Conversation Two—At a Funeral Home Visitation:

Widow's Friend: "I'm so sorry. I wish I could have come into town sooner."
Widow: "It's OK. It's good to see you."
Widow's Friend: (Motioning to sit at a bench) "Did he, you know, was he in a lot of pain."
Widow: "No, actually, he went quite peacefully."
Widow's Friend: "Well, that's got to be of some comfort to you."
Widow: "What? That he died peacefully?"

Widow's Friend: (Feeling awkward) "Oh, I didn't mean to …"
Widow: "It's alright. But you know as well as I do that Sam and I haven't been … weren't … close for a very long time."
Widow's Friend: "But you had many good years together."
Widow: (Bitterly) "That's what everyone says, don't they? 'Together for 34 years.' 'What a success!' 'They must be doing something right. After all, they stuck it out through thick and thin.' Sure, I stayed. That's what I was always taught—' … 'til death do you part.'"
Widow's Friend: "What are you saying?"
Widow: "I'm saying that everyone is expecting me to be so sad. And that's just it. I'm not. I'm … I'm actually relieved. It's over. It's over, and I'm glad."
Widow's Friend: (Jaw dropping) "You're glad?" "Glad that he's dead?"
Widow: "No, not that he's dead. He was a good man, a good provider. He never mistreated me. It's just that … we weren't happy. Not really. Not like when we were young and still dating. But after we got married something happened. Something died … died between us, a long time ago."

Two very sad stories, but what's even sadder is that we all know people like these two couples whose relationships started out so well, and then things became *different*. In fact, if you've been married for a while, you might be relating all too well to *the change* that comes once the honeymoon is over.

The following chapters of this book are an attempt to look honestly and openly at this very phenomenon. While almost all couples, married or not, report transitioning from intense fires of passionate love to a calmer sense of contentment—especially after living together for any length of time—again and again we hear of love disappearing *altogether* soon after a couple gets married. Even couples that lived together happily *for years* often speak of having lost something once they "finally made a commitment," and many break up within a few months afterwards.

Of course, attempts at living together in a successful relationship fail all the time and for a host of reasons. Regardless of whether a couple chooses to be married or to simply cohabit, they can run into all sorts of serious trouble—being too young and immature, not having good communication skills, interference from family members, financial stress or just plain, old being incompatible. When a couple splits up over any of these obvious causes, we're usually not all that shaken. In fact, break ups like these are often seen coming from miles away. And when they finally play out, there's more often a sense of relief than dismay.

What does rattle us, though, is when we learn about a couple splitting up that seemingly had one of those "marriages made in Heaven." This kind of break up has a way of reaching out and stabbing at the hearts of everyone around them. On one level or another, it forces us to wonder, "If the happiest couple I know can't stay together *and be happy*, then what hope is there for the rest of us?"

To put the same question in a somewhat, more hopeful way, just what can those who are married do when they realize that, not only have the flames of passion gone down, but that they've completely gone out? Should they resign themselves to stay together permanently simply because they vowed to do so? Or should they get divorced and try to "get it right the next time"?

A considerable number choose to stay in their dried up marriages, resigning themselves to low expectations and the singular reassurance that they are, at least, sticking to their vows. They remind themselves about the thousand different ways they'd been warned all their lives that love was doomed to die. Even if they had once hoped for better, when the day finally arrives that they no longer feel anything for their spouse, they quietly say to themselves, "So it's happened just as I'd been told it would." After this, "love" gets a new definition that's devoid of any positive feeling, on the order of "staying together no matter what," "putting up with someone," or even "quietly taking abuse."

Many others, though, opt to divorce with the belief that they just didn't marry the right person. They often say, "I'm gonna really be picky next time," comparing each potential new mate with a "laundry list" of higher expectations. They don't want to have to redefine love, or at least, they want to be better compensated when they do. Unfortunately, that list tends to get longer and longer with every disappointing attempt at a relationship thereafter.

Still, they keep trying. Nowadays, it's not uncommon to find people who have been married two, three, even four times. Even those who've lost huge sums of money to divorce court attorneys and suffered through horrendous custody fights and property disputes, both men and women alike will sign up again and again, each time thinking, "This time, things will be different." Why?

For more than a few, the answer is a cynical one. To these the idea of being happy in love for any length of time is regarded as a farce, and a "good marriage" is simply the lesser of evils as compared to single life. One hears their cynicism in the ever constant complaints they make about the woes of married life, only to be confounded by the reality of these same complainants either staying married or quickly remarrying once they finally divorce.

Comedians would be at a significant loss for material were it not so common for those who are so unhappy in marriage to marry and marry again—"So and so must be crazy for getting remarried, doesn't he know the definition for insanity is doing the same thing over and over, each time thinking that the result is somehow going to turn out differently!" Or my personal favorite, "Marriage is like the military. Everyone knocks it, but you'd be surprised to learn how many re-enlist!"

Why, then, do people marry with such optimism—thinking they have finally found Mr. or Ms. "Right," only to be repeatedly disappointed? Why do so many more finally throw their hands up and settle into a marriage with a Mr. or Ms. Will Do?

And just to make the mystery of love and Marriage even tougher to figure out, why is it that every now and then we run into a couple that does, indeed, seem to have the perfect relationship?

Like most people, I never bothered to question why we married, or why marriage so often failed, until I found myself reeling from a painful divorce of my own. My first wife and I were, by all accounts, a perfect match. We dated for years. We even waited until our wedding night before we "went all the way." We had two wonderful, healthy children. It should have been all a couple could ask for, but no sooner was my second son weaned, it all fell apart. In what I now know to be an all too familiar tale, we soon found ourselves caught up in a costly and emotionally traumatizing custody suit.

But unlike what happens to most men, I was able to prevail in the suit. It took a year and three months of agony, and not to mention $50,000 in legal and other professional fees, but I was awarded the custody of my two young sons. Afterward, I was led by every expert involved to think that the only reason all this happened was because I had picked the wrong person to marry. Presumably, then, I could now go on to find someone else who would make a good wife and mother.

At first I bought this logic, and determined to press on as a single parent, and in time, I tried dating again. But as the years went by, my sons got bigger, and I went in and out of several relationships, a pattern was emerging in my love life that was anything but encouraging. It was as if I were seeking a mirage that would disintegrate each time I thought I'd finally found someone with whom I could have a happy, as well as an enduring, union.

I was haunted. Somewhere deep inside, I felt that something was still very wrong. It's hard to say exactly why, but as I asked myself so many of the common questions about love, attraction, relationships and marriage, for some reason, I found myself wondering about a question that no one else seemed to be willing even to think about, much less verbalize, "Could it be Marriage itself?"

No sooner had I begun to question whether Marriage itself might be the culprit behind the failure of so many relationships—and especially once I began to voice those questions out loud—I quickly discovered that I was already deep in territory where angels feared to tread! Every time I said something even remotely hinting that Marriage could do love in, I got the same look that said, "How dare you?" It was as if everyone in the world had bound themselves to some secret agreement that no matter how many married couples are unhappy, we can only blame anybody and anything but the institution itself.

I was taken back at first, but the more I heard others protest, the more intrigued I became, and the more I wondered, "If there's nothing wrong with Marriage itself, then why all the resistance to merely asking?" I finally decided that I was going to get to the bottom of this mystery ... no matter how long it took.

Thus began my odyssey which, indeed, was to last as long as the adventures of Homer's famous hero. And just as long as Odysseus' journey home, it was only after a full decade of contemplation, research and hundreds of personal interviews, that I finally discovered the *main* reason why so many happy relationships run afoul after saying "I do."

Sure, not understanding certain things about the opposite gender, getting involved with someone who has serious problems, and searching for love in places where people with serious problems tend to hang out, don't lend themselves to having healthy and lasting relationships. But none of these are the biggest threat to enduring love. No, the biggest problem in most relationships after marriage, even those that have everything else going for them, stems from what is all too often overlooked—*that there is something wrong with Marriage itself.*

Regardless of how much our culture reveres the institution of Marriage, the time has come to call the institution itself into question. Our society clings steadfastly to Marriage no matter how much sadness people experience in relation to it. The institution is lauded and protected ... even though it's universally understood that marital happiness dissipates rapidly after the honeymoon. The anecdotes which matter-of-factly point up the ubiquity of marital discontent, are without number, and yet, when one openly challenges Marriage's legitimacy, more than a few cry, "Heresy!"

I quickly learned that, regardless of how unhappy so many were *in their marriage*, it was the *idea* of marital happiness—however fleeting it may be for them personally—that was so difficult to part with! Try asking if there isn't something about "tying the knot" that chokes love to death, and you're likely to hear, as I have hundreds of time, the protest, "Why that can't be true! I know some people who are happily married!" Even if people can't explain exactly what good Marriage does for love, they cling steadfastly to the belief that it must do so, and base this leap of faith on the rare observation of at least a few happily married couples.

These protests miss the point, though, and the logic they are based on is faulted. As I hope to demonstrate to the reader in detail, the problem with the assertion that Marriage does something good for love cannot be based merely on the fact that there are some examples of happily married couples. To do so is to presume that the *reason* these couples are happy is *because* they are married. But it is also very possible that the *cause* of their ongoing happiness with each other is something else, something which is somehow still operating with no help at all from their having said, "I do."

Let it be made clear, then, that the thesis of this book is *not* to say that it's impossible to be happy *and married*. We can all probably think of at least one married couple that is as much, if not more, in love now than ever before. Instead, the far more important question—which *is* the principle assertion of this book—is that those married couples who are truly happy, are not happy *because* they are married! To put it another way, in those cases where a married couple's relationship *is* good, what's making it good is doing so *in spite of Marriage … not as a result* of it.

From that assertion, I then go on to provide what I am convinced is the answer to the next logical question, an alternative to Marriage as we know it and the way our society practices it. It was not enough for me to merely discover what disease was behind the failure of lasting love, but to find a cure for it. Having learned that the institution of Marriage, as we know it today, does nothing to enhance, and is also a principle contributing factor to the sickness of many, if not most relationships, it behooved me to find a healthy alternative to it.

Of course, the assertion that a cure for unsuccessful marriage hinges on just what people mean when they use the term "successful," in the context of Marriage. For many, "a successful marriage" means nothing more than not divorcing. As long as a couple is staying together under the same roof, even if there exists domestic violence, chemical addiction, no sex life and a great deal of personal unhappiness, their "commitment" is deemed "success." Conversely, many of those who define "success" in this way also regard their separation or divorce as a "failure," even when a couple had many happy years together *before* things changed and they broke up as a result.

For the purposes of this study, though, a "relationship failure" will refer only to a *general and persistent* state of discontent between sexual partners who've lived together for a substantial length of time. Being "unhappy" with one's partner, here, is to be understood as a *chronic condition*. It is not to be confused with intermittent periods of time where, due to an argument for example, a couple may *temporarily* not "feel happy" with each other. I also hope to distinguish clearly between chronic unhappiness and the tendency for sexual passion to "calm down" after a couple begins living together. I will attempt to explain why it is only natural that intense passion is usually replaced by a calmer sense of general contentment that remains in tact even when there are periodic fights or times of difficulty.

When, therefore, in this work I speak of a relationship *failing*, I mean something quite different. It is only when a couple's ardor is *substantially* extinguished, and they find themselves in a state of *chronic* discontent, that I describe their relationship as "failing." Those who stay married after entering this chronic state of unhappiness are (in this book anyway) regarded as not succeeding at anything other than prolonging their misery. Likewise, a couple could end a long term relationship but still regard part or even all of their past experience together as "successful." The idea here is that, just because their togetherness didn't last an entire lifetime, there's no reason to pretend those good times never happened once they've stopped.

Now, some might take my definition of relationship success the wrong way. Just because I don't believe staying together for a lifetime is, by itself, a mark of success, this book is by no means advocating against life-long relationships. I only mean to make the case that fundamental relationship happiness outweighs longevity. I will show, for instance, that while staying together doesn't always mean both partners are happy with each other, *being happy with each other almost always results in couples staying together.* Simple as this last sentence sounds, it's a profound truth that we'll be fathoming again and again.

No doubt, there will be a number of persons who won't be able to grasp the idea that it's even possible to have a relationship "'til death do us part" without some external power—whether the State, the Church, or both—*forcing them* to do so. These folks will likely misconstrue the assertion being made here that *it is Marriage, not Unmarriage, which is the far greater threat to the longevity of happy relationships.* For those who are loath to openly admit that Marriage comes down to a matter of *compelling* people to remain bedfellows, when they would otherwise choose not to, this read is going to be a painful one. I go to considerable length to expose the fallacy of assigning any virtue to the notion of compelling love, but I do try to explain the history and identify the social changes which led to the creation and perpetuation of this false virtue.

Though it's already been implied, the term "Marriage" will be used throughout this work to mean that state whereby a couple obtains sanction for a sexual relationship by legal contract and religious ceremony. We will, therefore, make a distinction between those who are "legally married," and those who simply wish to cohabit in a sexual pair bond. Many other works—especially by anthropologists, sociologists and even zoologists—blur this line, even referring to an animal pair bond as a "married couple." While such broad usage of the term might be useful in other contexts, here it would be very inappropriate. For example, one of the supporting points in this work is that successful, long term, human pair bonding existed eons before the inventions of state licensing or religious sanctification of sexual relationships.

A note to any experts who are accustomed to reading long, scholarly works that are heavily documented and loaded with specialized vocabulary: This work has not been written primarily with specialists (such as anthropologists, sociologists, etc.) in mind. While I've taken care to be accurate and to maintain as decent a level of scholarship as possible, I've also tried to make this work readable for the average "Joe" and "Jane." Experts are, therefore, asked to be tolerant when details seem to give way to what might appear to be over-simplifications.

A couple words also to conservative Christian readers who tend to very literal interpretations of the Bible, especially those who are very sensitive to having their beliefs called into question. This work will reference quite a number of Biblical passages to demonstrate how the Bible has been used to enforce sexual standards that were established long before the Bible was written. Some may take this use of the Bible as a form of sacrilege, and conclude that it's my intent to attack their faith. The truth is I have simply focused on getting answers to questions about human sexuality that have vexed humanity for thousands of years. It's neither my purpose to defend nor to attack Christianity. However, when there is evidence that demands a verdict (sorry Josh, I couldn't help it), and when the judgments of Reason show up some of the claims of the Church to be false, then they are presented with no apology.

To those readers who have difficulty with the idea that every living species owes it's specific, genetic traits to evolutionary forces because they cannot bring themselves to believe that Life itself may have arisen due to natural forces, it's my hope that they will, at least, be open-minded to the evidence that supports the Neo-Darwinian view of how species have changed since life first began. One may very well believe that a creator God spoke the universe into existence and made from nothing the first living organism, and still accept that God also saw fit to employ Evolution as *the means* by which that original creation could respond and mutate itself to adjust to ever changing environments. After all, it would only make sense for an all-knowing Deity or Superior Intelligence that had made from nothing the first living cell, to also give it the ability to adapt by virtue of a process that science calls Natural Selection.

I have become fully convinced in the theory of Evolution as it pertains to the way living beings became what they are today, including my own species, *Homo sapiens.* Much of the reason I've become so convinced is because, time and again, the instinctive behaviors of both man and beast, from the humble amoebae to Albert Einstein, have no good explanation to them ... until we see them under the light of Natural Selection.

Sometimes also called the "Survival of the Fittest," this natural process rewards certain organisms with survival and reproductive success whenever otherwise random *mutations* give them a better edge over their fellow organisms in adapting to their environment. The better adapted live on, reproduce and pass on the new, mutated genes to their successors. Thus, all living creatures evolve.

We often think of mutations as being bad. The very word "mutant" immediately brings to mind images of horrific, two-headed monsters or pitiful victims of birth defects. But the word is really just another way to designate genetic "change." Rather than being a "freak occurrence," as population geneticist Spencer Wells has pointed out, genetic changes to DNA that are passed on to subsequent generations—what are also called "polymorphisms"—happen all the time. In fact, they occur at a very predictable rate—for humans, 20 to 30 per individual, per generation—and for the most part, go unnoticed.[1] They serve as a genetic first aid kit that, just like the ones at home or work, may even collect a lot of dust until a special situation arises, and then they're suddenly needed. Evolution occurs at the point where one of these genetic variations gives one organism a one-up on survival and reproductive success over other members of its species. Those carrying within them the less adaptive genes, don't reproduce as well, and eventually die out, taking their less adaptive genes with them. In this manner, species change, favoring genes that ultimately determine the size of our brains, what we look like and how we behave toward the opposite sex.

In this discussion of Marriage, we'll be looking very closely at how the process of Natural Selection acted to encourage certain behavioral traits that did much to help our species adapt and survive during it's longest period of existence—The Hunting and Gathering Era—and how those innate tendencies affect us today. We'll also look at how many of the genetically induced behaviors that effect most of the ways we behave sexually developed millions of years before hominids ever came along. To be sure, our species and our closest, hominid ancestors were tweaked by Natural Selection a bit differently, and I spend a good portion of this study remarking on these distinctions. But on the whole, males and females of most every species—from insects to birds, from reptiles to mammals—contend with very similar "primary directives" when it comes to sex and sexual relationships.

For any who are interested in a much more in depth understanding of these issues from a strictly biological science perspective, I highly recommend *The Myth of Monogamy, Fidelity and Infidelity in Animals and People* by authors David P. Barash, Ph. D., and Judith Eve Lipton, M.D. I mention this work in particular because it does such a good job of differentiating between social pair bonding and sexual monogamy. We often assume that these terms are interchangeable, but the evidence for both our kind and most every other sexually reproducing species tells us otherwise. Falling in love and making a home with a mate is natural, but so is the tendency to eventually stray from home to have sex with others. I address these issues as well, but from a much broader perspective, and hopefully, from one a little easier for the lay person to grasp. In any case, my quest for an answer to enduring love was only completed once I found what might truly fulfill that which Marriage only promises—fidelity!

I began my research for this book with a very different hypothesis from what is contained herein. I began thinking sexual monogamy was a natural state, and that it could be obtained and happily maintained if we could only shed the coercion of Marriage. But I had to eventually abandon any notion that monogamy was possible to happily maintain without honestly accepting the reality that it *never* comes naturally … not for very long anyway. The traditional answer to this dilemma is a simplified one—fidelity can only be accomplished by brutal force, by capturing and caging natural desire by sacred vows, legal restrains and social deterrents. So, I was confronted by the even bigger question, "Ought we to abandon the idea of fidelity altogether in favor of living in harmony with our natural state or resign ourselves to the traditional view of resignation to a life time of suppressing what we really want." Neither of these prospects sounded very good to me. Was there not a better way?

While Marriage does most of the damage to otherwise happy relationships by *shortening* the period of time one will naturally desire to be with only one sexual partner, I realized that maintaining happiness in love was going to take more than merely avoiding Marriage. The evidence for sexual infidelity being very common—especially from genetic studies in recent years of the paternity of offspring in of a multitude of species, including our own—was overwhelming. And if sexual monogamy is only encouraged by Nature for limited periods of time, than was my quest for the way to enduring love all for naught? Would avoiding Marriage only, at best, delay the inevitable? Thankfully, that third path finally did become visible after wading through a thick forest of questions and research, leading to more questions and even deeper research. It was somewhere in the middle of that dense forest that a light broke through, and there it was. I've given that rarely treaded path or process a name, "Fooling Mother Nature."

I'm frequently confronted with the question, "Don't many people who just live together also cheat, become unhappy with each other and break up just like married couples often do?" And the answer is, "Yes, indeed." As hard as it is to convince others that Marriage is a major threat to enduring love, I found myself equally bound to explain that it's not enough to simply cohabit with a lover. If I may resort to the forest paths metaphor one more time, yes, it's important to get off the wrong path of trying to compel love, but equally important, we need to find the right path and follow it until it gets us to where we want to go. In this case, the end of that path is enduring love, the kind of love where fidelity is the *effect* of natural causes, not the *cause* of unnatural impositions. It behooves us, then to learn how our sexual nature can be manipulated to work for us, instead of against us, and that is done largely by developing the skill of *mimicry*.

The answer to happy, sexually monogamous relationships, therefore, is two-fold. One, is to avoid, if it's not too late, the external constraint of legal bondage, the fear of social rejection or the threat of divine punishment to *make us* stay faithful. For the unmarried, this step is easy—don't fix what isn't broken by getting married. For the already married, it's a much more difficult process of getting out of the marriage mentality, something which is doable, but which requires considerable effort. However, that's only the first step. It's also very important to actively accommodate the natural tendency to stray by mimicking those conditions under which monogamy does come naturally ... in order to prolong it indefinitely. In the later chapters of this book, I devote considerable space to how this can be done.

For any who might wonder what exactly are my expert credentials that give me "the right to speak with any authority" on the subject of Marriage, relationships and so on, please allow me to explain—I don't have any. I do *not* claim to be any kind of authority whatsoever. Instead, this work is a *naked* presentation, void of the trappings so often made by those who claim to have some special knowledge, revealed only to a privileged few. In other words, if there's any validity to the arguments I bring forward here, they will speak for themselves without any need on my part to cloth it, as it were, with any authoritative claims.

Most everything I present in this book are the results of two things. One, is the personal research I conducted for over ten years, and two, the lessons I gathered from my own mistakes. There's no better teacher than Experience, and there's no better school than the one I went to for a very long time—"The University of Hard knocks." But if the lessons I got—pretty much from repeatedly doing everything the wrong way, for the wrong reason, at the wrong time—will help others to avoid similar pitfalls, then the wounds I suffered won't be all in vain. I have, therefore, very intentionally presented my arguments so that they will either stand or fall *on their own merits*. If anyone reads this book, and subsequently becomes convinced of any of the ideas herein, I want them to be convinced by the weight of the arguments themselves, and not because *I* presented them.

There are hundreds of books written by people who do lay claim to have some authority on the subject of Marriage. Some, like "Doctor" John Gray, author of the well known *Men Are From Mars, Women Are From Venus*, got his doctoral degree from one of those mail order universities. His specific focus is on the differences of the genders, and he's actually on to something there. Others, like Helen Fisher, whom I quote several times, has a real degree from a real university, and has a lot of great, specific things to say about things like the phenomenon of relationship obsolescence, and with some good research to back her up.

What I've done, however, is unique. I have sought to find as much legitimate information as I could—on Marriage, cohabiting couples, what we know about early human history and comparative studies in the animal kingdom—and then *bring them all together* with my many years of personal research and observation. From there, I present my findings, and let you, the reader, be the judge if they make sense or not. If what I believe to be true about Marriage is backed up by reality, then I don't need to *tell you* it's right. You will—as well as you should—find out for yourself.

I don't think the crucial pieces to the puzzle of Marriage's damning effect on lasting love are that far out of reach from the lay person or the experts. However, almost all those who have discovered the same facts I present in this book either fail to piece them together, or if they do and they've seen the picture that emerges, are apparently unwilling to talk about it out loud and even much less willing to put it in writing. No doubt, there is great fear for the repercussions one might suffer by openly calling into question the beneficence of Marriage (and I will admit that I've had to consider what some militant religious fanatics might do if they ever find out where I live!). Whatever such risks, I've chosen to take them, and it's my hope that all who read this work, whether they ultimately agree or disagree with my conclusions will at least appreciate my willingness to open up the discussion for debate.

Therefore, let the reader be forewarned that I am in no way offering any legal or expert relationship advice, nor am I telling anyone what they should or should not do regarding their love lives. I have my opinions, of course, and I invite all to read them, consider them or even challenge them. In the end, though, each of us must decide for ourselves what to do when we think we've met someone with whom we're considering making a home together, and to take full, individual responsibility for the results.

Consequently, I strongly urge anyone who is thinking of moving in together with a lover to first consult with an experienced, certified family law attorney in the state where you live. You need to understand as clearly as possible what the legal ramifications might be. (Too bad this isn't a requirement for people getting legally married.) Some states still have common law marriage provisions that a couple might unwittingly fall prey to. So make certain, before you cohabit, that you don't inadvertently meet such provisions, unless of course, you actually wish to be legally married.

And while I'm talking about things legal, I have quite intentionally avoided getting bogged down by the million or so Marriage law trivia questions which could be speculated upon. It's beyond the scope of this book to decipher in detail every minor change which might become necessary should Marriage ever be privatized. The only legal question contemplated in this work at any length is a very general one—that the State should not be in the business of licensing sexual relationships of mutually consenting adults. Otherwise, I defer to expert attorneys and legislators to argue over those details.

I ask readers, therefore, to use their common sense when it comes to all other legal speculations, and not to waste any time on those that are plainly foolish. For example, removing Marriage from the necessity of State licensure is by no means an endorsement of humans marrying animals (Yes, I've had someone ask me!) or of college roommates claiming the same tax breaks currently offered only to married couples who file jointly.

Just as the Emancipation Proclamation resulted in sweeping changes in the language of federal and state laws and local city ordinances, so too, Privatization, were it ever to occur, would no doubt result in the same. We've made such adjustments before, and while it wouldn't by any means be easy, we certainly could overcome any difficulties with those who would want to justify animal abuse by claiming they ought to be allowed to marry their dog (if I must answer such ludicrous questions), for example, by continuing to hold them accountable under other laws which prevent such behavior on the reasonable basis of animals being quite unable to give their consent.

Let me also clear up another misconstruction. I truly believe it's a wonderful thing for couples who are still unmarried to establish a permanent home together

... as I said, as long as they can avoid common law entanglements depending on which state they live in.

So it may come as a surprise that I also believe it is not, I repeat, *not* a good idea for those who are already married to seek a divorce, unless they intend to permanently separate from one another. However damaging Marriage can be to a healthy and happy relationship, current family law requires those seeking divorce to trek across a veritable minefield of adversarial court procedures before finally letting them go their separate ways. No matter what the good intentions are of a couple who wants to return their relationship to the way it was before they got married, it's too risky, in my opinion, to get divorced in order to do so. Instead, I devote most of the later chapters of this work to the already married to help them undo the damage they may be suffering from having already become part of this institution. They may have to work harder at it than cohabiting couples, but there is hope for them as well.

Some may also find it rather ironic that a liberal like myself who supports gay rights should be arguing for the privatization of Marriage just at the time when gays in the US are in a monumental struggle to be allowed to legally marry. Yes, I do understand that there is a keen sense of legitimacy that gays hope to achieve by winning the right to marry, even if the institution is severely flawed. Nevertheless, I don't hear gays saying that they would be opposed to Privatization as a solution to prevent our leading institutions from discriminating against domestic couples of either sexual orientation. In fact, I've heard them argue that their work to make Same Sex Marriage legal is primarily a pragmatic solution to the discrimination they experience. It remains to be seen, though, which route will be the more difficult to take, whether it's to pragmatically end discrimination or gain the more illusive state of social legitimacy.

While on the topic of same sex relationships, let me point out that I have intentionally restricted the focus of this work to heterosexual behavior. Though some of the principles I outline do have some correlation in gay relationships (which might apply if there's any truth to the popular notion that there is usually one partner who tends to behave as the "female" and the other, the "male"), there are many other works devoted entirely to theories of same sex attraction by people much more expert than I. Therefore, I defer to them and their research.

In this work, I have done my best to speak to every issue in as respectful a manner as possible, hopefully even with a bit of amusement every now and then. On the other hand, I have not shied away from being very frank about certain of my findings when they fly in the face of what is currently regarded as politically correct. Within our culture, for example, we are very loath to admit that love springs from sexual desire. We're told repeatedly that "true love" is something else—something "above" sex, or "better than" sex or "more important" than sex. Well, whatever else love might be in some other abstract dimension or spirit world, I have chosen rather to stand on the hard evidence—that we humans are creatures of flesh and blood, that the matrix of emotional attachments we call "love" are the direct result of genetically induced, biological forces, and that there's no reason to think badly of romantic love just because it is a "carnal" phenomenon.

Now, before we can address the serious question of what exactly is the reason behind Marriage's adverse affect on the bonds of love, we must first try to get some idea of what Marriage really means. Unfortunately, even this preliminary portion of our study is quite challenging. We are talking about an institution that has gone through some very big changes in recent decades. So, I've first begun by trying to distinguish between what Marriage means today from what it meant to our great-grand parents. We'll then look at where, when and how Marriage originated, and how it evolved over the following millennia. Then, once we've gotten some background on where Marriage came from, what it was up until only a couple generations ago, and what it is now, then we can try to predict where it's headed in the future ... and most importantly, whether it's wise to go there.

1

"Traditional Marriage" is History!

o o o o o o o o o o o o o o o o o o o o o o o o o o o o o o o o o o o

"My boyfriend and I moved in together about a year ago … and we plan on getting married next June."

—*Typical young fiancée of the early 21st Century*

This Ain't Your Great-Grandma's Wedding

It wasn't all that long ago that the concept of Marriage for most people included a number of presumptions that are no longer present today. Sure, a couple of generations ago, the average person might agree (as would most people today) that Marriage is a legal contract between a man and a woman who love each other and want to form a permanent home together. But there would have been a whole lot more to it. When Great Grandma was in her 20s, she would have very likely added that Marriage is absolutely necessary *before* any couple can have sex, live together, and bear "legitimate" children "or else "they are subject to the wrath of God." To have premarital sex was to "fornicate," and to cohabit unmarried was to "live in sin."

Nowadays, it's almost the other way around. It's very common for couples who've dated for a while to begin having sex. Rarely do they feel the need to first get official sanction from the Church and State before becoming intimate. If a relationship forms, many couples will begin cohabiting. More interesting, perhaps, others who know these cohabiting couples, even those who still think they are doing something wrong, will tolerate their behavior as long as its with the understanding that they intend to *eventually* get married.

This trend toward "trial marriages," as they are sometimes called, is not only becoming more common, but the length of time couples cohabit is increasing. Sometimes cohabiting couples only begin to seriously discuss getting married after they learn they're going to have a baby.

In fact, the number of cohabiting couples who are either delaying Marriage longer, or never marrying at all, is increasing so much that the gap between the married and the cohabiting will eventually close! According to the US Census Bureau, in the year 2000, there were 5.5 million people in the US who were cohabiting with an intimate partner, a *58% increase* from the 1990 Census of 3.2 million.[3] At this snowballing rate, the percentage of cohabiting couples will outnumber married couples by the year 2150. And while a good number of cohabiting couples in North America eventually get married, the number of couples who cohabit permanently is also increasing dramatically.[4]

For Better or Worse?

Then there is the issue of divorce. When Great Grandma was a young adult, being a divorced woman meant carrying a lot of stigma around (though the incidence of divorce had been steadily rising since the 1900s, almost in exact proportion to the number of women that worked outside the home). Divorce was something that happened "only under the worst conditions," usually only after severe and chronic physical abuse, adultery and drunkenness, and even then, something "to be very ashamed of."

A "Godly woman" who was the victim of a brutal husband was expected to do all she could to endure and suffer silently. The vow "for better or worse," was interpreted quite literally. Abused wives were offered much sympathy, but only as long as she remained faithful to her vows.

No matter how justified, a woman who left her husband was viewed with an eye of suspicion. To be a divorcée was to be thought of as a "loose woman," and much more likely to succumb to the sexual advances of men. She was now "marked," "used," "damaged," because no matter the reason, she had "gone back on her promise to remain forever true." It's no surprise, then, that most women who divorced did so as discreetly as they could.

It's also understandable why most divorcées remarried as quickly as they could, if only to other divorcées. For divorced women, remarriage was particularly important as a way to regain some kind of social legitimacy, even if they had to aim much lower by "settling" for a widower or another divorcée. The stigma attached to women who had "failed at marriage" was way too much for most never-before-married men to consider. Moreover, there was the onus of being single and not a virgin. "No red-blooded American man would ever consider marrying a woman who had been with someone else," was the common logic at this time.

Add to all the above the idea that "divorce was bad for children." It was very common in Great Grandma's earlier days to hear of couples that were very discontent with each other, but who were nevertheless staying together "for the sake of the kids." It was just assumed that it was the duty of married parents to stay together no matter how unhappy they were, no matter how abused they were, no matter if there was adultery, financial mismanagement or chemical abuse. No matter how much the domestic suffering for everyone in the family, it was presumed that it would be even worse for their children to see them separate. Staying married was the lesser of evils.

The family courts did a lot to encourage this view. Normally, one had to have "a really good reason" to get divorced, and to be able to prove it in a court of law. Since family courts were created and designed after the same model as criminal courts, at least one of the spouses had to essentially be proven guilty or "at fault" for the failure of the relationship. *Suspecting* a spouse of infidelity wasn't good enough. Drinking to excess, violence, abandonment, all had to be proved with a "preponderance of evidence" before a divorce could be granted. It wasn't unusual for a couple to go through a harrowing and costly divorce procedure, only for a judge to deny the divorce and order them to counseling.

Thankfully, attitudes about the alleged benefits of constraining married partners to stay together began to change in the 1950s. Multitudes of adult children of unhappily wed parents offered their testimonies to state legislatures, and told of the misery it caused them. Along with hundreds of family counseling professionals, they persuaded one state after another to change their divorce laws to make it less difficult for married couples to permanently separate. Overwhelmingly, their message was the same—"We wish our parents had divorced or divorced sooner; we would have all been much better off." Research on children of divorced parents since then has consistently noted that permanent separation *reduces*, rather than amplifies, the emotional trauma caused by children having to live with incompatible parents.[5]

In 1953, Oklahoma became the first state to introduce "No Fault Divorce." This meant that a spouse could get a divorce without having to prove anything against a partner. More simply put, a spouse could end a marriage simply because he or she wanted to, at least in theory.

No Fault didn't make divorce easy, in that issues of cost, custody of children, child support, alimony, separation of property and all the remaining negative social implications were still prohibitive enough to discourage many from divorcing. Nevertheless, it was finally *legally* possible to get out of a binding sexual union for the asking as long as one was willing to go through the process.

The Oklahoma law was condemned by conservative politicians and preachers all across the country. It was viewed by traditionalists as "just a way for people to back out of their marriage vows." The public, as a whole, wasn't quite ready to accept the idea that people should be allowed to leave a marriage except under the most severe of circumstances. However, for those directly effected, the idea of No Fault Divorce was welcomed as a godsend. Married couples who'd been separated for years and anguishing in long and costly court proceedings could finally hope for closure.

Then, in 1970, the time seemed just right for a change in the general public's attitude toward divorce, as a popular actor-turned-politician led the way. Ronald Reagan—who was at the time governor of California and himself, a divorcée—signed into law a No Fault Divorce provision that many other states quickly imitated. By the end of the 1970s, legal Marriage in most states had gone from "'til death do you part unless there are some very severe problems" to "when either partner wants out." By 1985, all 50 states had legalized No Fault Divorce.

Not surprisingly, the incidence of divorce rose dramatically, and for a time it appeared that the trend would continue until it was almost statistically guaranteed that all marriages would eventually end in divorce. But even with most women working and with every state providing No Fault Divorce, the trend finally leveled off in the 1990s to about 50% for first time marriages.

Why? Traditionalists began to preach that the level off was tangible proof that there must be something very good about Marriage. The problem with their reasoning, though, was it's circularity. To say that people are staying married because it's good to do so, and that it must be good because, well, so many people choose to stay married, doesn't really tell us anything.

Certainly, it would be fanciful to conclude from this data that half of all married couples are happy. Buy the high price of divorce may be the better explanation behind the 50% "success rate" of first time marriages. Though fault is no longer necessary to prove, the divorce process can still be very emotionally traumatic, financially devastating and exhaustively time-consuming. Its adverse consequences remain to this day a strong deterrent to any married couple considering a permanent separation even if they are quite miserable with each other.

Though it is still generally accepted that being a divorcée no longer means that there is something morally wrong with the divorced individuals themselves, the tide of this social toleration of divorce appears to be changing. In recent years, ultra conservatives have argued for a return to some form of Fault Divorce, and have even persuaded three states already—Louisiana, Arkansas and Arizona—to institute "covenant marriages," a legally binding agreement in which couples volunteer to limit the grounds on which they could legally divorce. The state of Michigan is currently looking at proposals that would constrain a divorce petitioner to provide proof of fault if the other partner refuses to agree to the divorce.

The reason for this shift backward certainly has much to do with the political organization and advances of the Religious Right in the past decade or two, but it may also have to do with society's short term memory and, ironically, the successes of No Fault Divorce in preventing domestic trauma to children. After two generations of marrying and divorcing, the reasons for allowing No Fault Divorce in the first place seem to be all but erased from human memory.[6] Without the advantage of having untold thousands who could today personally testify about the horrors of growing up with parents who couldn't stand each other, it's difficult to bring an effective defense against those who are arguing once again that Divorce is, in and of itself, bad for kids.

Another big change since the advent of No Fault Divorce is the definition of Marriage. For most, long gone is the notion that Marriage is an inescapable obligation to the death. While most every marriage ceremony will repeat the words of the famous vow, the fact is that most everyone is quite aware that the expression "'til death do us part" is really just a nice goal, nothing like the gravely serious and very literal obligation it was only a half century before.

◆ ◆ ◆

Clearly, something has radically altered the meaning of Marriage in just the last half century or so. The main reasons people used to give for getting married are for all practical purposes gone with the wind, and yet, the institution itself has survived. There were more than a few social scientists who, back in the 1960s, had predicted that everyone would quit getting married once they quit believing Marriage was necessary for a sexual relationship to be "pleasing to God." But so far, they've been proven wrong. If we could compare Marriage to a building, it's as if the interior has been ripped out and remodeled, and yet, the original framework is still firmly in place.

Why then, if most people, even church people, don't really believe they first need a license from the State and sanction from a minister of God in order to have sex, live with a sexual partner, and even have a baby, do most people get married anyway? Are there other good reasons besides avoiding damnation from

God in order to participate in this institution? Or is it possible that, while many *rationally* conclude in their heads that they need not marry, they still feel so much guilt about not being married that they eventually comply to assuage their consciences? Or is it for the promise of legal protections in the event of a later breakup? Or do people still marry for another reason altogether—thinking that once their partner vows to the death never to leave them, they'll be liberated from the fear of eventual abandonment?

In order to find out the answer to these and other related questions, let's first take a closer look at what getting married really meant to Great-Grandma.[7]

2

What Was Marriage Like For Great-Grandma?

o o o o o o o o o o o o o o o o o o o o o o o o o o o o o o

"Still not expecting? There must be something wrong; they've been married now for over a year. She should go see a doctor!"

—Typical relative of a yet-to-become-pregnant 40s newlywed

Marriage and Sex in the 1940s

Imagine if we could go back in time to ask the average man and woman of the 1940s to talk about their views on Marriage and sexual relationships.[8] Unfortunately, no sooner than asking our first question, we'd immediately run into a problem—very few people are even willing to talk about sex … even within the context of Marriage. Let's recall that this was a time when sex, no matter the context, was still a very taboo topic of conversation. It was considered something "dirty," and a subject no "decent" person would talk about … unless … it was in a "shaded" environment such as a locker room, a night club or an alley way, away from "polite company" and even then, only in whispered voices.

The Double Standard

For the sake of simplicity, though, let's just say that after looking long and hard, we finally found at least one typical man and woman who are willing to reveal their views. We proceed, then, to inquire about the connection between Marriage and sex, and sure enough, we initially get a pretty consistent response—Marriage means, among other things, getting to have sex for the first time. However, it becomes clear as the details of our interview are slowly revealed that "waiting until Marriage to have sex for the first time" has two meanings—one for men and another for women. For men, "waiting until marriage before having sex" meant "that a man shouldn't have sex *with his fiancée* until they are married." But for the bride, "waiting" meant that she *ought not to have ever had sex at all,* not with anyone![9] The woman was to be a virgin.

The typical bridal dress and marriage ceremony traditions reinforced the expectation that a bride should be a virgin. Take the white wedding gown, for instance, which clearly proclaimed the "purity" and "cleanliness" of the bride's body (implying that sex somehow makes one "impure" and "dirty"). Note the wedding veil which was "lifted by the groom" only after the minister proclaimed the couple lawfully married—a subtle symbol of her husband gaining access to her vagina which had previously been "veiled off." And let's not forget the tossing of the bridal bouquet—yet another image of the bride's imminent "pollination" or the "taking of her flower." No "red-blooded American man" would ever consider marrying a "bad girl," i.e., a non-virgin. Regardless of whatever the groom had done before with other women, when it finally came time for him to "settle down," a man was supposed to find a "nice girl" to settle with, meaning one who had preserved her virginity until her wedding day.[10]

Young women were often told that having premarital sex would seriously jeopardize their future marital security as a way to frighten them into abstinence. A woman who had premarital sex was characterized as "betraying her future husband." She would reap very severe repercussions, ruining her chances for a successful and happy marriage, for "how could her future husband ever trust her to be faithful if she couldn't wait until their wedding day?" Once it was learned that a woman had sex before marriage, she was labeled a "slut," a "tramp," a "whore," and so on. She was forever relegated to the "bad girl" category, someone "no decent man would ever want to marry."

In contrast, the requirement that men not have premarital sex was clearly an afterthought. Never were men punished or scorned by society in the way a woman was for having "given in to the temptation of lust." It was a brazen, but widely accepted, double standard. A man who'd had premarital sex, was at worst, only slapped on the hand, and was generally tolerated for having "sowed his wild oats," that is, as long as it was with other women.

A man could get away with having all the premarital sex he desired as long as it was done discreetly and only with "bad girls." All that mattered was that he make sure to find a virgin when the time came for him to get married. This hypocritical standard even went so far as to require that, should a man ever persuade his virgin fiancée to have sex with him before their wedding day, it was his duty to break off the engagement or else suffer dishonor to his reputation![11]

The Hand Slap of Guilt

There were limits, though, to just how much even men could get away with as far as premarital sex goes. True, relative to the way sexually active women faired, men found to be sexually promiscuous were only hand slapped. Society *tolerated* men who'd "had some experience." But societal toleration didn't mean that men were completely free of guilt, shame and fear regarding their sexual desires and indulgences in them. Inwardly, many men were very conflicted about their sexuality. There were many who—in spite of escaping the severe ostracism, sexually-active, single women suffered—were nevertheless heavily influenced by church preaching and felt deep guilt for their sexual "transgressions," even for just having sexual fantasies![12]

Interestingly, sexual guilt, shame and fear were heaped on men in measured quantities, in pieces just big enough to make them feel badly for their indulgences, but not so much to constrain them into actual abstinence. Regardless of how men behaved sexually Monday through Saturday, as long as they felt just enough guilt to come to church on Sunday to confess their "weakness" and contribute some money, the Church was content to ignore the disparity of the lower sexual standard society expected of them as that compared to women.

In fact, the Church may have encouraged the lower standard for men. Christianity is by no means the first religion to discover that, by equating certain biological drives to "sinful desires," they could guarantee an endless supply of guilt-ridden supplicants. People who are made to feel guilty will time and again pay good money for the absolution services of religious priests and ministers. Since there are very few alternatives to ridding one's self of the sex drive—no more than for ridding one's self of the biological drives to eat, sleep or eliminate—one can never be "cured" of it. For every man the Church convinced that his sexual feelings were coming from his "sinful nature" (instead of naturally occurring hormones), another steady client was assured.

Sex Under the Radar

This begs the question though—"If premarital sex was so forbidden to women, but not so much to men, then with whom were these men sowing all their wild oats?" To be sure, intercourse with prostitutes and so-called "loose women" (who presumably had multiple sexual partners) partially explains the math behind men having more premarital sex than women. However, beginning with Alfred C. Kinsey's landmark studies, *Sexual Behavior in the Human Male* (1948) and *Sexual Behavior in the Human Female* (1953) and then the Masters and Johnson work,

Human Sexual Response (1966), it turns out that the premarital sexual experiences of women—yes, even when Great Grandma was in her 20s—had been severely underestimated, to the tune of at least 30%. And due to the reluctance on the part of women at this time to report their pre-marital sexual behavior, this percentage likely erred on the low side.

Whatever the precise numbers, one thing is sure, even before the so-called "Sexual Revolution" of the 1960s, far fewer women then what was popularly thought actually abstained from premarital sex until their wedding day. While it's fair to say that a decent percentage of women actually did wait, as the 1985 movie *Back to the Future* portrayed, much of what was bandied about as the normative sexual mores of the 1950s were very frequently violated … as long as it was done with discretion, and vehemently denied if later confronted about it.

Recall the scene from in the 1942 movie classic *Casablanca* where the young bride-to-be seriously considers giving up her virginity in exchange for passports to freedom and her determination to "lock the secret in her heart forever." Clearly, this film take would have landed squarely on the editor's floor had the typical movie-goer not been able to fathom that a young bride-to-be of the 1940s might secretly not be a virgin. The very fact that most Americans would find it very difficult to imagine their Great-Grandma having been sexually active prior to marrying is not so much a testimony to her chastity as to the degree to which women went—and were expected to go—to conceal their pre-marital, sexual behavior.

Marriage in the 40s, then, carried with it something of a promise of relief, especially for women. The realities of human sexual nature resulted in ministers having to privately counsel many an engaged woman, overcome with guilt "for having succumbed to temptation" to seek God's forgiveness and regard their now chaste—and usually shortened—engagement as an opportunity to have their "virginity renewed." For many women, even back in the 40s and 50s, Marriage offered the hope of finally getting to have sex without guilt and no longer having to ask their lovers "will you respect me in the morning?"

Saved Through Childbearing

Unfortunately, the promise of relief from sexual guilt by getting married was usually a fleeting one. For women, there was still one more hurdle to jump. It would have been great if being married actually did result in guiltless, shameless and fearless sex for most women of the 40s. But many newlywed brides still had trouble making the adjustment to "wholesome sex," and for good reason.

For most people in this time period, getting permission from Church and State to have sex was not the same as saying that sex was something good, something to be proud of, and something beautiful. Sex was still regarded as "a necessary evil," even *after* marriage! The Christian Bible (Hebrews 13:4) summed it up this way: "The marriage bed is undefiled." In other words, sex is *permissible* for those who are married; it won't "defile" you any more. However, it's clear from the use of the term "undefiled" that getting married only met a minimum requirement. It was a permit only—but still nothing close to a ringing endorsement! The Apostle Paul puts it even more plainly in I Corinthians 7:36-38, where he says, "those who marry and have sex are not sinning, but those who don't marry and don't have sex, do better."

Much of this ongoing guilt, shame and fear about sex was due to the lingering notion from the Medieval (Catholic Christian) Church position that even marital sex was only permissible for the purpose of having children! Christian Protestantism had formally differed with this view, but that difference had as yet by the 1940s to make it socially acceptable for a healthy woman not to get pregnant soon after her wedding. If by her first anniversary, she had not yet "been expecting" (No, you couldn't just say "pregnant" out loud), a young married woman was "surely having problems." Why?

In practice, the only real justification to society for a woman having sex, even for a married woman, was if it ultimately resulted in her having a "legitimate" baby.[13] It would have been unheard of for any married woman, who was young and healthy enough, to say that she just didn't want to have children. A "decent" married woman didn't have sex for pleasure. She only submitted to intercourse as part of here twofold "marital duty": 1) to please her husband, and 2) strictly in the hope that "offering her body as a sacrifice" would lead to pregnancy.

The sin-staining act of having sexual intercourse, for a woman, even a married woman, could really only be washed away on the day she gave birth. Only then could she be saved from her sinful, sexual self. Once again, the New Testament was often used to perpetuate this view: "Adam was first formed, then Eve. And Adam was not deceived, but the woman being deceived was in the transgression. Notwithstanding she shall be *saved through childbearing* [emphasis mine], if they continue in faith and charity and holiness with sobriety," I Timothy 2:13-15.

In all fairness, a careful exegesis of this passage makes it clear that it is not at all saying marital sex is sinful unless it results in pregnancy. The apostle Paul was actually just pointing out that a woman could still get salvation for her soul in spite of the curse of painful childbirth that God had allegedly put on all women thanks to Eve's having eaten that apple. Nevertheless, ministers and priests frequently interpreted this passage in their preaching to mean that sexual intercourse was indeed permissible by God only for the purpose of procreation. Even to this day, the Catholic Church condemns the use of "artificial" contraception because of its historic position that sexual intercourse is still sinful for a married woman if her *motive* for doing so is other than to try to get pregnant! Modern Catholic women can be glad that the Church has finally said it's OK for them to enjoy sex "while they're trying" to have a baby. Perhaps it's no coincidence that among Catholics there are quite a number of experts in "natural" birth control methods like the Rhythm Method which allows those for whom the method actual works to keep them "trying" for years on end, and thus, staying within the letter of the church law!

A Wife's Duty

Unsurprisingly, there was extremely little information available at this time on how sex could be pleasurable for a woman. A "Godly woman's" pleasure was to come from becoming the mother of children fathered by her husband, never from the sexual acts themselves that made motherhood possible! Women were still subject to the popular thinking of the previous 19th Century in which the prudish Queen Victoria of England had set the standard of what a "good wife" did and didn't do in the bedroom. This Victorian attitude even went so far as to advocate that, during sex, a "virtuous wife" was supposed to remove herself mentally to "thoughts of God."

We have to remember that the idea that a woman could ever, even within the confines of marriage, really enjoy sex for the simple pleasure of it was still decades away. Until then, the notion that pleasure ought to be derived from marital sex was solidly reserved for men. It was "a man's right" to have sex with his lawfully wedded wife, and in most parts of the country (remember, this was a good two decades or so before No Fault Divorce became possible in most states), a man could divorce a woman and avoid paying alimony, on the grounds of prolonged "shunning."

None of this, however, is to say that *all* married women of the 40s failed to enjoy sex. A very poignant episode of the hit TV series of the 1970s, *All in the Family*, reminded us of this. In one episode, Edith Bunker responds to her daughter's question as to whether or not she'd ever enjoyed having sex by saying: "Why, shoooore," to her daughter's surprise. Then she explains, "Of course, your grandmother asked me on the day before my wedding if I was ready to perform my marital duty. And naturally I said yes … but I thought she was talking about doing the dirty laundry!"

The small number of women at this time who did manage to enjoy marital sex did so, not because of, but in spite of the strong social and religious expectations to the contrary, and that was largely by accident.

Uncommon Law Marriages

We see, then, that a few women were able to enjoy sex, married or not, in a relationship or not, and that such enjoyment had to be kept far under the radar screen of social observation. It should almost go without saying, then, just how much more taboo was cohabiting with a lover prior to matrimony. While Common Law marriages had been tolerated to some degree in frontier areas—usually in remote areas of the country "where no minister was available," society by this time made little distinction between a Common Law marriage and "living in sin." The argument that one's live-in sex partner was a Common Law wife was becoming very difficult to make by the Mid-20th century by which time the frontiers of the Old West had long been gone.[14]

◆ ◆ ◆

For most people at the time Great Grandma was in her late teens, there was really only one practical way to live together with a sex partner—after getting married first. And regardless of what was actually going on in secret, it was just taken for granted six decades ago that getting married meant that a couple would be having sex on their wedding night for the very first time.

What a difference only a few generations can make.

3

Where Did Marriage Come From?

o o o o o o o o o o o o o o o o o o o o o o o o o o o o o o o o o

"And the Lord said to me, Go, take unto thee a wife ... so I bought her for six ounces of silver and ten bushels of barley."

—The Old Testament Prophet Hosea

Why "Husband" Originally Meant "Farmer"

Having some grasp, then, of what Marriage and sex meant for the average man and woman of the 1940s, leads to an important question: Where did these beliefs and attitudes come from in the first place? To get the answer we'll, once again, have to journey back in time, but a whole lot further this time—6000 years ago.

It may be more than just a coincidence that Christian Fundamentalists who believe in a "recent creation" have calculated that God made Adam and Eve, the so-called "first married couple," around six millennia ago. As is the case with many mythical tales, there's a grain of truth to the Adam and Eve story, for history also tells us that the institution of Marriage first began at about this same time. However, instead of resulting from a deity's sympathy for a lonely guy with a rib to spare, Marriage as we know it was actually founded in response to a radical change in the way humans got their food—from hunting and gathering to farming, or what used to be called in Old English, *husbanding.*[15]

Homo sapiens and our hominid ancestors had for hundreds of thousands of years roamed the savannas of Africa, eventually fanning out into Asia and Europe, hunting for meat and gathering plant food. This period is often referred to as The Hunting and Gathering Era. During this vast time, there were only two ways to get food, and each gender played a vital role in the process. Usually, females gathered plant food from the wild, while males hunted and scavenged for vital meat supplements.[16] For the majority of our species' history, this is how we got our breakfast, lunch and dinner. And how we got our food had a big impact on how each gender treated the other.

Bringing in food had the effect of determining one's social status in the Hunting and Gathering Era. Since both genders played a vital role in this all important process, both men and women normally held relatively equal status in their traveling communities.

The reason food provision so directly determined social status at this time was because we and our hominid ancestors had no means of storing food. Each day was a new challenge to survival: for women, to find edible roots, berries, nuts and leaves, and for men, to hunt down a beast or scavenge for carcasses of animals that had recently been killed—by accident or by some other predator—which still had some meat left on it. If the women were skilled in knowing where to gather, and the men in knowing how to hunt, they could hope to eat and live another day. However, no matter how much food they gathered up or hunted down, any leftovers would quickly go to waste. Fruit rotted and meat decayed, so the search would start all over the next day. Our ancestors lived from hand to mouth, and all hands, both male and female, were equally needed.

Then something remarkable happened roughly 10,000 years ago, after the last surge of the Ice Age had retreated. The climate in many parts of the world began to favor vast grasslands of edible seeds (the cereal plant predecessors of wheat and barley). Soon, our ancient ancestors discovered that they could eat these seeds and that they had a special advantage. Unlike fruits or meat, seed (or cereal) didn't rot in a matter of days. If you found a bunch growing in a meadow somewhere, you could load up as much as you could carry, bring it back to camp and store it for long periods of time—like squirrels do with their nuts—as a backup for times when other food was scarce. This was a huge improvement on the hand-to-mouth lifestyle which had previously been the only means of getting sustenance since the dawn of hominid existence.

The initial attempts at food storage weren't efficient enough to stop people from living on the road all the time. But the ability to store food encouraged those early traveling bands not to go as far afield as they once did. Instead of having to always find a new home territory each time the food resources dwindled, they began to move from one familiar seasonal camp to another (where they might have left a buried store of seed food) in a circuit.[17]

The gathering and storing of wild seed food went on for hundreds of years, and for thousands in some parts of the world, until someone made an even bigger discovery. We don't know exactly how it happened, but it could very well have gone as follows: One rainy day, while walking along a familiar path with a load of wild seeds, a "cave woman" tripped on a rock and spilled some of her collection. The seeds got all full of mud. Too dirty to bother with, she just left them. But a couple weeks later, when our clumsy cave girl just happened to be walking on the same path, she saw something that amazed her—there were plants growing at the very same spot where she had spilled the seeds, the same kind of plants that made the same kind of edible seeds she had earlier spilled there! Suddenly, it dawned on her that she could save herself a lot of trouble having to search every day in the wild for those plants that bore edible seeds by intentionally putting some of them in the muddy ground where they could easily be found later.

This change in the way *Homo sapiens* got food by planting seeds instead of roaming the wild in the hope of finding them is often referred to as the Horticultural Revolution. No more did humans have to *find* food, but thanks to learning how to plant seeds by hand—i.e., gardening—they could actually make it grow in a pre-determined spot. The end result was that humans could now settle in certain places for extended periods of time. And with the brand new experience of staying somewhere for months instead of days, a remarkable chain of events followed. (Bear with me a bit longer here; we'll soon see what all this has to do with Marriage.)

This era of primitive gardening went on for hundreds of years, but in a rather hap hazard manner. People could now stay in one place as long as the plants would grow and yield (fertilizer was to come much later), and as long as the ground in these places was moist enough (and therefore, soft enough) to dig in by hand. Along the way, though, someone had yet another stroke of genius and figured out that plants yielded more seed when planted in ground that had been "stirred" or tilled. A simple tool was invented, the *hoe* (which was, at first, just a stick), which allowed for more seeds to be planted in less time with less effort, for much improved yields. This allowed the pre-historic traveling bands of humans to spend even more time in one place, at least until soils were depleted of nutrients. This invention, along with other nifty stone tool innovations, marked the beginning of the very last chapter of the Stone Age, also known as the Neolithic Era.

As long as the soil wasn't too arid, a hoe was pretty sufficient to till the ground. This fact is important for our study because the hoe didn't require any particular brute strength to wield. Therefore, women as well as men—who typically have a 15% to 20% advantage on women in terms of raw, physical strength—were able to till the ground with more or less the same level of productivity. This helped preserve the relative equality between the genders during this new era in that women continued to do as much of the bread winning as the men, just as they had done before as gatherers.

It wasn't until the invention of the *plow* that the ground could yield enough food from one location to allow people to settle down permanently.[18] It was the discovery of the first plow (basically, a stick with a shaped rock tied to it that was then pulled by a person or a domesticated animal) that made farming as we know it possible. With the ability to plant and grow all the food one needed from one place, or Agriculture, came civilization. And when *Homo sapiens* settled down for good, to begin husbanding the earth in earnest, many other changes came in its wake, especially in the way men and women related to each other.

The End of Gender Equality

As noted, during the Hunting and Gathering Era, the first and longest era of early hominid and later human existence, there was relative equality between the sexes. They were both dependent on each other, and this mutual dependency balanced their status most of the time. We've also noted how this equality continued through the Horticultural Revolution. However, when men truly began to husband, i.e., to farm, the brute strength which was required to command the primitive plow elevated men above women as principle breadwinners and pushed women into utter dependency.

To be sure, there had been some exceptions to the Neolithic tendency toward egalitarianism. Whenever there were scarcities of vital resources (inability to locate herds for hunting or harsh weather that made gathering plant food unusually difficult), this often led to war with neighboring tribal bands. When there weren't enough resources to go around for all the groups roaming in a particular area, warring against a neighboring band to either kill or run them off was the better alternative to starvation. The more often a tribal band became war-oriented, the more the status of women went down as men would tend to use brutal force among their own after honing brutality on the battle field.[19]

Turning to war was the exception, though. Most of the time, it was just easier to move over to the next valley, beach or forest whenever resources thinned, and gender equality normally prevailed as a result. Unfortunately, this fragile balance between the sexes all came apart at the seams when men began to farm.

From Territoriality to Ownership

With farming came a new possibility—a steady, year-round food supply, all coming from one place. There was no more need to continuously roam about, searching for what food grew in the wild or following herds for meat. There was a catch though. The need to constantly travel was replaced by the need to constantly stay in one place, to guard the land where the food grew! This need for the guardianship of land quickly translated into a concept that has ever since revolutionized human society—*ownership*.

Back in the good old hunting and gathering days, the idea of owning anything, except for the few items one could carry on one's back, was a rather vague notion. To suggest to early humans that land could be "owned" might have made as much sense as owning the sky or the moon![20] Nevertheless, human communities all over the world began to quickly adopt the ownership concept almost the same day as it was introduced to them. In a matter of a few hundred years, the idea of ownership was found in every inhabited continent. It seems that humans only needed to stay in one place long enough in order to begin feeling like that place belonged to them.

The speed with which the ownership concept took hold suggests that our species may have in some way been predisposed to embracing the idea that things can be "mine." Perhaps, the seeds of such a predisposition were first germinated eons earlier in pre-hominid history when an instinct to protect a certain place was first favored by Natural Selection.

Many creatures, from insects to mammals, evolved some sense of "exclusive rights" to the general area where they dwelt or found their food millions of years ago. We call this tendency to feel protective of certain general locations "territoriality." A similar tendency developed from the need to guard mates from rivals and to protect young from predators.

We don't know which brand of territoriality came first. Perhaps, the first creatures to evolve an instinct to feel that a given territory "belonged" to them, did so because it helped them better guard their mates. If so, then territoriality for a physical area was merely an evolutionary expansion of a primitive sexual instinct which had evolved much earlier. Or maybe the mate guarding instinct came later as an extension of territorial guardianship.

Either way, the primitive behavior of territoriality seems to have set the stage for what we now think of as ownership. It's not likely that *Homo sapiens* would have ever come to think in terms of any specific person, place or thing as being "mine" had our primitive ancestors not developed a general instinct for territoriality first. The fact that humans coming to think they could own property took place independently all over the world—from the Indus River Valley to the plantations surrounding the Aztec pyramids of Mexico—suggests some kind of territorial predisposition.

The seedling ability to instinctively feel one had exclusive access to some general space was already planted deeply in the early *Homo sapiens* mind, if only dormant, until the day came when people finally rested somewhere long enough for it to burst forth into full fruition. Once they did, humans quickly got the idea that the specific area of dirt where their food was coming from was "theirs." And like a snowball, this clear sense of "mine" didn't stop with land.

No sooner did humans begin laying full claim to plots of land, they quickly got the idea to extend their claims of ownership. A remarkable domino effect took place in the minds of these original farming men that went more or less like the following: "If this land can be 'mine,' then the things located on it can be 'mine.' The animals on it can be 'mine.' Anything can be 'mine' … even other human beings!"

"Property" Expands to Include Women

The new, agricultural view of the world as a giant storehouse of claimed or unclaimed property led to a mad scramble to stake out as much as one could, and this property rush resulted in the female gender being utterly displaced.

The primitive plow required a lot of brute strength to command. In no time at all, it became clear that men were far better suited than were women to take over this new technology for acquiring food, leaving women with only a secondary role. Once removed from the direct role of bread-winning, overnight it seemed, the value of a woman was reduced to one thing—the extent to which she could successfully bear a male child for her farmer/owner. In other words, women had become sexual slaves, not much different from any of the other domesticated animals that were also claimed as property, and subsequently bought, sold, branded and bred accordingly.

However, the new order was for a time anything but orderly. It took a while for people to sort out some kind of practical system for preventing conflicts between men who were asserting ownership of everything and everybody they could. There was a lot of fighting at first, with no clear winners. A lot of men staked out claims for the same land, the same animals, and the same women. Some tried to barter and trade, but these exchanges often erupted into feuds over who sold or traded what for whom. Some verifiable method for deciding which piece of property belonged to whom had to be devised to keep everybody from killing each other.

Then one day, someone came up with a plan, "Let's put some kind of markers around each piece of land, and appoint some village elders to witness whatever agreements are made as to which lots belong to which man." If someone tried to bully another by simply taking his land, the bullied could appeal to the village elders to step in. The new system wasn't perfect, but it was a big improvement over the initial chaos. In other words, the first *property laws* were invented. Word of the innovation spread rapidly until villages all over the world had some simple set of rules to bring order to staking claims, trading property and keeping track of it all.

This, however, was only the first property problem that needed to be resolved. Difficult as it was at first, land disputes turned out to be the easiest to settle. At least land was stationary, and boundaries could be marked off with sticks, stones or some kind of descriptions that would be clear to the local inhabitants (e.g., "from the edge of the river bend to the large Oak tree," etc.). Even though reading and writing hadn't really taken hold yet, some form of public records, however rudimentary, could be kept by a village elder, and stiff penalties for moving a boundary marker helped early land owners to live in peace with each other … most of the time.[21]

What to do, though, about "mobile belongings" like domesticated sheep, pigs or cattle? Animals had a way of roaming all over the place (and still do in many rural parts of the world). For example, when a farmer traded one of his cattle for a pig, what was to stop him from backing out of the deal later on if the pig turned out to be sickly and died prematurely? If farmer A said, "that calf is mine," and farmer B said, "No, it's mine, you sold it to me for a pig," what was to prevent a violent confrontation from ensuing? So, along with some crude means of making it clear which land plots belonged to whom, something similar had to be done to clarify to one's community the trades made of any other "property" as well, so any later disagreement or question could be settled without violence and chaos. For the most part, this meant the establishment of some simple, standard trade ceremonies, rites that could readily be witnessed and remembered.

The First Marriage

Now, if the preceding pages seemed like a ways off the beaten track, perhaps it will now become clear what these original trade ceremonies have to do with Marriage. On the very heels of the virus-like spread of the ownership concept came the imperative to secure farm hands and to maintain control of the land. Insuring a loyal and perpetual supply of strong hands, male hands, to protect and keep the all sacred land was the big issue of the new day for those early pioneers of the Agricultural Era. We don't know who first came up with the answer to this challenge. What we do know is that someone somewhere got an idea that went something like this: "If I can own land and animals, then I can own women, and if I can own women, I can own the children they bear me. And the males that she bears me will be my ticket to security when I am too old to farm any more. My sons, then, shall be heirs to the land, who will continue to till it and protect it even after I am gone. My seed, like the seeds I plant, will be my way of living on, even beyond death."

To us, it might seem odd that ancient farming people drew a connection between their belief that plant seeds contained some supernatural essence, which passed from one generation of plants to the next, and the idea that there was something of themselves in the semen of men which had the potential to similarly carry on their own essence for generations on end (and this was thousands of years before anyone knew what DNA was). It made sense to them that if generations of animals and plants inherit something of the essence of their ancestors, then so must humans. Thus, the need to ensure that one's "seed" (which was thought to be passed only through males) could not only provide security in one's old age, but a man's seed could also extend his existence in the afterlife.

Soon men came to believe that as long as one's descendents cared for their graves after they were buried—the way farmers cared for their fields—their essence or life force would likewise be preserved after death, just as seeds which had been buried in the ground would bring forth new life if tended to properly (watering, weeding, etc.). Of course, this only worked to the extent that the children *your women* bore were biologically *your seed.*

Paternity, therefore, suddenly became a very big issue![22] Just as it had become necessary to establish some formal way of making clear which land plots belonged to whom, and then which animals belonged to whom, it became even more important to establish which females belonged to whom. The new order of the day for women, then, was to ensure that no one but their rightful owner/farmer, or *husband*, bred with them.

And so it began that men in village after village, then town after town, and later, city after city, began to use the same kind of simple public rituals—originally designed for land and animal exchanges—to make it as plain as could be who owned which women. From then on, whenever someone wished to buy a mobile "good"—whether a young, healthy horse or a young, healthy woman—the innovation of gathering together at the village gate, before the elders, to make such exchanges "legal" seemed the perfect solution. Then, if someone other than the recognized owner/husband was later caught studding his cattle with a bull that wasn't his, or having sex with a female that wasn't "his," something could be done about it. All in the village would know whether or not the persons so caught had legitimate access to the "property" they were caught with.

It was then, around six thousand years ago, in some small, ancient farming community where, before a handful of village elders who served as formal witnesses, that a father/owner of a young woman first announced, "I sell this woman to so-and-so, in exchange for his camel" (or some other beast or valuable). By making this transaction public, there would be no question that the buyer, and only the buyer, now had the right to be intimate with her. The eyes of the entire community could then serve as enforcement should there be any subsequent attempt by anyone other than the new rightful owner/farmer, i.e., the husband, to lay with the woman he paid for.

Just as with the exchange of land, animals or material property, the reason for using a public ritual as the means to make such trades was mainly because reading and writing was in its very infant stages. The recognition of goods traded fairly and squarely had to be done in some fashion other than through a written document. Of course, written documentation of such transactions were eventually added on, but by then the overt rituals had become well-established traditions. Even today, sales contracts are usually accompanied by some overt ritual—a hand shake, a toast, sometimes a business dinner, and so on.

At first, these ritualized transactions were very simple—a father/owner would make it known that his daughter was *available*, i.e., old enough to bear children and that he was willing to sell her.[23] Negotiations would take place, often with a sex slave broker (the forerunners of the later matchmakers) who made it his business to know who was in the market for a new woman and what he had to offer to any prospective seller.[24] Once a deal was struck, *a date would be set* for the transaction. On the appointed day, the father/owner would lead his daughter on a formalized *march*, usually down a specially designated path (or *aisle*) through the village as a way of notifying everyone who could come to witness the exchange. In some traditions, a leash made of personalized rope was tied around the nose *ring* of the young woman to be traded, which he untied when they arrived at the village gate where the elders and formal *witnesses* were assembled.[25] If the exchange was for a female that was a virgin (who, of course, would be much more valuable in that virginity was tantamount to a 100% guarantee of the new owner's paternity of any child that should come later), she would be *veiled*, as a way of stating the guarantee publicly.[26] Finally, he would *give her away* to the new owner, who then, would *take her hand* and *tie the knot* of his personalized leash to her nose ring, thus sealing the transaction.[27] Sometimes, the woman was then branded with her new farmer/owner's family name. In other words, *she took the name of her husband* … right onto her skin!

Do any of these practices and rituals sound familiar? Well, they should, because it was this first woman to be sold as a sex slave, by one man to another, through a public rite in order to ensure formal recognition of the sale, who became the *first wedding bride*! It was because she was purchased by one of the early farmers—in whose hands most of the wealth was concentrated, the wealth necessary to afford the purchases of those women most fit for breeding—that the original term for farmer, "husband," eventually became synonymous with any man taking a bride. And it was this crude but effective form of a business transaction, wherein women were bought and sold like animals, that constituted the first marriage.

As Marriage evolved around the globe, the rites and rituals of these trades varied from one culture to another. Often, the "quality of the product sold" had to be "guaranteed," especially when the seller claimed the product to be "brand new." In many cultures, a consummation rite followed the wedding as a way of closing the deal. One of the most well known of these required that a white cloth be laid on the bed where the marriage would be consummated. The new owner would, in due course, emerge after having sex with the woman he'd just purchased, and hold up the cloth before witnesses who were in attendance outside. Their task was to make sure the cloth was stained with her hymen blood. The blood-stained cloth was the "warranty seal" of the father/seller's claim of her virginity. The cloth was then presented to the father/seller to keep … just in case there was ever any question later on.[28]

It should go without saying that women were not always pleased with the men to whom their father/owners sold them. It was not uncommon for women to try to run away or to resist intimate contact with their new husband/owners. In response to these "complications in taming," (and in manners not too dissimilar from those used to tame wild animals to become domesticated) women were often shackled before they were sold in order to prevent them from trying to escape. Restraints made of rope or leather were put around their necks, wrists and feet. Later on, metal shackles were sometimes used. These restraints were especially necessary when their new owners were first having sex with them, and if need be, were used as long as the bride would not submit to her new owner and accept her new circumstance.[29] Violence was also a regular part of "taming" a new woman, who often had to be flogged into submission.[30]

The onset of the Agricultural Era gave a huge sexual advantage to some men. Those who accrued the most land (or the most animals if they were herders), i.e., those who were the most wealthy, could afford to purchase a disproportionately larger number of women than most other men, and they did just that. This practice is what we normally think of as polygamy (literally, "many mates"), or what is more commonly termed among experts as polygyny ("many women").

Involuntary Polygamy

There were also some men of the previous era, those who were the more dominant in any one group, who also had a big advantage when it came to having more sex with more women than others. The difference between the two, though, was that the Pre-Agricultural harem keepers didn't have to enslave or buy women; they came to them of their own accord.[31]

The 18th Century philosopher Jean-Jacques Rousseau believed men and women lived in entirely egalitarian societies until land ownership came along. Before that, he concluded that there must have been nothing to restrain men or women from having more than one sexual mate and to partner in any number of ways whether it was several women with one man or the other way around. None would have been bound to any single person, especially as was the case after the Agricultural Revolution when a small number of men began to accrue large numbers of women in harems. However—as we shall see later in this study—there is much more to the story of polygyny.

For now, though, suffice it to say that, to whatever extent women volunteered to polygyny before the Agricultural Era, things changed dramatically thereafter, as Barash and Lipton explain: "The early evolutionary prospect of human mating systems is unclear, but here is a possible quick-and-dirty scenario: Our early ancestors roamed the Pleistocene African savannas in small bands. Most current hunter-gatherer human societies are [socially] monogamous (although with adultery relatively common). Only a small number of men—typically 5 to 15 percent—are active polygynists, and even then, it is extremely rare for one man to have more than a few wives. With a hunter-gatherer lifestyle, it is almost impossible for one man to obtain a monopoly of resources, or even a preponderance: Luck is often involved in hunting, for example. Besides, when game and gathered vegetable foods are at issue, it is difficult to store excess. Then came agriculture, providing the opportunity for some men to own large amounts of land and, with it, large surpluses. The rich were able to get richer yet. Out of this came enhanced competition as well as the prospect of enhanced success—especially more wives—for the winners. In a sense, maybe Rousseau wasn't altogether wrong, after all, when he suggested that people were primitively egalitarian, with this Eden disrupted by the invention of the private property!"[32]

Thou Shalt Not Covet Thy Neighbor's Purchased Female

All the laws of early civilizations that had to do with what we now call "adultery" originated with the imperative to make certain that women would only bear children by the men who purchased them. As with any laws that early societies came up with, it was expedient to get religious hierarchies to chime in with various supernatural threats and punishments awaiting any transgressors in order to promote conformity. This is how the "sin of adultery" was first created. Rather than originating with some deity who wanted to make clear his intended use for sex, religious priesthoods were merely reinforcing the primitive rules village societies had already established long before.

They would usually do this by claiming that someone of notoriety—an honored ancestor, a legendary figure or a popular military leader—had a vision of some deity who gave them a special, supernatural insight. These "insights" or "visions" were conveniently supportive of the policies that the religious hierarchy and their allies in government wanted to impose. Sometimes these visions and the laws they inspired were pragmatic and agreeable with our modern sense of ethics—"Thou shalt not steal." Other times, they were quite cruel and barbaric—" if a man suspects one of his wives of committing adultery, but doesn't know for sure, let him give her a poison from the temple, and if she lives, she is innocent."[33]

One influential priesthood of a small tribal kingdom in the Middle East proclaimed that a prophet named Moses had received ten commandments directly from their tribe's principle war and sky god, Yahweh. They wisely included a commandment (based on a much older village custom) against covetousness—having such a desire for someone else's property, that one is willing to try taking it for himself outside of a proper trade agreement, "Thou shalt not covet thy neighbor's house, thou shalt not covet thy neighbor's wife, nor his manservant, nor his maid-servant, nor his ox, nor his ass, nor any thing that is thy neighbor's," Exodus 20:17.

Notice how this commandment gave no particular significance to any one piece of property a land owner held. His "wife" was just another item on the list! Also note that it was possible to own women for other purposes. There were some who just did menial work—the "maidservants," and though not mentioned in this verse, there were others whose status lay in between, those who served primarily as sex toys—"concubines." Any of the children born to concubines were normally regarded as slaves and unable to inherit property as the children born to the official wives of the husband/owner's household.

The term "adultery" had a very different meaning in ancient times when it came to men having sex with women. In the Old Testament, for instance, we read time and again of "married" men having all kinds of sexual encounters with numerous women, but not getting into any trouble for it! Only if they had sex with a woman who'd been purchased by another man for the purpose of producing an heir, might they get into hot water, and even that depended on who the owner was (e.g., it was much more serious for a man of low social status to have sex with the wife of a man of high, social standing.[34] It was, by far, a wife who suffered the greater scorn and punishment for being caught in the act of adultery, meaning sex with any man aside from her owner/husband.[35]

Originally, then, adultery had nothing to do with prohibiting *men* from having sex with someone other than their wives. They could have sex with prostitutes. Many prostitutes were the sex slaves of the priest classes who generated large revenues for the operation of their temples. Any children born to them merely became the next generation of temple prostitutes. Men could have sex with concubines, either the ones they had purchased for themselves or the ones offered to them while guests in the homes of a friend or relative. Again, paternity was no issue. If a concubine got pregnant, her child normally just became another slave in the household.[36] In times of war, one of the rewards for military service was getting to rape the women of the conquered, and then to take for themselves as wives or concubines if they so desired. When it was possible, men could also have sex with women who were bound to no man at all, though this was rare. Only a woman, for example, who may have been the widow of a man of great wealth or high social esteem who had no other male heirs, might obtain such independent status.

Adultery, then, was a "sin" designed for one gender only—the female. But it was also a sin that could be passed on to certain males—her children. While natural jealousy played a part, the real offense of adultery was voiding the guaranteed paternity of the offending woman's children. Any children born to a wife impregnated by someone other than her owner/husband were damned by both social and religious institutions. They were permanently cursed and forever labeled as "bastards" or the later, not much better term, "illegitimate children." Without a recognized "pedigree," these children were doomed. They were not allowed to own land, and for much of Christianity's history, were thought to not even have a soul![37]

Thankfully, most of the worst aspects of the ancient female sex-slave trade have since been outlawed, modified or toned down, though their remnants remain. In Western nations, fathers may no longer sell their daughters to other men in exchange for a cow or a horse, yet they continue to "give away the bride" at weddings. Brides are no longer branded with their owner's insignia, but they still take their husband's last name. It wasn't all that long ago that a dowry was expected at the time of marriage. (A dowry served as compensation to parents for whatever work their child would have otherwise performed for them had they not left home.) Today, it's the bride who receives direct payment in the form of costly rings, or the couple in the form of wedding gifts. Most modern wedding rites still include a symbolic taking of the hand of the woman after the father has led her to the groom, and every now and then, we hear about an "old fashioned" suitor who asks his girlfriend's father, "May I take the hand of your daughter?" The nose ring which once ensured a new bride would follow her new owner wherever he led, is now placed on the bride's finger, and the literal knot once tied around it has been reduced to a mere expression, though it's thought to be just as binding.

Where Had the Love Gone?

Since the marriage rite began as a financial transaction—and remained so only up until the last couple centuries—romance was regarded as an unwelcome complication. In fact, love was often labeled a demonic evil, a force that could upset the societal order, and was therefore something that ought to be quenched at every turn. Likewise, sexual desire was labeled a mortal sin by the Church. Some states instituted severe penalties, even capital punishment, for those caught committing premarital sex. Women were constrained—as is still the case in many Islamic nations—to cover their bodies almost entirely whenever they went out in public. The powers of societal rule did whatever they could to restrain natural sexual behavior and to prevent natural love bonds from forming in the hope of maintaining Marriage as the foundation of all permanent sexual relationships. Even so, their efforts often failed.

Tyrannical as the man-made, sexual order was toward women after the Agricultural Revolution had taken hold, not all lost the ability to experience parental and romantic love. Sometimes, fathers truly loved and cared for their daughters, even if they did legally own them. While they might sell them off as soon as they attained puberty, they would at least lend some care while negotiating whom they would sell their daughters to. These would often take the bride prices paid to them and turn right around and hand it over to their daughters as a way of helping them get started on the needs of a new home.

In the early cultures where "marriage by capture" was commonly practiced, the woman was not always being taken against her will. Sometimes, she was an active conspirator with a man whom her father may have disapproved of, and she merely feigned being taken by force. In some cases, she would even ask her captor/lover to strike her on the head so her bruise would later prove that she had at least resisted.

Sometimes, a young man, would naturally fall in love with a girl, and if he were not the leading male in his household (because only the "patriarch" or eldest father of a family could conclude business decisions), he might plead with his father to purchase the girl for him. The Bible gives us several accounts like this. In the 29th Chapter of Genesis is the story of the young, unemployed, patriarch-to-be Jacob, who falls in love with a girl named Rachel. He wants to be with her so badly that he makes a poor bargain with her father (who probably saw how head-over-heels he was) to work as an indentured servant for seven years in order to pay for her!

As one sided as the deal already was, when the wedding day finally rolled around, Rachael's father pulled another fast one on Jacob by tricking him into taking his other, not-so-attractive daughter Leah instead. How? Since virgin brides had to be completely veiled and a big celebration followed the wedding, Jacob didn't really get to see whom he'd purchased until he woke up the next morning ... with Leah (not remembering anything from the night before, probably due to a lot of alcohol consumption). Needless to say, he was more than a little disappointed! Now, he was stuck (a deal was a deal), but he still loved Rachael so much, that he agreed to add another seven years to his servitude to get her in addition to Leah.[38]

In a later chapter of Genesis, a young man named Shechem becomes completely obsessed with a girl named Dinah, who just happened to be the daughter of the now older Patriarch Jacob. At first he abducted her and seduced her sexually, according to the common practice of "marriage by capture," but afterwards he implored his father to, "get me her as a wife." His father agrees and goes with him to meet Jacob. During their business proposal, Shechem says to Jacob, "Let me find grace in your eyes, and what ye shall say unto me I will give. Ask me whatever so much dowry and gift, and I will give according as ye shall say unto me: but give me the damsel to wife" (Genesis 34:11-12).

Unfortunately, things didn't go so well afterwards. Dinah's brothers ended up killing poor, love-lost Shechem along with his family, because they were very offended that her virginity had already been taken. The reason for their outrage, however, wasn't so much out of concern for her as a date rape victim, but for their family's business reputation: "Shall he *do business* [emphasis mine] with our sister as with an harlot" (Vs. 31)! In spite of Shechem's "blank check" offer, they were still very angry that word might get out that they had been manipulated into selling their sister after her market value had been so diminished. In other words, they punished Shechem because he should have known better than to "open the package" prior to a proper sales transaction with her proper owner!

These are just a few of the multitude of examples we find in ancient literature showing us how futile was the repression of natural desires. Even the severest laws never fully succeeded in stopping people from wanting to have sex and falling in love. The need for sexual fulfillment and loving relationships were still very much a part of the human condition. In a way, the harsh repercussions levied at adulterers and premarital lovers were signs of just how futile the effort was. No matter how hard authorities tried to eradicate naturally occurring sexual desire and love relationships, they continued to happen in spite of them. In fact, forbidden love stories have become the basis for countless dramatic tales replayed in our arts over and over again (take Romeo and Juliet for example).

"Losing" Virginity and the Law of the Marketplace

As sexual relationships were turned inside out by the events following the Agricultural Revolution, the commercialization of women, from sexual beings into sexual products—like any other product for sale—became subject to the laws of the marketplace. Just as any good or service can fetch a better price when supply is low and demand is high, so it soon went with sex. Women as sex products began to be "distributed" with this principle in mind. The high demand to ensure paternity, translated into higher prices for young women who were, not only attractive, strong, and healthy, but "yet to be touched by a man."

This sense of loss was, at least in part, due to medical ignorance about human reproduction. Though the ancients knew that women didn't always get pregnant after having sex, they had no particular reason not to think a woman might carry a man's seed within her for years before having his child. Where might they have ever gotten such an idea? Well, primitive farmers had noticed that plant seeds could be stored for great lengths of time and still maintain their fertility. So they just assumed that the same held true for their human "seed." Ancient husbands concluded, therefore, that the only sure guarantee that the offspring of any female they had purchased would be theirs was if she had *never* had sex before!

Of course, non-virgins were sold and traded as well. However, as "products" they were marketed at bargain rates, much in the same way a modern car dealer might sell a used car. To put it another way, a non-virgin was sold "as is," with no guarantee. They might still fetch a pretty good price as a concubine, especially if they were young, attractive and healthy. Concubines were still good for sexual pleasure, household work and, as noted earlier, bearing more slave children. But normally, their children could never become heirs to the land, which explains why they were traded for much less and with much less fanfare.

Therefore, *it was out of the concern to determine the legitimate control of property* that a great sense of loss was attached, the proverbial "loss of virginity," to any woman who had had sex before she was properly sold off as a potential mother of an heir. Unfortunately, long after the original reason for placing such a high premium on female virginity was forgotten, society continued to regard a woman's non sexual experience as if it were a thing of value. Equally unfortunate, and perhaps much worse, society also continued to label sexual experience as a damaging loss to a woman's value as a person.

The perceived advantage of acquiring a virgin over a non-virgin as a guarantee of the paternity of her children was also extended to issues of loyalty. This was especially the case when women were taken as part of the spoils of war. A good example of this comes from the Old Testament Book of Numbers in the 31st chapter. We read here that Moses had sent the Israelite army to attack the Midianites. The Israelite army was victorious, and to complete the victory, they put every adult male to the sword and brought back all the women and children, together with the Midianites' livestock and goods, as their compensation. Moses, however, became very upset when he saw the returning army and the Midianite women and children in tow. No, not because they needlessly executed all the Midianite men instead of taking them as prisoners of war. Instead, he rhetorically asked, "Have ye saved *all* [emphasis mine] the women alive?" (verse 15). According to the story, Moses went on to chew out the military commanders for failing to recall how "the Midianites" had previously influenced the Israelites, through a priest named Balaam, to commit idolatry, and how God punished them with a plague as a result. So with this justification, he ordered, "Now therefore kill every male among the little ones, and kill every woman that hath known man by lying with him. But all the women children, that have not known a man by lying with him, keep alive for yourselves." (verses 17, 18).

The women taken from this other tribe who worshipped other gods represented a threat to the priests and prophets of Yahweh, a theme that is repeated over and over throughout the Old Testament. Time and again, the priest class blamed foreign wives for tempting Israelite men to worship their idols. However, it's quite interesting to see that virgin girls were not regarded as threatening in this manner. Behind the overt justification Moses gave in this instance, it's very possible that it was just assumed by all that virgin women could be counted on to become loyal to their new masters, as well as to their deity, because they had not yet been intimate with other men, and given birth to their children.

Most importantly, though, allowing only the virgins to be taken alive ensured that none of them would ever give birth later on to a child of a deceased Midianite father who might one day realize a sense of connection to his real father, his father's heritage, and his father's beliefs and values, and then rise up to avenge him. Of course, at no time was there any concern expressed for how these young girls might have felt about becoming the sexual property of the very same men who had massacred their parents, male siblings and other relatives.

Variety Trumps Monopoly

Virginity, though perhaps regarded as ideal, was not as critical a factor in the mate selection process during the Hunting and Gathering Era. To borrow an image from the business world, the rules of attraction in that earlier time were geared more to being the best competitor than trying to gain a monopoly. In the "business" of a male's reproductive strategy, Nature had not really encouraged a few men to take sexual monopoly of *all* the women. Instead, men evolved instincts which, to be sure, inclined them to want to have sex with a lot of women, but drove them to primarily focus on finding and copulating with the kind of female who is most likely to finish the job that he and she start when they have sex—successfully giving birth and rearing his children. This meant trying to mate with young, healthy women, those who were *more likely to be* virgins, but not necessarily *because* they were virgins.

In every other human endeavor, it is the experienced we honor, and mastering a skill is encouraged and praised. In fact, we expect our young to learn a great number of skills by certain ages, and if any are to be chided, it's those who fail to meet these benchmarks in a timely manner. Believe it or not, a similar sense of disappointment would have been the normal reaction of pre-agricultural societies toward any young woman who had failed to learn the arts of lovemaking not too long after attaining puberty.[39]

We can better understand the ancients' "liberal" sexual attitudes, though, when contemplated rationally. When we think of sexual experience in the same manner as any other human skill, the idea that a female is "losing something" simply because she's had sexual intercourse for the first time is absolutely ludicrous! No one loses anything, other than inexperience, when they do anything else for the first time, whether taking a first step, riding a bicycle or driving a car. Lovemaking would have, at that time, been thought of as just another skill the young need to learn as part of growing up. Quite to the contrary of all that was to follow, sexual experience didn't connote any kind of loss, but a gain.

Hunting and gathering societies, therefore, were usually practical with their young adults when it came to things sexual. Upon attaining puberty, one wasn't expected to immediately be good at lovemaking, in much the same way that we moderns don't expect teens to be good at driving. Understanding this, ancient societies often took measures to begin schooling their young on sex so they would be well prepared by the time they crossed the threshold of puberty, again not too unlike the way we send our teens to driving school. A young woman often had the benefit of several of the mature women of her traveling community to educate her. Her first attempt at sexual intercourse, in many of the pre-agricultural societies, was with a mature male that could patiently teach her what and what not to do to make her first experience as enjoyable as possible. Young men were often introduced to sex in a similar manner, with an older female.

If making sure the young were sexually educated seems perverse to us, imagine how perverse the first sexual encounter our typical modern young—between two inexperienced, ill-advised, and often unprotected teens, that's done and over with in a few minutes—might have seemed to the ancients! It would have been very irresponsible in their minds for a caring adult community not to give their young practical training in such a very important area of life.

Obviously, attitudes toward a young woman's virginity changed dramatically once the plow came along. However, it may also be that the Agricultural Era exploitation of virginity didn't happen in a complete vacuum. Maybe there was something about human nature itself that added some bounce to the leap toward regarding virginity as a thing—a thing worth a lot of gold—that can be lost.

Therefore, at the risk of arousing the ire of those who can't see the forest of what actually makes us find someone attractive for the trees of what some think should, I provide the following elucidation.

Perhaps, there was something deep within the primitive part of the male brain that, indeed, predisposed him to prefer a woman "never before touched by another man" if he should have a choice. The mere fact that men are universally attracted to those physical characteristics most common to a young woman who has recently entered puberty, but who also has as yet to bare a child, may very well have set the stage for the Agricultural Era extreme of placing a premium on virgins. Why?

Because even without a need to insure paternity for inheritance' sake, a primitive instinct to prefer a virgin female above all others would seemingly be a good candidate for reward by Natural Selection. It would only be logical that Evolution would favor the genes that prompted men to mate with a woman before anyone else did. Getting his seed inside her first better ensured that he would impregnate her. If he did, then he would be more reproductively successful, and his genetically inspired tendency to prefer virgins would have been passed on accordingly. Later, when the need to insure paternity for the sake of maintaining control over land came along, what started out as an elementary, biological preference, graduated to a social imperative.

Some cite the universal sex appeal of women who have flat stomachs, smooth skin absent of stretch marks, and firm breasts (in other words, a lack of the physical signs of having given birth and nursed an infant) as proof that men are naturally inclined to find virgins more appealing than others. There is also evidence from animal studies that seems to indicate a basic preference for virginity. But there are other factors to consider which contradict this Virgins Go First view.

We must also consider that pre-agricultural mothers were not as likely to gain much weight during pregnancy (thanks to a subsistence diet), and they were not as likely to be unexercised (thanks to their much more physically demanding, gatherer lifestyle). Thus, the figures of young mothers had a much better chance of "bouncing back," and post birth "flabbiness" and stretch marks were probably negligible. Nursing an infant probably took its toll on the firmness of a young mother's breasts—but as with modern men—not to the point where they would be considered so unappealing, ancient men would not want to have sex with them anymore.

There's another problem with the Virgin's Go First theory. If the reason men are naturally attracted to the typical, outward features of a young woman who has not yet had her first child is because it would give them a better chance at reproductive success, then one could just as easily ask why Nature didn't incline men to be even *more* attracted to those features which indicate a women has had at least one child already! Why would evolutionary forces reward male inclinations toward a woman who has apparently never given birth more than to those who have clearly proven they are fertile? If anything, droopy breasts would be a bigger turn on than firm ones![40]

The answer is probably because the physical traits which most arouse male attraction are as much an indication of "health" and "youth," as they are of virginity. A younger woman is, in most cases, going to be fertile, so getting her pregnant is something of a given. But being able to get pregnant is only one factor in the equation of successful reproduction. Only if she's also strong and healthy, can she carry a child in her womb successfully, give a live birth. Only if she is young can she survive long enough to care for it afterwards.

Moreover, there's another phenomenon in both animals and humans that contradicts the idea that being the first to inseminate a woman automatically translates into greater reproductive success. It's known as the Last Male Advantage. For animal classes like the Mammalian, it's the *last* male to have sex with a female in heat who is more likely to be the father of the offspring she bears, not the first.

So how can we account for these apparent contradictions between men most preferring women who are past puberty but yet to give birth, and the principle of reproductive success which would seemingly incline men to prefer a woman who was a proven baby maker?

The reason for this seemingly contradictory pattern in male attraction may have much to do with the evolutionary change from primitive egg laying and external fertilization to the relatively late development of internal fertilization and giving live birth. Our most primitive male ancestors who lived in the sea and reproduced by spawning were more likely to father the female's eggs *if they got to them first.* All the competition between males over who got to fertilize a female's eggs took place out in the open sea. This primitive instinct is likely still deeply embedded in the "lizard" area of the male brain. However, later evolutionary development turned this order on its head once fertilization began to take place *inside* the mother. While males continued to compete among themselves for access to the most fertile and healthy women, the field of the contest changed. In other words, once sexual intercourse came along, the vaginal tract became a veritable competition arena, a place where male sperm can, quite literally, battle with each other to see which man wins by getting to the egg first. However, it was the winner of the fight who got to proceed to fertilize the egg, not necessarily which sperm "got in the ring" first. For reasons which will be elaborated on in more detail in a later chapter, the advantage in the contest for successful fertilization shifted away from the first male on the scene to the "last man standing."

The idea that pre-agricultural men preferred younger women *just because* they were more likely to be virgins is, therefore, probably stretching the truth. The reality is that men, then as now, didn't have that much trouble being just as attracted to an "experienced" young mother as they would to an "inexperienced" young woman who is yet to become a mom, as long as they are both pretty, i.e., bearing all the signs of "health." No one needs to be a rocket (or biological) scientist to know that men's primitive desires are not that discriminating.

This is not to say that a genetically induced preference for virginity doesn't exist. A primitive man might have opted for a virgin first whenever circumstances were such that he had to choose only one of two equally attractive young women!

But if he thought he had a decent shot at both of them, the order in which he made his conquests was probably not that significant. An inherited preference for virgins, then, if it exists at all, appears to be a marginal one at the most.

If we keep in mind that the goal of Natural Selection in all of this was overall reproductive success, then it's not so confusing. The mammalian male reproductive strategy likely preserved the more ancient inclination to regard signs of having gotten to a post-puberty female before any other guy as a nice, added extra. However, it was a benefit that was tempered by no sure signs that she would get pregnant. His investment (a few minutes of his time, and a small dose of semen), after all, was not so costly. Therefore, it would have been much more to his reproductive benefit—and therefore, Natural Selection began to modify the male's inclinations—to want to have sex with *any* young woman who was pretty, i.e., those who had the signs of being strong and healthy. If a guy could get a girl who was likely fertile and healthy, and get there first, all the better, but not by much.

The Code of the Oppressed

One would think that after learning where Marriage came from that women everywhere would be so offended that they would be the first to abandon it by the droves. But alas, it has as yet to occur. Why then—even women who've studied anthropology and who know the ancient history of their gender—do they still get married? Actually, there are many reasons for this reluctance to abandon Marriage even though, clearly, it originated as one of the worst forms of sexism. In order to understand why modern women are still saying "I do," we have to go back, once again, to the early Agricultural Era. There, we'll look for a deeper understanding of their reaction to the great loss of social position and esteem they experienced. Part of the answer to Marriage's continuing popularity lies in what women began to do at that time to make the best of a very bad situation.

After descending to the lowly state of servitude in the nascent agricultural world, just what were women to do? Well, as with any group of oppressed people, they found ways to fight back ... if only indirectly. And one of the best ways for any oppressed group to offer resistance—especially if they are too weak to confront their oppressors openly—is through strongly enforced codes among their own. By extending *direct* pressure on one's peers—and punishments if need be—the unity that is achieved can put a lot of *indirect* pressure on a group's oppressors to extract compromises and win benefits.

Take union workers, for example, when they go on strike. As individuals, workers have very little power compared to their bosses. But they can get around this weakness by calling on all workers to abide by an often unspoken, but clearly understood, code. This code helps them pull together, so that while as individuals they are weak, together they are often stronger than their oppressive employers. They might threaten a strike in order to get better pay. The company could fire a few individuals, but not everyone at once, without going broke. The union, then, makes sure to levy threats of one sort or another against any who dare cross picket lines, and many a collective bargaining contract are won as a result.

Codes, therefore, empower those who are individually weak, so they can prevail over their oppressors by reserving direct confrontation for those peers who fail to hold ranks. Similarly, women of old began to join together for their mutual protection, and they soon developed a code amongst themselves to ameliorate the worst aspects of their fallen condition.

The challenge for women who were old, unhealthy, unattractive or no longer fertile was to find ways to prevent becoming marginalized or worse. Even the once highly valued young and beautiful brides had to be concerned. As they aged, their value shifted from sexual pleasuring, to mothering, and then to menial labor. Sooner or later, even serving as a maid might become too much, especially if they became sickly or disabled. Those too old or too sick to do any more work, might be cast into the street.

The answer was for women who were less regarded to bring their joint influence on the most prized women—those regarded more highly for their youthful appearance, their health, their beauty, and thus, their fertility—as a way of getting them to act on their behalf. The young and beautiful still had all their natural charms which could in turn be used on the men who, legally, owned them. Often, husband/owners could be persuaded by one of their tantalizing young "properties" to offer better treatment to the not-so-tantalizing women in the household. A young and beautiful woman could also use her sexual charms, offering her body willingly to her owner, in return for his agreement to purchase her mother or aunt or sister who might be in another household where they were being mistreated, because they weren't as desirable or useful anymore.

The favored women could use negative means as well to get what they or their "sisters" wanted. They could make life for their male owners rather unbearable by the way they spoke or the kind of food they cooked (or didn't cook so well) if he denied the favors she asked. He could refuse, of course, but then he would have to take the trouble to discipline her, and contend with her resistance, endless complaining or bickering. In some cases, a husband could even be convinced to put the elder women in charge of the young, their homes and sometimes, in charge of their businesses, rather than to put up with their nagging them to manage things differently. An attractive woman, though taking the chance of losing the favor of her male owner, knew she would face even worse discipline from her older and less attractive female peers if she failed to use her position of influence to act on their behalf. Generally, it was in her best interest to use her place and her charms to gain rewards or use passive resistance to wear down her owner into giving concessions for the benefit of the other women.

The Code was especially important within the female "sisterhood" of a harem. What if, for example, a young, attractive, and the current "favorite wife" were at first unwilling to help her less attractive "sister wives" of the harem by using her influence on her farmer/owner to treat the older wives better? She might be subjected to any number of passive forms of punishment. She could be ostracized. She might become the subject of virulent gossip, or be exposed to her master/husband whenever she broke a house rule. In severe cases of unwillingness to help, out and out lies could be told, even that she had sexually betrayed her husband/owner! The mere threat of such discipline was usually all that was needed to sway the favorite wife to do her part to help her less favored sister wives, as well as to win their friendship and support.

Many of these innovations to bring pressures to bear on those who had influence—birthed out of the necessity of that time—were kept in practice long after female sexual slavery morphed into the less abusive forms of Marriage more familiar to us today. In time, and with the help of men of lower rank and religious institutions, husbands were eventually obliged to return to women who had for millennia been pressed into accepting life-long, monogamous commitment, a mutual obligation never to abandon them, even long after they had served their "original purposes."

That said, there were, even at the worst points of male domination over women, male landowners who were not cruel and void of empathy. True, it was just a given that they owned their women. However, just like a horse breeder might be very fond of his horses, there were certain men who took pride in being very good to their women.[41] Underneath the oppressive system, natural bonds still formed and sometimes thrived between men and their female sex-slaves in spite of the social inequality between them. While an older male/landowner might continue to keep a fresh supply of younger concubines on hand—if he was wealthy enough to do so—he wouldn't necessarily stop holding some affection for the aging mother of his "legitimate" children, or even for a barren concubine who once pleasured him for nights on end. In most cases, they could always have some place in their households, and there, be taken care of, if not for what services they once provided or others more menial, then for the fact that they had formed and maintained an affectionate bond with their husband/owner. If natural affection failed, though, it was The Code which offered a kind of insurance for the security of women, and a means to prevent a lot of abuse.

But The Code also had a side effect. For lack of a better term, women eventually became addicted to the new system, especially as they came to feel secure within it. Perhaps a few analogies can help us understand this phenomenon. For instance, it's a known fact that long-term prison inmates become so accustomed to having everything decided and provided for them, that they often have great difficulties adjusting to living in society upon their release. In some cases, they will intentionally commit an offence, just so they can be returned to the relative security of prison life. After the Emancipation Proclamation, there were many, newly liberated black slaves who were utterly frightened by the prospect of having to make a living on their own. Numerous freed slaves implored their former masters to keep them on their plantations, if not as servants, as hired hands. By a similar process, women also got so used to being cared for (whether is was good care or bad care) that the idea of being "free and independent" would have been very frightening to most of them.

Before women could truly emerge from their servitude, another ally had to join in before any real women's liberation could take place. As we shall see in later chapters, it was ultimately those men who were *not* the beneficiaries of the sexual slave trade who, for their own reasons, helped turn the tide. These were the males of lower status, those who were excluded from buying the kind and the number of women they really wanted. It was those males who for millennia were the indirect victims of the female sex slave trade, who ultimately formed a union of their own in order to exact concessions from those elite males who had for millennia taken all the prized females for themselves. Not to diminish the tremendous efforts of many a pioneer of women's rights, as we shall see, the present day ideal of monogamous marriage was not so much the triumph of oppressed women who fought their way out of harems. Instead, it was much more the result of a collective bargaining agreement won by oppressed *men* over the powerful to get a better share of prized women that ultimately gave women a substantial measure of equality! And for all this progress toward equality and fairness, modern women remain as competitive as ever when it comes to winning men of the highest status possible.

The Competition Continues

Though The Code set limitations on what the more marketable women could do at the expense of the less marketable, by no means did it do away with female competition altogether. The sense of ever being in competition in the "meat market" survives to this day … and it can get rough! Older women will sometimes communicate a considerable amount of disgust with the younger, shapelier and prettier who offer themselves to older, single men, for a deep down fear of leaving none available to them. Even women competing "in their own league" in terms of age, health and beauty, will tear down and ridicule any whom they feel might have a clear shot at a desirable man they believe is within their reach.

In general, the less desirable a woman feels about herself, the more likely she is to ridicule and try to discourage other women whom she perceives to be more desirable from seeking out male sex partners whom she might think she would otherwise have a chance at attracting. We see this, for example, when a much younger woman dates an older bachelor. An older woman who also fancies the bachelor often gets very angry, calling the younger woman, a "bimbo" or "whore" or "gold digger." Why? The stated motive might be because it offends her religious sensibilities or because she's allegedly concerned for the bachelor's well being in that he won't have much in common with the younger woman if they should form a relationship. But underneath those scruples and alleged concerns, there's likely a more fundamental motive—because it drives down the "market demand" for sex, and thereby, lowers her own "sexual market value." In other words, discouraging the availability of better sex partners encourages men to resort to the imperative, "Better to have sex with older, less attractive women, than to have no sex at all."

On the flip side, the more attractive women will do as much as they can—within the limits of what their society will tolerate—to make themselves as sexually appealing as possible, especially when they go out in public.

Men are frequently mistaken about the principle motive a woman has for wearing a skirt that hardly covers her buttocks or a top that reveals much of her breasts. They are completely baffled when a woman dressed so provocatively gets upset if she notices *them* "checking her out." They ignorantly assume she's dressing this way so *every man* she encounters will look at her and be "turned on."

While it's true she wants to look attractive in the event she encounters a certain kind of guy, she is just as motivated, if not more so, to wear "sexy" attire by the need to establish her "higher rank" among other women! In other words, in order to properly position herself to get that one special guy, once he comes along, she first has to be all decked out to impress, and if need be, to intimidate other females into getting out of her way! So when the right guy finally does come along, she's already in "front position" to win him over her female competitors!

Why Alimony?

To combat the loss of sexual market value, particularly in relation to aging, women were able—over the centuries, and with the help of sympathetic men—to argue for some compensation in the event a husband abandoned her. This was the principle logic behind the creation of alimony payments, and regarded by many a conservative as a civilized restraint against the brutishness of men's primitive instincts. And yet, we can find in this compensation a clear remnant of an even greater brutishness, for contained therein is the principle that money is due for sex with young women—a socially acceptable form of prostitution.

In almost any alimony court hearing, the refrain of the "abandoned" woman goes something like this: "I gave him the best years of my life … and then he left me for that young floozie." Though it is rarely stated overtly, the expectation is that part of the price a husband has to pay for his sexual access to a woman while she was younger—and therefore, more sexually attractive—was to commit to supporting her in her later years after she had aged and was therefore, not as attractive. If he should later choose to do otherwise, especially after the wife of his youth was not as likely to fetch another man, at least none as equally desirable, due to her lack in youthful beauty, the least he could do is compensate her for her loss … loss of sexual market value.

Today, alimony is not as commonly awarded as it once was, largely because of women's advances in the workplace. Before, the overt rationale for expecting divorced men to pay alimony or "maintenance" was because women were less likely to find work adequate to support themselves after having stayed home to rear children. But the clearly understood, if covert, rationale was to compensate them for their reduced ability to sexually attract and secure another man of equal or better status to care for them. To underscore this rationale, alimony payments were usually terminated whenever a divorcée remarried.

Paternity Equals Eternity

We need to further digress a bit in order to grasp the importance of paternity to ancient farming cultures, not just to this life, but the next. We've noted already that one of the first ideas men of the Mesopotamian River Valley, the Cradle of Western Civilization, got about how they could "live beyond the grave" hinged on their biological male heirs inheriting their land and honoring their memory. The afterlife for the ancient farmers of Mesopotamia was something very different from what is taught in modern Sunday Schools. The idea that one could have an individual, full-fledged consciousness in some utopian dimension after death—in other words, what "Bible-believing" Christians of today think of as a soul going to Heaven—would have been very foreign to the minds of ancient Mesopotamian culture. Ironically, though, we can still get a very good idea of what the Mesopotamians did believe about the afterlife from reading the older parts of the Christian Bible, The Old Testament.

The people of the Mesopotamian River Valley—the original home of Abraham, the legendary patriarch of three of the world's largest religions (Judaism, Christianity and Islam)—viewed the afterlife as a semi-conscious state, where one didn't live as a "wide awake" soul, but only as a sleepy shadow or shade of one's former self.

Unfortunately, this difference isn't always clear to the first time reader of the Old Testament, because the translators of the King James Version Bible (the popular translation with all the "thees" and "thous" in it) often used the word "soul" to translate the Hebrew NEPHESH—for what is left of one's self after death. However, a much better translation for this word is "shade," meaning something akin to "ghost," but a ghost whose existence is very tentative. The reason "shade" was used as a metaphor to describe the dead was because the ancients thought of the them as having an existence that could either fade or strengthen depending on how close one remained tied to the world of the living. Just as the amount of shade under a tree would fade or strengthen, depending on how sunny or cloudy it is, so it went with the shades of the dead.

They had no concept of an idyllic Heaven or Paradise, nor a punitive Hell or Hades, where an indestructible soul went after death, depending on how good or bad one behaved in life. Instead, what a man hoped for in the afterlife after burial in the tomb of his fathers was for his shade to abide not too far away in the upper level of an underworld cave refuge called Sheol, and there, rest in peace. If all went well, he could enjoy something like a permanent Saturday morning sleep in, where he is mostly dreaming of the good times he had in life, feeling content and snoozing, not really awake or conscious most of the time.

The strength of one's shade, as with an actual shadow, was contingent on the degree of "light" which shown upon it. As with a natural cave, it was thought that the upper part of this netherworld cavern had more light since it was closer to the surface of the living world. Further down however—again, as with any natural cave—it becomes darker. In the upper part of Sheol, a shade was distinct, but were one to cascade downward to the "bowels of the pit" or the bottom of Sheol, one's existence faded quickly and could turn into nothingness, just as shadows become one with the darkness the deeper one goes into the abyss of a natural cave.

Now, a shade could be "stirred up" or awakened every now and then. And upon waking, they could be in either a good or bad mood. To awaken a sleeping shade could be a good thing if it was done by descendents visiting their ancestor's grave with respect and soft words. (Ever notice how everyone still feels they need to be quiet at a graveyard?) Sometimes, for example, it was thought that a shade might stir with a smile when one of his sons or grandsons came to his grave to pay his respects and recite some nice story about his departed ancestor. However, one could also awaken a sleeping shade in a rude way. The Bible story of King Saul who, one time, clandestinely sought out the help of a medium (the "Witch of Endor") so he could consult with the departed shade of the prophet Samuel was one such rude awakening: "Why hast thou disquieted me, to bring me up?" says the shade to Saul.[42] The departed Samuel had been "resting in peace," and was a little put out that someone other than one of his respectful children had forced him to "get up"!

It was also believed that descendents could ask and receive favors of their dead ancestors, to bless them with prosperity and so on. They would usually make these requests by going to their ancestor's gravesite, where they were "close enough" to hear them. The reason they believed this possible, was their belief that tombs located on the family's land, allowed the dead buried there a portal between Sheol below and world of life above.

The main connection, then, between the dead and their living descendents was the land upon which the departed originally dwelled, and whether their male descendants were on that land, honoring them, carrying on their memory, and keeping them close to the world of light by repeating the stories of their ancestors' accomplishments and carrying forward their name.[43] These were the requirements for keeping the silhouette of one's post earthly existence distinct, staying near the top of the Sheol Cave, in close connection to the living.

We can imagine, then, the fear men must have had of not meeting these obligations. The last thing a man of this era ever wanted to happen was 1) to die without an heir, 2) not to be properly buried on his land and 3) to be forgotten.

What in most of the Old Testament was translated by the Christian Church of England scholars in the 17th century as "Hell" in the King James Version, was not the fiery, place of punishment with devils and pitchforks the modern imagination leaps to. In the Mesopotamian mind, the word "SHEOL" is more accurately translated as "pit" or "cave," the netherworld we've been talking about. Eternal life had nothing to do with keeping commandments or accepting a personal savior. That all came much later. But when one was left with no male heir, or if killed out in the open and the body left to rot, or if one's land was overrun by invaders, then one's shade would begin to descend further down into the bowels of the pit, or the deepest part of the Sheol Cave (Isaiah 14:15).[44] This wasn't a punishment for having committed evil deeds; it was just what happened to anyone who had lost his inheritance, hadn't received a proper burial, or whose children had been killed before they, in turn, could reproduce. As a shade descended deeper into the Sheol cave, the light from the surface faded and any distinction between one's silhouette and the darkness became less and less pronounced until, finally, there was nothing left—oblivion![45]

Another biblical example of this belief comes from the Book of Job. The famous story of Job is a confounding one, indeed, unless we understand it in the context of how important descendents were to the ancient Mesopotamians as the key to eternal life. The tale begins with the well-to-do animal breeder Job who is tested by Yahweh (God) whom he worships. In the story, Satan challenges God's assertion that Job is steadfast in his faith: "Doth Job fear God for naught? Hast not thou made an hedge about him, and about his house, and about all that he hath on every side? Thou hast blessed the work of his hands, and his substance is increased in the land. But put forth thine hand now, and touch all that he hath, and he will curse thee to thy face."[46] God then gives Satan permission to kill all of his children, seven sons and three daughters, all of his oxen, sheep, donkeys and camels, and most of his slaves. To make a long story short, Job basically passes the test of his loyalty to God, not turning against his deity though he has suffered such a great loss. The "happy ending" of the morality tale has God rewarding Job for his faithfulness by giving him twice as many animals and servants as he had before, and another seven sons and three daughters (who are described as "the fairest in all the land," and therefore, worth much more). He is said to have gone on to live to the age of 140, getting to see "his *son's sons* [emphasis mine], even four generations."

Of course, to many of us, the rewards for Job's faith, are overshadowed by the trivialization of the death of his apparently replaceable first ten children, and the image of Yahweh as a cruel and heartless dictator who places his reputation above the value of human life. As with many old tales, though, the real value they contain is separate from any literal interpretations. We need not believe God "permits Satan" to do evil things for any reason—much less just to make a rhetorical point to an adversary—in order to appreciate the insight this story provides on the importance of having descendants at this time in Mesopotamian history.

The death of Job's children was, we're told, the result of God allowing Satan to test him. The good news was that God only does this sort of thing temporarily. If one will pass the test by remaining faithful to God, then he will not only be compensated, but rewarded. Job gets an even better set of kids the second time around. To us moderns, who for the most part, see every human life as being unique and irreplaceable, Yahweh's reward just doesn't sound like that great of a dividend. But when we look at the story from within the prevailing mindset of Job's time—when children equaled your ticket to eternal life—then at least, the logic behind the "reward" is clear. Getting more children to replace the others was, for Job, good compensation, in that he could once again be assured of a posterity. In the end, there's not a word about Job "going to Heaven," but he does get to see for himself that he would leave the Surface World with four generations of sons. The more sons he leaves behind, the more likely he will have descendents who will remember him, visit his tomb, and allow his shade to rest nearby them in peace for as long as he could imagine.

This ancient attitude also explains why, for example, in the story of Abraham—who was childless and already well past his prime when he first meets God—was so focused on Yahweh's promise to give him a son. The "gospel" to Abraham was that "his descendents would be as numerous as all the sands of the earth," and just as important, that "his seed would inherit all the lands (of Palestine) as far as he could see."[47] No mention of Abraham having the "assurance of going to Heaven after he dies." "Going to Heaven" would have made no sense to Abraham and would not have been appealing to him at all.

Adultery: Man Made For Women

Now, we need to tie all these strange stories about Sheol, paternity, land and posterity together with our main theme. Hopefully, the reader has already anticipated how critical it was to be certain that any child who was to become the heir to a man's land was in fact his biological son. This led directly to laws strictly prohibiting women from having sex with anyone except the husbands who bought them. What we now call "adultery" originally had nothing to do with God having some problem with men having sex with more than one woman. The sin of adultery was made to ensure that women, not men, would be sexually monogamous.

Just in case one is tempted to think this is an exaggeration or merely a "secular myth," let's take a closer look at what the Bible actually says, like the account in Deuteronomy 22:13-20, and see what was required under Mosaic law to ensure a woman's virginity ... and why. The passage reveals how a newly sold bride was to lay out a special cloth on the bed where she was to have sex, presumably, for the first time. When she bled after the breaking or tearing of her vaginal hymen, the blood-stained cloth was to be delivered to her father—"proof positive" of the integrity of the "product" he had just sold.[48] If for any reason her husband were to later claim that she was not a virgin at the time of their consummation, her father merely had to produce the "proof of his daughter's virginity" in order to prevent *him* from being put to public shame for having sold a "used item" as if it were brand new and, only incidentally, to keep the terrified girl from being stoned to death! The overly suspicious husband (who was likely too drunk to remember) who was thus proven wrong, had then only to pay a fine to the girl's father to compensate him for having slandered his reputation. (After all, what if you had six other daughters to sell, and the word got out that you couldn't be trusted to deliver an "untarnished product"? Such could lead to serious problems when later negotiating for their bride prices! Right?)

Note that no compensation was paid to the girl who must have been terrified out of her wits while she could only hope that her dear old dad would be able to find and produce the bridal cloth. Any question about the condition of the product/daughter was treated in the same way a modern vendor might insist on "a proper receipt" whenever a customer comes back with a complaint about the product before he even begins to consider giving him a refund.[49]

There's the story of David (the same one who killed the giant Goliath with a sling) who at a later point was asked by King Saul to consider purchasing his daughter for "no dowry except a hundred foreskins of the Philistines."[50] What a deal this had to have been! Nice to know that this sacred institution could be had for killing a hundred people, mutilating their bodies, and bringing some body parts back to your future father-in-law, who received them with a look of satisfaction only a Hannibal Lector could fully appreciate.

As with any rudimentary property laws that dealt with special circumstances, the ancient Law of Moses was no exception. What to do, for example, when a man raped a woman before she had been sold (what we would nowadays regard a felony crime against the woman)? Or what to do about a similar crime that was not uncommon at this time, often referred to as "marriage by capture"?

It wasn't unusual for a man to make an offer to a father for his daughter that just wasn't good enough, or perhaps, not enough to sway him from his intentions to keep her for domestic service. The man then might opt to kidnap the girl and force himself upon her in some hideaway until she was pregnant.[51] By taking her virginity and forcing the conception of a grandchild that he had fathered, he could then hope to leverage her father to accept a lower price for her, and keep his silence about his initial resistance … if only to avoid public embarrassment.

In either case, the Law of Moses sought to restrain this kind of behavior by declaring that the rapist/kidnapper had to be punished … well, punished somewhat—by obligating him to purchase his rape/kidnap victim for no small amount of change! He was required to pay her *father* 50 shekels of silver (about a year's pay for an average worker back then), and then he had to take the girl home as his bride![52]

Sure, the fine was pretty hefty, but notice who got the money? It boggles the mind to think what it must have been like for a rape victim who was not only denied the satisfaction of a fitting punishment for the perpetrator, but who then had to become his property to boot! The only person this Mosaic "rape" law really protected, as well as the only one who was compensated, was the victim's owner/father who would have otherwise been so put out because his daughter/product had been so devalued.

Now in all fairness, there are a few exceptions in the Bible when it comes to love and women finding creative ways to survive, and sometimes thrive. Though the principle reason for Marriage—insurance of paternity—was by no means ever excluded, now and then, we can see in the JudeoChristian Scriptures how women were in some instances able to make the best of a very bad situation. The book of Ruth is one such example.

The story of Ruth is often referred to as "the Bible's best love story," which most assume was between a Jew named Boaz and a gentile (a non-Jew) woman named Ruth. A closer look at the story, though, reveals that the real love story is not about a man and a woman, but a mother and her daughter-in-law.

The story begins with a famine in Judah that was so bad, one Jew decided to pack up and leave for the neighboring Gentile land of Moab. There, his wife Naomi gives birth to two boys. They grow up, and each marry two local Moabite girls. But tragedy strikes again. Naomi's husband and both of her sons die. In frustration, Naomi decides to go back home, but one of her daughters-in-law, Ruth, insists on going with.

When they get back to Judah, things are pretty tough, until one day, a relative of her late husband named Boaz spots Ruth and is immediately attracted to her. The next thing ya know, he's in love and is willing to do anything to win her heart. Though Ruth is a widow (and therefore, by no means a virgin), Boaz is still so crazy about her, he not only agrees to buy/marry her, but he also agrees to re-enfranchise Ruth's widowed mother-in-law, Naomi, by purchasing the land Ruth's late husband's father owned before he left for Moab, and making a home for them all there. The reason he gives for making the "package purchase" is "to raise up the name of the dead upon his inheritance."[53]

Does this logic now sound a little familiar? As noted above, nothing could have been worse for a man of this era than dying without leaving any male descendants on his land. Naomi's husband only sold and left his land out of great desperation. He likely had every intention of coming back, and redeeming it after the famine had passed. Unfortunately, he and both of his sons died before he could do so. But, as bad as it was for Naomi to lose her owner/husband and her two sons, what made it all the worse was the disenfranchisement from the land. The reason? Because her fate in the Beyond was intimately tied to the fate of her deceased husband's property. The fact that she had no living sons on her husband's land was both a terrible shame to bear in the present, and quite a frightening prospect for her in the afterlife.

She had to have felt like she had been cursed. Until her daughter caught the eye of the wealthy Boaz, she had little hope that her husband's shade could ever be recovered from the deep darkness of the lower pits of Sheol. Were his family land never recovered, then her shade would also disappear into the Abyss along with his. These ancients understood that wherever a shade was in Sheol, he took his human property with him, whether slaves, concubines or wives. Naomi was still his wife/property, and therefore, her fate beyond the grave was tied to his.

Of course, the story silently asks us to look past the fact that a male child born to Boaz and Ruth would never be a direct biological descendent of Naomi's dead husband. However, Boaz was a relative of the dearly departed—probably a cousin—the next best thing. At least some of the "seed" that was in Boaz was the same as what had been in Ruth's father-in-law. They knew this because they shared one ancestor, most likely, a grandfather. "Raising up the name of the dead on his inheritance," then, was just another way of saying, "reproducing the family seed on the dead man's land," and thus, releasing the magical power of Seed and Land to retrieve and keep his shade close to the land of the living. As long as Ruth could bear a male child with Boaz, he would be genetically close enough to keep the shade of her dead father-in-law from fading into the depths of Sheol. No doubt Naomi became aware of this possibility after they returned to Judah, and heard that one of her husband's kinsmen was in the market for another woman. Perhaps, it was more than good fortune that Ruth just happened to be "hanging around" Boaz' fields?[54] Let's get back to the story and see.

Ruth had come to love Naomi so much, that she was willing to go back to Judah with her. This was quite a step since she was leaving behind all she'd ever known to go to a foreign country. It's not too odd, then, if Ruth was willing to go this far just to be with her mother-in-law, that she would also be willing to become the sexual property of a man she may or may not have been attracted to (Boaz was probably a lot older and not all that handsome) just so Naomi could die in peace.

On first arrival, the only way Ruth and Naomi can get food is by "gleaning," a social custom requiring farmers not to harvest the corners of their fields so the poor can have something to eat—a kind of ancient Food Stamp provision. One day, a land owner who just happens to share an ancestor with Ruth's father-in-law spots Ruth gleaning in the corner of one of his fields, and he just goes head over heels for her. We're told that it was Boaz who, to get her attention and win her favor, instructs his farmhands to leave even more grain behind than what was required. But as women have sometimes been known to do, then as now, perhaps Ruth was dressed and behaving in such a manner that it was not too much of a surprise that Boaz found her so sexually appealing. Like so many modern men often do when they are madly in love with a woman, especially one that is out of his league, Boaz eventually offered to do anything if she would agree to be his wife. (A woman, who wasn't a virgin and who had no father/owner dictating terms, had a little more say in such matters.) Sure enough, she took the opportunity of Boaz' blinding affection to be agreeable to her purchase, as long as he would take in her mother-in-law as well and redeem the land that once belonged to her late husband's father.

Now for all we know, Ruth came to be as interested in Boaz as he was in her, but the point is how women, regardless of how they felt toward their owners, were able to use their sexual appeal to bargain for the best accommodations possible. Though the new system of the Agricultural world had greatly displaced and demoted the female gender, this didn't exclude all men from naturally loving and caring for their women. And though they were still the property of men, women often found ways to use what naturally occurring lust and love remained to, at least, become property that was well cared for.

Perhaps some who read of how women were forced to go to extraordinary lengths sometimes to make the best of their property status in biblical times would be tempted to think, "Oh, but that was just in that mean Old Testament." If so, then let's take a quick look to see if things really became all that much better by the time a little Jewish sect, started by the close followers of a certain Jewish peasant healer named Jesus, began to write their own versions of what God wanted people to do and believe.

Thou Shalt Not Divorce

Though the gospels provide very little information about Jesus of Nazareth's views on the institution of Marriage, what little there is has had Christian theologians scrambling for centuries. The main reason for this scramble are the two seemingly contradictory messages of Jesus regarding Marriage. One was to discourage the unmarried from marrying which has been taken to mean by some that he was against Marriage, and the other was Jesus' adamant opposition to divorce for those who were already married, which has been taken to mean by some that he supported the institution.[55] We'll first examine the latter view.

In the Gospel of Mark (in a passage most likely to be an original teaching of Jesus according to biblical scholars because of it's multiple attestations in a number of early manuscripts) in chapter 10, verse 11, Jesus states: "Anyone who divorces his wife and marries another commits adultery." The Gospel of Luke reiterates pretty much the same in Chapter 16, verse 18, and interestingly, Matthew 5:32, a gospel written much later than Mark, adds some "clarification." The ban on divorce is repeated, but Matthew adds some interesting language when he quotes Jesus as saying that a man who divorces his wife "*forces her* [emphasis mine] to commit adultery also." It would appear that Matthew wanted to make it clear that women who were turned out by divorce often *had to* either remarry or become prostitutes in order to survive. And then, he adds an exception to allow divorce "for the cause of prostitution."

Many Bible scholars believe that Jesus originally made no such exceptions, but that later Christian communities modified his stern opposition to divorce as being too impractical to follow. Some even go so far as to say that the reason behind Matthew's exception was because some situations would have just been too much for any man to bear, such as "a wife leaving her husband to become a prostitute." But one need not be a biblical scholar to question the logic of this simplified explanation. How often did a wife just get up one day deciding, "I've had enough of this relationship, I think I'll go become a hooker!" Then as now, becoming a prostitute was usually a last resort for a woman's survival.

More likely, this exception clause was added as a convenient euphemism to reinstate and justify the previous norm of men divorcing their wives at will. How? Because it was generally only when a husband divorced a wife, that she would find it necessary to become a prostitute in order to survive. So when later asked, "Why did you, a Christian, divorce your former wife?" the self righteous ex-husband could claim, "because she turned into a whore!" Though in fact, it was *he* who put her in a position where she had no other choice than to sell her body to survive. The cause and effect of divorce were reversed.

Some radical Christian sects who still advocate against Remarriage for any reason mistakenly interpret the old English word "fornication," the one was used in this passage in the old King James Version, to mean "pre-marital sex" instead of the more accurate "prostitution." Thus, they try to argue that Matthew was only saying that a man who discovered on his wedding night that his bride was not a virgin—presumably because after having sex he found that her hymen had already been broken and therefore, must have had sex at least once before—could have the marriage annulled, and he could marry someone else without violating Jesus' commandment. But as it turns out, since their interpretation of the original Greek word is inaccurate, and as stern as the Anti-divorce and Remarriage hold outs are, Jesus may have in fact been even more radical, requiring even men who unwittingly married a "slut" to either remain married to them or else leave for a life of celibacy.

In any case, the question still remains at to whether Jesus' opposition to divorce necessarily means he advocated Marriage. Perhaps, the Marriage teachings attributed to Jesus in the New Testament are not all that contradictory. It's quite possible that he, on the one hand, regarded Marriage as a life long obligation to God with no exceptions, and at the same time, a compromised state that a follower of his could indulge in, but preferably not. Other biblical passages, together with the early Church's tendency to promote celibacy and monasticism, seem to indicate this double-edged view.

The two teachings attributed to Jesus, discouraging Marriage and forbidding divorce, are seemingly reconciled by the basic agreement he implied to his disciples, as recorded in Matthew 19:10. After Jesus teaches against divorce for any cause, his disciples react with such shock to Jesus' view of the Marriage pact as so permanently binding, they conclude that it's "better not to marry at all!" Jesus (in verse 12) doesn't overtly affirm their logic, but he doesn't deny it either. Then, he goes on to say, "some men make themselves eunuchs for the sake of the kingdom of God."

Perhaps Matthew, as in the earlier quote, was re-imagining the original event and replaying it to a later audience who was finding it difficult to deny divorce for everyone in their community. Perhaps, he was also trying to help those who had believed in the Gospel but who were feeling guilty for not having given up sexual relationships altogether as many of the apostles had done, and that he was trying to assure them of their status before God in spite of a tendency to confer "First Class" Christian status upon the celibate. By the time the early church was well established, regardless of whether Jesus taught Marriage to be indissoluble or not, it was largely excepted that he advocated celibacy.

Why then didn't Jesus merely advocate celibacy for *all* his followers? Perhaps, as much as he might have preferred that everyone just drop everything, forgo sex completely along with every other earthly attachment and focus solely on spreading his message, he was also pragmatic. If we look carefully at these two teachings, when Jesus is speaking of his ban on divorce, it's almost always in the context of women. When he speaks of being celibate for the kingdom, he's talking to men. It's no coincidence that almost all of the disciples who were "eunuchs for the Kingdom" were men. Single men had a great deal of flexibility. They could come and go wherever they pleased, and were relatively easy to provide for in their missionary efforts.

Single women, on the other hand, were another story. The society and culture of Jesus' time just wouldn't have understood, much less tolerated, women going all about on their own. They were still regarded as livestock; property that had to belong to someone, and property that ought to be kept in their proper places. They just couldn't be allowed to run loose without someone keeping them corralled. For women, single living was just not a practical alternative in the culture of Jesus' day.

But there's an even better explanation for these two seemingly contradictory views of Marriage—that Jesus' teaching against divorce was out of sympathy for the plight of women in his time. Surely, he was quite aware that, after having been used sexually, women often faced destitution whenever they were "put away."[56] Unless a woman was fortunate enough to have a relative or friend who was willing to put up with the stigma of taking in a divorced woman and see that she was cared for, she was simply out on the street and in the cold. Older women, the unattractive and those who were sickly were particularly vulnerable to destitution and starvation. If a woman found herself so disenfranchised, and she was no longer marketable for her youthful beauty or ability to do menial labor, there was little else to do but become a beggar. By banning divorce, he may have simply been addressing this threat to women in a practical way that would have been more palatable in a culture that was no where near ready to give up the female sex slave trade, but might be convinced to treat those slaves better—"once you buy a woman, you have to permanently take care of her." Therefore, Jesus' ban on divorce was actually quite an improvement, relative to the state of women at this time in history. His effort was not too unlike recent efforts by animal rights activists who have persuaded many a state legislature to establish laws against pet owners abandoning their cats or dogs should they later on grow tired of them.[57]

The Early Church—while not at all interested in removing the institution of female, sexual ownership—applied Jesus' teachings in other ways that, relatively speaking, improved their care. For instance, in I Timothy, Chapter 5, Paul gives instructions on who may be eligible for a church charity that provided assistance for widows. He first advocates that all widows who have relatives be excluded, and he actually curses any families that refuse to provide for them! Then, of those who have no family, and are under the age of 60, he directs that they be remarried as the preferred way to be taken care of. But those whom he felt were "widows indeed" were offered assistance.

As much as the Apostle Paul, like Jesus, preferred male believers to be single, he gives no slack to married men looking for reasons to get divorced. At the same time, he uses his apostolic authority to subdue any inclination by married women to become more self willed, and he does what he can to take the pressure off of husbands who were clearly becoming weary in maintaining their wives. In his letter to the Ephesians, he makes it clear that "the husband is the head of the wife," and that every wife was to "see that she reverences her husband."[58] In the same letter, though, he also orders husbands to love their wives. Paul gives a similar command to husbands in Colosse, but with a telling addition, "husbands, love your wives and *be not bitter against them*" [emphasis mine].[59] In the apostle Peter's first letter, we find a similar attitude: "Wives, be in subjection to your own husbands," followed by a command to husbands to "… give honor unto the wife, *as unto a weaker vessel* …" [emphasis mine].[60] Clearly, the Early Church leaders were all for making some improvements to the status of women, but by no means were they ready for an all out liberation of them.

We need to segue here to note the Early Church's acceptance of a concept that originated with the onset of the Agricultural Era, namely, that one could be *ordered* to love a superior, with the expectation that such "love under duress" could actually work. In the Old Testament, we even find a commandment to the people of Israel: "… thou shalt love the Lord, thy God.…"[61] Though our practical experience tells us that no one can ever be made to love someone, how often do humans wish they could! Then as now, ancient men also tried all they could to constrain their prized purchases to have affections for them. It seems that they believed it quite possible, maybe because they too were often told by their deities' priests to love their gods … or else!

And so it followed that, just as men were ordered to love their gods, women were commanded by (the priests of) their deities to love the men who had purchased them. By reminding women of this divine obligation, they hoped to pressure them into being affectionate toward them, if not in response to any earthly motivation, then with fear from above.

This illogical concept of compelling love, born within the practice of enslaving women as sex slaves, is alive and well today. Even though the female sex slave trade has been largely done away with in Western societies, the idea of compelling love has found a very comfortable life in its descendent institution, what we now call Marriage. Clearly, the institution of Marriage has, to this day, carried with it the idea that one can be constrained to love. Though invented for women, the only difference is that it now also applies to men. We see how modern marriages offer the hope of compelling love where there is fear of eventually losing it. By getting a man to vow to God and "make a commitment" until death, the bride is led to believe that she is getting some insurance that her husband will be forced to love her when, as feared, he will be tempted to abandon her for someone else when she's older, not as attractive, "lets herself go," or he's simply grown weary of being with the same women.

Getting back to the Early Church, it's clear that the apostles believed the place of women was in direct subordination to their owner/husbands. Both Peter and Paul justified this hierarchical order by their presumptions of female inferiority. Paul relates, as a commonly accepted fact, that a wife can't think for herself; her husband is, therefore, "her head." Peter says a wife is a "weaker vessel." True, their presumptions were tempered by their admonitions toward the "superior" male to follow through with the greater responsibility of good caretakership, but it most certainly came from a condescending position.

While a very long way from what we would today call "women's liberation," the teachings of the Church did lead to some improvements in their condition compared to the previous norms. Before, it was simply up to each male owner to decide for himself how he may treat his "purchased property." As we will see later, though, it may have been precisely because of such reforms, that Marriage became palatable to later, more humane societies which otherwise might have done away with it altogether.

The Story of Tamar

While there were some modest reforms of the institution of Marriage by the early Christian Church, whatever net improvements achieved, they were tempered by the Church's perpetuation of anti-sexualism. Many people assume that the Bible consistently prohibits both men and women from having sex with anyone accept one's lawfully wedded spouse. However, the idea that a man should feel any fear, guilt or shame for having sex with someone other than his wife came thousands of years after holding only women to this standard. If one merely takes the time to read the Bible, one finds that it was originally only prohibited for a man to have intimacy with the wife of another man who was of equal or higher status. Otherwise, it was not at all a problem for men to have sex with any other woman, whether he had a wife (or wives) of his own or not. This point is clearly made in the story of Judah and Tamar, as we return to the Old Testament Book of Genesis, and read the 38th Chapter.

Judah had three sons, and had purchased a wife for the oldest named Er. Unfortunately, Er met an untimely death, leaving his widow Tamar in a bad position. "Bad" because, having been purchased for a man to produce his heir but dying before he could impregnate her, meant her "purpose for being" was gone.

As already noted, ancient laws and customs, though primitive, had been devised to deal with special situations where inheritance and paternity were concerned. As an example, "What to do if a landowner dies, after a wife has been purchased but before she bears him a male child?" Well, the crude laws of the patriarchs had the answer.[62] Under this circumstance, a dead man's eldest brother was obliged to take in his widow, impregnate her on his brother's behalf, and then take care of her and the child until he was grown and could inherit his father's land.

It was a nice insurance policy for the dearly departed man, but was often a heavy obligation for his brother who'd have to support a woman and at least one child without receiving the benefit of inheriting any portion of his brother's land for himself. Instead, the child would eventually get the property in honor of his deceased "father" (who was biologically his uncle). In order for a brother to pass on his own inheritance, he would have to be in a position to support at least one additional wife, and this was often difficult as most men could barely afford to buy one. So taking on the care of a deceased brother's widow was not always gladly welcomed, especially since it meant getting nothing in return.

Sure enough, Er's oldest brother Onan didn't really want to be so encumbered. When the time came for him to raise up a seed for his brother, he only went through the motions of attempting to impregnate Tamar (employing what we'd now call the "withdrawal method" of birth control).[63] Tamar continued to remain childless, and as fate would have it, Er's brother also met an untimely death, and poor Tamar was once again in socioeconomic limbo.

According to the common law of this time, Judah could have next arranged for Tamar to become the wife of his youngest son Shelah (even though he was only about 10 years old), but after losing his first two sons, Judah held off for fear that he might die too. He suspected that Tamar had brought some curse with her to his elder sons' beds. But he had a ready excuse to put Tamar off, claiming that there was no point in giving her to Shelah until he attained puberty. To do so would have only served to give Tamar a better standing, and Judah was not about to arrange a marriage of convenience just to help her, and certainly not at the risk of his last remaining son's life. Instead, he ordered her to "remain a widow until Shelah was grown," which was pretty much the same as demoting her to a slave. Tamar had no say in the matter because, after having been sold to Er, or more accurately, sold to Judah to give to Er, her fate now rested with the family patriarch even though she was now widowed and "temporarily" returned to her father's house.

Tamar dutifully complied, but she may have already anticipated what was to come: when Shelah finally hit puberty, Judah did nothing and failed to reinstate her by giving her to him as a wife.[64] Surely, Tamar must have felt very cheated. But as we've already seen, women in bad situations like the one Tamar found herself in often came up with ingenious ways, if sometimes risky, to turns things around.

While being a wife meant sexual slavery, it was a lot better than being a de facto worker slave in her father's house. We might compare this situation to those of African American slaves prior to the Civil War who were relatively fortunate to work inside the plantation mansion instead of having to sweat and toil in the fields. Similarly, the female sex slave purchased to produce an heir, usually got better living quarters, better food, better clothes, and so forth, not necessarily because the owners cared for these slaves more, but by virtue of their proximity to the owner. Whether a Pre-Civil War, southern house slave or the wife-slave of a landowner in ancient Palestine, it was necessary that they reflect the elevated status of their owners. Tamar's plight was like that of a mansion slave forced to work in the fields who is trying to figure out some way to regain her former, relatively better position.

Tamar, therefore, waited for a chance to do something about her situation, and luckily, one came along. We don't know whether she had made plans in advance or on the spot, but it's clear that Tamar knew what she was going to do by the time she got word one day that Judah was on a trip to see a friend of his who lived nearby. Quickly, she changed her clothing and headed out to the road that led to the friend's home. As Judah was hiking along, he spotted a young woman on the side of the road whom he took for a prostitute. The woman, of course, was Tamar, who had covered her face (and no doubt put on some kind of otherwise revealing attire), which at this time was the way in which prostitutes advertised themselves and which also provided a convenient disguise. Clearly, Tamar must have known enough about Judah's sexual habits to have thought this plan had a decent chance of working.[65] Sure enough, Judah saw her, liked what he saw, and stopped to do a little pricing. He made an offer, promising for her "service" a young goat from his herd.

There was just one problem—he didn't happen to have the goat with him. What to do? They didn't have credit cards back then. Or did they? As it turned out, Judah did have with him some highly personalized items which could, indeed, be used in lieu of "cash." In this case, the items were a staff (which likely had the names of his ancestors written on it), a cord (with colored strands particular to his tribe, not unlike a Scottish tartan) and a signet ring, items difficult to duplicate and therefore, unmistakably the owner's. So Judah agreed to let the woman have his staff, cord and ring, as a kind of security deposit, ensuring that he would give her the goat later on, and thus conducted their business. Afterwards, Judah left, and later on sent a friend of his with the goat as promised to find the prostitute, pay her off and get Judah's things back. But by the time he got there. She was gone.

Now, let's stop here for a moment to take notice of something. Remember, this is the Holy Bible we're reading, "God's Word," to millions of people who believe this same book teaches against things like extra marital sex. But lo and behold, Judah's sexual encounter with Tamar, as a prostitute, is *never once* deemed inappropriate, not by anyone in the story, not by the author, no one.

Back to the story. When at first Judah learned that the woman could not be found, he only became concerned that his business reputation could be hurt—that someone might think he couldn't be trusted to pay his bills—not that anyone might learn he'd "had sex outside of marriage." But he comforts himself by saying, more or less as someone might do when they forgo an apartment deposit for the same amount of their last month's unpaid rent: "She can just keep those things, so I won't be shamed." In other words, since Judah gave her some collateral, and he made a good faith effort to pay his obligation, then by letting her keep the collateral, his reputation should be protected … or so he thought.

The story gets a little twisted, though, when later on Judah finds out that the woman was actually Tamar, the widow of his eldest sons who'd suffered the untimely deaths. Three months after Judah's little whoopdeedoo on the road side, Tamar comes up pregnant. Still in the dark, Judah is furious when he first learns of the pregnancy, and actually threatens to have her burned to death. Never minding *his* sexual escapades and the fact that the only reason Tamar was in sexual limbo in the first place was thanks to Judah's procrastination, he yells at her for daring to violate her obligation to have sex with no one until she is given to another rightful owner. Imagine his surprise, then, when she produces his staff, cord and ring, thus proving that it was Judah's child she was carrying!

Embarrassing to say the least, but again, not for the reason we in our modern mind set would readily suspect. Yes, the revelation made Judah feel very ashamed … but not because he had sex with a girl he thought was a hooker, and not even because it became public knowledge that he had had sex with his daughter-in-law, both outside of wedlock. No, he was ashamed of himself only because

Tamar's daring act exposed Judah for his phobia and inaction—that he had failed to give her as a wife to his younger son Shelah, so their first male child would then be heir to the land.

In other words, the moral of this tale (and thus, the reason for telling it) was not that Judah shouldn't have been a fornicator or an adulterer, nor was the lesson about how bad it was of him to have displaced Tamar (which we only learn as an incidental). No, the intended lesson was that Judah should not have allowed his superstitious fear (that his youngest son might also die were he to share a bed with Tamar) cloud his good senses from seeing his most important obligation—*to make sure that the names of his sons who'd died were raised up on their inheritance.* The story of Tamar (who, by the way, came out the better in the end after becoming pregnant with an heir, allowing her to move back into Judah's home with full, de facto wife status) gives us a clear view of the double standard for sexual behavior that was quite acceptable among "God's people" up until some changes that followed centuries later.[66]

Until then, even a cursory study of the Old Testament reveals numerous accounts in which "chosen men of God" pretty much got a whole lot of sex from a whole lot of women other than their first wives. The only times they were punished by God, criticized by priests or condemned by prophets for getting all this "extra action" was when they were violating the wife of some other man of status.[67] It was only much later, after influences from other cultures, particularly that of the Greeks, that men began to be seriously impugned for giving in to their lustful desires.

Stoics, Cynics and "True Liberty"

In 333 BCE, Alexander the Great swept through Palestine as part of his conquest of the Middle East, wresting away domination from the Persians. Palestine in the 4th Century BCE, included a remnant of the Jews who had returned after their ancestors had been carried away into Babylonian captivity several hundred years before.

Not long after the Babylonians had completely conquered Judah in 587 BCE, they themselves were conquered by the Persians in 539. The Persians were a little more sympathetic to the Jews, and eventually permitted a remnant to resettle in their ancient homeland. The returned Jews, though vassals to Persia, had adapted to living under the Persian ways of doing things. But when the Greeks came crashing in, the Jews became subject to a new culture—Hellenism.

Alexander the Great's conquest of Palestine brought Greek culture, including several schools of Greek philosophy into the mainstream of middle eastern societies. The ideas of Socrates, Plato, Aristotle, and other schools once limited to the Mediterranean world, now traveled East. Two very influential Greek philosophical schools, the Stoics and the Cynics (not to be confused with the term "cynics" as is used today to refer to people who are very skeptical of others' motives), became very well known and began to have an impact on the culture of the restored Jewish settlements. For some Jews, these Pagan philosophies weren't entirely flawed, and their ideas began to filter into Jewish religious thought.

Both of these schools taught that material attachments were the source of all of mankind's woes, and that if one could only separate himself from being dependent on any thing or anyone, he could then truly be free and at peace (oddly enough, not very different from the basic teachings of Siddhartha Gautama—Buddha.) The Stoics taught that this detachment was largely a mental and emotional one—"I can have a coat, a cup, a house, a wife, etc., but I should never be emotionally attached to them." The Cynics, on the other hand, taught that the only way to be truly free was to not actually possess any more than what was absolutely necessary.[68] The Cynics were what we might now call "anti-materialists," and while few people imitated their bare necessity lifestyle, they came to be admired by many for giving up so much for their beliefs. This was particularly the case among the poor.

When the Cynical school of thought was introduced into Palestine, it quickly became appealing to those peasant Jews who didn't have a lot to give up in the first place, and who were constantly being told that their poor estate was a sign of God's disfavor. At a time when most religions and philosophies, including Judaism, equated prosperity with God's favor, Cynicism gave the poor grounds to not only assert a degree of moral equality with the well-to-do, but even to see themselves as morally superior!

As the Jews had for centuries been dominated by others, and had very little to show for the hay day of the Kingdom under Solomon the Great, the basic ideas of Cynical philosophy filled a wide vacuum in the Jewish consciousness. Within time, there would arise a number of Jewish versions of the Greek school that despised the material world, earthly kingdoms, political power and sexual attachments as base, animalistic, and unbecoming to the state of man that ought to be devoted to the "purity" of religious devotion. Eventually, one Jewish peasant in particular, in the grand tradition of Cynical philosophy, would begin a revolution that would change the world and result in taking the stringent sexual rules originally made for women and turn them upon men as well.[69]

Jesus and Paul—Jewish, Cynical Teachers

One need only lay side-by-side the sayings of Jesus (easy to do with one of those handy "red-letter" bibles) next to the sayings of the Cynical philosophers to find they had a lot in common.[70] Again and again, we find Jesus attacking the rich, reaching out to the poor and displaced, and making virtue out of being content to have only the bare necessities of life.

The New Testament is rather silent about Jesus' early life with only a vignette or two about his childhood. For all we know, Jesus had attempted marriage in his younger years. Maybe he had sex with women outside of marriage, maybe even with prostitutes. Perhaps, he had some very bad experiences with women that ultimately led him to find the teachings of Cynicism on "the oppressive bondage of sexual attachments" and their many accompanying woes appealing. We will likely never know.

What we do know is that the picture we get from the New Testament is that Jesus had little use for sexual relationships, and many of his later followers—most notably Paul the Apostle—swore them off in order to devote themselves more fully to the work of evangelism. As an example, look at the practical advice Paul shares with the Corinthian Christians on this very topic in response to their question about whether it was OK or not for a Christian man to ever have sexual contact with a woman: "Now concerning the things whereof ye wrote unto me: It is good for a man not to touch a woman. Nevertheless, to avoid fornication, let every man have his own wife, and let every woman have her own husband. Let the husband render unto the wife due benevolence: and likewise also the wife unto the husband. The wife hath not power of her own body, but the husband: and likewise also the husband hath not power of his own body, but the wife. Defraud ye not one the other, except it be with consent for a time, that ye may give yourselves to fasting and prayer; and come together again, that Satan tempt you not for your incontinency. But I speak this by permission, and not of commandment. For I would that all men were even as I myself. But every man hath his proper gift of God, one after this manner, and another after that. I say therefore to the un-married and widows, it is good for them if they abide even as I. But if they cannot contain, let them marry: for it is better to marry than to burn."[71]

Paul set the stage for how sex was to be treated by the Church for hundreds of years in this letter that was to eventually come to be regarded as part of the Word of God. He didn't go so far as to say that having sex was a sin under every circumstance, but he made it perfectly clear that if one wanted to be a First Class Christian, he'd better do without it.

Paul didn't view sex as a gift of Nature and the principle "mortar" by which humans bonded together to form the fundamental structure of society—the family. But let's not be too hard on Paul, or Jesus for that matter, if they only viewed sex as a carnal distraction from what they believed to be far more important—"spiritual things." In the world they lived in, sex was hardly given the place that Nature had conferred upon it. Rich men had sex with their wives to ensure a rightful heir to their property, but went right on to have sex with prostitutes, concubines and even children! Women were frequently displaced and left destitute by divorce. Temple priesthoods regularly made use of enslaved prostitutes whose incomes brought in the lion's share of their livelihood and the maintenance of their orders. It was standard procedure for conquering armies to rape and enslave the women of the conquered as part of their compensation. The contemporary sexual behavior of 2000 years ago was overwhelmingly a tragic state of affairs. Loving sexual relationships existed, but they did so in spite of the dominate sexual milieu, not because of it.

Given all the abuse of sex and women at this time, perhaps its not surprising that later Church leaders ultimately interpreted the ascetic examples of Jesus' and Paul's celibacy to mean that all believers ought to imitate their example if they could and that sex was a necessary evil at best.

It took several centuries for the Church to decide it's exact position on sex. Initially, there was quite a hodgepodge of traditions that all claimed to have an inside track on Jesus' original teachings. Some were quite "libertarian" about human physical desires. Others were more inclined to interpret Jesus' and Paul's choices as proof of their special callings, but not a universal requirement to abstain from sex. But it was the most radical group, the sexual ascetics, who prevailed in having the most influence on church teachings and rules for sexual behavior.

Augustine and Neo Platonism

The Early Church of the first and second centuries was composed of many different kinds of Christians. Some were very libertarian, like the Christian sect of Manichaeanism (a kind of Christianized version of Greek Stoic philosophy). Manichaeists, for example, would agree with other Christians that pursuing sex for the sake of pleasure is sinful … but an unavoidable pursuit while dwelling in a world corrupted by sin. They reasoned that one's fleshly sins would be forgiven, thanks to Christ's sacrificial death, and that real freedom from earthly attachments was for most only attainable in the next life.

But the Christian philosophy that eventually came to dominate the Church ran side-by-side with the Greek schools which took a dimmer view of the material world. To be sure, the ascetic Christians took their inspiration from the traditional stories of Jesus and his teachings (or perhaps were responsible for preserving those they agreed with and suppressing those they disliked), but also from a number of contemporary teachers who in their turn had been heavily influenced by Cynicism and the later teachings of Aristotle and Plato. Apart from Jesus, Paul and the original disciples, perhaps there was no teacher so influential and charismatic as the early 5th Century North African bishop who put his stamp of sexual asceticism upon the Church as no one has since—Saint Augustine of Hippo (354-430 CE).

The story of Saint Augustine's personal journey to Roman Christianity helps us to understand how he came to regard the place of human sexuality within the context of a world view that he defined as a mere testing ground to determine where each soul was to dwell for eternity. In his youth, Augustine had at first come under the influence of the more "liberal" Manichaeists. As such, he accepted that his earthly desires were evil, but that there was little to do about them other than to believe in Christ's forgiveness for his fleshly indulgences. But this left him very conflicted. The sect offered no solution toward overcoming fleshly desire and attachment during earthly life.

Augustine had at least two mistresses and indulged in a number of sexual pleasures as was common for a middle class youth of his time. In his book "Confessions," he revealed how he came to feel increasingly guilty about caving in and being controlled by the desires of his body.

In time, Augustine renounced the Manichaean sect, and moved to Italy. There, he began to attend—probably as a superficial gesture to advance his teaching career—the church where a Roman Christian Bishop named Ambrose skillfully impressed him by his eloquent oratory and knowledge of Greek philosophy, especially Cynicism, and it's later incarnation, Neo-Platonism.[72] Augustine eventually accepted baptism into the Roman Church, and adopted a very ascetic style of Christian philosophy, no doubt incorporating into his new found faith the anti-materialism and anti-sexualism of the Neo-Platonism of his day.

Augustine's distinctive scholarship and reputation for excellence in oration propelled him into church leadership, eventually becoming the bishop of Hippo in Northern Africa. He went on to write profusely and preach vehemently in defense of the Roman Christian Church, calling upon all to be baptized into the "one, true faith," and to persevere with all one's conviction to shed the pleasures of the present world in preparation for the next. Though monastic orders had already been founded by the time of Augustine's conversion, his influence upon the faithful led thousands more, both men and women, to abandon all fleshly pleasures, to take oaths to celibacy, and to "forsake all to follow Christ."

For what reasons specifically, we may never know, but Augustine's compulsive battle to convince Christians to do without as much sexual pleasure as possible in the here and now was perhaps his own way of giving himself some catharsis for the guilt he felt for the sexual indulgences of his youth. For having allowed himself to become so attached in such a carnal manner (and what greater emotional and carnal "attachments" are there but sexual ones?), so anathema to the high ideals of Cynical purity of thought now recycled into the purity of Christian spirituality, he spent the rest of his days sounding the call to renounce fleshly desire and refuse sexual satisfaction. From this time all the way until only the last 3 decades, sex was generally viewed by the Christian faithful as an evil.

The Absolution Industry

For a millennium to follow, the Church openly sought to subdue, in both genders, one of the most basic of human biological drives. It wasn't long before ecclesiastical regulation even called upon the married to abstain from sex on so many "holy days" of the year that there were more days when sex was prohibited than permitted.[73] To be sure, the Neo-Platonic influences on the Early Church had a lot to do with this onslaught. But perhaps the Church had some other reasons to embrace such a severe stance against a fundamental, biologically driven behavior that surely was impossible for most to overcome, even temporarily.

Some have suggested the reason was to protect property. In the middle ages, the second born sons of noble families were expected to become priests, leaving the first born males to inherit all the lands of the feudal kingdoms. If the Church had become a bastion of second born males, it's not unthinkable that many of them would have been jealous of their elder brothers' who were grabbing up all the land. To get back at them and to retrieve some of that property, the Church instituted an array of prohibitions against sex and other behaviors that would serve to prevent the first born from reproducing: No sex on the scores of holy days throughout the year; no divorce, even if a wife was barren; prohibitions against the use of wet nurses (in that breast feeding causes the body to naturally prevent eggs from being fertilized); and prohibiting marriage between cousins (which made it difficult to find an eligible woman in that nearly everyone was so closely related at a time when travel was so limited). To a considerable extent, the strategy worked. The Medieval Church accrued more property than ever before.

Nevertheless, there was an even larger advantage to restricting sex to such a bare minimum. The Church had also discovered that the best way to promote ecclesiastical security was to establish an unending need for ecclesiastical services so they would always be in demand. The "beauty" of making sex an evil, for both men and women—even if it was being conducted specifically for the purpose of procreation—was ideally suited to the Church's monopoly over the means of getting absolution from sexual sin through the Sacrament of Confession.

Since priestly absolution was only good until the next infraction and could only be secured for a price, providing absolution translated into a vicious cycle of never ending payments for the sinner, and thus, a cycle of never ending revenue for the Church! Though Christianity didn't invent the Absolution Industry, it most certainly found unprecedented ways to exploit the faithful for their natural desires and nurtured their guilt for having them. It's not beyond the veil of imagination to wonder if most of the great Christian cathedrals of Europe and beyond were built with funds that came from the masses of people who were made to feel chronically bad about themselves.

Due to differences in their sexual nature, women were better able, on the whole, to abide by the restrictions on their sexual behavior that had already been imposed upon them millennia beforehand.[74] But it was pure, evil genius to have found a way to take advantage of men's overwhelming sex drive in order to finance the Absolution Industry. The oppression that for thousands of years had been reserved for one gender, was now expanded to both.

The Inoculating Effect of Marriage Reform

As noted above, the efforts by the Church to repress male sexuality had the benefit of leading to some changes that helped the estate of women. However, making improvements to the state of sexually enslaved women was a two-edged sword. To be sure, the Church did help remove some of the worst aspects of the sexual slave trade. Divorce was banned as a way of deterring men from casting aside a wife who no longer suited any purpose. Fathers were required to give away their daughters at weddings instead of selling them. And though polygyny continued for several centuries, it was eventually prohibited by the Church and states of Europe.

Can we, though, really think of these changes to the institution of Marriage as having somehow weeded out the bad and left only the good? Or did these "reforms" only serve to inoculate society from realizing that, no matter how much we try to dress it up and make it look appealing, the institution is still at its core a bad thing that just needs to be abolished altogether? If this sounds shocking to some, imagine for a moment that another institution that was founded almost at the same time as Marriage, African slavery, instead of being abolished altogether, had been merely reformed.

We can only be grateful that the plantation owners of the Pre-Civil War South hadn't conceived of the kind of rhetoric that is nowadays used to "protect the institution of Marriage" in order to preserve African American Slavery. What if they had gotten the idea to modify slavery just enough to make it less obvious to most people that it was in fact an evil through and through? They could have, for instance, drawn up laws that required plantation slave owners to provide better living quarters, ordinances prohibiting the separating of family members in slave auctions, and punishments for any who sexually violated slaves against their will. They might have instituted a process of "voluntary servitude," whereby Africans could have been "asked to voluntarily make a commitment" to life-long slavery in order to justify punishments for later changing their minds to want their freedom as a violation of their own vows.[75] What if the Abolitionists could have been put off, as the whipping of insubordinate slaves and the hanging of runaways were done away with in favor of fines or periods of confinement, making abolitionist books like Uncle Tom's Cabin less likely to have been written. Perhaps, in time, even minimum daily requirements for their feeding might have been added. Imagine if the South had developed a propaganda campaign that lauded the great benefits plantation owners provided for their slaves. We might very well have never fought the Civil War, and every African American today might still be the property of well-to-do whites!

Would such "positive improvements" have really been the right answer to the evil of slavery? Hopefully, most would answer with a resounding, "No! Of course not!" The slavery of Africans was just plain wrong, and even though the emancipation of slaves resulted in far reaching changes to the order of American society—some of which we are still adjusting to today—most anyone with any good will understands that it was still the right thing to do. How short of the mark of true social justice our society would have fallen had we settled for anything less—like reforming slavery, making slavery better, fixing slavery, or helping blacks to find the secret to a happy slave life!

Likewise, reforming Marriage, making Marriage better, fixing Marriage, finding the secret to a happy marriage, are all efforts that fall far short of what really needs to be done. While removing the worst aspects of what Marriage used to be was certainly an improvement—it's just not enough to stop there. Marriage, therefore, ought to be completely privatized.[76] In a later chapter, we'll examine in detail the idea of privatization, but for now, we'll return to the history of Marriage.

State Licensure of Marriage

Whatever the original teachings of Jesus of Nazareth were (or those of the first century Church for that matter), by the time the Christian religion was legalized and adopted by the Roman Emperor Constantine in the early 4th Century, the Church had already begun to argue for the exclusive right to sanction all marriages before God, i.e., to make Marriage a sacrament. By making Marriage a sacrament, the Church was able to extend a powerful influence over all of European civilization. The only way to have a sexual union validated was by an official religious rite by an ordained priest of the One, Holy, Roman and Universal Church. Only the heirs of such sanctified unions then, would be considered legitimate. The Church had seized upon the vacuum that Roman Law had left behind where marriage rites were largely regarded a family matter.

The State had nothing to do with recognizing, licensing or registering marriages. They were exclusively processed by the Church and through its priests. It was the Church which had the only say as to whether a sexual union was recognized in the eyes of God as well as man.[77] It was only when the Protestant Reformation of the early 1500s began that this power was finally challenged.

In England, the challenge began as a political one. When King Henry VIII's first wife, Catherine of Aragon, couldn't provide him with a male heir, Henry had his Lord Chancellor Thomas Wolsey, Archbishop of York, appeal to Pope Clement VII for an annulment.[78] Unfortunate for the king, though, was the pope's dependency on Charles V, Holy Roman Emperor and nephew of, you guessed it, the same Catherine. The Pope steadfastly refused.

By 1533, King Henry gave up on getting any help from Clement VII, and boldly moved to assume full control of the Church of England. As the new church head and "Defender of the Faith," he promptly decreed his right to divorce, and was remarried to Anne Boleyn the same year. The Church of England carried on with pretty much the same kind of authority to sanction sexual unions as did its Roman cousin, but with one big difference—the Church was no longer separate from the British Crown. Though it retained some independence, from this point on the Church in England was regarded as an extension of the State, and so whatever the Church did in the name of God was also done in the name of the King, including the process of sanctioning sexual relationships.

Under English Common Law, a couple didn't necessarily have to go to a church to be married, though most did. As long as they were of age (males had to be at least 14 and females at least 12), they could simply agree between themselves that they were married, thus the term, "common law marriage." For good Christians, though, a church sanction was a necessity, and besides, it was still a relatively simple process of making arrangements with the local priest, and proclaiming a "bann," a verbal announcement of their intentions at their local church, assuming of course, they wanted everyone of their friends and family to know they were engaged.

When the Church first came under the control of the British Crown, the Crown allowed the Church to stipulate its requirements for marriage according to it's canon law, and to keep all the records of who was married to whom. The British Government didn't get directly involved with Marriage until a crisis arose in the middle 18th Century over the issue of "clandestine marriages."

With the Industrial Revolution quickly narrowing the gap between aristocrats and a rising middle class, and with more people coming to live in the cities, soon men and women of different classes began to meet, find each other attractive, sometimes becoming intimate, and also, wanting to marry. For the wealthy, prominent and upper classes, marriage across the diminishing gulfs between them and someone of the proletariat was anathema! As time went on, though, more and more cross-class intermingling went on, and in order to avoid interference from protesting parents and other family members, many couples took to marrying outside of a formal wedding in the church proper to marrying in secret.

In other words, a growing number of couples began looking for a way to still get the church's blessing on their union, but in a venue that was relatively inexpensive, available without any notice and most importantly, discreet. To meet this demand, as well as to satisfy the minimum requirements of the Church of England's canon law (which only asked that the service be read out of the Common Book of Prayer), a new class of clergymen of questionable training and ordination emerged. Many of these men were either defrocked priests or perhaps not even priests at all. Not unlike the more familiar Las Vegas wedding chapels, marriage booths began to spring up in every major city. The ordinary rules were often bent to accommodate any couple willing to pay the standard fee, such as backdating their marriage date records in the event a bride was already pregnant. In London, most of these marriage shops were set up next to the famous Fleet prison. Soon, the term "Fleet Marriage" became synonymous with a clandestine marriage.

Needless to say, many an aristocratic parent of a daughter whom they wished to "marry well," were not at all pleased with this growing institution. Finally, they found a champion to help them save their daughters from being "stolen away" by men of lower birth.

To save the day came a certain Lord Chancellor Hardwicke who, in 1753, managed to convince Parliament to pass the Marriage Act. Far from being a move to protect the interests of women, the new act was clearly designed to slow down the ever increasing number of aristocratic daughters running off and marrying "rogues"!

The Marriage Act of 1753 took control away from the Church to preside over the legal recognition of Marriage. Severe punishments were set forward for any priests who married couples under the age of 21 without parental consent. There were penalties for the performance of marriages by laymen posing as ordained priests and defrocked priests were similarly prohibited. And banns became a requirement, not only as a verbal announcement, but to be put in writing and kept, not as a church record, but as a legal instrument in a local office of the Crown, in effect, created what we now think of as the Marriage license.

Up to a point, the Marriage Act of 1753 did reduce the number of clandestine marriages and ultimately put the Fleet Street marriage market out of business. However, the efforts of the Blue Bloods to stem the tide of inter-class marriage was in vain. This was largely because the New Economy was replacing agriculture based wealth, and thus, blurring class distinctions and making it increasingly easier for the young of different classes to marry.

On the northern European continent, there was a clean swap made between the Church's and the State's authority over Marriage. During the German Reformation, the authority of the Church to legitimize sexual unions was directly confronted by Martin Luther, who went into very specific reasons in his eight-volume Genesis Commentary for why Marriage should no longer be a sacrament: "Marriage is a civic matter. It is really not, together with all its circumstances, the business of the church, and therefore, out to be handed over to the State to license, register and govern." The Church's only role in Marriage, as far as Luther was concerned, was to offer its blessings and ministerial support.[79]

It's difficult to imagine just how revolutionary Luther's redefinition of Marriage was. On the surface, couples continued to come to church and exchange their vows. Both men and women were supposed to be virgins before they married, and were supposed to remain monogamous thereafter. However, gone were the notions that church ceremonies were absolutely necessary to have legitimate children. Couples could opt for a civil ceremony if they so wished, and their union would be recognized just as much as any who'd had a church wedding ceremony.[80] The Reformation, therefore, struck the first of several blows to follow against the Church's power over the most intimate of human relationships. Soon, another great change came over Europe that, in time, wrested away even more of the Church's control over the bedroom.

The Fall of Bride Prices and Rise of Dowries

During the Middle Ages, Europe became a network of feudal states. The once vast Roman Empire had dwindled to a weak regional power in Northern Italy, replaced only by the religious influence of the Church. The Roman Republic had been founded by citizen land owners, the wealthiest of whom usually made up the Senate. But after Rome's demise, this changed. The basis of all power, land ownership, maintained its economic and political significance, but a new idea was brought in which asserted that only the King really owned all the land—Feudalism. Land owners were replaced by barons and knights who were "permitted" the use of lands in return for their loyalty and pledges to defend the king's realm. The difference between a Medieval feudal baron's estate and a citizen farmer of the Roman Republic was seemingly a matter of semantics. But the fact is Feudalism removed people from the more intimate connection to the land they once had before, the same connection that precipitated the original Marriage Institution.

The Renaissance and the discovery of sea routes to the East took this disconnection to yet another level. By the time of the Protestant Reformation of the 1500s, more and more people were beginning to earn their living, not from farming, but trade. In many ways, the Reformation was led by the new Middle Class who owned property for the purpose of conducting trade, such as a shop or a ship, while farming was left to others.

This new division of labor had a large impact on the relative economic value of children, and in turn, the wives who bore them. In an Agricultural society, the more children one has, the more loyal and harder-working farm hands one has. Children in agricultural societies are, therefore, an economic asset. However, as Europe began to move slowly but surely away from being organized strictly around agriculture, and more toward trade and business, the economic value of children began to drop, especially for females.

To be certain, children were employed in shops and markets just as they had previously been employed in the farm fields, but the rising costs of feeding, clothing and housing them wasn't as well offset by putting one's children to work in the shop in lieu of a hired employee. As a consequence, the ancient customs of purchasing women began to fade. A young, attractive, healthy virgin, in a strictly agricultural society, was very valuable, and a hefty bride price could be gotten for her—well worth the years of feeding, clothing and housing her. But in the emerging world of trade and rudimentary business adventures—as was the case by the time of the Reformation—Christian men seeking a permanent mate weren't about to compensate her parents for taking her care off their hands. In fact, the opposite began to take place, especially for the well-to-do aristocrats.

In aristocratic circles, maintaining a female was a costly affair, as society and tradition required that she wear the right clothes, be attended by a proper number of servants, and live in a proper (i.e., expensive) home. The advent of mercantilism had so changed the economic equation of marriage that the pendulum swung all the way from a bridal market over to a suitor's. Soon, parents of brides began *paying* dowries to the family of the new husband, as it became less expensive to pay a man to take her than to put up with the on going costs of supporting her.

Though the wealthy and aristocratic owners of lands continued to exchange dowries for several more centuries, for commoners, such payments had already evolved into symbolic gifts, as is still the case in most modern weddings where presents are still pretty much expected, but now go directly to the couple instead of one or the others' parents.

◆ ◆ ◆

In summary, the institution we now know as Marriage began shortly after humans settled down to permanently farm—in most parts of the world, 3000 to 6000 years ago—as a rudimentary sales transaction in which women were bought, sold and traded as sexual slaves. The laws first codified by ancient civilizations regarding adultery, had little to do with restricting men's sexual activity, but were designed to prohibit women from having sex with anyone except their owners/husbands in order to guarantee the paternity of the heirs they bore. It wasn't until 2000 years ago, that influences from Greek philosophical schools that scorned physical attachments combined with the success of early Christianity, to apply a few of the same kind of restrictions on the sexual behavior of men.

Some of the worst aspects of the female sex trade were modified by the Church, but in the long run, these "reforms" only served to perpetuate the institution by making it less distasteful. For the next millennium, the Church assumed complete control of sanctioning all sexual unions—having turned Marriage into a sacrament—which in turn gave the Church considerable political power as it alone determined the legitimacy of all heirs.

The Protestant Revolution, however, brought an end to the Church's monopoly over legitimizing sexual unions, and shifted these powers to the State, conjoining until the present day the role of the state to license sexual unions together with the Church's to sanctify them.

The rise of the Middle Class also served to modify the way people viewed Marriage, as land ownership became less the occupation of men, who left farming to work in the burgeoning factories of the Industrial Age. As the acquisition of wealth moved from exploiting farm land to factory production, children began to lose economic value as vested farm hands, and the benefits of holding on to daughters for the domestic labors they performed or the bride price they might fetch began to drop below the costs of their upkeep. As a consequence, bride prices (or dowries) began to be paid instead of received. In time, however, even these were replaced by wedding gifts, along with the Marriage tradition of fathers selling their daughters gradually morphing into a mere formality where they "gave them away."

4

What Preceded Marriage?

o o o o o o o o o o o o o o o o o o o o o o o o o o o o o o o o o o

After Sunday School class, a little boy asked his mother, "Mom, were Adam and Eve the first married couple?" "Why yes," she answered. "So were Adam and Eve, and Cain and Able, the first family?" "Yeeeeesss," Mom reassured. The boy paused for a moment, and then said, "No ... that can't be right!" Caught off guard, the mother inquired, "Why do you say that?" The boy's wheels turned for a moment, and then he asked, "What about the Flintstones? Weren't they a family too?"

The Real Garden of Eden

The Bible believing have countered the brutish history of Marriage with claims that all was different before Original Sin ruined God's plan in the garden of Eden where Adam and Eve were naked and innocent, and as God looked on, all was good ... at least until the Serpent came along. For most people of reason, though, the biblical story of Adam and Eve is a myth, not unlike the story of Santa Claus—which is told again and again to children from one generation to the next, but isn't really meant to be taken as a literal, historical event. Nevertheless, a myth can be helpful in giving us some understanding of a deeper truth that might have otherwise been lost to us, such as the lesson behind the Santa Myth: being "nice" brings reward; being "naughty" doesn't.

Oddly enough, the Bible is in general agreement (if not in the specific details) on the original state of human sexuality. Relative to what happened after the invention of the plow (which took place at more or less the same time God is said to have created Adam and Eve according to those who take the Bible literally)

Homo sapiens did, indeed, dwell in something of an Eden-like state as far as sex and sexual relationships were concerned.

Before men became farmers, and sexual relationships deteriorated into a system of trade, and women became sexual commodities, human beings had for thousands of years joined together in lasting, loving sexual relationships as the fundamental building blocks of their traveling communities, and they did so without the need for States or Churches to compel them to stay together.

What Kept the "Cave" Men and Women Together?

In the previous chapter we looked at what happened when humans first began to settle into permanent communities to begin farming in earnest and settling down long enough to fully embrace the concept of ownership. We then examined the subsequent downfall of the status of women, especially with regard to their sexual relationships. But now we need to back up even further. Upon learning that Marriage was first conceived as the answer to nascent civilization's need to bring order to the enterprise of sexual slavery, the next logical question is, "What was the state of sexual relationships beforehand?"

Of course, the staunch advocates of preserving Marriage would have us believe that there was no such thing as a stable family—loving, caring and lasting relationships, and communities of mutual empathy and protection—without some external institution that forced people to stay together. They would have us believe that, were the State to suddenly declare it will no longer license and obligate people to remain together, it would immediately result in families coming apart at the seams, and millions of children would be abandoned in the streets! They do all they can to frighten the masses with subtle suggestions—and sometimes, not so subtle fear-mongering—that without the State's legally binding pressure to compel monogamy, the unbridled lusts of men would explode like the opening of Pandora's box, wrecking sexual havoc everywhere! Hopefully, the readers of this work are not so readily taken in by such baseless rhetoric of paranoia.

The facts paint for us a very different picture. Any thoughtful contemplation of what sexual relationships were like before the Agricultural Revolution should at least suggest that they must have been ordered well enough so as to make the survival of our species possible—otherwise we wouldn't be here! Indeed, *Homo sapiens* would never have survived the tens of thousands of years spent in the harsh, pre-civilized world—including a number of Ice Age surges—were it not for some other phenomenon binding men and women together. Without some form of cooperative bonds, early humanity could not have survived long enough to eventually make the discoveries of farming which, in turn, made civilization possible.

Men and women had to have some way to mate, have and care for children and support one another. Somehow, someway, long before any church (issued marriage sanctions), and much longer before the existence of any government (that issued marriage licenses), the human family not only survived, but thrived ... maintaining a basic social framework that provided protection and support for the young, the weak and the elderly.

It is so taken for granted nowadays that a permanent relationship is only possible if two people commit themselves to a holy and legally binding obligation not to leave one another. Many who today advocate for the necessity of State license and Church sanction (which carry with them very negative repercussions for those who later back out and divorce) argue that such are absolutely necessary in order to deter people, especially men, from abandoning their spouses and children.[81]

However, these presumptions are not supported by actual experience. For one thing, it is usually women who first petition for divorce by a margin of two to one.[82] Moreover, all we know about our early human and our hominid forbears tell us that our very survival was first and foremost due to the strong, familial bonds that promoted the kind of teamwork and mutual care that kept us from going the way of the Saber Tooth and Wooly Mammoth.[83]

So if there was no external institution or force holding them together, what did? For example, what made early humans share their very-hard-to-come-by food? Since growing food on a farm was not yet invented, finding food, was the principle occupation of all. Typically, women did most of the gathering of the plant foods—roots, nuts, fruits, certain edible leaves and so on, while the men went out to hunt or scavenge for meat. Why didn't the women eat all the plant food they had spent the day gathering instead of saving some for the men who could be gone for days? Likewise, why didn't the men consume all the meat from the animals they had hunted down? Why did they carry the heavy carcasses of their prey all the way back to their home camps and share their food—which they often risked their lives to obtain—with women, children, the infirm and the elderly too weak to hunt anymore?

The Bonding Effect of Perennial Sex

The answer is that at some point in the distant past of biological evolution, the ancestors of our species developed the ability to form sexual relationships that naturally resulted in deep emotional bonds between males and females. These bonds, in turn, created a profound sense of mutual loyalty and empathy—what we now commonly refer to as "love." It was these loving bonds between men and women that formed the nuclei of their larger, extended families who were also then very loyal and empathetic one toward another.

These very close relationships among the traveling bands of early humans resulted in the cohesiveness necessary for survival in the very inhospitable environments of pre-history. Though our hominid ancestors lacked most of the natural defenses and weapons that many other species had—hard shells, sharp claws, great speed or coats of fur—they were able to survive by virtue of their wits and mutual empathy, that deep down sense that says, "I feel what you feel."

This empathy translated into working together for the common good—once one loves someone and feels what they feel, one is more inclined to also care for the persons that person cares for. A man loves a woman, hence he comes to care for her children, her parents, her friends. A woman loves a man, and therefore, comes to care for his siblings, his parents, and so on. Just as a spider web is first constructed with main threads that are anchored to some solid objects, so too, the web-like interconnection of relationships within a human community are also built around "firmly anchored" relationships.

What was it, therefore, that anchored humanity's earliest core relationships? Nature's answer was sexual bonding. This deep inclination toward mutual care and concern was the result of the deep bonds which *naturally* form between humans engaged in repetitive, sexual contact. Sex was the "social glue" that continuously reinforced the bonds of the principle relationships that all others in those earliest communities were built on.

Therefore, assuming that repetitive sex was Nature's way of ensuring the tight cohesiveness of early human communities, imagine what would have happened to these groups if they were incapable of having sex with any frequency? Were our hominid ancestors like most all other mammals who only have sex during certain parts of the year, such bonds might have easily fragmented.

Well, Nature provided a special answer by giving human females—and perhaps our closest, living, primate "cousin," the Bonobo Chimpanzee—the ability to have sex all year long.[84] All other female mammals copulate only when they are "in heat" or in estrus, meaning the time of the year when their in-utero eggs are ready to be fertilized by male sperm. While it's true that human females are only capable of becoming pregnant for about one week out of every month, they are nevertheless physically able to have sex almost any other time, assuming of course, they have found someone with whom they'd like to have intercourse.[85]

The importance of this one variable that makes humans so distinct from almost every other member of our mammalian genus cannot be understated. For many other species, sex has one purpose only—reproduction. The time and trouble it normally takes for most every other animal to find a mate and have sex, from the salmon to the deer, is critically timed to coincide with the female's ability to have eggs at the ready either to be externally fertilized, as in the case of Salmon, or to be in the proper cycle to get pregnant, i.e., internally fertilized, as with deer in heat. But for humans, sex also serves a very important, secondary purpose, so much so that it almost rivals reproduction itself.

There are still some people who claim that the only purpose of human sex is for making babies. Were this true, though, why then should Nature (or God if one prefers) have gone to the trouble to make us so different from all other mammals? Why provide us the *ability to* have sex, and the powerful drives within us to *want to* copulate, when there is no chance of fertilizing any eggs?

Successful reproduction is very important, to be sure, and it remains the driving principle behind Natural Selection. However, for humans (though it is certainly also a factor in bonds formed among other species), sex also ensures that very deep and empathetic emotional bonds are formed and continuously reinforced between mating partners. The development of this unique, human ability to copulate year round—no matter what the season—was one of the most critical stages of hominid evolution. To be human is to be capable of perennial sex.

What is Love?

Before we go any further, we need to pause for a moment to address some faulty conclusions that some might have prematurely drawn about the evolutionary addition of love to sex. While it is asserted in this thesis that it was the development of our hominid ancestors to have perennial sex that made love possible, by no means does this suggest that sex *is* love. Also, no one should construe from this discussion that every time one has sex with someone else, that it will in every case lead to love.[86]

With these disclaimers out of the way, the point here is that sex, the ultimate form of intimacy, is the one human activity which *best lends itself* to the formulation and maintenance of loving relationships. When sex occurs between partners with any frequency, it provides the best circumstance where deep emotional associations can form between the intense, pleasurable, physical sensations of intercourse and the person with whom one is copulating.[87] Once our ancient ancestors began to experience these associations on a regular basis, what we now call "love" was born.[88]

The first well known experiment that led to an understanding of how certain behaviors can be linked to primitive, biological responses—so much so that a seemingly unrelated stimulus can, with enough consistent association, produce the same response as a directly related stimulus—was conducted by a Russian scientist named Pavlov.

Pavlov had some dogs that were fed at the same time each day. Just as food was being brought to the dogs—resulting in an increase in salivation in anticipation of eating—he rang a bell. The simultaneous ringing of the bell together with the presentation of the food was repeated over and over, every feeding time. Then one day, Pavlov came to the dogs and, with no food at all, simply rang the bell. Sure enough, the dogs began to salivate all the same.

Pavlov's experiment is credited for first demonstrating that it's possible to condition behavior by repeatedly putting a direct, native stimulus together with an indirect, foreign stimulus resulting in the same reaction, a process known as *association.* Other experiments later confirmed that people as well as animals also respond to the association of stimuli in much the same way.

The discovery of association helps us to understand why we may suddenly recall an event that happened decades ago, for example, by stumbling on to a particular odor that was inadvertently part of that experience.[89] Association is also a phenomenon that is frequently exploited by those who hope to influence, and sometimes manipulate, others.

Political and commercial ads go to great lengths to create associations between direct and indirect stimuli in the hopes of persuading someone to vote for a candidate or buy a certain shampoo.[90] Much as we might hate to admit it, we are all quite susceptible to such ads or else politicians and advertisers wouldn't spend the billions they do on producing, distributing and showing them.

Notwithstanding, it was Nature, not Wall Street or Washington, that first figured out a way to associate two unrelated stimuli with each other in order to get a similar response. Through a marvelous process of evolution, the great degree of physical pleasure which can be derived from sexual contact became linked to a similar pleasurable response to the person with whom such contact is made.

The high concentration of nerve endings which evolved in the male penis and the female clitoris provided the conduits to the first rewarding response, nerves which ultimately trigger the release of powerful "feel good" hormones in the brain. Then, as hominids engaged in repeated instances of sexual intercourse with the same partner, and for longer periods of time until the process became year round, other "feel only good when I'm with this one person" hormones started to kick in. The conditioning toward love was assured.

Just as Pavlov's dogs came to associate the ringing of the bell with the imminence of food appearing and automatically began to have the same physical responses, likewise we humans tend to experience a pleasure similar to that of coitus just by being with the person with whom we've had, or hope to have, sexual intercourse, i.e., when we fall in love.

The conditioning that results from the association of the sexual pleasure and one's sexual partner (or even the anticipation of such pleasure) can have negative as well as positive results. Once in love, we seem to acquire a strange ability to tolerate behavior that would normally disgust or greatly agitate us, and for some, love keeps them bound to persons who are downright bad. We all know of at least one couple that seems to always be in conflict, sometimes in very abusive and violent ways, and yet, they stick together no matter what.

So what's behind this phenomenon? What is it that seems to magically change inside of us, to start out wanting *to do* something very pleasurable with someone, only to later find ourselves wanting to be with that *someone* even more? Ancients were convinced it was the work of certain gods, like Cupid, who were supernaturally manipulating our feelings. But science has in recent years begun to help us understand that the strong attachments we often, though not always, develop after we begin to have sex with someone are actually the result of powerful chemical reactions igniting deep in the brain.

The Mother of All Drug Dealers

The "pleasure centers" of the brain, those which release powerful hormones that give us that great sense of pleasure and euphoria during sexual foreplay, intercourse and orgasm, are the same hormones released by highly addictive drugs. And just as with street drugs, some people get addicted more easily than others.

Not unlike the experience of those who can experiment briefly with a powerful narcotic, enjoy its effects, and then go on to never use it again, sometimes people can have sex with someone once or twice and develop no attachments at all. On the other hand, we all know of other circumstances where two people merely kissed, and they were immediately inseparable, not unlike those who become addicted on their first try of heroin!

We might say that love is also an addiction, a direct result of the brain's responses to intimacy and sometimes, just the mere possibility of it. Once in love, we *need* to be with our sex partner. As already pointed out, so strong is this dependency that sometimes, even if one's sexual partner is mean, selfish or even cruel, it may be less painful to put up with such bad traits than go through the withdrawal symptoms sure to accompany leaving.

This need to be together often goes unnoticed. For couples who live together, they may go for months, years or even decades without any particular feeling of a longing one for the other, and they might even complain about how they just don't feel what they used to when they were first dating. In a real sense, they, like street drug addicts, no longer get the same high as they did at first, but are just "maintaining."

But all changes when there is a sudden separation of the two! They find that they can't hardly stand to be away from each other, even if they didn't really get along all that well and fought and argued most of the time.

The reason for their strange inability to part is simple. While being together, they were getting uninterrupted "fixes," a slow but steady release of the love chemicals deep inside their brains. Just as many drug addicts can function almost as normally as anyone else until there's an interruption of their regular supply, many a couple who are constantly together only notice just how dependent they are on each other when they are suddenly separated.

In spite of the "unintended" negative consequences of sometimes falling in love with the wrong kind of person and literally becoming addicted to someone who might be mean, cruel or unfaithful, Nature's innovation of this "addictive attachment" has actually been a very successful one on the whole. There were specific benefits for our species' survival and evolutionary advances that were only possible because of the evolution of this "addiction to love." Love, indeed, forces us to get along and to put up with things that, absent this amazing, emotional Super Glue, we'd never otherwise endure. This led directly to an unsurpassed level of cooperation, mutual loyalty and support between our primitive forebears. Thanks to the chemical magic behind perennial sex and these lasting bonds leading to such dedication one to another, our ancient ancestors had that "one up" on the Saber Tooth who might have otherwise picked them off, one at a time, until they were all extinct.

We're not just guessing here. Modern scientists have actually tested the brains of people who had recently fallen in love, and have produced evidence to show that specific chemicals are released whenever one is with or even just thinking about the object of one's affections.[91] The same chemicals are released in animals as well whenever they form mating bonds. Researcher and anthropologist Helen Fisher sums it up this way, "Lust is associated primarily with the hormone testosterone in both men and women. Romantic love is linked with the natural stimulant dopamine and perhaps norepinephrine and serotonin. And feelings of male-female attachment are produced primarily by the hormones oxytocin and vasopressin."[92]

Interestingly, the release of these various brain chemicals tend to follow each other. As one paves the way, then the others more readily kick in. The "lust" hormone testosterone in particular seems to be especially suited to serving as a catalyst for these other drugs to activate.

At the risk of overusing the street drug metaphor, it appears that the release of these powerful natural drugs inside the human brain indeed follow the same pattern as the much ballyhooed risk of using certain "gateway drugs" like marijuana. We're told by anti-marijuana advocates that, while many of those who smoke pot never go on to use "hard drugs," almost all those who do end up using hard drugs began by first smoking pot. While many questions remain about the whole concept of gateway drugs when it comes to street narcotics, there's mounting evidence that this principle is surely at work in the context of the natural "lust" chemical testosterone. The brain chemical testosterone which drives us to want to have sex, also serves as a kind of gateway drug to more powerful and addictive ones, the chemicals that cause us to become deeply attached to a certain person.

The scientific reality of where love really came from is rather ruinous to all the lofty and romantic notions that our traditional culture has attributed to it. For millennia, people have sought to explain love in terms of some kind of spiritual force that is somehow separate from the physical body. They try to separate "physical" lust from "spiritual" love, as if they are forces from two entirely different dimensions. But evidence coming in from science is showing us that both lust and love are anything but from another world, originating neither from demons, nor from gods.

Instead, what we see is Nature first coming up with a primitive concoction which drove our most ancient forbears to coitus, the gateway brain drug, if you will, testosterone. And then, after millions of years of successful reproduction, Nature went at it again, adding new chemicals on to those behind the primitive sex drive, so the genders would not only *get together* to copulate, but *stay together* to raise increasingly helpless infants together. Why? Because as one species after another grew bigger brains, it was necessary that their larger brained babies exit a mother's womb faster, meaning longer periods of dependency and the need for more help to raise them. In other words, this new array of addictive brain chemicals which compelled mates to stick together longer, and which may have at first seemed like a cruel escalation by the Mother of all Drug Dealers, had a wondrous consequence, the evolution of larger brained species like Homo sapiens.

Love Without Sex?

Just as squares are always rectangles, but not all rectangles are square, there are many times when people succumb only to the gateway desire for sex, and after copulating, they each go their separate ways. Most people who have had some sexual experience can testify that they have had sex with someone whom they never loved and didn't really want to have a relationship with. Few would disagree that it's quite possible to have sex without love.

But what about the converse? Can two people be romantically in love, and not have sex, i.e., if there's no external obstructions keeping them from being intimate? Let me put the question another way. If the brain chemical driving us to want sex is indeed a gateway to more powerful hormones causing us to become attached to a certain person, can those stronger attachment drugs keep on working indefinitely without the gateway drug?

I assert that the attachment drugs the brain produces when we fall in love can and do persist long after two people in love are for one reason or another unable to have sex … but only with some painful consequences! The reason is because testosterone is, for us humans anyway, more than a gateway drug, and the sex it drives us to is more than a kind of bait used to catch a mate.

Though a different set of brain chemicals take over, and the amount of testosterone decreases the longer a couple is together, it doesn't go away altogether as a relationship endures. Just as a couple might begin by meeting up for "casual" sex, only to later fall in love, and then form a relationship wherein the sex still goes on but there's much more to it now, the chemicals inside of their brains go through relationship changes in tandem. At first, the couple is principally driven to satisfy a desire that requires each other's close, physical cooperation—sex itself. Then, they begin to find themselves wanting to be as close as possible to the person with whom they enjoyed such satisfaction. Finally, in order to continue to satisfy the second desire, they find that *the best way to do so is to continue joining with each other in the most intimate way possible.* In other words, while sex might have been what first *got them to* love, sex also turns out to be the *best means of keeping them* in love. To deny or prevent someone from having sex with the object of his or her romantic desire means, not only frustrating the more primitive desire for pleasurable coitus in general, but removing the satisfaction otherwise retained from the ultimate expression of attachment to someone in particular. Sex, then, is not only a gateway taking us *to* love, but a gate that can also be shut to *keep* us there as well.

The answer, then, to the question, "Can one have love without sex?" is "yes," but it's a very incomplete response unless we add the caveat, "but it sure is frustrating." In time, love so prevented from being both satisfied and reinforced by physical intimacy will often result in anger and despair. Separated lovers will often go to great lengths to overcome whatever obstacles lie in their path just to rejoin with their beloved.

It's no surprise, then, that—even among the very religious who believe God will damn them to hell for committing the sin of pre-marital sex—only a very small number of people in love can manage to carry on as celibates for any length of time without becoming at least mildly neurotic and obsessive. If they are prevented from openly joining together, they will most often find some clandestine way to do so. If they can't find a way to be together, their desire for each other pushes them to extreme behaviors, in some cases, even suicide.

On the other side of this coin is the phenomenon commonly referred to as "growing apart" or "drifting away." Many a relationship counselor has documented the high correlation between the state of a couple's bond and their sex life. Should a couple begin having less and less sex, it's very likely that their relationship as a whole has begun to fragment in the same proportion. The bedroom is any given couple's relationship in microcosm, whether good, bad or indifferent.

In spite of society's many attempts to thwart sexual attraction by propagating lofty notions of "spiritual" love while installing and maintaining all kinds of other barriers to keep people apart—from laws against pre-marital sex to the requirement of chaperones on dates—the power of the biological chemicals behind the physical sex drive together with their hormone partners who fashion love, almost always prevail in the end. Thanks to Nature's chemistry, people in love who stay in love, are normally people who have sex together on a regular, year-round basis.

We need not, however, mourn the loss of unrealistic notions of love as a spiritual force when we consider just how special the physical reality of love is. Indeed, the ability to fall in love is a miracle of Natural Selection! Evolutionary forces favored those early hominids who had the genetic predisposition to go from the gratification of seasonal sexual desire which only temporarily brought the genders together—something all mammals have in order to procreate—to perennial sexual copulation and deep attachments forming as a result. Perennial sex so helped to reinforce such strong, emotional bonds, that it gave a small group of ape-like creatures such an advantage, they eventually stood upright, and became the crown of the animal kingdom. While other hominids formed bonds in other ways—perhaps in manners similar to the way modern apes do, for example, by spending hours on end picking fleas off each other—none could compare to the fierce loyalties and deep empathy that year-round sex facilitated.

Female Sexuality and the Goddess

We can gather some idea of what the relationships of our ancient pre-agricultural ancestors were probably like from the information that anthropologists and other experts have gathered from remotely located tribal peoples survived until modern times.[93] While we might see some similarities in the attitudes primitive peoples have about sex and sexual relationships, there are also some striking differences between the sexual mores of our modern society and theirs.

In general, the natural process of falling in love was usually regarded by primitive cultures as a sacred and honorable gift from the gods. Whenever it became apparent that two people in a given community had fallen in love, their friends and family would typically take some time to give thanks to their deities for the gift of love they had received. The couple's experience was often thought of as a visible expression of their fertility gods' cosmic mating, whom were often perceived as falling in love with one another just as humans do, particularly in the springtime.

These primitives believed there was a direct link between the mating habits of their deities and the rebirth and renewal that Nature would display at certain times of the year. Consequently, the earthly, sexual union between two partners was not at all regarded with the kind of negativity that was to come much later in human history. On the contrary, sex was celebrated as a joyous gift, a sign that Life was triumphant once again!

In fact, a pre-agricultural woman who could successfully give birth was not only considered "blessed" but sometimes even "possessed" by a deity. There was a great deal of reverence and awe generated in early human communities when a woman gave birth. A woman who could deliver a healthy child was regarded as having a special connection with The Creative Power which gave life to all things. Often, a fertile female was thought to have become a medium of the Great Mother through whom She came to bring a new member to their number. This relationship between an earthly mother and the Cosmic Mother greatly elevated the earthly mother's status, and thus, helped to make her quite desirable.

Not too surprisingly, once agriculture came along, the sacred associations with female sexual desire, love, and birth, were pushed to the wayside along with the worship of the Goddess. As if a mirror to the heavens, the less Western Civilization venerated female sexuality, the more its divine imaging became strictly male.

"Sexy" Equals Fertility

Then as now, when sexual attraction in the Hunting and Gathering Era led to copulation, it didn't necessarily always result in two people falling in love, even if it sometimes resulted in pregnancy. Fortunately, what was not all that long ago labeled as an "illegitimate" pregnancy in our society carried no such stigma for early humans. Nor did it present the kinds of disadvantages that a modern single mother faces.[94]

Instead, a female who became pregnant within a pre-agricultural community would actually *gain* status regardless of whether or not she had a relationship with the man who impregnated her. Though having a man at her side while nursing an infant was a definite advantage, he didn't necessarily have to be the baby's biological father. And single mothers of older children could take their time to find another mate because weaned children within the traveling bands of old were looked after by pretty much everyone else.[95]

There's a possibility that, while humans of this era might have suspected a relationship between sex and pregnancy, they had no conscious way of being certain whose child, biologically, belonged to whom. A woman, for instance, might have formed a love bond with one man while she was in the early stages of pregnancy from a different sex partner. Even so, she could expect her contemporary mate to be supportive of her regardless of whether the infant was biologically "his" or not.

Any pregnancy was proof positive of a female's fertility and a sure sign that her womb was blessed by the gods. Even if a woman became pregnant while she had no ostensible mate, far from being stigmatized, she would have been regarded all the more attractive and desirable. Upon delivering a healthy child, she actually became more, not less, likely to find a man.

This ought to make us wonder. Did pre-agricultural women appear to be more desirable to men merely because of primitive beliefs that it was due to the favor of fertility gods? Or were these beliefs more a primitive expression of something much more fundamental about human attraction that merely found a voice in their religious beliefs. In other words, might there be a direct, biological link between a woman's ability to conceive, deliver and successfully nurse an infant … and sexual attraction?

To see if there is any scientific evidence for an innate connection between what men find attractive about a woman and the likelihood of successful reproduction, a survey was taken by researcher Devendra Singh of some tribal men living in the remote jungles of Ecuador. The reason for going so far a field to do the survey was to exclude the possibility that the subjects' ideas about what made a woman attractive were not simply due to the influence of modern advertising.

The survey was simple. The men were shown a number of drawings of women of all shapes and sizes to see whom they would favor as the most attractive.

Some of the interviewers on Singh's team had anticipated that, because these young men had never been exposed to the influence of modern Western stereotypes of what constitutes an ideally attractive female—shapely bodies, smooth skin, large breasts and so on—that their choices would be different from those typically portrayed on the cover of Cosmo. But to their surprise, the native men cited the exact, same things Western men do—round, symmetrical facial features; flat waists; large breasts; proportionate legs, thighs and buttocks; and the same, "hour glass" waist-to-hip ratio![96] The only thing that was different was the reason the men gave for their selections. All of them stated that the features which made some females more physically appealing were signs that they were more likely to bear many, healthy children.[97]

The Alpha-Beta Scale of Attraction

Attraction—for men and women—is very much about stratification. No matter how much one might rationally believe in the value of fair play, deep inside the base of our brains where the raw "wiring" of what makes us find certain members of the opposite gender sexually appealing, there's no such thing as "fairness." There are specific qualities which render some members of the opposite sex "hotter" than others, and they don't necessarily coincide with other qualities that we would reason to be "good" as far as mate choices go.

Most of us are pretty familiar with the consensus men have about which women are sexually attractive. We could assemble almost any combination of a hundred men, mixing up their ages, races, cultures, socio-economic backgrounds and so on, have them look at any group of women, and almost all would be able to agree on which ones are "attractive," and which ones are not.

Further, men would likely finish this task very quickly. Men can seemingly look at any group of women and almost immediately determine which ones are, for lack of a less-crass term, "doable." In fact, not only do men have this uncanny ability to assess in a matter of seconds which women they *could* have sex with, they would also agree, if they were being honest, that these would be the same women they *would* have sex with, if they were not prohibited by social, religious or legal barriers to do so.

For men, there is only one test for choosing which woman to have sex with—is she "hot" or not, and they can take and finish this exam in a matter of seconds.

Women asked to evaluate the attractiveness of any assembly of men would also be in general agreement on their initial findings, that is, if given a chance to interact with them long enough. Unlike the men, though, women would need more time to make their evaluation.

But the reason they need a bit longer is not what most are tempted to think it is. Though women often say that they must first "get to know a man" before they can be physically attracted to him, the female's selection process doesn't depend on asking lots of questions to find out if this guy or that would make a suitable mate. In fact, a woman could have a tally sheet of a hundred great qualities that she would, *rationally* speaking, want to have in a man. But even a guy who had every one of these hundred traits wouldn't necessarily make her *feel* any attraction. Rather, a woman needs to *interact* with a man long enough to either begin *feeling attracted* to him, or *feeling repulsed*, regardless of whatever she might reason his qualities are.

Unlike the men who need only to get a good look, women need more than a picture of a man. And as already noted, even a detailed resume is of little help either.

Women make their assessments in a different way and with some additional steps. At first, they employ a kind of a "screen test" to put men in one of two general categories—those who are causing them to feel attraction, and those who aren't. But the test is very general in nature. Though like men, these initial results are widely agreed upon, unlike the men's test, it doesn't mean the women would be willing to go on to actually mate with everyone who makes it into the Attractive category. Further screening must follow to see which ones will make them feel even more attraction.

As attraction increases, the number of acceptable male candidates for mating begins to narrow. The closer women get to actual sex, the more narrow the number of acceptable male sex partners becomes.

Now, before we try to sort out the specific dynamics of attraction, it's important to first review one of Nature's favorite ways of getting us to do things that are in our reproductive interest. Time and again throughout this study, we have and will continue to refer to men and women reacting to certain characteristics of the opposite sex because they do or don't lead to better chances of reproductive success. But when a man sees a woman that he wishes to copulate with, he's not thinking consciously (as we might imagine Mr. Spock from Star Trek using his pure logic to decide what to do next): "Ah! Here's a woman who has all the familiar, outward markers that indicate she is fertile enough to get pregnant and healthy enough to successfully give birth and care for a child at least until weaning." Sure, a man might rationally draw such conclusions were he to stop and think about an attractive female in a purely rational way.

But Nature would have had a tough time getting any life form to evolve at all if the ability to reason so had to come first. It was, instead, imperative that attraction be an *instinctive* response from the primitive brain. There had to be an "automatic" way drive prehistoric creatures to copulate first with the best choices available. In fact, we could even go so far as to say that the primitive origins of the brain—what is sometimes called the "lizard" section of the modern human brain—began with the development of this purely reactive ability.

Therefore, when it comes to how we select our sex partners, we are primarily motivated, not by conscious choices, but by instinctive urges planted in us long ago by Natural Selection. And Nature developed this process as a selective one, giving our forebears progressively more intensive desires for those who had all the "signs" of being better reproductive "choices."

Of course, when we speak of "Nature giving" or "Evolution predisposing," we're not talking about a conscious process here either. We only mean that any genetically-based preference for a mate that happened to make their offspring a little better off, resulted in those same genetically induced preferences being passed on to succeeding generations.

To be certain, early humans, having finally evolved large brains that could temporarily override their instincts had a one-up on many other species who could only do as they were programmed—"Ah, there's a fine young, cave girl I'd really like to copulate with ... but there's also a Saber Tooth lurking nearby. Maybe, I'd better call her later." The ability to reason gave us advantages when circumstances that were normally suited to sexual "auto pilot" changed into a temporary disadvantage. But switching to "manual override," from instinct to reason, was the exception, not the rule. Most of the time, it was instinct, not reason, that led our early ancestors to make good mating "choices," at least as far as the overall reproductive success of our species was concerned.

In modern times, though, our sexual instincts often create problems. Our world has changed so rapidly that Evolution has had no time to help us out by re-wiring our natural, sexual instincts to coincide with our best interests in the world of today. We are still subject to finding certain members of the opposite sex very attractive based on what *were* the better mate choices for millions of years before. Now though (some might be tempted to say "especially when"), the persons we are most attracted to don't necessarily possess any of the qualities that one would rationally regard as better for reproductive success in our society of today. As a matter of fact, our over-populated world has made successful reproduction itself a bad option for us all.

Let me digress a bit to explain the word device I've chosen to compare and contrast those persons who possess or lack attractive qualities—"The Alpha-Beta Scale". In this study, I've chosen to use the first two letters of the Greek alphabet to help us grapple with the manner in which attraction works for men and women. Those who have the characteristics that trigger the "attraction mechanisms" deep in the "lizard" part of our brains, are called "Alphas." Those who don't, I call "Betas." An Alpha Male is one whom women find almost irresistibly attractive. An Alpha Female is one whom men find equally desirable. Beta men and women are those that just don't "turn on" the opposite sex.

Now if this device sounds over simplified to the reader, then you would be right. In reality, there are many degrees to attraction just as there are degrees to the lack thereof. And just to make things even more complex, the range within which a particular member of the opposite sex may be perceived as an Alpha or Beta can shift depending on several different factors. A "Beta," as used here, is really a catch-all term for anyone who can't seem to attract the opposite gender … at least, one whom the Beta would find attractive. Objectively speaking, though, a Beta could be anyone, from those who fall a little short of the Alpha, to those who are at the rock bottom. Moreover, depending on how far up or down one might be on the proverbial "1 to 10" scale, someone who might be an "Alpha" to one person, is a "Beta" to another. And there are other ingredients. The degree to which a potential sex partner resembles an Alpha or Beta may vary according to certain circumstances, such as how many others are around to compare with or how long it's been since one's last, satisfying copulation.

"Confusing!" to say the least. This is why I felt that the best way to make some sense of how human, sexual attraction works, especially because of all the variables, was to begin with a bit of oversimplification until readers can get their footing.

So taking it a bit slow at first, I begin with a simple definition of an "Alpha" as anyone who arouses sexual attraction from the opposite gender upon initial encounter, and a "Beta" as one who doesn't.

"Settling"—A Sexual Back Up Capability

No doubt some might already be asking, "Why isn't sexual attraction a matter of absolute characteristics?" Why, for instance, would a woman who gets only a moderate amount of men's immediate attention in a big city, be the "best catch" in a sparsely populated, rural area? Why is it that a woman eagerly accepts a proposal from a man she is certain to be The One, only to later think of him as a wimp? One could put it another way, "Why is the Alpha-Beta Scale of Attraction, more like a bunch of different scales, each with different ranges on them, and with people jumping from one to another, rather than a simple 1 to 10 range that could be applied to everyone, under any circumstance?"

I recall a story my father, an ex-Marine, once told me about a comic strip he saw in a military newspaper while he was stationed on Midway Island during World War Two. The cartoon depicted a soldier who'd been on the island for quite some time—long since he'd been in the company of American women—who began to find the native females very pretty. The cartoonist did this by depicting a soldier looking at a rather homely and overweight native female. Thanks to the cartoon "cloud" floating just above him, allowing the reader into the mind of the soldier, one could see a ravishing, athletically figured version of the same female and the soldier responding accordingly with a wolf whistle. In the next caption, however, the soldier sees the same female after he'd gone on a furlough to the mainland where, presumably, he'd had a chance to be "in the company" of other, more appealing women. Then, the cloud image of the native appeared exactly the same as the one standing in front of him. No whistling this time.

One of the reasons behind the complexity of sexual attraction has to do with an instinctive ability which Natural Selection has endowed us with that I call "Back Up Desire." Were we only capable of finding an absolute number of partners sexually desirable, then what to do if no such persons are around? In our modern world, where there are, if anything, way too many people on the planet, finding oneself in a place where there are no potential sex partners around is rare, and even when one does, it's more a personal problem than a threat to our specie's very existence. This, however, wasn't always the case.

What if, for instance, somewhere early in our human history when human populations were so thin, one of our ancestors was having trouble finding a suitable mate because there was no one around who was "his type"? Had we not the ability to desire someone among a limited number of available partners, even if it was someone that we wouldn't otherwise find suitable when there are better options available, *Homo sapiens* would have gone extinct. It was critical, then, that our early forebears had the ability to be flexible when it came to finding someone sexually attractive, and that ability is still with us. Though we tend to think of "settling" only in negative terms, it really isn't all that bad … nor is it all that uncommon.

The same holds true with any of our biological drives. The more hungry we get, the less discriminating we become about what food choices we make. Something we'd normally never think of eating, might appear appetizing if one has not eaten for a long period of time. Then once regular food becomes available, we go back to having a more discriminating pallet.

We've probably all heard stories of what starving people have done under extreme circumstances, such as the South American rugby team who resorted to cannibalism after being stranded in the Andes mountains after their plane crashed. Who hasn't, at one time or another, urinated or defecated in some unpleasant location (perhaps even a public one) that one would otherwise never consider, if the urge to go were strong enough and one could no longer "hold it." Under normal circumstances, our drives are less intensive, and we tend to be more selective as to how we satisfy them. But Nature inclines us to be less discriminating at times of shortages of food, restrooms … and yes, even mates, so we can survive.

For us as individuals, it may seem a cruel trick that Mother Nature has played on us by putting such a back up system inside of us. We might feel especially foolish if we went out with someone at one time in our life only to look back with dismay at how we "stooped so low." However, it was this "cruelty" that allowed our ancient ancestors to reproduce and keep our species going at times when death and disease and limited resources allowed for only a few choices. As the late Luther Vandross put it, Nature gave us the ability to "love the one you're with."

Why Are Men So Attracted to Alpha Women?

Why, then, specifically do men seem to always find pretty, young, shapely women more attractive than others? What compels some men to cheat on a caring, loving and intelligent wife with a whiny, immature and uneducated 20-year-old, just because she's, well, a very pretty, 20-year-old? Even more mysterious, what is going on when a woman marries a man thinking she'd gotten a really good catch until another guy comes along who redefines for her what a "real man" is? What's going on when, all of the sudden, she's meeting with some scruffy dude she barely knows in a cheap motel, and her loving, supportive, nice-guy husband is at home, all alone, crying, and wondering where he went wrong?

We'll first attempt to answer these questions by examining the relatively easier question first, why men are so attracted to Alpha women? Then, we'll tackle the greater mystery of female attraction to the Alpha Male.

As pointed out already, the idea of "love at first sight" is truly immediate for men! A "sizzling hot babe" is recognizable to most men within seconds of spotting her. Why does this happen?

The answer is twofold: 1) All the visible traits we associate with an attractive female are the signs she is a good candidate for reproductive success, and 2) it was important to the survival and evolution of our species that these signs be easy to spot.

The connection between the universal markers of preferred female sexual partners and fertility is not readily apparent to the modern mind where the thought of having children is usually put off until a woman is well into her twenties or later. However, if we can leave the mindset of our modern society with all of its demands for a higher education and the prolonged period of preparation for adulthood that we often refer to as adolescence, the relationship becomes clear. The physical features that most men would say are the most attractive, if they are honest, are those most common to young, healthy women just after they attain full puberty and can successfully procreate. Things like the "hour glass" figure; smooth skin; firm, protruding breasts, and facial symmetry are universally considered the ideal, and therefore, the most attractive female body features.

Why? Why should *these* physical features be signs of a female's good chances of successful reproduction?

The answers are practical An hour glass waist-to-hip ratio is a sign that a woman has a birth canal large enough for a baby to pass through it. Protruding breasts are a clear signal that a woman can breast feed a baby. Smooth skin indicates a greater likelihood of not having yet suffered from too many of life's wears and tears. Symmetry is a giveaway that a woman has good genetic stock, that she is likely to be free of other, not so readily apparent genes that lead to birth defects and susceptibility to later diseases.

OK, so the good health of a potential mother is critical for the good health of her children, but why should the signs of youth be so important?

Let's think about this for a moment. The genetic tendencies predisposing men to prefer younger women evolved at a time when life was short, brutal and dangerous. Some scientists have estimated that the average life span of early humans was around 30-35. There was little time to waste. Just as soon as a female *could* reproduce, it was imperative that she get on the job right away! But this brings up a rather delicate subject in that today's women enter puberty at a very young age. Did Natural Selection mean to actually place a strong desire in men to find girls so young attractive? Or did something else happen along the way to foil Mother Nature's original intentions?

The Double Punch of Accelerated Puberty and the Creation of Adolescence

The fact that men find the physical traits most common to very young women is a disturbing one for us in modern times to contemplate because of the very young age at which girls become "adults" in the strictly biological sense of the word. Nowadays, girls become physically mature years before they are mature in any other way. This disparity has led most states to create statutory rape laws.

As a society, we don't tolerate, and rightly so, older adults who initiate sexual relationships with young teens, even if they are physically very adult looking, for fear of the disadvantage they would be at emotionally and mentally, and not to mention, the far more serious consequences of becoming pregnant in our society at such a young age. But this wasn't Nature's original plan.

It's mostly taken for granted nowadays that puberty just normally sets in around the ages of 11 or 12 years old. But this is actually a relatively recent phenomenon. It's only been in the past 100 years or so that puberty began setting in so early in life. Before 1900, the average age of the onset of puberty was much later—more likely to start in the mid-teens, and much more in keeping with the mental and emotional maturity necessary to handle sexual relationships and parenthood.

Man biologists believe that the reason for this acceleration comes from the modern diet which is very high in animal fat, protein and enriched starches. Before 1900, the diet of most children contained no where near the high intakes of sugar, meat, milk and other animal products kids of today ingest. The result of this dramatic increase has been kids getting heavier quicker, and it's been documented that puberty tends to set in, especially in girls, once they hit a certain weight. Now, the onset of puberty has been so greatly accelerated that some girls are now having their first period as young as 9 or 10 years old!

Fortunately, for the young of the Hunting and Gathering Era all the way until the 20th Century, puberty didn't come along until every other form of maturity did too. Back then, men didn't have to worry about whether the post puberty woman they found attractive was "underage" or as some put more crudely, "jail bait." Girls had plenty of time to mature emotionally and to learn all they needed to know about sex, love and making babies *before* they developed the physical qualities of puberty which would attract a potential mate.

But as if the acceleration of physical puberty were not problematic enough, it occurred at a very bad time—right on the heels of our society's extension of emotional, educational and financial dependency! Only in modern times has the way we raise our young *prolonged* their immaturity in every way but physically.

There was a time when a 16-year-old was as adept at farming as well as any other adult farmer in his 20s, 40s or 60s. It was not at all unusual at one time for young teenagers to marry and begin having their own families in the same way we now take it for granted that 15- or 16-year-olds should begin driving cars on their own.

It wasn't until the Industrial Age that child-like behavior was encouraged and tolerated past the point of physical puberty and when society began to delay the age at which the young were expected to behave as adults. This delay increased in proportion to the greater number of complexities the Industrial Age made necessary, which in turn, required many more years of education and training before one could truly enter society as an independent adult. And as the expectations changed, our young responded accordingly. A whole new stage of human development was artificially created as a result—that tumultuous time we've come to know as *adolescence*.

Adolescence is a time when one is no more a child, but not yet an adult, a time when adult desires have already kicked in, but when society requires further child-like restrictions on one's behavior. For teens of the 1800s who found themselves being asked to stay in school longer, and to delay truly joining the adult world for anywhere from 1 to 5 years, the time was agonizing. Then again, they were still only hitting puberty at the age of 15 or 16.

Now add to the delay of social, emotional and legal maturity which began around 1800 to the hastening of physical puberty which began around 1900, which in effect doubled the average period of adolescence to 10 to 12 years!

This double punch has resulted in a host of social ills, from the commonplace domestic struggles between parents who find themselves at their wits' end while dealing with "teenage rebellion" to young women getting pregnant and having babies long before they and the boys who impregnated them are prepared for modern parenthood. And then to make the situation for teens even worse, they often get treated as if there is something wrong with *them* for merely responding to natural desires which, at any other period of history, would have been taken as normal.[98]

In contrast to the troubles we now encounter with regard to the deeply instilled, biologically driven preferences for the physical traits common to females shortly after arriving at puberty, this preference made perfect sense in the world of our prehistoric ancestors. Our pre-agricultural ancestors took these desires in stride very well, largely because, they knew how important they were.[99]

We've already noted how life during the Hunting and Gathering Era was short. Knowing this, our ancestors understood the imperative of children learning all they needed to know about the responsibilities of adulthood by the time they reached the age of puberty. There was food to be gathered, meat to be hunted down, and the new adults—again, who were somewhere in their mid teens—had to get on with the business of reproduction as soon as possible.

To be certain, the idea of teens—even at the ages of 15 or 16—becoming full-fledged parents is unpleasant to our modern ears in our modern Western society, and for good reason. It's very impractical to start having babies in a society where one is still going to high school, and hoping to get at least another four years of college. But we must understand that children in ancient hunting and gathering societies were much more emotionally mature than their modern counterparts of the Industrial and Technological Age.[100] By the time a young woman in an ancient, pre-agricultural society reached puberty, she was far more mature than most young women in modern societies are by their mid 20s. And Nature ensured that something else would change at that very same time in her life, that she would begin to desire the best men she could find, and that men would begin to desire her as one of the best females around.

So it was only fitting under these circumstances that Nature would endow—deep within the base of the male brain where the sex drive is seated—a strong preference for those women who were beyond their first period and ready to reproduce! To put it another way, Evolution made sure to make the outward markers of a young, adult woman look sexy because the young adult is most likely to bear a child and live long enough to take care of it.

Now then, I hope the reader has a firm grasp on why the issue of a woman looking young is one of two major factors in the male's instinctive attraction mechanisms. Assuming this is so, let us return to the other part of the equation of what makes women sexually desirable to men—beauty.

The Original Certificate of Good Health—Symmetry

As alluded to already, the other aspect of what men think makes a woman *pretty* is in reality those features which signal *health*.

Male attraction to young women was important to our species' survival, but if she was sickly or of poor genetic stock, the odds of successful reproduction would still be low. Unfair as it may seem, our kind's survival hinged on Nature's directing men's instinctive desires to focus, not only on young women, but on those young women who were in the best health and had the best genes.

How to know who the healthy were? There were no written certifications of good genes and freedom from disease a woman could carry with her whenever she was out and about trying to attract a man. Or were there?

As it turns out, Nature did, indeed provide a kind of "written certificate of good health," by linking certain external traits to what goes on inside the human body, even down to one's genes. This "certificate" is actually known all through nature and is a major factor among many other species finding certain mates attractive or not. From bugs to people, we can pair down most every feature that is normally regarded as "attractive" to one concept—*symmetry*.

Think of every model you've ever seen, and you'll notice that they have balanced sets of eyes, ears, shoulders, breasts, lips, hips, buttocks, you name it. Now think of every woman you've ever thought of as homely, and the opposite comes to mind. They tend to be asymmetrical, one feature after another being a little bigger or smaller than the other.

As it turns out, the more symmetrical one is, the more one is indeed likely to be more healthy, and to have gone through less physical trauma. Scientists have repeatedly documented that the more symmetrical a parent is, the more healthy her kids are.

Ancestral males who had a genetic predisposition to prefer symmetrical or "pretty" women, along with the flags of young adulthood, were therefore rewarded by Natural Selection with a disproportionately higher number of progeny, who in turn carried within them these same preferences.

The endowment of these preferences occurred millions of years ago, and served not only the best interest of early humans, but all of our preceding ancestor species. They were helpful because they encouraged males to mate first with those who had the best chances of reproducing, and we are here today as a result.

But it bears repeating that the world has changed dramatically since the Hunting and Gathering Era subsided. Though women are nowadays anything but ready to successfully reproduce right after puberty, the male brain hasn't had anywhere near the time necessary to evolve and adapt their "hard wired" preferences in sexual attraction to suit these, relatively speaking, brand new circumstances.

Perhaps, in a million or so years from now, evolution will catch up and incline men to be primarily attracted to older women who are smart, educated, easy to get along with and more successful at their work, and youthful appearance will take a back seat. Perhaps, those women who only look healthy, but who are not, will reproduce less and less, and in time, men who are not as turned on by pretty, symmetrical features will pass on their bias to succeeding generations more successfully. But alas, for the present, men's preferences are unchanged!

How often, then, do we see many a modern man finding himself irresistibly attracted to "hot looking women" with no regard whatsoever for any other quality? Despite how immature, uneducated and lacking in social graces, men of all ages are often smitten with them, for they have the best procreative markers which communicate to the male's powerful instincts: "Here's a woman who can get pregnant, carry your child successfully to birth, and then be strong and healthy enough afterwards to care for it." Even though he's unaware of it consciously, his instincts are responding to that which was working just great for millions of years, but which now might put him in bed with someone who'll bring him nothing but trouble.

Now, none of this is to say that older or less attractive women of prehistoric times were completely left out when it came to sex and sexual relationships. Then as now, Nature also gave mature women and those with average looks the ability to have sexual relationships since sex also served as the social glue of primitive human societies. Every adult was normally part of a sexual bond, and a minimum of sexual bonding for all is what promoted and preserved the cohesion and loyalty among all members of any given band. The point here is not that older and less attractive women were excluded from sex and relationships, but that Nature made sure that those women who stood the best chance of successfully procreating, the Alpha Females, got "first dibs."

The natural and universal physical male preference for Alpha Females also explains why modern women who don't have (or perhaps due to aging, have lost some of these preferred attraction markers) will go to considerable lengths to modify their appearance in order to continue projecting them—dying their hair, working out at gyms to flatten their stomachs and paying thousands of dollars to get breast implants and lipo-suctions and wrinkles removed. One need not necessarily be young to have the markers of the young, and thus, get the same results!

The same can be said of those qualities which we normally think of as distinguishing the pretty from the ugly. From make-up regimes to plastic surgeries, there's just no end to what is offered to women who weren't born with the outward signs of superior genetic stock, but who can afford to and are willing to do what it takes to add them on later.

Nature's original purpose in making men more attracted to women who were actually younger and healthier is often outwitted by older and less healthy women who've done and spent a lot to look the part.[101]

Hopefully, this section has served to confirm what most of us, male or female, already knew. In spite of all that's alleged in polite company, men know what they really want, and so do women, i.e., women also know what kind of women men want.

But what about the converse? What do women really find most attractive in men? This question has almost all men baffled, and while most women might know what they like when they find it, they often have difficulty explaining why?

Why Are Women So Attracted to Alpha Men?

For females of the Hunting and Gathering Era, the rules of attraction were, then as now, very different from what work for men. Instead of being automatically attracted to the "nicest guy" in the camp, women tended to be far more attracted to those males who were the strongest, the most dominant, the men of status, those who are sometimes called "Alpha" males. Why?

Mainly because it was the dominant males who had the best genes and who could best protect and provide for them and their children.

Just as the "triggers" for male sexual attraction are not always helpful in a modern context, so also do the triggers that arouse attraction within females often result in unfortunate side effects. Evolutionary "hard wiring" deep within the reactive areas or "lizard portion" of the female brain to find dominant men sexually irresistible, leads more than a few modern women to men who are abusive and violent. What worked so well to ensure a woman and her children's protection thousands of years ago, doesn't always serve so practically in modern times. So strong are the biologically triggered reactions to traits that communicate "strength, dominance, and status," some women find it impossible to remove themselves from relationships where they are subjected to chronic abuse. This same biological phenomenon explains why rock stars, famous politicians and pretty much every guy who rides a Harley have a steady stream of women throwing themselves at them as their fame, riches or persona project the compelling traits of an "Alpha Male."

While this seems to be unfair to weak, needy, and submissive men (just as men's sexual preferences seem unfair to older, overweight, and unattractive women), let's remember that Natural Selection isn't driven by a sense of fairness, but by whatever best ensures survival! Evolution placed a strong preference deep inside the female psyche to be most attracted to strong, dominant males, to those who could best "bring home the bacon," fend off enemies, and better protect them and their young. The Alpha Males also had some physical markers which told women, here's a guy with good genes. As we shall soon see, though, a guy's looks didn't count as much as his personality.

Genetically determined preferences for strong males evolved over millions of years, and are now firmly fixed in the female brain. But just as modern women who are not actually young and healthy can successfully mimic the flags which trigger attraction in men, so too can modern men do the same to women. Those men who "give off the signals" of being strong, confident and self-sufficient will trigger the "Alpha attraction" mechanisms in women even if they are not, in fact, wealthy, powerful or even very physically strong!

So just what are the signals that turn on a woman's primitive, sexual desire? And perhaps more importantly, what signals turn it off?

The Upward and Downward Spirals

One of the clearest signs to a woman that she is in the presence of an Alpha Male is whether he comes off as "needy" or not. Depending on whether a man projects that he's got all he needs and then some, or is as needy as can be, results in either a very rewarding or a very frustrating process that I describe respectively as the Upward and Downward Spirals.

A male who is in an Upward Spiral naturally attracts women, and therefore, is much more likely to succeed in having sex. These men may be great guys, but not necessarily. Sometimes, men who are selfish jerks will project such an "aura" of self-sufficiency, status and strength, that women will find them irresistible. In either the case of men who actually have these traits or of those who just take women for granted and merely "come off" as strong and dominant, they will both act as if they are very sexually "full," even complacent! And guess what? Both will naturally attract and succeed sexually with women as a result, because there's something about a man who doesn't seem to need a woman that makes women want them. This phenomenon seems so contradictory, at first, but it actually does have a logic to it once we look deeper at what's really going on in side the female's Sexual Reaction Center when a guy's behavior suggests to her, "I can take you or leave you."

Guys who come off as already sexually satisfied are much more likely to attract women, and, you guessed it, be even more sexually satisfied. This success reinforces their sense of confidence, and depletes any sense of needing women. The more a male is confident that he can get a girl anytime he wants one, the more he sends the message, "I'm a winner. You better do what you can to get with me before someone else beats you to it!" He comes off as an Alpha. The more one projects Alpha confidence, the more likely one is to have sexual success with women, which in turn, makes it all the easier to project even more confidence. The spiral just keeps going up.

On the contrary, a male who finds himself in the Downward Spiral gets just the opposite reaction … one that is also reinforced again and again. If he comes off as sexually needy, he'll signal weakness to women, that he is a Beta male. He is, quite unconsciously, transmitting messages to women that he's "not gotten any" for a long time, and his needy behavior is a warning sign to every woman he meets, "I'm a loser; stay away!" Because he comes off as so needy and weak, he is anything but attractive. Because he is less attractive, he's less likely to "score" and be sexually successful. And sure enough, the less success he has with women, the more sexually needy he becomes! He's already sliding downward, and the momentum keeps pulling him down even further.

Women easily spot a Beta male because he unwittingly tells them, by everything from his body language to his speech patterns, that he must not be a strong Alpha. This is especially so when he meets an attractive woman. Immediately, he's signaling, "Oh wow, I want you so badly!" But it's his out-of-control desire that makes it that much more unlikely he'll get what he wants. If only he could act like the nonchalant Alpha, then it would be *she* who needs him, not the other way around.

Beta males are usually the guys who are always trying so hard to win women over by buying them drinks, offering to take them out to dinner and sending them flowers … but who rarely get any where. In their minds, they're thinking they can somehow bribe or persuade a woman to be attracted to them. What's worse, when these tactics fail, they often resort to trying even harder, doing even more of the same, and yes, getting only more of the same bad results!

Their repeated failure leads them to become even more needy, more desperate and, therefore, even more unattractive. They are the big losers in the game of Natural Selection. The spiral just keeps going down.

What's So Great About Alpha Men's Genes?

To understand how women evolved their preference for Alpha Males, imagine a time in our ancient past in which two hominid females have each found a mate, one an Alpha, and the other a Beta male. The female who found the Beta male attractive and mated with him would not have been protected very well at times of danger. Her mate would not have been as good a hunter, nor as good a defender. His lower status in the traveling hunter/gatherer band meant he was less able to summon help at times of need. Their children, therefore, would have been less likely to survive, and any genetically induced preference for the traits of a Beta male which she passed on to her children perished with them.

On the other hand, the children of the woman impregnated by the stronger, dominant, Alpha Male would have been better protected and better fed. The mother would have gotten more help in times of trouble because she would have been better able to summon aide thanks to the better status and popularity of her Alpha mate. Her children would, therefore, have been more likely to survive than any child born to the mate of the weaker Beta male. Thus, the genetically induced preference for the Alpha Male that this mother had would have been passed on to the next generation and to the next and the next.

In reality, these preferences were instilled long before hominids came along. It was actually many millions of years ago when some female who became the mother of all the sexually reproducing species that followed had—by some neutral, mutational quirk—a personal preference that inclined her more toward the stronger males of her kind. Whatever that genetic influence was that initially predisposed her to like the stronger, more "macho" males resulted in her offspring having a greater advantage in survival. Because those children carried that same genetic trait within them, it spread generation after generation thereafter … all the way down to us. And as it spread, it became more deeply embedded, so much so that an Alpha Male tends to be almost irresistible.

Unfortunately, this predisposition to find a "strong man" almost irresistible led to another negative consequence for women along the road of human history in addition to a tendency in modern times to date a lot of "bad boys." It may very well be that the deep-down wiring in the female to so desire an Alpha may have paved the way for women to more readily accept their oppressive state that almost immediately followed the Agricultural Revolution.

Inequality of Mate Preference

Having learned about the Alpha-Beta Scale of Attraction, we shouldn't be surprised to learn that, despite the *general equality* between the genders as a whole prior to the invention of farming, there was still a considerable degree of *individual inequality* in terms of who was the most preferred sexual partner. This inequity was not so pronounced that only a select few got to mate, fall in love and have children. But it did translate into a definite, stratified order in which everyone mated.

The mating preference for those who would most likely contribute to successful reproduction helped to ensure our species survived. But once this "primary directive" was met, sexual partnering still took place, even among those who were not likely to procreate at all. Why?

Let's recall once more that the purpose of human sex is two-fold—procreation and social bonding. Sure, reproduction had to come first, but had not everyone in those early communities been able to have at least some kind of sexual relationship, the resulting discord would have sealed the fate of *Homo sapiens* long ago. What kept humans living and working together effectively enough to overcome the challenges of everyday life in the harsh environs of the pre-historical world was their sexual bonds.

Yes, the Alpha Males and females had more sex with more partners and, therefore, had more kids, but they didn't have it *all*, and for good reason. Had only the best mated with the best, whatever evolutionary advantages might have been gained would have been lost to the adverse social consequences of sexual deprivation suffered by those who were left out. Early hominid communities depended heavily on social cohesion, and those community bonds would have flung apart had there been any number—much less a large percentage—of their members sexually excluded while a handful of Alphas were having non stop orgies.

Most other mammals, who can only mate for brief times of the year, spend the mating season in highly intensive competitions. Males often fight with each other to see who will prevail and get to impregnate all the available females. In some cases, the sparring can lead to serious injuries.

Once the fighting is over, it's Winner Take All. Among the deer, for example, the Alpha Male indeed does get all the girls, and all the other males just have to do without.

It's a good thing these times of intensive competition are short. As any deer hunter knows, a buck preoccupied with finding a female in heat and fending off competitors once he does, is a lot easier to shoot. There are even products sold in hunting stores and magazines boasting to mimic the same scent that does in heat give off as a way to attract bucks to their doom. Their sexual preoccupation makes them more susceptible to predators whom they'd otherwise evade with relative ease.

Imagine, then, if Nature had expanded the breeding season to a year round enterprise for these mammals without making any other changes to compensate? Surely, the entire mammalian genus would have perished long ago were such the case. It's bad enough that the loser, Beta males of these species have to deal with their sexual frustration for only a few weeks out of the year. Any longer than that and all the males would end up killing each other.

For humans, though, who are different from most other mammals in that we are sexually active on a year round basis, allowing only a few men to satisfy this fundamental desire would have, indeed, been a disaster! For a species like *Homo sapiens* whose mating season never really ends, and most especially for a species that depends much more on social cooperation, sexual competition had to be ameliorated, and the Winner Take All strategy had to go.

Humans are the exception to the normal rules of mammalian mating. While the principle benefit of the more primitive sexual strategy of promoting the strongest and most adaptable genes was preserved by a strong sense of selectivity of mate choice, Nature found another purpose for human sex—to ensure cohesive, empathetic bonds among all members of any given human band. It may not be readily apparent, but the two purposes are designed to work together.

Human communities of both the pre-historic and modern era function best when everyone has at least one mate, so everyone is getting their "minimum requirement" of love. At the same time, there always seems to be a handful of "beautiful people," the Alphas, those who are in the "Major Leagues" of procreation, who are "jumping from one bed to another."[102] They don't "get it all," but the Alpha Males do tend to breed with a disproportionately higher percentage of the Alpha Females, and the Alpha Females tend to breed with a disproportionately higher percentage of Alpha Males, even if they don't always live together. The Betas don't have as many kids per capita as the Alphas do, and more often than we might care to know, Beta males end up raising children who were fathered by Alphas.

The Alpha-Beta Paradox

This brings us once again to a principle of Nature that often baffles, frustrates and sometimes makes us modern humans very mad—that which is good for a species as a whole turns out to be not so good for certain individuals of a given species! As it pertains to reproductive success, it's clear that Nature has seen fit to predispose our deepest and most powerful drives to ensure some to winning and others to losing. As it pertains to sexual monogamy (not to be confused with an ostensible pair bond which may or may not be a *sexually* monogamous one), all the evidence shows that when sexual fidelity does occur, it's usually a one-sided affair!

As noted above, males are naturally inclined to want to copulate with as many females as possible, beginning with the most desirable first—the younger, prettier, shapelier, i.e., those most likely to successfully reproduce. But this doesn't mean they will all succeed in satisfying their desires.

Beta males—those who are (or who come off as) weak, submissive, unsure of themselves—tend to turn females off, and their sexual advances are normally rebuffed. If they're lucky, they'll find one female who will mate with them in a pair bond. They would copulate with others if they could, but they can't spend much time gallivanting around for opportunities to have sex with other females (even if they could find some willing partners), because they have to spend most of their time guarding the one female they have in order to prevent the advances of other, sexier males from cuckolding them.

His female mate can take some solace in this knowledge. The more attractive or "Alpha" she is, and the more Beta her mate, the less likely he is to cheat on her. Not so much because he doesn't want to, but because he can't! She doesn't have to worry very much about him running off with some other girl, because his best strategy for reproductive success is to just stay home and help with the kids. As a matter of fact, Beta males are much more inclined to be better parents than Alphas.

One would think, then, that women would be very happy to mate with Betas, to raise their children, and never would they jeopardize the level of security having a Beta man offers by cheating on him with some Alpha guy. Having a sexually monogamous pair bond with a Beta male would be the best way for her to go … *if* all a female's most primitive instincts cared about was the fidelity and parenting aid of her man.

Alas, this "if" turns out to be quite a big one! The reason is because that which inclines the male in this type of relationship to be sexually faithful—his membership in the Beta category—is exactly what is most likely to lead his mate to be unfaithful to him!

The female may appreciate the fact that she has a "nice guy" for a mate, one who helps change diapers and drives the kids in the mini-van to soccer games. But the longer they're together, the more he just doesn't do it for her. Beta men tend to get only a modicum of sex, just enough to barely get by, and the more the female he's with is an Alpha, the more having sex with him becomes just another chore to her.

What's worse for the Beta male's reproductive success, what little sex they do have together tends not to result in pregnancy. Scientists have documented that submissive, less dominant, pair-bonded men produce less sperm, have shorter and less firm erections, and are less likely to engage their partner at the time of her menstrual cycle when she is most fertile.

Oh, but should an Alpha come around, her passion is suddenly re-ignited! She finds him nearly irresistible, and will often find a way to sneak off and copulate with him. And wouldn't ya know that even the briefest of affairs with a strong and dominant male, as modern genetic research has revealed, often results in pregnancy! When Alpha men are gallivanting and cuckolding Beta males, they produce more sperm, have longer and harder erections and tend to turn women on the most while they're at the most fertile point of their ovulation cycle.

And sure enough, long after the biological father is gone, the faithful Beta guy often ends up, unwittingly, rearing the Alpha's kids.

What is going on here? Why would a woman who has such a great guy in her life be so unappreciative, and throw herself at some stranger who only has his way with her a few times and then moves on? Are these women crazy? Are they "sluts"? Or are they responding to some primitive instinct that, at one time anyway, served a very important purpose?

While it seems so unfair to poor Beta guys (who are not getting very much sex, neither from their mate nor from other females on the side, and more often than not, raising kids that are not even their own), such a "mixed reproductive strategy" for females makes a lot of sense from the viewpoint of Evolution, and Nature's ultimate game—successful reproduction.

Her strategy to prevail is two-fold. A female's first priority, whether she is conscious of it or not, is to get the best genes of the best man she can find. Regardless of how kind, caring and well off a potential mate is, if he doesn't have the "right stuff," the biological children he has are not going to survive and themselves successfully reproduce. Sure, it's nice when a girl can find a guy who has it all—good genes *and* all the other qualities that go into a good mate and father. But this is a rare fortune. More often, some improvising is necessary. "Get the quality seed first, and then worry about getting help around the house," is the order of priority for a woman's sexual instincts.

Since getting a good domestic partner is secondary, and it's not always possible to find both in the same guy, cheating then becomes a very practical way for a woman to win the game of reproductive success.

Zoologist David P. Barash and physician Judith Eve Lipton, explain: "For most females, genetic partners are easy to come by. Behavioral partners are a different story. Males are typically more than willing to contribute some squirts of sperm in return for a chance at reproductive success. Harder to come by are males willing to be behavioral fathers, not just genetic beneficiaries. The optimum female strategy—as in many other species—would be to get the best of each: Mate with genetically promising males and gain other benefits from wealthy, paternally inclined individuals. If all this can be obtained from just one individual, so much the better. If not, then a bit of deception may be worthwhile."[103]

There is, however, some poetic justice to these "cheating ways" of pair bonded females. Should a female be socially mated to an Alpha Male, then quite the opposite takes place. In this scenario, it is now *she* who is the one not at all inclined to want to stray—she's already getting good genes to make better kids, plus the benefit of some of his direct support. For the Alpha Male, it is now *he* who needs not worry about his mate going astray. Therefore, he doesn't have to stay home all the time to guard her from other males.

Of course, this only makes it that much more likely that he'll have the time and opportunities to have sex with other women on the side. And because he is an Alpha, he is much more likely to find willing females, single girls or women socially mated to Betas who are instinctively on the lookout to upgrade their genetic supply.

To be certain, this cheating phenomenon flies in the face of what we've been led to think is instinctive behavior for women. At the very least, we'd expect only an unhappy or "desperate housewife" to "give in" to adulterous sex with a secret lover because he's led her to believe he is willing to eventually take her as a permanent mate. We've come to think that women who find themselves in a torrid affair with a man who has no intentions of making a home with her, is bound to become very disappointed. We've been taught that only a "slut" would ever have sex with a man whom she knew would never become her mate. No "decent woman" would ever settle for sex just to get his sperm.

Such expectations, though, only come from the influence of tradition, religion or the cover stories women have had to fabricate to explain their irrational sexual behavior. The reality of the female's mixed reproductive strategy we are learning about from science tells a different story.

From the perspective of Natural Selection, it makes good sense for women to cheat on their Beta mates in the "hope" of getting pregnant by an Alpha, even if he's just passing through. If he doesn't tell her his name or leave a phone number, it's OK, and she's not upset that the Alpha didn't invite her into a relationship, though certainly, that would have been even better.

As long as she can get pregnant by the Alpha Male, her instincts are pleased enough. Why? Because she's made an advance, genetically speaking. If possible, she'll lead her Beta male into thinking he's the father of her "love child" in order to get him to help support and care for it. But even if this fails, the female still contents herself because she's got offspring with better genes, and for that, she's even prepared to do all the parenting by herself, if need be, even without the Alpha father's or any male's help.

Imagine then, how the female's instincts respond when they do get an invitation into a relationship with an Alpha? While it was already quite a benefit to have simply gotten some Alpha genes, once the prospect of making an even greater advance is realized, the female is even all the more pleased.

Now before anyone goes, "Ah, ha! I knew it!" hang on, and don't let present day traditional expectations draw you to a premature conclusion. The kind of second step up we're talking about here may not be what you think. Sure, a woman who has progressed from just getting to have sex with an Alpha to an invitation to live with him may not seem all that surprising to us … until we consider that we're not talking about a monogamous union! The Alpha may simply be adding her to a number of other, special women in his life. In other words, this next, higher level of primitive satisfaction is so strong that it doesn't even matter that she is not getting to have the Alpha all to herself! And what seems even more bizarre to us, is that it could very well be that it is *precisely because* she's not getting him all to herself that her sense of achievement is all the greater.

It's no coincidence that in societies where males tend to be domineering, i.e., more Alpha-like, women there tend to "look the other way" when they happen on evidence of their husband cheating on them.[104] As it turns out, not only are the women in these societies willing to put up with this rather unfair situation, but the fact that he's got so many other women is somehow part of what's making him so attractive to her in the first place!

Perhaps this bears repeating. We're talking about the Alpha Beta Paradox, a strange but common tendency toward sexual fidelity when the object of one's faithfulness is doing anything but reciprocating.

So far, it doesn't sound like Mother Nature is being very helpful toward those who would like to have a happy, enduring and monogamous relationship … and so far, that would be correct. But for those readers who seek a faithful and happy union, try not to despair too much. We'll be coming back to the Alpha-Beta Paradox several times more, and toward the end of this work, I've taken up some considerable space to explain what's going on behind the scenes of this "cruel trick" of Mother Nature as well as to offer some practical advice about how to turn these strange instinctive responses around to the advantage of long term, monogamous relationships. Before we do, however, it's necessary that we come to grips with a number of other phenomena that add to the challenges ahead of any couple hoping for enduring and enjoyable love, the most powerful of which is jealousy.

Is There a Jealousy Gene?

What did ancient humans do when they suspected or discovered someone with whom they had formed a sexual/love bond was having sex with someone else? Did it inspire a fit of jealous anger? Or was the situation so different for our Hunting and Gathering Era ancestors that no one would have thought a thing about their partner having sex with someone else? Did jealousy exist back then or did it arrive later on?

There are two main theories about the origin of jealousy in sexual relationships. One view (popularized by Rousseau) is that the tendency to become jealous over sexual mates is a learned behavior that wasn't present throughout most of *Homo sapiens*' existence until the Agricultural Revolution introduced the concept of ownership.

Ownership is a word that describes any particular outward realization of the inner sense of possessiveness. Possessiveness is a deep down, assertive feeling of having—or having the right to having—exclusive access to or control over a thing, a place or a person.

The logic that jealousy is learned is based on the notion that, since early humans could never own anything other than the few items they could carry on their backs, neither could they have developed an inner sense of possessiveness motivating them to own. With no sense of possessiveness, then there could neither be jealousy, that negative emotional reaction to the loss or the threat of losing a possession.

According to this view, jealousy—whether over the threat of losing an object, a place or a woman—only became possible after it became conceivable to own in the first place, and it was the outward possibility of ownership that eventually gave us the inner sense of possession.

The idea that sexual jealousy is learned presumes that pre-agricultural humans were not sexually possessive since they could not be possessive at all. Only after the mad scramble for land possession did it become necessary to take possession of women in order to keep control over one's land through one's descendents. Unlike all that followed the invention of the plow, there couldn't have been any worry about one's mate being unfaithful, because if a man couldn't own land, then neither could his son, so it mattered little who his real father was.

If this theory is right, there was no great motive to be concerned about adultery—for there was no need to maintain control of land wealth and no implications for life in The Beyond. No need to have any rules and punishments for rule breakers to ensure that a child born to a man's mate was biologically his or someone else's.

There's other evidence to support Rousseau's hypothesis from the female's perspective. Early humans all lived together in one, big, extended family. The entire community kept an eye on older children, and while assistance from biological fathers to mothers of younger children was gladly welcomed, they were not entirely dependent on them. For instance, a woman could have an occasional lover who might be the actual, biological father of her child while another man, who was her ostensible mate, would still be supportive of her and the child by virtue of the strength of their relationship rather than the paternity of the child. Moreover, we see a similar lack of the need for a nuclear family consisting of biological parents among our closest living relatives.

The closest living animal species to humans is the Bonobo or "Pygmy" Chimpanzee. One could easily say that Bonobos live in communities where "free love" is the rule. Unlike so many other mammals, and even other chimpanzees, the Bonobo female's ability to mate is very much like the human female's due to her very lengthy estrus period which allows her the ability to have sex on nearly a year round basis. Also quite unlike their chimp cousins where there is frequently a lot of tension between males vying for dominance and exclusive rights to mate, the Bonobos' are very tranquil by comparison. Further, Bonobo males and females live in egalitarian partnerships, sharing responsibilities for the care of the young, as well as food and food gathering.

What's their secret? It appears that they truly abide by the motto to "make love, not war," for Bonobos are constantly having sex with each other, with no apparent signs of any one male or female getting jealous.[105] There would also be another advantage to having so much sex with so many different partners—genetic variety.

At first glance, it would make sense that Nature would also endow both the Bonobos and us humans with an drive to mate with as many different persons as possible in order to vary the gene pool. The greater the variety of genes in every generation, the more options Natural Selection has at its disposal to adapt to ever changing environments.

However, such an intensive, natural drive wouldn't necessarily exclude the possibility of a contradictory (and often frustrating) inherited behavior like jealousy. In fact, it actually serves to invite jealousy in. Why? Because as the old saying goes, "you can have too much of a good thing."

In the race of Evolution, a wide open "primal horde" of "everyone doing everyone else" would treat good genes and bad genes all alike at the sexual "starting gate," the female vagina. The potential gains made in varying the gene pool would be lost because many of the poorly adapted genes would not be sifted out in advance. With an even start, some of them might succeed in fertilizing eggs ahead of better genes, only for those eggs to produce weaker offspring who were less likely to survive.

Without jealous competition, a man would not give any care whether his mate had sex with other men. He would do no mate guarding, and therefore, would increase the chances of men with inferior genes impregnated her. As a result, the child born to her would not be as strong and healthy. The baby would be more likely to perish before growing up and herself reproducing. In terms of the mother's long term reproductive success, this would be a waste of her time, energy and resources. If she were an Alpha, she could have otherwise brought a genetically superior child into the world.

Sure, Natural Selection would still be at work to weed out the *environmentally* maladaptive, but this means working at a very slow pace, and not very efficiently.

Enter, then, the next view (as well as the one which I am convinced of) which revolves around the notion of *competition* as the driving force behind the evolution of genetically induced jealousy. This second view rejects the idea that sexual jealousy is a learned behavior, and instead holds that the Agricultural Revolution was not what first introduced possessiveness to humanity, but that which only greatly exaggerated an innate sense of exclusive access that had been in place already for millions of years.

The evolutionary benefit of competition offers an explanation for the universal human conflict between the desire to have sex with more than one person, and the intensive amount of jealously that arises when anyone else attempts to sexually attract one's mate or mates. Just as Nature uses competition between predators and prey to constantly improve upon the adaptability of both, so too there's formidable evidence that Nature favored a genetically induced tendency to assume a right to exclusive access to a mate in order to create sexual competition.

Here's why jealousy acts as a genetic sieve. Just as the common wire mesh kitchen utensil allows only some food product through and keeps other things out, so do the actions of a jealous lover. Whenever the sense of exclusive access seems threatened, jealousy arises to force a competition to decide who is too Beta to get past one's jealous defenses, and who is so Alpha that those defenses will fail to stop them. Jealousy actually works hand in hand with the drives of both men and women to want to have sex with others, as it often does stop a mate from taking the risk of enduring a jealous rage over someone whose genes are in question. On the other hand, not even the most intensely jealous mate can stop the super attraction an Alpha projects toward his partner, and she will abandon all cares to get his superior seed. In this way, jealousy kicks Natural Selection into high gear, by sifting out bad genes and promoting good ones even *before* sex and fertilization take place!

The slower form of selection, the one we ordinarily think of as "the Survival of the Fittest," is passive. Weaker organisms are only manifested as weak by how they ultimately survive in their environment. The parents of these less fit organisms invest a lot, only to eventually have their offspring perish before they can reproduce. This passive elimination process is ordinarily acceptable to the prime directive of Natural Selection when both parent organisms are of weaker, maladaptive stock.

But what if one of the parents had good genes, and was only prohibited from passing them on by having made a poor selection of a mate? It would have been very wasteful of Mother Nature to work in such a hap hazard way. To allow for the genetically adaptive to be weeded out simply because they combined their DNA with some less fit ones is just not very efficient. So Nature came up with a solution, a whole new level of competition that actively works to prevent bad genes and good genes from getting together in the first place. We call this *sexual competition*, and long, long ago, Mother Nature introduced sexual competition by evolving within our primitive ancestors powerful instincts for sexual possessiveness and jealousy.

Sexual possessiveness, then, gives those with better genes a better chance of reproducing only with others of good genetic stock. Those who prevail in the resulting sexual competition have kids who are much more likely to survive.

Anthropologist Helen Fisher explains it this way:"… possessiveness has genetic logic. Jealous males of any species will guard their partners more assiduously; thus jealous males are more likely to sire young and pass on their genes. Females who drive off other females, on the other hand, acquire more protection and gratuities; because of their jealousy, they have acquired additional resources—so their young are more likely to survive. In this way possessive creatures bred disproportionately across the ages, selecting for what we call jealousy."[106]

Of course, the benefits of the conflict between wanting more mates for ourselves and possessiveness of our mates to keep them from following our example are not for everyone. The benefits go to the winners and the species as a whole, not those individuals who end up in the Loser category. In other words, our species evolved better because the winners of sexual competition successfully reproduced … and the losers didn't.

The "losers" would be those who, even if they could temporarily get the mild interest of a an already mated female by fooling her into thinking he was an Alpha, could still be kept from breeding with her by virtue of her ostensible mate's jealous guardianship. The "winners," on the other hand, are those real Alphas who rise up and overcome the obstacles a jealous partner might put in his way. Jealousy, then, is indeed a handy devise to filter out the sexually mediocre from polluting the gene pool.

That pool, in turn, is filled by those superior females who could beat the competition in winning the seed of superior males and by those superior males who spread their seed far and wide in spite of the efforts of jealous Betas to prevent them from doing so.

A League of Their Own

I'd like to elaborate a bit more on why the "purpose" of the jealousy gene was not to prevent "cheating" altogether, and how this behavior is critical to an overall mating process this is very stratified.

I've already noted that jealousy works to reduce the regeneration of maladaptive genes. If males of inferior genetic quality could keep *all* the other guys away, then their possessiveness would have only preserved the genetic status quo. But the mate guarding behavior prompted by natural jealousy works only up to a certain point. Beta males can normally keep away those who have nothing better to offer. Their guarding, then does well to screen out the weak, sickly and maladapted. However, their efforts are usually all in vain when confronted by the powerful attraction Alpha Males project.

Time and again, females will find a way to elude their guardian long enough to reproduce with the strong, healthy and better adapted. To put it another way, jealousy works well to prevent intruders of lower genetic rank from spreading their inferior genes to one's mate, but it isn't very good at impeding those of higher rank from bringing in their superior DNA. When those of lower rank do succeed at "fooling around," they are normally limited to getting only with those within their "league," or more often, those in an inferior one.

Certainly, we see a strong tendency today toward sexual partnerships forming along well understood strata. Even the apparent exceptions prove the rule. Under the rare circumstances where a woman in a more "advanced league" dates a guy who appears to come from an inferior one, we tend to react, "What did she ever see in him?" Or if the converse, when an "inferior" man is seen going out with a woman "way out of his league"—"How did he ever get her?"

More often though, we hear of men who are caught cheating on their wives with someone who doesn't seem to be all that comparatively more attractive. Why? Not because they didn't want a younger, prettier looking woman. If they could have convinced a woman from a higher league to bed with them, they would have. But their advances toward women in higher strata were shunned because Alpha women would have nothing to gain by having sex with them. Instead, they had a much better chance to seduce a woman of lower status, because he may seem to her, relatively speaking, a trade up.

Was there ever a time, therefore, when we were free of jealousy as Rousseau believed? I don't think so. It doesn't seem likely to me that our ancestors behaved as a "primal horde," as it has sometimes been called, in which hominids were having sex with anybody and everybody. It's more likely that there existed a kind of pre-historic eugenics program (thankfully, nothing like what eventually took place in Nazi Germany). The younger, healthier, more fertile females, those in the "major leagues," were only attracted to dominant males who were either in their league or a superior one. A Beta male might try to make a play for a major league female, but he would have been shunned. Fortunately, he could still find someone else to have sex with and perhaps even form a relationship, but in all likelihood, she would be a Beta female also.

In other words, humans evolved a mating strategy that is somewhere in between that of the Winner Take All, polygynous gorillas and the "free love communes" of the Bonobo chimps. For our kind, Natural Selection saw to it that there was enough competition to promote good genes, but not so much so that the inferior members got left out altogether. This compromise reduced the stress of sexual competition to a tolerable level while leaving a good deal of sexual stratification in tact.

Even today, there exists a general resignation toward the sexploits of the Alphas by those who perceive themselves as lower ranking. Much as they might envy them, it's just taken for granted and accepted that the "average" man or woman could never have a chance to mate with the higher ranking. Their envy for the "beautiful people" is subdued … even to the point of admiration.

We seem not only to put up with, but in fact, take great interest in the many sexual dalliances of movie stars, rock stars, the wealthy and the powerful. Were we to remove every story from every magazine, gossip column, novel, soap opera and movie that detailed the sexual behavior of the elite and beautiful, how much material would be left? Not much, I suspect, and I don't think we'd have this kind of resignation among the lower leaguers if it were not for a genetic predisposition to do so.

It appears, then, that there was indeed a jealously gene which had been a *considerable* factor in human sexual behavior until the invention of the plow, which then became The Factor soon thereafter! Perhaps, the very same phenomenon that propelled those who first settled down to farm to quickly stake out claims of exclusive ownership of all arable land, also helped stir up this genetic predisposition to guard one's mate into the extreme possessiveness that followed.

It bears repeating that if there is any one principle that is to be found in all of Nature, it is competition. Were it not for competition, for food, for water … for mates, Biological Evolution would never have occurred. Again and again, we find that, whether we are discussing the mating habits of dragonflies or chimpanzees, there is always some form of competition going on between the most suitable individuals of any given species and those who aren't, with the result of reproductive winners and losers.

Millions and millions of years ago, during Life's early beginning, those viral and single celled creatures whose individual genetic traits made for improvements to their survivability, passed those traits on every time they split in two, but only at a snail's pace. The reason is because the earliest living things reproduced all by themselves, or asexually, passing the same genes on, one generation to the next. The only means of evolutionary improvement was from the rare, adaptive mutation. The pace of change was, therefore, very slow. But once sexual reproduction came along, the pace of Evolution stepped into high gear.

With the advent of sex, regeneration became a matter of combining two halves of a set of genes from two different members of the same species in order to create a unique combination of genes in the very next generation. Those who could win more sexual partners, partners who were healthier, partners more suited to their environment, were immediately rewarded with reproductive success. Those who didn't were conversely "punished" by leaving fewer or no successors to carry their genes forward.

The "instant variety" of each generation's DNA package that sex made possible led to better and faster adaptation, a very good thing for the evolution of species. But the price of this "high speed evolution" was the forced participation in a fast paced race among the individuals of species to win the best mate or mates. If there are winners, then there are losers, and thus, competition has been a part of the mating process ever since.

It didn't take long for defensive strategies to evolve along with the offensive ones, meaning that it wasn't good enough to just get the best possible mates, but upon "getting them," to keep others away. So let's now take a closer look at the defensive strategy most common to sexual possessiveness—mate guarding.

Mate Guarding

What to do when someone who first formed a bond with you—perhaps because you seemed like a pretty good catch at the time—has bumped into someone far more attractive? What to do when you can just tell that your mate is getting the attention and interest of this other who seems to have more to offer?

Go to any beach, where women tend to wear only a modicum of attire, and one of the things that you'll notice is just how much boyfriends who are there with their girlfriends have their hands on them. It's almost as if they feel the need to advertise to every other guy on the beach, "Hey, this one is mine, so you better keep your distance!" The reason? Because they are, in deed, advertising that the woman their hovering over is their sexual possession. They are mate guarding.

Though we might think this to be a uniquely human dilemma, it is in fact very common in most other species as well. And just as we humans do when others threaten to cuckold us, so also do most sexually reproducing creatures respond to similar threats by mate guarding. Males of many species—insects, fish, reptiles, mammals, you name it—tend to hover around their mates whenever it appears that they might stray to find another "lover" who seems to be a "trade up." And just like human males, just because a male of some other species is spending most of his time mate guarding doesn't mean he wouldn't be tempted to seduce the female mate of another male … if he thought they had a chance of getting away with it!

Something else to mention here. Though we've been talking mostly about males guarding their female mates, because it's so much more obvious, females guard their male mates too. It's just that they tend to be more subtle about it. Going back to the beach example, ever notice that once in a while there's a guy who has a girl just hanging all over him? Usually, the guy is acting aloof, seemingly impervious (and often on the verge of annoyance!) to the fact that he has a bikini clad beauty wrapped all around him and who just can't keep her hands off. Most of the other guys on the beach would pay anything to get one date with her, but they know they don't have a chance. Her eyes are glued on this one guy.

But if you watch more closely, the reaction of the women in the surrounding area is even more telling. Often, other women observing this behavior will begin to ridicule the girl for "hanging on him like jewelry." Why should they be so bothered by what this girl is doing with this guy, unless of course, most of the women are actually finding this guy very attractive, and it's clear to them that she is marking him off as "hers."

Why are the roles here reversed? Because in this case, the guy is an Alpha Male, and it's now the female who must be careful to show all the other women in the surrounding area that he's with her!

As mentioned already, the irony of mate guarding is that, while it does help fend off *most* intruders from seducing one's mate, it has the disadvantage of preoccupying the one doing all the guarding from doing unto to others as they would do unto him. And the less attractive a male is, the more he's got to worry about his mate cheating, so he has to mate guard more, leaving him with even less time or opportunity to break away to cheat with some other male's mate.

But even when these Beta males do get out and about, it's most often a big waste of time because other females are unlikely to be interested. Just as their in-pair mates don't find them all that attractive, and thus the need to guard them, neither do females paired to others.

Conversely, the more a male meets the Alpha criteria, the less mate guarding he has to do. His in-pair mate, if he has one, has already got what she wants—a male with the best genes around who has invited her into a relationship with him, so she is very unlikely to "trade down" and copulate with some loser Beta male. Ironically, her fidelity serves to free up her Alpha mate so he can gallivant and spread his DNA even further. This why the Alpha Male on the beach wasn't pre-occupied with making sure at all times that he had his eyes and hands on his woman. *She* wasn't going anywhere with anyone … although *he* very well could.

Then as now, most of early *Homo sapiens* males who had a woman felt a strong sense of exclusive, sexual access to her, and if they were Betas, an accompanying sense that they had better protect that access. Since they lacked that seemingly magical quality of attraction that Alphas had to get girls left and right, their best bet for reproductive success was to find one female, entice her to form a pair bond with him, stick to her like glue, and hope for the best. As long as he didn't snare a female that was too far out of his league, he might be able to ensure her fidelity. If he succeeded, it wasn't so much because he found a girl that had such a high moral standard that she would never cheat on him, but because he found one that would see him as the best she could get.

Monogamy, if it happened at all, was when both partners perceived the other as belonging to a higher league, when in fact neither of them were, and therefore, wouldn't be worth the trouble of any better leaguers to find them attractive. Because they each thought the other so much better, they would both be very preoccupied with guarding each other, and thus, doubly ensuring that neither would ever stray.

We can imagine how such a commonplace tendency to be jealous or protective of a mate could quickly turn into full scale bondage once *Homo sapiens* settled down long enough to fully grasp the concept of ownership. In a very real sense (borrowing from the recent television fad of "reality" shows), the subsequent sexual slave trade of women was simply a transition from ordinary to extreme mate guarding.

Which Came First? Territoriality or Possessiveness

The first humans to take up farming might have also been predisposed to the idea of sexual ownership by another common behavior found in a multitude of animal species, one which echoes back to the earliest days of sexually reproducing species—territoriality. Just because our Hunting and Gathering ancestors lacked the *specific* sense of ownership that we have, doesn't mean they had no *general* sense of exclusive rights to certain territories, especially at times of stress on the natural resources contained within them. Though we're all somewhat familiar with the infamous purchase of Manhattan Island for about $24. worth of trinkets by Pieter Minuet, those same Indians who thought the idea of owning a specific area of land as ludicrous were generally conscientious of the territory in question. Otherwise, they would not have understood what it was that they had purportedly sold for such a large take of cheap jewelry.

The typical, human traveling band of the Late Hunting and Gathering Era often camped in the same locations year after year, moving to others only when resources there were depleted. They would have occasionally felt threatened if, for example, another tribe began to encroach upon the territory that they were accustomed to having all to themselves when the resources there weren't enough for all.

Usually, it was easier to just pick up and go on to the next hill or dale. But if not, the result was war. The status of women tended to go down in proportion to the extent that their tribe found it necessary to war with other groups for its survival.[107] In these relatively isolated cases, we see something of a precursor to the way women were treated after the Agricultural Revolution where competition over land-based resources became a nearly universal issue of confrontation.

Whatever qualities that encouraged early hominids to be violently protective of the territories they generally dwelt in when resources were limited, may very well have been the same genetic traits that, in time, gave rise to the more severe forms of female oppression that were to follow. It was, therefore, very possible that a deeply embedded "territoriality gene" also predisposed us to an extreme expression of sexual jealousy, shortly after the invention of the plow.[108] So strong now is this sense of possession that most every modern experiment in group marriage, open marriage or polyamory (a term coined from the Greek literally meaning "love of many") end within a short period of time, rarely lasting over one year.

Swinging Grandparents

Though it's not something most people feel comfortable telling the world, there are a substantial number of the daring couples who try overcoming their innate sexual possessiveness by attempting to allow their mates to have other sex partners. These are people who are generally much more honest with themselves about their desires to have sex with others. Rather than fall prey to all the hurts that follow the typical experience of cheating, not to mention the guilt and shame that comes with having to lie to one's most intimate life partner, these brave folks try another approach. Most who try, fail to stay with it. However, some do succeed.

To make sure things are clear, we're not talking about cheating partners, but *those who are trying to head off the temptation to cheat.* Here, we also don't mean the rare polygynous family where only the men have multiple wives. We're also not talking about those who are single and just "playing the field." We're talking about couples who have sex with at least one other person while maintaining a steady relationship where both the males and females have other partners. What is it about these adults who seem to be the exception to the rule of jealousy?

The answer is that the very small number of people who manage to hold together sexual arrangements of three or more persons by informed consent of all parties involved, have only done so with much determination, usually in social isolation (such as the rare, often cult-based, "free love" communities located in remote areas), and even then, all the while still battling feelings of jealousy that well up on a regular basis.

These paired men and women who engage in multi-partner sex can be subdivided into two groups—*swingers* and *polys.* Swingers are those whose "swinging" means they get together with other partners strictly for recreational sex purposes. They do all they can to avoid any emotional attachments from forming. The polys, which is short for "polyamorous," do just the opposite. They intentionally form emotional bonds in sexual partnerships of three or more people, and form what are sometimes called "group marriages."

But whether we're talking about polys or swingers, there's a very interesting fact about these "sexually liberated" people that helps them overcome the powerful jealousy instinct—the women involved tend to be, or more precisely *appear to be* at or above the usual age at which menopause occurs. And since women normally form pair bonds with older men, both the male and female polys and swingers are almost uniformly old enough to be grandparents! In other words, those who manage to successfully adopt the swinger or poly lifestyles, are normally couples who are too old to have children anymore.

Why should being too old to have kids help reduce jealousy? It's likely because the jealousy gene—having been favored by Natural Selection for the competitive edge it provides in reproduction—has served its purpose already, and therefore, it wanes in its strength as couples mature.

How did this waning evolve? Let's recall that it's reproductive success which fuels the engine of Natural Selection. Once a woman can no longer bear children, her mate can no longer lose ground to a competing male, not directly anyway. So he's not going to be as threatened by other males. Cuckolding the mate of a post-menopausal woman is not going to result in any reproductive disadvantage for the cuckolded male. Neither is it a reproductive advantage for the intruding male. Any instinct, therefore, for a male to become jealous when his mate was younger, fertile woman—instincts so heavily encouraged by Natural Selection beforehand—begins to atrophy once she can no longer reproduce.

Of course, older couples who engage in extra-relationship sex with the informed consent of all partners involved represent an extreme minority. What is much more typical of mature couples is to have, relatively speaking, less trouble with jealousy issues than younger couples. For instance, the mature are more likely to be tolerant of a partner that ogles at other attractive members of the opposite sex ... "as long as they don't touch." They may have no problem with their mate going to exotic nightclubs ... "as long as they don't go to brothels," Or they may even go together to very sensual plays or live, Vegas-style shows, featuring very scantily clad performers. They may even be well aware that their partner fantasizes about other people while they make love, but are quite tolerant of these fantasies "as long as they don't make it too obvious." (More about the use of such fantasies later.) Once having children is no longer possible, the bonding effect of sex assumes predominance over reproduction, and while jealousy doesn't exactly disintegrate, it normally declines in its intensity.

For younger adults who are still reproducing, jealousy works at full capacity. This is especially the case with mothers of young children. It's really not too difficult to see how Evolution brought this about. With the exception of polygynous families, a male who acquires another female sexual partner "on the side" means only one thing to his young woman at home—she has more competition for his time, attention and resources while trying to care for her young children. If a woman was not "Alpha enough" to be accepted into the harem of an Alpha Male, and she has "settled" for a Beta, then at the very least, she is going to do all she can to have exclusive access to him and what he can do for her and her young by driving away other females who might seem a little too interested.

The only women of child bearing age who tended not to become jealous over their mate's having sex with other females were those belonging to an Alpha Male. But even then, the only reason the Alpha men were able to keep female jealousy at bay was because they were skilled hunters and strong leaders who had the means to provide for all of them adequately. This threshold explains why even Alpha Males were limited to no more than four or five women in their harems during the Hunting and Gathering Era.

However young or old, there just seems to be no easy way to deal with the competing impulses of desire for more than one sexual partner and the equal, if not stronger desire, to keep one's sexual mate all to oneself. No one has as yet to come up with a magic formula that can overcome millions of years of Natural Selection to completely rid us of all temptations to stray. Both the tendencies to stray and to become jealous are here to stay.

The big question, then—which we will be addressing specifically toward the end of this book—is if we can't get rid of either one, how to cope with, and if possible accommodate, these contrary desires simultaneously? Many of the religious advocates of Marriage argue that it's our "sinful nature" that causes us to "lust" after others, and therefore, one must simply resign to living with these temptations or else suffer the legal, social and eternal repercussions awaiting any who cheat. Trouble is, even those who buy into the belief that we are incurably damned by a sinful, lustful nature and therefore, must accept the restraints of church, state and society as necessary evils, more often than not, find themselves cheating anyway! And even those who don't actually cheat in outward deed spend a lot of time wishing in their minds and hearts that they could.

But what if there was another, better, less pessimistic way? The good news is that there is better way to deal with these competing urges within us that seem to make a monogamous pair bond impossible to happily sustain. There is a way to love someone and to be content without having to resign to the pitiful state of always wishing for some one else. Using a crude analogy here, there is a way to acknowledge having a "hunger" for some "food" that we know is bad for our health, and yet find a way to avoid the temptations to eat unhealthy food by filling up on something else first that is much more healthy (as opposed to putting locks on the refrigerator door)! In other words, there is a way to take advantage of our instincts that naturally lead us to be temporarily monogamous and then extend their normal "lifetime." But before we examine this alternative strategy, we must first understand why and how monogamy ever naturally happens at all, even if only temporarily.

The Three Stages of a Pair Bond

Common experience tells us that people fall in love every day, and that at least for a time, they feel no need or desire to have intimacy with anyone else. In other words, whether one is a Christian Fundamentalist in the American Bible Belt or a heathen aboriginal that has as yet to encounter civilization, there is very little disagreement that people can and frequently do enter into monogamous unions … at least for a while. We'll call this Stage One of a pair bond. This first stage is often compared to a shooting star. Two people meet. They become very attracted to one another. They "fall in love at first sight." Soon, they begin to have intimate contact. They make love repeatedly, sometimes all night long. They can't seem to stay away from each other. The furnace of passion is on full blast! During this stage, both partners might have opportunities to be with other sexual partners, but they have little to no desire to be with anyone else. They are monogamous in thought, word and deed … at least for a few weeks to a month on average.

People in this stage will stay up all hours of the night, making love again and again. Later, they'll look back and wonder with amazement how they ever got to work the next day. It almost sounds like a form of insanity, and in a sense it is. It's no coincidence that a couple in this stage is often described as being "madly" in love. Why would Nature do such a thing? Well, this physically, mentally and emotionally taxing phase makes sense once we see it in terms of successful reproduction, the "Primary Directive" of Nature.

By having sex practically day and night for at least two to four weeks, the odds of a pregnancy resulting are pretty good assuming both partners are healthy adults—a female who is producing eggs and a male with a decent sperm count. This is time enough for most women to ovulate while (thanks to the non stop sex) millions of fresh sperm are "in play." Regardless of whether a deeper bond forms after Stage One is complete, the most important function is accomplished—reproduction. The highly focused desire for one person only, long enough to result in pregnancy (since human females are only capable of getting pregnant for about one week out of every month) was a perfect solution of Natural Selection to get the job done in a timely fashion.

The ecstasy of a Stage One bond and the memorable moments it leaves behind are as addictive as any hard drug. The "high" resulting from this stage leads many to wish that it were somehow possible to prolong it, even for a lifetime. But beware. Anyone who makes a wish like this better hope they don't get what they ask for. Were it not for the natural down turn in the "fuel flow" after a month or so to reduce the blazing fires of passion, we would literally die! In case this sounds like an exaggeration, just think about other species who don't have a sexual passion safety valve like we humans do.

Take Salmon for example. When Salmon spawn, they go into such a breeding frenzy that by the time the females complete their egg laying and the males their fertilizing, they are both so physically spent, they die within a few hours afterward! Apart from those many nights (or days) of Stage One love, humans also feel a great deal of exhaustion after having sex. We tend to go right to sleep afterwards in order to recuperate our strength (which, by the way, is the reason we equate "going to bed" with "having sex"). However, were we compelled by instinct to continue for months on end being "madly in love," we'd end up just as dead as the "sexuasted" Salmon.

From Hot Blazes to Warm Embers

Intensive Stage One bonds, often morph into deeper and more lasting connections. In these cases, the "naturally occurring" sexual monogamy dissipates, and the maddening kind of love gives way to a mellow state that we'll call Stage Two or Contentment. Since the two people involved still feel very good just to be with each other, or perhaps more accurately, don't feel so good when they're not, this stage is characterized by a social form of monogamy. If Stage One seemed like a hot blaze of fire, then this one is more like a glow of warm embers. Though less arduous, this second stage provides sexual partners a good deal of satisfaction, most of the time. There may occur instances where they will disagree, have fights, and for brief periods of time, not always feel a great deal of attraction for each other. But this is the stage where a deep bond can form, and once established, it can be very difficult to pull away and separate for any length of time. Even if there has been a major fight or disagreement, they soon kiss and make up.

Couples who have moved into Stage Two often report that they don't make love as much as they did when they were first together. But at the same time, they'll say that they are getting as much as they want … from each other. The reason is because the purpose of their sexual behavior has now shifted from being primarily about getting pregnant, to creating and maintaining a deep emotional bond between the woman who is either already pregnant or soon will be, and her sex partner who can be of extra help and support while she is pregnant, giving birth, and nursing an infant. However, Stage Two bonds also have another function—to serve as the basis for a cohesive community. As people get older, the need to breed decreases, but in proportion to the increase in the need to be empathetically connected. We'll be discussing more about post menopausal sex later on.

Lastly, there's a third stage that many couples eventually find themselves in where their bonds just seem to have withered away altogether, and occasional tiffs become chronic battles. Sometimes, these couples are able to reinvigorate their relationship, and move back to Stage Two. However, the longer a couple lingers in Stage Three, the less likely they are to recover. They may still be living together, but if so, they're not very happy about it. It's not unlike the feeling people have when they can't stand the apartment they're living in, but they have to stay there anyway because they can't afford to break their lease.

There are a lot of people whose relationships have moved into Stage Three. And unfortunately, these are probably many of the married people you know. Their passion is all gone. If they do have sex, it's rare and mechanical. If they speak to each other, it amounts to no more than chit chat. If they feel compelled to remain together superficially in order to conform to religious, legal, social or familial expectations, they often assume a state of resignation. They may report that they have a happy relationship, but this is very often, not because of any real satisfaction, but because their expectations were low to begin with.

Why do so many monogamous unions tend to break down into Stage Three? Are so many people doing something wrong? Are so many people just not finding Mr. or Ms. Right? Or is it possible that *Homo sapiens* was never designed by Nature to mate monogamously in the first place … at least not for a life time? The answer seems to be, that while we are naturally inclined to monogamous sexual unions for a while—sometimes even long whiles—we are equally inclined to eventually end them.

Built-In Obsolescence

Even though humans are naturally inclined to fall in love, begin living together and have a child, it is quite unnatural for us to mate with only one person for an entire life time. In fact, statistical reports from all around the world reveal that there may exist deep within the human psyche a genetically induced time limit on pair bonds, which shows, on average, to kick in after about four years. A four year itch, instead of the proverbial seven.

One explanation for this built-in obsolescence is that during our hunting and gathering days, it only made sense for Nature to encourage humans to form close, intimate partnerships for a few years, while the woman in the relationship was pregnant and nursing a baby. This ensured that a new mother had the undivided attention and care of at least one male during a vulnerable period of her reproductive years—from pregnancy to the time her child was weaned.[109] But for reasons soon to be addressed, once the child was old enough to eat regular food, the main reason for the pair bond forming in the first place was no more. Then, unless the mother became pregnant again, the relationship between her and the ostensible father was likely to disintegrate.

To our modern ears, this seems very tragic, especially because of the hardships modern breakups typically cause for families in our society, especially for children. However, a parental break up was not such a bad thing during the Hunting and Gathering Era. One reason was because children who no longer needed their mothers' milk didn't have to worry about who was going to feed or look after them.[110] Once children are weaned, they became part of a juvenile play group—the Hunting and Gathering Era version of public school—where kids would spend much of their time mimicking the activities of adults, i.e. playing, as a critical part of their education and preparation for adulthood. Since everyone—the adults, the older children, as well as parents and grandparents—were all part of the band that lived together, ate together and shared resources, there was no particular difficulty for a mother to provide for her older, weaned child. The father (or surrogate father) could continue to maintain a close relationship with the now older child, but the mother wouldn't need his support as much as when the child was young and she was still lactating. While a couple's relationship could go on from this point—especially if the mother were to soon become pregnant again after the first child was weaned—the evolutionary imperative to have as much genetic diversity as possible explains why the "itching" to look for a different partner becomes particularly acute after the child and mother no longer need extra care.

Did Adam Have Eyes Only For Eve?

The Church, of course, has always characterized the "itch" and the breakups that often follow in simplistic terms—"a surrender to lustful desires that arise from the fallen nature of man." Churchmen would argue that having any feelings of sexual desire for someone other than a lawfully, wedded spouse is the same as adultery.[111] However, one only needs to follow the path of this logic out a little ways to see just how crooked it becomes. If lust or desiring someone sexually is purely the result of sin, then it would follow that had Adam and Eve not fallen from grace, then Adam would have been incapable of having sexual attraction for any one other than Eve. The Fundamentalist presumption is that Adam must have had two "sexual desire switches," one that was flipped into the "off" position as far as any other women were concerned, and the other in the "on" position only as far as Eve, his "God-given wife," was concerned. Following their logic, had Adam steered clear of that apple, every man and woman since would have only experienced sexual desire on the day of their marriage! Presumably, had it not been for Original Sin, no man would ever select a woman for a wife on the basis of her looks and no woman would ever be tempted to find another, more dominant male sexually enticing.

Accordingly, the ability to "lust" for a woman prior to or outside of the marital covenant had to have been a direct result of the corruption to man's nature after the Fall in the Garden of Eden. If this were so, then it would be due to one of two things. Either God directly "rewired" the base of our brains or Original Sin somehow mutated the base of Adam's brain to create a generic "lust switch" for women other than his spouse, and made it so it could easily flip to the "on" position! The same could be said for Eve, though the analogy of a lust *dial* seems to be more fitting than an on-and-off switch. In any case, poor Adam and Eve—and all the rest of us since then—are now doomed to find ourselves very easily tempted to be sexually turned on by people other than our lawfully wedded spouses. The best we can hope for is to resist these "impure thoughts" and "sinful urges" and place ourselves under as much external pressure as possible so our "fleshly lusts" will be reigned in until we get to Heaven where things will presumably be different.

Unfortunately, the logic of the Fundamentalist explanation for the origin of pre-marital and extra-marital sexual desire—and their remedy to subdue it by means of legal contract and sacred vows to the death—is only about as effective as the futile attempts by the poor soul under the Curse of the Wolf Man. In an effort to restrain his inner beast, he would tie himself up on the eve of every full moon, knowing that he had no other way of preventing his behavior once the wolf inside of him manifested itself. But just as the Wolf Man always managed to break out of his chains anyway, so too does the human sex drive, sooner or later, overcome the restraints put upon it by church, government or society.

Attributing sexual desire to a fallen, spiritual state may have served as a convenient explanation in times of past ignorance for the common experience of often desiring that which Society, Church and State said was forbidden. But in the same way we can now dismiss superstitions that were widely accepted hundreds of years ago—that flies originated from decaying meat, that the earth was flat, or that having a black cat cross one's path was a sure sign of bad luck—scientific evidence offers us a far better explanation as to why humans lust for more than one sex partner.

Germ Warfare

While there are a few species who are truly monogamous, they are the rare exception. Most species, especially mammals like us, are by Nature very sexually outgoing … and for good reason. Our very survival depended on, among other things, staying as many steps ahead as possible of the throngs of parasitic viruses and bacteria that secretly attack our bodies every day. And one of the best ways to dodge disease causing germs is to have as varied a genetic makeup as possible. This way, our microscopic enemies have to continuously mutate themselves just to "pick the locks" of a myriad number of DNA combinations in order to break through the cell walls of our bodily tissues and attack them successfully.

Rather than simply waiting hundreds for occasional mutations to provide the DNA variety needed to throw germs off the trail of our most ancient, sea-dwelling ancestors, Nature came up with a much faster way to mix things up genetically speaking—sex. Sexual reproduction is perhaps Nature's best invention yet to ensure genetic diversity.

To review, asexual reproduction is a simple splitting apart into twin versions or exact clones of the parent organism. Many micro-organisms still reproduce in this manner, and when they do, their offspring each has exactly the same DNA. The only way their genes can change is on the occasion of a naturally occurring mutation. Since most mutations provide neither benefit, nor advantage, it can take a long time for those mutated genes which provide for better adaptation to come along and show their stuff. It normally takes so long, in fact, that it gives their enemy parasitic germs plenty of time to mutate themselves enough to be able to find chinks in the organism's "armor."

On the contrary, sexual reproduction allows for a rapid jumbling of the genes, with each new fertilized egg getting a unique combination of one half of each parent's DNA.[112] Every generation is a brand new puzzle, genetically speaking, which forces germs to work a lot harder and change a lot faster in order to catch up.

Germs are pretty good at catching up though. Sexual reproduction helped to keep things pretty well confusing for them, but at some point on the Tree of Biological Evolution, a little fine tuning of the genetic shell game led to an even greater advantage in the arms race with germs. To understand this next advance by Natural Selection, let's suppose we could actually talk to the little critters to find out whom they would prefer to attack if they had their choice.

If a group of parasitic germs were to invade a small community of early humans where all the children were born to the same sets of parents—as our modern cultural ideal of a "traditional family" would prescribe—they'd have quite a fight ahead of them. Unlike some other creatures, such as asexually reproducing reptiles who all have the exact same DNA, and therefore, the very same defensives and weaknesses, the germs know that they've got to mutate and change faster than ever. But once past the genetic locks of one person, they'd stand a fairly good chance of infecting the rest of that person's close relatives because they would have so much in common, genetically speaking. However, if they were to attack another human community where each and every individual has a different set of parents, the enemy germs would be much more likely to lose. Surely, the germs would prefer to go after the purely monogamous community. Natural Selection, therefore, favored those early ancestors of ours who were genetically predisposed to have kids by as many different mates as possible. More of their kids survived, as well as their genetic inclination to diversify their posterity.

Serial Monogamy

Nature had no good reason, then, to encourage our hominid ancestors to be monogamous on a life-long basis as far as reproductive success is concerned. So why bother with relationships at all if they're bound to eventually fizzle out? Why not just have "a quickie" and move along, as so many other species do? Why not let the most "macho" males focus solely on impregnating, let the females do all the child care, and let the not-so-macho males look on with envy? The short answer is that Nature did something a little weird with our kind, and the first part of the explanation has to do with the human ability to have sex even when human females are not ovulating.

This doesn't make any sense at first glance. It would be a total waste of evolutionary pressure to equip us in such an odd fashion … unless there was some other reason besides reproduction for encouraging humans to have sex all the year round. As it turns out, indeed there was. The ability to have sex with the same person on an ongoing basis—which in turn, led to the formation of deep emotional bonds with a sexual partner for significant periods of time—helped provide an extra layer of support for new mothers and their vulnerable children.

Though we normally think of vulnerability as a bad thing, it was the development of a long period of relative helplessness that gave human infants a developmental advantage on other species who are born or hatched with the ability to immediately walk, crawl or swim away and live on their own. This expanded time gave human infants more time to develop larger, more complex brains. Thanks to that thing we call love, a young mother had the extra care, extra food and extra protection needed while she was nursing a helpless baby for so long a time. One can therefore rightly say that it was the evolution of sex into love that helped our brains get bigger. Had our forbears not evolved this ability, infants who were taking too long to be weaned, because they were growing larger brains, may not have survived long enough for all the other adaptive advantages bigger brains made possible.

But what happened after the child was weaned? At this point, the reproductive advantages of the pair bond begin to wear off. Unless the pair goes on to have another child, and with that, the risks of genetic similarity, there's really no more benefit to maintaining the love bond in terms of reproductive success. And sure enough, we often see the bond of couples who have been together a number of years weakening—as mentioned, at just about the time a child was normally weaned in ancient times—and they begin to drift away to find other lovers to reproduce with. Why?

Again, because having children by separate partners translated into an increase in the odds of infant survival. Deadly parasitic germs attempting to invade a given human camp would have better odds at killing the children who share many of the same genes because they have the same parents than the children born to no same two parents.

This why we can say that our species' survival was enhanced by a mixed mating strategy which provided for both the genetic advantages of sexual mate variety over a lifetime, together with the social advantages of ostensible monogamy on a limited time basis. The name for this mating strategy is *serial monogamy*. The ingenious combination of two, seemingly contradictory impulses—1) to be sexually multifarious and 2) to form socially monogamous pair bonds—provided for the best of both worlds. Genetic diversity resulted from desires encouraging us to have children with many different sexual partners, while other natural impulses moved us to form deep, empathetic pair bonds to help look after these genetically diverse children while they and their mothers are most vulnerable.

Today, we continue to feel the same competing urges deep within ourselves just as our ancient ancestors did. At first, we long to find partners as close to our ideal preference as possible to have sex with. Then, if one has sex with the same partner for any length of time, an intense emotional bond may form—we fall in love. At least for a time, this emotional bond becomes the dominant force, and tends to suppress the drive to seek out other sex partners.[113] (Curiously, some seem more prone to stray than others, even when the social bond is still strong and a long ways from naturally disintegrating. We'll address this issue in more detail in a later chapter.) Eventually, though, even these strong pair bonds of love begin to weaken, and most are inclined to seek others once more, and the process begins anew.

We could complain that this was a bit unfair of Nature to place within us such contrary desires. Then, again, Nature is rarely "fair." Think about the myriad number of creatures who never get a chance to hatch or grow up after live birth because the majority of them must serve as nutrition for other species higher on the food chain. We humans could have gotten a far worse deal. By all logic our species should have been the first to go during the first surges of the Ice Age for our lack of thick fur, great speed, hard shells, sharp claws, and Bloodhound like noses.[114]

We were naked apes on the fast food menu for scores of hungry carnivores and about as vulnerable as sheep before the slaughter by armies of parasitic germs. But we made it anyways thanks in part to a drive to mate with many different partners throughout a lifetime. Serial monogamy helped keep us at least one step ahead of extinction.

Aging and Lasting Love

We've touched on the change our society made in the latter half of the 20th Century upon realizing it was the lesser of evils to lift the most weighty obligations on women to be monogamous for a lifetime. Since obtaining more equality in the workplace and with the removal of Fault Divorce, most young women—i.e., women in their best child-bearing years—will often choose to get out of a marriage once it slips into Stage Three. Unlike Great Grandma's generation who would have found it very difficult to end a marriage, nowadays, unhappily married women have the means to exit, and they usually do. Social and religious conservatives still argue that our society should have never gone the route of condoning No Fault Divorce, and blame all manner of ills on it. However, what we have instead, serial monogamy, is really the far older and more enduring pattern of human mating behavior! Though we witness everywhere the reality of relations lasting only for so long, we cling to the ideal that love ought to last, even if it doesn't. Are we, therefore, programmed by Nature to spend all of our earthly lives going from one relationship to another? Asked another way, is the ideal of lasting love purely a myth?

It might seem so based on all we've examined up until this point ... but that's only because we've focused on the mating patterns of young adults, that is, those who are best suited to reproduce. For them, love just doesn't tend to last more than a few years. That said, there does appear to be some hope for enduring relationships after all—when we get older!

We're all familiar with the comment typically made upon learning that someone who married their high school sweetheart has just ended up in divorce court—"They shouldn't have gotten married so young." One need not be in a relationship or marriage statistician to know that the younger a couple is when they try to form a permanent relationship, the more likely they are to eventually split up. But the trend to break up with a lover begins to slow down as we move from the teens to the 20s. By age 30, the tide begins to turn. The age at which most divorces occur in the US peaks at about 30 years old which is—you guessed it—four years past the peak age of successful female fertility![115] Relationships from this point forward begin to last longer, and most all that either begin or have lasted until a woman's menopause, will remain intact until one of the partners passes away.

Once again, this phenomenon makes sense in the context of early human history. Our hunting and gathering ancestors were not monogamous in the sense of having only one sexual mate until one of the pair dies. However, once the primary directive of genetic diversity was satisfied (by producing children with as many different mates as possible), the built-in obsolescence that tended to kick in each time a child was weaned … lost its strength. That tendency is still with us today, and as a result, the older we get, the longer relationships last.

Perhaps we all know of at least one older guy that was quite the "ladies' man" when he was young, but who eventually settled down with one woman, and has been with her ever since. The same is also true of women, though they have a harder time admitting to having "been around the track a number of times" in their youth because of our tenacious, cultural taboos that are much more harsh on women who are open about how many sex partners they've had. This is more than just a coincidence.

The Granny Factor

The tendency to form permanent sexual bonds in the latter part of life contributed greatly to the cohesiveness and stability of our prehistoric ancestors' communities. In fact, one of the biggest advantages that allowed our species to monopolize natural resources better than the Neanderthals—eventually resulting in their extinction—was the Granny Factor. Because human females ceased being fertile long before their life spans were over and because they tended to settle into permanent relationships that provided them with added support, human grandmothers could devote a considerable portion of their time and energy to assist their daughters in the care of their grand children. Cave Granny had the same advantages she did when she was a young mother thanks to a stable, sexual relationship with a Cave Grandpa … but without the burden of having to care and nurse an infant of her own.[116]

The poor Neanderthals didn't have a support system like this. Their average life span lasted only about as long as they were fertile—30 or so years. Unlike humans, their females didn't have the extra help and the benefit of their mothers' wisdom at the time when they needed it most. This meant spending more time caring for young children and less time gathering food, and probably doing neither one as well as human mothers who didn't have to learn everything from scratch with every generation. Yes, the Neanderthals managed anyway, and for a very long time … until some real competition showed up. Pitted against early humans who had advantages in their social organization like Cave Grannies, they were no match when it came to who first got to the limited food resources of prehistoric times. Therefore, it's been speculated that the Granny Factor may have been one of the main reasons why Cro-Magnon Man (an early form of the modern human) overran and replaced the Neanderthals in such a relatively short number of years (5,000 - 6,000) after they arrived in Europe around 35,000 years ago.

Once again, Evolution had provided *Homo sapiens* another edge. Early human communities benefited from the greater distribution of child care thanks to the help of Cave Granny and Cave Grandpa. At the same time, the young and fertile tended to shuffle from one mate to another, maximizing genetic diversity.[117]

In our modern society, we tend to think of having several children by different partners as "irresponsible," "bad" or at least "very difficult," but having children by more than one mate is not inherently evil. To be certain, today it is more difficult, but only because our society does blessed little to support families who don't live up to the so called "traditional family ideal" of biological parents living together with all of their biological children. Our society makes it very costly for parents to separate, as divorce lawyers laugh all the way to the bank, doing all they can to get parents to litigate over custody, child support and property division. Our society ostracizes single parents, and we practically persecute any alternative family structures, such as same-sex couples that want to adopt children.

But what if our society were to find ways to imitate the truly old fashioned family structure that our ancient, hunting and gathering communities had? What if we were more accepting of our tendency to have several relationships over a lifetime? What if we were supportive, instead of punitive, of single mothers, step families, or blended-families? What if we didn't think of non-traditional family structures as "failures?"

The fact is that we humans have already come very close to full circle in our mating patterns, and the sooner we face it, the better. Women who have (or obtain) the ancient markers of fertility and health are very likely to engage in short-lived, Stage One bonds with males who have (or learn to come off as) strong and dominant. But once in their early 20s and out in the working world, most go on to form Stage Two bonds. After that, Stage Three comes along, and while many try to stick it out no matter how discontent they become, most finally break up and divorce.

However, even after the most painful of break ups, people try again. Second marriages tend to last about as long as first time marriages, especially for those in their 30s when women are still capable of having children with few complications. But as women get closer to menopause, and even as men who in their youth were "lady killers" at the disco but now in their 40s can no longer dance with the confident agility they once had, they tend to settle down to one mate, and many of these relationships actually do endure "until death." Our perception of what ought to be is still a long ways from catching up to the way things are, but lasting love is neither an unrealistic dream, nor is it going away altogether. It's just becoming more and more evident that it takes getting older to achieve it.

◆ ◆ ◆

Now that we've examined how and why Nature endowed us with mating behaviors that made so much sense for our species' sexual relationships during the greater part of our existence, the Hunting and Gathering Era, it ought to be easier to comprehend the havoc that was wrecked upon those relationships after the Agricultural Revolution. We've looked at how the demise of women's status to that of property in the sexual slave trade resulted in the kind of sexual restrictions and double standards that continued right up until the time Great Grandma was first saying "I do." But as we are all very aware, much began to change in the way our society looked at Marriage and sex within the decades that followed Great Grandma's wedding. While we tend to think that most of those changes happened in the 1960s, many of the events that were to transform the Marriage Institution—from Great Grandma's lifetime obligation to a single sexual partner to the relatively temporary unions we observe today—had begun long before she was born.

5

The Sexual Revolution

o o o o o o o o o o o o o o o o o o o o o o o o o o o o o o o o o

"If it feels good, do it."

—*Oft quoted mantra of the "Hippy Philosophy"*

American Dreams

While it was by no means the first time in history that a society made some dramatic changes in its attitudes and beliefs, what is often simply referred to as "The 60s" is one of those times of change that stands out the most in living memory. It was during the 1960s, that the so-called Sexual Revolution came to fruition. However, the changes that seemingly intoxicated an entire generation during that one remarkable decade had actually been brewing for centuries.

For many of the "untrustworthy," over-30 generation of the 60s, the new ideas about human sexuality were shocking. Though men and women had already been having pre-marital sex in greater numbers, though divorce had already been steadily rising since the beginning of the 20th century, and though women were increasingly leaving "their place in the kitchen" to fill up the factories, America's "greatest generation" didn't really awaken to these changes until it was laid on their doorsteps in broad daylight more or less culminating in the most famous rock festival ever—Woodstock.

This was the generation that had struggled through the Great Depression, fought in World War II and had come home heavily pre-occupied with getting all the material things that they were denied in their youth. A large number of the women who had taken men's places in the bomber, tank and battleship factories, came home to have the babies (of the Boom fame), and throughout the 50s, Great Grandma and Great Grandpa set out to buy all those things deprived of them when they were the children of the Depression. They were keenly focused on achieving the "American Dream"—owning a home, filling it up with the latest material goods, and having a nice car in the driveway to get away from it all.

Television programming of the 50s seemed to say it all with Ozzie and Harriet, Leave It To Beaver and Father Knows Best, depicting the ideal, white, suburban lifestyle, where teens only got in trouble for getting poor report cards, not for getting pregnant! But even though the reality for most Americans was a far cry from the ideal family most aspired to, it truly came as a shock to most of the "older generation" when they saw TV reports of young men and women frolicking naked at the first Woodstock festival. They hardly knew what to make of middle class, white teens smoking some illegal narcotic called marijuana, coinciding with a steady increase in news headlines reporting more and more American military casualties in a strange, far away country named Vietnam. When they finally did awaken from the American Dream in the 1960s, the older generation was at a loss as to what was happening. It seemed as if all they had expected, all they had believed, and all they had hoped to pass on to their children had all vanished overnight!

Many got heatedly angry, and sought out some scapegoat to blame for it all. Some blamed it on "Communist infiltrators," others on the Martin Luther King, and believe it or not, there were more than a few who were absolutely convinced, "all these hippies, rock music, drugs and [illicit] sex started when those Beatles came over here with that long hair!" But in fact, what boiled over in the 60s, had been heating up long before the British Invasion.[118]

The Growth of Democratic Principles

If we really want to pick a time to when the Sexual Revolution of the 1960s got started, we'd have to go back 200 years, to the 1760s. This was a time of great change, not just on the American Continent, but all through Europe and around the world. On the heels of the Protestant Reformation and European colonial expansion, came a tremendous increase in literacy and learning called The Enlightenment. Actually, we should probably go back even further, because the "Age of Reason" can be traced back to the trailblazing ideas of people like the 13th Century monk Francis Bacon—who laid the groundwork for what we now call the scientific method, the invention of moveable type by Johann Gutenburg—which made books affordable for the common man, and oddly enough, the Protestant demand that all believers learn to read—"in order to study the Scriptures." In any case, by the 1700s, it was clear that Western Civilization was no longer dominated by those who insisted on telling everyone else what to think, what to believe and what to do, at least, without having to supply a reason for doing so.

By the 1700s, a considerable percentage of the American colonial populace was literate. Many had gone to school and learned to read in the same building which served as the town church. Once having acquired the ability to read, though, they didn't stop with the Book of Revelations. Reading also opened their minds to new ideas, new discoveries, and most importantly, a new way of defining what was true—Reason.

We take it for granted now, but there was a time when most things that most people thought to be true, were so considered because that's what they were told. To question was to sin. To wonder why, was to wonder into hell. But once the sparks of intellectual inquiry began to fall on the general populace, a wildfire soon followed. True, people didn't immediately abandon all that they'd previously been told to believe. And almost just as quickly as the saying "Prove it!" became common, there arose a number of people who began to use their increased knowledge to manipulate human behavior in ever more insidious ways. Nevertheless, those who would have otherwise dictated our every thought no longer had the monopoly they once enjoyed. The playing field on which science and superstition competed was much closer to being level.

The ideas of the Enlightenment figured greatly in leading many of the Founding Fathers of the United States to finally reject dependency on the British Crown in favor of a government by the people. Thanks to the resuscitated virtue of Common Sense—as opposed to Church or Monarchical authority—American colonists came to see independence and free will as inalienable rights, instead of the vices of a rebellious and sinful rabble.

For so very long, ignorance and fear had kept the masses of humanity locked into control. But once they began to think for themselves, the deep down sense of liberty which had been largely lost since men and women freely roamed all over the earth to hunt and gather, was revived. By the time the US Constitution was ratified, the idea of people, average people, all people, getting to live their lives the way they see fit, and not simply for the purpose of pleasing someone else, whether a king, a bishop, a master or a husband, had fallen on fertile ground and begun to grow and flourish.

To be certain, the struggle to make this noble ideal become a practical reality has been a long, arduous, and often, bloody one. The right to elect government representatives, for instance, did not by any stretch of the imagination extend to everyone overnight. In the beginning, only white, male landowners could vote. It took a civil war to even nominally extend the vote to men of every color. A century and a half before allowing female suffrage.

Women's Suffrage

The Women's Suffrage Movement of the late 19th and early 20th Centuries was the next logical step toward liberation from millennia of sexual oppression, culminating in the passage of the 19th Amendment on August 26, 1920. However, the "Suffragettes" (a term which was originally used as a demeaning epithet) were as much a religious movement as they were political and social reformers.[119] Many of the women who were fighting for the right to vote were also advocates of "Temperance" or the prohibition of the sale of alcohol. Ironically, about one third of the membership of the Temperance Movement were also part of a popular, Protestant revivalist movement of the late 1800s—the Sanctification Movement.[120] Most of the women who partook in the effort to give women the vote were motivated by otherwise very conservative issues—preservation of the traditional home and family with mothers as faithful home keepers and fathers as reliable bread winners.

Protestant Christians in general were united in the hopeful belief that their efforts to Christianize the world by virtue of a social gospel would pave the way for a New Millennium, and what better way to change society for the better than to use the power of the voting booth. And what worse evil in society to first be rid of than booze?

Underneath the surface of the Women's Suffrage Movement was a strong current of homemakers who were determined to save their husbands from the Saloons. "By getting the vote," these women reasoned, "they could rid the country once and for all of the curse that was alcohol." Men, they believed, had been so corrupted by the "devilish brew," they would never quit drinking on their own. Women's Suffrage was seen as the means by which "Godly women" would get men out of the saloon and back in church. While modern Feminists can proudly look to the Suffragists as the pioneers of women's liberation, the fact is most of those who fought so gallantly to win suffrage for their gender would be quite shocked by the radical changes that their efforts ultimately helped make possible.

In any case, the efforts of a broad alliance of Protestant optimists to win female suffrage and rid the land of alcohol might have prevailed sooner, had it not been for the American government's preoccupation with the political powder keg that was soon to explode in Europe … into World War One.

World War and the Protestant Schism

The millions of deaths and other evils that came with World War One took the wind out of the sails of many 19th Century religious optimists about humanity's ability to ever achieve a kingdom of God on earth. Before, American Protestantism had been fairly united in spite of several signs that their unity in influencing American culture was waning.

All through the 1800s, there was disagreement about the theory of evolution, the place of women in church and society and what to do about a small but rapidly growing Pentecostal movement. But they were able to set their differences aside while crusading together against their biggest enemy—alcohol. It was this one great banner under which all Protestants could unite.[121] This fragile unity came flying apart at the seams, though, once the Prohibition was enacted and the pre-war, patriotic fervor and optimism which had united the entire country gave way to the skepticism and pessimism following the horror stories soldiers brought back from World War One's trenches. By the end of 1920, there was nothing left to keep the Protestants together.

They quickly broke into two basic camps, the "Modernists" who were the more liberal-minded, and the "Fundamentalists," who were the more conservative. The Modernists hung on to the hope that good works were still the best way to show the world Christ's love. But even they had difficulty making their case with any confidence as the European Continent that had been Christianized for over a millennium lay in ruins, and almost every family had lost a loved one or was caring for a permanently maimed veteran. Their self doubt seemed to show no matter what their words, and visions of an ever better world rang shallow to an increasingly skeptical and secular society.

The Fundamentalist faction adopted a more pessimistic view of their role in the world. They had basically given up on the Social Gospel as a lost cause, and held that the world could only be remedied by Christ's literal return. They adopted a garrison mentality where they focused on getting individual converts into their pews, and there, they would await the "rapture of the saints" to Heaven.[122]

The schism left both sides too busy vying for dominance over each other to be all that concerned with politics and the rapid changes taking place in society. With each side retreating from their confident, turn-of-the-Century idealism, their influence on the outside world diminished significantly. The resulting vacuum allowed for Secularism to assert a greater role than ever before in guiding societal values. What the Church had to say about sex was still being preached from pulpits everywhere, but it sounded from a lot further away, no longer loud enough to drown out the voices of others.[123]

The Roaring 20s

Adding to this vacuum, quite a number of inventions and events helped precipitate swift changes in social behavior and attitudes, whether toward human sexuality or anything else. Air travel, movies, radio, the Victrola, the telephone, the affordable Model T, and for the first time, more people living in cities than in the country, all acted together to fuel a furious rate of information exchange and exposure to many different ideas, lifestyles and values.

In the 1800s, most people lived in the country or in small towns. Even if they did live in a big city, it was normally in a neighborhood where everyone spoke the same, dressed the same, belonged to the same race, the same religion, and the same social stratum (Recall the Italian neighborhood, for example, dramatized in the movie, The Godfather II). It was hard for different groups of people, that were rather homogenous within their own communities and so isolated from each other, to think about challenging ideas, beliefs and behavior. They hardly ever ran into anything different from what they'd ever seen, learned and came to expect before. But the rapid changes of the early 20th Century, in things like rapid modes of transportation and the exchange of ideas through the new mass media, forced people to confront values very different from their own on almost a daily basis.

Moreover, there was a remarkable surge in prosperity for the average family, thanks to the many successes of the Union Movement, in giving workers a greater portion of the business profits that had previously all gone to the top financial barons. Times were relatively better, and with the spare cash to afford it, the attraction of the big city with so many new things to see, to experience and to have, was too compelling to resist. As life on earth got better, the need for hope of deliverance in a next life didn't seem as pressing a matter.[124] The promise of streets of gold and freedom from all fleshly deprivations in Heaven, just didn't have the punch it had before as the riches and satisfaction of fleshly desire came within reach in the here and now.

Soon, the long skirts and long sleeves of women's clothing gave way to the short skirts made notorious by the Flapper Girl. Women began smoking in public. Though illegal, booze flowed as never before in the "speak-easys," and a new, sensual music called Jazz was bounding over the airways of the latest marvel of technology called "radio." The Model T gave mobility to the average man, and with that mobility, minds were broadened even further. As more and more people went to and fro, they discovered that not everyone thought and believed the same.

Needless to say, just having a car was, by itself, a great advantage for young lovers to get away and have some privacy. The back seat became *the place* to first experience sex, and all over the country, any road that provided the seclusion "to park" was soon dubbed Lovers Lane. As in the contemporary novel, The Great Gatsby, love affairs were no longer a forbidden topic, tolerated only as "back alley talk."

In many respects, the 20s was a precursor to the 60s. There's no telling just how far American society might have gone to overturn the sexual values that had been in place for centuries, had it not been for a very fateful day at the stock market in 1929.

The Great Depression

The stock market crash that set off the Great Depression of the 1930s brought an end to the embryonic sexual liberation of the 20s. The Fundamentalists began to regroup, and they took advantage of the financial distress of the times—some going so far as to claim that the Depression was God's punishment for a nation that had gone astray—a claim that has been repeated in many other forms ever since. With not as many places to go, and not as much money to go there, the glitter of worldly things, worldly music, and worldly fun was, once again, too far out of reach for most. A backlash had begun against the indulgences of the 20s, and as the Fundamentalists found their footing, they were somewhat successful in calling people back to traditional values.

However, not everyone was prepared to go all the way back to the values of the previous Victorian century. The poverty of the depression which helped shift society back to a more conservative place in their sexual values, also led them to call into question their place on the economic ladder. Historically, the Church had been a ready ally of the rich and powerful by reinforcing another "traditional value" that taught everyone to be content with their place in society, especially if one was poor. "The rich and the powerful are there because God put them there, and if you're poor, well, that was God's way of helping you to be rich in Heaven," so went the message from the average pulpit. Nevertheless, the common person of the 30s would no longer endure such economic fatalism. In the rural society of the 1800s, one was rarely exposed to material extravagance, and when it happened, it was in brief encounters and from a long distance. But now the poor and the rich were side-by-side in the big cities, and the Have Nots were acutely aware of what the Haves possessed. No more could the common worker endure the excuses of the wealthy. The suffering of the Great Depression ran along side a keen sense of injustice, and laid off workers began to unite as never before to demand that the wealth made off of their backs ought to be more evenly distributed.

FDR and the New Deal

The response to the Depression took us one step closer to the ideal that individual happiness and prosperity was not the privilege of a blessed few according to God's favor, but a right that everyone deserved. In 1933, Franklin Delano Roosevelt became the 32nd President, bringing with him the New Deal which was built on this very concept. After several years of widespread poverty and starvation, Americans were quite ready to narrow the gap between the lavishly rich and the wretched poor. The old school idea that each person was completely responsible for himself and his family, and that big business had no obligation other than to line the pockets of their stockholders was on it's way out. This new political ideology became the accepted standard. The government was now expected to act as a balancing force on behalf of the common laborer against the imperatives of Wall Street to cut costs and expand profits no matter who lost or gained. The idea that the individual deserves at least a minimum of earthly happiness and care, regardless of what might await in the next life, would continue to reverberate until the present day, even if its effects on sexual attitudes were not immediately apparent.

At first, the new vision had to address basic needs of food, clothing, shelter and employment. Public works programs helped get people back to work, and there was gradual progress. But the Depression really didn't end until events in Europe had once again, gotten out of control.

World War II and Women in the Work Place

World War II was very different from the first Great War. Instead of hundreds of thousands, this time millions of American men left home to fight in several different parts of the world. This time, they were gone for years, instead of months. As a result, women began to fill in the void in the multitude of weapons factories opening up and as the other war related industries expanded their labor roles. All over the country, workers were desperately needed to mobilize and sustain the country at a time of total war, and as more men left for the European and Pacific theaters, women took their places on the assembly lines. It wasn't just young, unmarried women either. The need for human labor was so great during the war that even mothers of young children were encouraged to join in the effort. But this presented a problem—what to do with the nursing children? Sure enough, American ingenuity came up with the answer—the baby bottle! The innovation of the baby bottle was held out as a "great liberator" by World War II "propergandists,"as they were called, since it made it possible even for nursing mothers to put on the hard hats their husbands had left behind for helmets. Nursery schools, too, were opened in record numbers to accomplish the same end.

The great influx of women into the workplace was regarded as a necessary but "temporary measure" that would surely end after military victory over the Axis powers. But the sense of independence millions of American women got by having their own money resulted in a permanent change to the American family.

When the war ended in 1945, a decent percentage of women, though a minority, stayed on the job. Many of the nursery schools closed, but not all of them. Even the single women who did leave the work place to marry and have children (resulting in the Baby Boom of the late 40s and 50s), didn't forget what it had been like to have the independence and power that making one's own money provided. As the 50s progressed to the 60s and as the baby boomers got older and started going to school, many of these same women—longing to have that sense of independence again—returned to the work place for good. This return translated into the advantages a second income provided in acquiring many of the goods now deemed "necessities" to put inside the homes that were being built in record numbers.

The change didn't go unnoticed by Ultra Conservatives. Preachers protested long and loud, reverberating again and again, "a woman's place is in the kitchen." But it was too late. Wall Street had realized that an entire new market of women with money to spend was now available, and the promise of profit was a lot stronger than the threats from the pulpit. With more and more women leaving housewifery and coming into a position of less financial dependency, it was just a matter of time before they would begin to challenge their dependent sexual roles as well.

Korea and Vietnam

The sense of national unity and confidence in authority that went hand-in-hand with the effort to defeat Nazi Germany and Imperial Japan was short lived. Upon the defeat of Fascism, support for the US military leadership's call to fight a new international enemy, Communism—and thus to maintain pressure on society to continue setting aside government criticism, individual needs and liberties—began to erode. This erosion became very evident by the end of the Korean Conflict, where no clear victory was won, and the American boys who came home in coffins were buried very discreetly. Those who survived, received no parades and no speeches in their honor. Parents and loved ones of the Korean veterans were justifiably embittered. While their discontent remained largely muffled, especially during the period of anticommunist extremism led by Senator Joseph McCarthy, a groundswell of distrust of government in particular, and traditional authority in general, was slowly but steadily welling up all through the 1950s. Flaws in the rationales of government authority were soon to be revealed and discarded.

When it became apparent by the mid-60s that the US Government was at it again, this time, in a little known country called Vietnam, the groundswell burst outward into broad protest. In spite of the shrill allegations of cowardice that conservatives voiced on TV and radio airwaves, there were many parents, widows, other loved ones and friends of those who died or were wounded in Korea and Vietnam who'd simply had enough. They began to shout, "No more!" Draftees, often with parental aide, began to pour over the US-Canadian border. College professors encouraged student protests, and the liberal clergy began to call for a withdrawal of troops.

The loss of government credibility helped fuel challenges to every other institutional authority. The patented answers of the Church were no longer holding sway on many an issue. Now that women were working and feeling more independent than they had for thousands of years, all they'd ever been told about their sexuality became open to question. And then, as if by some fate, a medical breakthrough came along that served as the perfect catalyst for a revolutionary change in sexual behavior. It became known simply as "The Pill."

The Pill

The fear of unwanted pregnancy, especially at a time when abortion was still illegal in most states, was all that kept many women from translating their new found financial independence into sexual liberation. So when the FDA approved the use of a convenient contraceptive that could be taken orally, the frustration of millennia of sexual repression was suddenly lifted. Women could now do what men had been getting away with for centuries—having sex for recreational purposes.[125]

We need to remember that paternity tests were at this time crude at best, and women who got pregnant outside of marriage were simply labeled as "sluts" and cast out of polite society with little in the way of negative repercussions befalling the men who'd impregnated them. But the promise of the Pill alleviated this concern. Coming available at just the right time, when many people were seriously questioning the authority of the Church and the State and all that was told them by their parents as "the way things are," led to thousands of women asserting sexual liberty and openly talking about it.

The Good Life

Sexually explicit magazines full of nude photos of women had been around since the camera was first invented. However, there was one such publication in particular that began a series of articles that fleshed out (couldn't help the pun) a philosophy that was emerging triumphantly in the 1960s. The series, written by the magazine's founder, Hugh Hefner, was entitled, "The Good Life." In summary, Hefner set forth his arguments for a lifestyle that was completely secular, one which understood the present life as an opportunity to become as successful as one can with the talents one has in order to enjoy the pleasures of earthly life to their fullest. The message found an audience that had grown weary of being told again and again that one's natural impulses, like sexual desire, were evil and something to be ashamed of. As more and more people of high social and political esteem stayed as guests at Hugh Hefner's large mansion or appeared on his late night show "Playboy After Dark," the stigma of being open and honest about non traditional sexual behavior began to fade.

Hollywood and Hippies

Hollywood didn't start the Sexual Revolution, but certainly movies, and to a lesser extent, television, helped move it along once it got started. Movies began to show more and more revealing sex scenes. Perhaps far more important than the increase in visible skin was the increase in depictions of heroes and heroines having premarital sex without any guilt or shame.[126]

The revolt against traditional sexual values was no where more evident than among the members of a youth movement that emerged at this time who were generally referred to as "Hippies." There's been a lot of debate about where this movement first began, and whether or not there was any one person who got it started. In any case, by the summer of 1967, the "Summer of Love," the streets of San Francisco became the epicenter for a nationwide movement of young people who were exploring a whole new way of defining the meaning of life. The "Hippy Lifestyle" was generally perceived by its sympathizers as living life more independently and freely, and by it's detractors as being rebellious and irresponsible. The shedding of traditional ideas by the Hippies was most acute when it came to sex.

A new sexual ideal was finding its way into the vocabulary of everyday Americans, whether they found it tantalizing or repulsive—"free love." Soon, images began splashing up all over American television sets and movie screens of these free spirits whose mantra was peace (mainly referring to Vietnam), love (mainly sexual love), harmony (often with the help of mind-altering drugs, especially marijuana), and music (and that, of course, would be Rock), and the media attention devoted to the movement helped to magnify its influence.

The young of today might wonder how their Grandma could have ever been one of those "wild and free" girls at Woodstock (i.e., the first one in 1970), bathing openly in the nude and living in communes. And their incredulity is actually quite justified. In reality, many people that might have been called "Hippies," were simply any of the young men that began to imitatively sport long hair or the young women who wore jeans with flowers painted on them, but who otherwise held on to many of their parents'values and deviated very little from them.

Though for a time "hippie communes" of various sorts had sprung up all over the country, only some of them made any serious attempts at free love or group marriages, and even fewer of these lasted more than a few months. With the exception of some isolated cults where personal behavior was highly regulated, most free love groups disintegrated as members would find themselves overwhelmed with feelings of jealousy and possessiveness for certain partners with whom they had naturally paired and bonded.

True, many more people than ever before were experimenting with drugs, going to rock festivals and having sex prior to marriage. However, for many young Americans, the Hippie Movement was a phase, especially as it applied to sex. Almost all of those who did experiment with multiple sex partners retreated from such behavior as they got older, and then settled into monogamous relationships. Many more, never got caught up in the movement at all.

Watergate

On June 17, 1972, police discovered five intruders inside the Democratic National Committee headquarters in a Washington DC hotel called The Watergate. As it turned out, the burglars were there to adjust bugging equipment they had installed earlier in May of that year and to photograph documents. Subsequent investigation revealed a vast conspiracy by Republican party elite, leading all the way up to President Nixon himself. On August 9, 1974, President Nixon resigned from his office after tape recordings of his office phone communications revealed he, himself, had knowledge of the Watergate break-in to the help the Republican president's re-election campaign.

The Watergate scandal was a severe blow to conservatives who were already reeling from their other losses (no "victory" in Vietnam, the legalization of abortion, etc.), and it served to confirm everything liberals had been claiming all along about their underlying agendas.

It took many Americans a long time to understand what had happened in the Watergate Hotel, but by the time of Nixon's resignation, it was clear to most that their government could simply not be trusted. If one could say that trust in government authority had peaked during World War II, then it might also be said that Nixon's resignation was the deepest valley of government credibility in living memory.

For a time, it seemed all that Great Grandma's generation had so undauntedly believed in, striven for and stood by would be completely abandoned. Authoritarianism, whether coming from the Church or State, whether with regard to politics or sex, had lost its influence for good … or so it seemed.

Abortion is Legalized

If the Sexual Revolution officially began with the introduction of the Pill, one might say that it officially peaked with the 1973 US Supreme Court Roe v. Wade ruling that legalized abortion. The Women's Liberation Movement, which coincided with the Sexual Revolution, had focused much of its energy on this cause. Once it was won—not unlike the disintegration of Protestant unity following the passage of the 18th Amendment to ban alcohol—the broad coalition of various interest groups who had united for a woman's right to choose disbanded to go into many different directions. A good number of the Feminists then turned to condemning many of the other changes that came about as a result of changing attitudes toward human sexuality—legalization of pornography, lighter sentences for sexual offenders and a toleration for sex in the workplace.

As the 70s moved forward, the momentum to realize the lofty ideals of the Hippie Generation like ending war, bringing social justice to the oppressed and freedom to the individual, lost their steam. By the mid 70s, having long hair, or wearing frayed jeans came to imply only a hedonistic lifestyle focused on sex, drugs and Rock N Roll. Recreational sex continued, but was soon to encounter a major set back in its social acceptance.

Herpes and HIV

Sexually transmitted diseases, or STDs, were nothing new. But treatments had improved so much that, by the 1960s, they were for a time regarded as more of an inconvenience than a real threat to one's health. The common perception was that one might have to briefly contend with "a little problem" every now and then if one happened to have sex with someone before checking to see if he or she "looked clean." All one had to do was go see a doctor, get some penicillin, and all would be cured.

In 1980, this perception changed dramatically. The National Center for Disease Control released reports of a new strain of the herpes virus which was transmitted by sexual intercourse, and which had no known cure. The disease wasn't fatal, but soon, Fundamentalist preachers and social conservatives began to take advantage of the fear of the new disease—just as they had done in the years before treatments were devised to render VD infections as "minor"—in order to frighten people into celibacy. Oddly, promiscuous behavior continued at pretty much the same levels as best as anyone could determine, but it was no longer as socially acceptable to be proud of it. The tide of the Sexual Revolution had turned.

Of course, the Herpes Scare was nothing compared to the revelation of a yet another sexually transmitted disease that would truly serve as the best weapon in living memory to try to frighten people away from bed hopping—HIV! By the late 1980s, it seemed that the days of sexual promiscuity were gone for good. The fear that one might actually die from being sexually promiscuous, seemingly overnight, changed the commonly accepted rhetoric about sex norms right back to monogamous relationships. Not only was it no longer "cool" to be proud of being sexually free, but once again, one had to be careful, especially women, about where one could talk openly about having more than one lover. But once again, even as the death toll from AIDs steadily raised, people were still having sex with just as many partners as before. The only thing that really changed was a moderate increase in the use of condoms.

The Instinct to Protect vs. Teenage "Rebellion"

Perhaps the most important factor leading to the end of the Sexual Revolution was when the Baby Boom generation got a little older and started having children of their own. However "wild" Baby Boom teenage girls and guys might have gone, something very different takes place after a teenager's tendency to assert his or her independence starts to give way to an even stronger instinct in their middle to late 20s. This is especially the case after they have a child. Instincts to protect naturally assert themselves with parenthood and override many of a person's independent tendencies or what many like to call "teenage rebellion." Suddenly, some of the old fashioned ideas one's parents had repeated over and over to deaf teen ears don't sound so bad after all to brand new parents still in their 20s.

When we look at what happens in many homes during the turbulent and normally confusing teen years against the background of Human Evolution, you guessed it, this phenomenon begins to make sense. In the interest of favoring genetic variety, Natural Selection rewarded our hominid ancestors who, upon entering puberty, were no longer content to be dependent on their parents or extended family. Those who subsequently struck out on their own—going off to begin a new traveling band if they took mates with them, or in some cases joining with others to find new mates there—spread their seed and offspring further and wider, helping to keep the gene pool more varied, and thus, more adaptable. The descendents of those ancient "rebellious youth" made for a richer genetic pool and so were more likely to survive, reproduce, and pass those traits on, even to the teens of today.

Nevertheless, once the task of getting teens out of the house and on their own is complete, and especially once they begin raising a family of their own, whatever hormones that fueled their drive to be so fiercely independent before wears off quickly. As a result, many a young parent turn right back to the ideals their parents first instilled in them.

Much of this regression toward more "conservative values" has to do with the overwhelming sense of responsibility that one is hit with, whether as a father or a mother, when that frail "bundle of joy" is first resting in one's arms.[127] When it finally dawns on young parents that they are in for at least 18 years of the largest obligation of their lives, often happening just when they themselves have barely gotten out of their parents' nest—it's easy to begin panicking in fear and scrambling to find any sure sounding voice that offers the promise of stability.

It's usually at this time in life when people who hadn't been to church in years, start going back. They might privately feel that what's being preached is superstitious non-sense. But if there's just the slightest doubt that maybe there is a God who throws people into a cosmic furnace for not doing what the Good Book says, the parental instinct to protect one's young, will compel them to put their kids in Sunday School regardless of their personal lack of faith "just on the off chance." It's hardly any wonder that beliefs which have not a single ounce of logic to them are perpetuated generation after generation in this manner.

As mentioned above, a great number of events and influences came together to make the Sexual Revolution of the 1960s possible. However, it may very well be that even if The Pill hadn't come along, if Hugh Hefner had never published his Playboy Philosophy, or if the Vietnam War hadn't occurred with all of it's disillusionment with government authority, the mere fact that there existed in the 1960s a disproportionately large number of teenagers, the Baby Boomers, the Sexual Revolution may have occurred all the same. Likewise, Ronald Reagan may have never been able to pull off his 1980 Conservative Republican election victory had it not been for those same Baby Boomers who, by that time, were in their late 20s, trying to keep up with one to two young children, and feeling the full impact of the protective instinct.

A New Gospel

Conservative church leaders went into a panic during the late 60s and early 70s. While many resolved to fight the Sexual Revolution by stepping up their rhetoric with even more Hell, fire and brimstone preaching, it became clear to many others that the "gospel of fear" was only serving to confirm what the hip generation was saying about them—that they were simply consumed with hatred, and therefore couldn't possibly represent a God of Love. The pews were beginning to empty, and these more pragmatic preachers realized they could either stay the course, keep pounding their pulpits, and look forward to losing an entire generation of church members … or make some changes and make them fast! Faced with the dilemma of either holding true to the anti-sexualism that was now depleting their church roles and coffers or compromising, they opted for the latter. Except for a few hard-liners, most church leaders made three major changes to their message.

The first was a relaxation of rules against the divorced. Before the 60s, there were still quite a number of denominations that would not even allow divorcées who had remarried to join their churches. Of those that did, most had strict rules forbidding them from having ministerial positions, not even deaconship. But by the 1970s, the vast number of divorced and remarried couples was too much to turn away. One by one, denomination after denomination began to reinterpret the harsh and unequivocal words of Jesus and Paul against divorce and remarriage to softer and more tolerant positions. Usually claiming "God's forgiving grace," they found a way to continue labeling divorce a "sin," but one which could be forgiven. But unlike the requirements normally expected to follow other forgiven sins (such as a penitent thief returning that which he stole) divorcées could not only remarry without reproach, but they could even serve as a minister.

The second big change had to do with the doctrine of eternal punishment. Most denominations still affirm a belief in a judgment day and that one can only go to Heaven by being saved through faith in Jesus. But the consequences of not having the right kind of saving faith is rarely ever now described in terms of active punishment in an overtly punitive Lake of Fire. Ask most bible-toting Christians today how a loving God can send any one of his children to Hell, and they'll usually respond by either down playing the gravity of hell, "Hell means 'being separated' from God for eternity," or deflecting the blame onto the sinner. "Oh, *God* doesn't send anyone to Hell. If you reject Christ, *you* are sending yourself to Hell."

The new message still carries the iron fisted threat of eternal punishment, but it's tucked inside a velvet glove of love and compassion. Christ is depicted, not as the Final Judge meting out the damnation of eternal torture to "hard-hearted" unbelievers, but crying and pleading with sinners to come into his loving arms to be saved from certain eternal doom … as if the dooming were being carried out by someone else!

The new emphasis proved very effective, and many who had at one time agreed that God was dead or who had dabbled in Eastern religions straggled back into church pews.

This strategy continues to work today as long as no one follows the logic all the way through to realize that the same "loving" deity who is pleading with sinners to avoid Hell and accept his "love" is the exact same deity who is stoking the fires of that very same Hell for all eternity![128]

The Marriage Bed Is Finally Undefiled

The third change, though, is the most remarkable, because it has so quickly become an accepted standard throughout all but a very small number of the most radical Fundamentalist Christian denominations. This change—which one might call the most enduring achievement of the Sexual Revolution—is the recognition that sex was created by God, not just for the purposes of reproduction, but also for pleasure's sake! Truly, it was only until a few decades ago that any major body of Protestant Christianity had ever embraced and sanctioned recreational sex … as long as the couple having that sexual recreation are married to each other.

Conservative Protestant church leadership had come to understand that they could no longer deny people one of the most compelling of human, biological drives … and keep their pews filled. Promises of greater reward in Heaven for abstaining from sex and threats of eternal damnation for not (or at least feeling very guilty about it when partaken of), just weren't working any more—not even superficially. In response, the religious hierarchy began to interpret the Bible differently so as to openly sanctify sex for pleasure alone, even for women, and even if there was no intention of having a baby.

Perhaps the best example of this new trend came from a very conservative, Protestant evangelical writer—now very famous for his "Left Behind" series of end time novels—the Rev. Tim LaHaye. His earlier book, co-authored with his wife Beverly Lahaye, *The Act of Marriage, The Beauty of Sexual Love*, first published in 1976, and reprinted in the millions, became a favorite study guide for thousands of special church classes that sprung up all over the country on "how to be a happily married Christian couple."[129]

For many church couples first reading the book, it seemed almost pornographic. Detailed discussions about mutual masturbation, oral and anal sex, and a number of other previously very taboo topics were set forward as perfectly normal and blessed of God. Multiple passages from the Song of Solomon, a Bible book that had for centuries been interpreted as a purely spiritual metaphor of Christ's loving relationship with the Church, were re-classified as having been about sex for fun after all! "Sex is a blessing of God," they now proclaimed, "as long as it's within the sanctified institution of Marriage."

Even the Catholic Church, which still opposes "artificial birth control" (condoms, birth control pills, spermicidal lubricants, etc.) has given it's passive blessing to the use of the "rhythm method" to prevent unwanted pregnancy. Obviously, this is nothing more than a last ditch effort to pay lip service to the historical church position that having sex is only acceptable for the purpose of procreation.

Of course, this only begs the question. If having sex purely for the fun of it is (at least since the 1970s) OK with God "as long as the partners involved are married," then why is it so terribly wrong for people to have recreational sex before they're married? The pat answer from contemporary Protestants is that sex is only "blessed by God" for couples after they get his sanction to have intimacy through the Marriage Rite. But this is just circular reasoning. "God blesses sex only after he gives his blessing to have sex"? No, the question, again, is, "Why should God bless or not bless recreational sex at all, for anyone at any time?" If it's fair to say that God really meant for sex to be an enjoyable activity among mutually consenting adults in their own privacy, *apart from the intention to reproduce* (the historical reason for Marriage, at least, for women), then it makes little sense that God should be so terribly upset at those people who don't feel the need to get a minister and vow never to have sex with anyone else before they do that which God, in principle, is happy to see people do. Nevertheless, this new claim for the recreational benefit of marital sex is a strategy that, as long as no one thinks it through more than two logical steps, has helped the church hang on to many adherents who might have otherwise left a long time ago.

Christian leadership also got a little help with this new win-back strategy on the sexual front. Odd as it might seem, the call to women everywhere to come back to Church and march down the aisle in a bright, white dress—no matter how many other sex partners they'd already had—appealed very strongly to women as a means to be set free from a deeply entrenched sense of guilt and shame in the female psyche, guilt and shame from millennia of conditioning.

Since the invention of the plow, women could only get full family, societal and religious approval to have sex once they had a baby, especially a male baby. Now that having children of either gender was no longer a priority as it had been during the Agricultural Era, a vacuum was left behind. How were women supposed to feel—really and truly feel deep down inside—that having sex for the enjoyment of it was really OK? What was to validate and sanctify their sexuality? Something was needed to replace the vindication that for thousands of years could only come in diapers, and sure enough, something did—the Marriage Rite itself!

6

So Just Why Are People Still Getting Married?

o o o o o o o o o o o o o o o o o o o o o o o o o o o o o o

"Who can tell the class about the Trinity?" asked the Sunday School teacher. One boy, pushing his arm upward as high as he could was finally selected to answer. "I know, I know. Father, Son and … and …". "One more," said the teacher. "Oh, now I remember," said the little boy, "Father, Son and Holy Guilt."

Saved Through Ring Bearing

We seen how for thousands of years women were subjected to every manner of constraint thinkable in order to keep them from having sex with more than one person—her husband/owner, and for only one purpose—to have his babies. We also took some time to address the issue of human conditioning, noting how easy it is to be manipulated. We've noted just how psychologically and emotionally vulnerable we must be, or else why would advertisers spend millions of dollars on commercials geared toward housewives, for instance, in the hope of creating an association between a certain feeling of warmth as when she sees a cute baby, and some kind of toilet paper! So imagine, if we are so readily influenced by such brief ads, that a housewife sees maybe once a day for just a few seconds that she switches to another brand of toilet paper as a result, what sort of cavernously deep influence would thousands of years of conditioning have on the female mind? How about a lot!

So when our social structure changed so rapidly that it was no longer imperative for a woman to have children, at least, not until she's in her 20s, 30s, or later, what was to become of that keen sense of sexual legitimacy that having a baby provided for Great Grandma when she was in her late teens or early 20s? How would she cope with an ever growing sense of guilt and shame for being sexually active, especially once her "rebellious teen" hormones begin to wear off? Thanks in part to the Church's sanctification of recreational sex, with the only caveat that it be enjoyed only with one's marriage partner, a surrogate event was made available just in time to provide legitimacy for female sexuality—getting married. Just as when Great Grandma could only be "saved through childbearing" once she became sexually active, women of today are only "saved," i.e., saved emotionally, mentally and socially, through ring bearing.

Let's remember that Great Grandma could, for a while, have sex after getting married with the toleration of society, but only because it was understood that she would eventually have a baby. The time period between her wedding night and the announcement that a "blessing was on the way," was often an awkward time for her, her friends and her family. For many, it was difficult talking about anything relating to her sexual life—the double bed she and her husband shared, the hotel room (note the singular) they stayed in, and heaven forbid, any physical problems she might have had related to intercourse! The fact of their intimacy was often carefully avoided in polite company. Even though no one normally said anything, she could just feel the lack of full approval.

Once she became pregnant and gave a successful birth, though, there was a very noticeable change. People became relaxed, even joyful whenever there was some reference made about their intimacy, even if they still refrained from talking too openly or directly about sex itself. And most women, being as perceptive as they are about how others are feeling around them, could sense it. It was almost as if they were saying out loud, "Oh, we're so glad now to know that you were doing 'you-know-what' for the intended purpose of giving birth." Most importantly, though, upon giving successful birth to a child, a woman not only got the full approval of society, her family and friends about her sexuality, but their approval, in turn, helped her to finally accept herself as a sexual being.

Likewise, single women today who are sexually active with a boyfriend will generally have the toleration of society, family and friends, for a while, but only as long as it's understood that they are eventually going to get married. As with Great Grandma when she was a newly wed, the family of a sexually active, single woman will often behave rather uncomfortably when any topic comes up relating to her and her boyfriend's sexual intimacy. They'll normally find a way to smile and nod until the topic changes, but the relief they'll unwittingly project when it does is almost palpable.

This doesn't mean she has to marry each boyfriend she gets involved with. It just means that once it becomes public knowledge that a woman is in a sexual relationship, *she must at least give the impression that the intended purpose of the relationship is to serve as a precursor to marriage.* She can even get away with having quite a number of sexual relationships with different boyfriends that for one reason or another didn't work out ... as long as each break up is described in terms of how far short her expectations fell after believing that he was The One. It takes a woman with a lot of courage and confidence to openly defy this subtle but constant pressure.

Great Grandma would have been scorned up one side and down the other by everybody she knew if she had let it be known that she and her husband had no intention of ever having children. On the rare occasion when a young married woman said as much, she was quickly labeled as "selfish." Why? Because then she would have been exposed as having sex purely for the fun of it (yes, even though it was within marriage), and not for "God's intended purpose."

Similarly, it is still quite unusual for a single woman of today who is living with a boyfriend to openly declare that she has no intention of ever getting married. This is not to deny that more men and women than ever before are choosing permanent cohabitation over marriage, because they are. However, many still find it necessary to avoid telling people about it, because when they do, they are likely to get a barrage of criticism.

For sexually active women, especially if they are cohabiting with a man, the persistent social rejection for not marrying weighs very heavily on them over time, and they begin to struggle with emotions of guilt and anxiety—inner voices saying you're "doing something bad," or "missing something good." Getting married then, if nothing else, promises to relieve her of these persistent, negative feelings. Thus, the marriage ceremony itself has now become the legitimizing, affirming and relieving event for sexually active women, whether she has a baby afterward or not.

This isn't the first time a symbol that was part and parcel of a long held tradition was swapped out with something similar in order not to disturb deep, emotional attachments any more than necessary. For example, the missionaries of the Medieval Catholic Church would frequently build their first chapel on the same location where a Pagan altar to various deities once stood. In some cases, they would simply leave the heathen shrine in tact, put a cross on top and rename the idols into Christian saints.[130] Not to be outdone, modern converts in predominantly Roman Catholic countries to Protestant evangelical churches that forbid the use of "graven images," such as statues of Mary, Jesus or saints, are encouraged to place picture frames with Bible passages written on them in the very same places in the home where they previously had a statue of Mary or Jesus. The reason? To reduce the sense of emotional guilt and anxiety that would otherwise result after years of bowing, praying or just taking in some sense of security by the mere presence of the objects in question.

Regardless of how liberal-minded and educated a modern woman is, and no matter if she logically accepts that it's unnecessary to marry her live-in boyfriend in order to avoid God's wrath or to go to Heaven, and even if she could not care less in the *rational* part of her mind what other people think of her moral choices, many of these same women will begin to *feel* a longing for some kind of an affirming, symbolic event to legitimize their intimate relationship.[131] In the absence of The Pivotal Event of female sexuality—giving life to another human being—the next best legitimizing experience which Western culture could come up with to replace it was the Wedding Ceremony.

It's unfortunate that most people, women especially, are given to understand that they only have two choices—either to forgo any affirmation at all or to buy into the Marriage tradition with all of its damning legal and emotional entanglements. Nevertheless, in a later chapter, we will explore an alternative to the marriage rite that avoids both of these extremes.

Monkey See, Monkey Do

There are many other forces at work today keeping the institution of Marriage alive. One such force is *imitation,* the human tendency to do things simply because they've seen "everyone else" do the same. More accurately, it's not literally "everyone" else, but those whom they look up to—those who serve as their role models, those who have some influence on them—that they will imitate, even without consciously thinking about it.

When a group of people begin imitating the same behavior which is done or experienced together, over and over again, we call this a "social habit." If a shared or social habit should pass from one generation to the next, largely through unconscious imitation, it becomes a part of their "culture."

Sometimes, social habits can last a long time. In fact, long after no one can remember how or why some social habit got started, humans often repeat it over and over again, for decades, centuries, even millennia. We're talking about a behavior that has little to do with reason or things we do as a result of thinking them through. This can happen thanks to the human ability to learn and behave according to "auto pilot."[132]

There's nothing bad per se about imitative behavior. Nature outfitted *Homo sapiens* long ago—as with many other species—with the ability to mimic behavior as a very efficient means of learning. This is particularly evident among children whose play often imitates what the significant adults around them are engaged in. Young girls will play with baby dolls or toy ovens and young boys will play with building blocks or toy trucks, as a way of preparing them for their gender-based, adult roles later on. Animal young do the same thing.

When human social habits that involve most everyone in a given society are passed on from one generation to the next, we call them *cultural traditions.* For the most part, cultural traditions serve helpful social functions, such as easing the transitions of major changes in life. Sometimes a cultural tradition is begun that may have had a sensible purpose a long time ago, but later on becomes impractical. This is particularly true of specific prohibitions known as *taboos.*

I recall during a visit to the countryside of a foreign country when I mentioned to the family who had invited me to be their guest that I was about to take a bath. We had just eaten dinner, and little did I know that these people had a strong, cultural taboo against bathing immediately after eating. The lady of the house assured me that I would die if I went ahead with my plan. I wasn't sure why these folks were so overly concerned until the mother of the family related the tragic story of a young man of their little town who, not long ago, had died for having ignored the warnings he'd heard all his life about not bathing after eating. As it turns out, though, he'd actually gone *swimming* at the nearby beach, went too far out in the deep water, got cramps, and drowned. No doubt, whenever this first happened to some poor victim, years, maybe even centuries ago, the villagers naturally concluded that what killed him was the water itself, not its depth, and so the taboo of never getting the body wet after eating was begun.

Taboos often come from similar faulty conclusions, usually for the lack of scientific inquiry. In this case, it was an inability to discern that it was only coincidental that one's entire body is wet when the cramps began due to a swimmer's body calling for more blood oxygen to digest food than to supply the muscular activity necessary to swim in deep water. As long as no one ever questioned why all those who died in violation of this taboo just so happened to be swimming in deep water, everyone just continued to think that the deaths were due to getting wet after eating.

Thankfully, we humans might be beset with a myriad greater number of foolish taboos and unhelpful cultural traditions if we didn't also have the ability to question. We humans have a distinct advantage over our animal cousins who are led only by their instincts or shared/learned, imitative behaviors; we can do something different. Nature went one step further with the evolution of our kind by giving us a frontal lobe that allows us to override our habitually acquired behaviors. When our mimicking "cruise control" needs to be turned off, we can do so.

Even some of our close, animal relatives have only limited versions of this override capacity, but nothing like ours. For instance, there's a special trap that is used to ensnare monkeys which takes advantage of their inability to override a primitive instinct. Some food is put inside a clear container that has an aperture just large enough for the monkey to slide his hand into. Upon seeing the food, the monkey will reach inside to grasp it. The grasping results in a fist that enlarges the size of the monkey's hand. When our poor, hungry monkey tries to retrieve his hand from the container, it's too big to pull back out. Unfortunately for our primate cousin, his brain is not equipped with the ability to figure out that he is only being trapped by his unwillingness to let go of the food.

More sadly, though, is the phenomenon of human beings, who have the ability to override habitual behavior *but fail to use it.* We see again and again, people who are very well aware of the sadness which most every married couple they know is experiencing, or even when they themselves have had one, two or three unhappy marriages before, who will nevertheless remarry anyway, simply because it's what they've seen everyone else do and are accustomed to imitating!

To be sure, traditions that have gone on for a long time are not easily changed, even long after it becomes clear how damaging they are. Chinese women of noble birth used to have their feet bound during infancy in order to intentionally cripple them, with the idea that they should have to be waited on for the rest of their lives. This was an accepted practice for hundreds of years. As time wore on, though, it became clear that foot binding was really just a way of keeping women born to households of high status from becoming too powerful. The practice continued as late as the mid 20th Century, and was only stopped after the Communist Government banned it.

Even as late as a hundred years ago, the first-born female of certain Mexican families was expected never to leave home and marry, so she could abide with her parents to care for them in their old age. In India, the practice of shunning the "untouchable" class by those born to higher "castes" also continued until it was strictly prohibited by law in the last century.

It's hard to predict the future, but the Marriage Tradition is so deeply entrenched that it, too, may only come undone when a government finally decides to stop licensing sexual relationships. Even then, many a religious organization will, no doubt, continue pressuring people to carry on with the ceremonial portion of the institution.

We shouldn't underestimate the raw force of cultural tradition, habit and imitative behavior. In spite of the fact that the Baby Boomers—who were in their impressionable teens during the Sexual Revolution with all its talk about free love and sexual liberation—have not only passed on the Marriage Tradition but just about every other social behavior they got from Great Grandma and Great Grandpa as well. It's quite likely that they will live to see many of their great grandchildren getting married ... simply out of cultural habit.

The Marriage Industry

Certainly, the financially interested of the Marriage Industry would be very upset at the very thought of Marriage ever becoming a thing of the past. Everything from bridal dress makers to the creators of "My Wedding Day" Barbie dolls—have no small stake in preserving this institution. According to Wedding Magazine, the cost of the average wedding in 2003 was $20,434.00.[133] Multiply this figure times hundreds of thousands of couples per year, and we're talking about a major financial enterprise. Add to this a whole new trend—"renewal of vows" ceremonies, very popular for women who either eloped or had a very bare bones wedding the first time around—for those who tire of not having the same elaborate wedding photo albums "all their friends do," and the coffer sums for the Marriage Industry stand to double. And do we even need to mention where the jewelry business would be if diamond engagement and wedding rings were not their lucrative mainstay as the modern incarnation of ancient bridal payment?

Even in times of economic uncertainty, the Marriage Industry is one of the few areas of unending expansion. Every time one turns around, there's another costly "necessity" if you "really want to have the perfect wedding." No doubt the huge profits being made by these slick marketers will continue to do all they can to keep people marching down those aisles.

The Marriage Repair Industry

Every day, all across the USA, millions of people are longing to know what the secret is to a happy marriage ... and they're spending millions of dollars trying to find it. There are literally hundreds of books, DVDs, seminars, vacation packages, online courses, training camps, you name it, all of them costing no small amount of cash, and all claiming to have the answers for people who find themselves in a lousy marriage to "make it work."

But if all this help is out there, then why is it that so many of the people who avail themselves of it, end up with so few positive results? The label I use here to designate all of these so-called experts, counselors, and whoever else is making a pretty good living off of unhappily married people is the Marriage Repair Industry. Next to the Weight Loss Industry, I can't think of a worse group of shady business practitioners. Why? Because most, not all, but most of them are offering "answers" that aren't really helping anyone ... and they know it!

And why in the world should they? If, for example, even 10% of the hundreds of How-to-Fix-Your-Bad-Marriage books actually did the job, then they would be out of business. While there's nothing wrong with compensating someone for a product or service that really does what it promises, most of the Marriage Repair Industry gurus out there are counting on their customers' continued unhappiness so they'll return again and again for even more of their "help." Some are even more brazen. They've got millions of people convinced that their problems are incurable, but with their never ending (and never paid in full) "assistance," they can help them "cope." The only real good this industry has done is give some insight into just how high the level of marital discontent has reached.

The Divorce Industry

As much as the Wedding and Marriage Repair Industries profit from couples getting married, they pale in comparison to the billions of dollars in profits taken from these couples and their children when they split up later on. The national average cost of a divorce, just in legal fees, is $36,000.00.[134] On top of this are all the other fees charged by a an ever growing number of divorce court professionals—psychiatrists, psychologists, social workers and therapists, who often work their way into a divorce suit, with courts orders to the litigating parties to pay their expenses. With over 1.1 million divorces each year in the US, this translates into an annual revenue of about $40 Billion dollars![135]

Divorce became a profitable enterprise thanks to the ingenious invention of a legal institution that holds itself out as a necessary protector of the weak and innocent, only to become their worst predator, the so-called "Family Court."

Oddly though, when most people think of what can go wrong during a divorce, they usually only think of one of the litigants getting a raw deal from the other spouse. If it should happen to be the woman, the story of a divorce gone bad plays like an old tear-jerker movie. We get a vision of woman dragging herself into a cramped apartment after putting in a 12 hour shift at a minimum paying job. Her several kids are running wild. Her bills are piling up. Her ex-husband hasn't "sent" her any child support. While the divorced woman is barely putting food on the table, we see him riding around in a new sports car, with a young blonde in tow, living it up, and not giving a single care as to what's going on with the children he's fathered.

There's another scenario, though. In this one, it's the divorced man who is dragging himself to a cheap hotel after trying and failing, once again, to get to see his kids. His ex-wife has moved herself and their children half way across the country, and he can hardly afford the air fare to go see them. Child support and alimony is taken out of his check. He is alone, broke and on the few occasions he can see his children, they keep referring to some strange guy as their "Dad."

There is truth to both of these extreme scenarios. In some divorce cases, the results are not much different than what we find in these two examples. But most of the time, it's really not a matter of one person winning everything—custody, house, car, bank account, a new and better sex partner or partners, and so on—and the other losing all but the shirt on his or her back and being cast out in the snow to freeze to death.

Most of the time, *everyone in the family* is the loser! The man, the woman, and the kids, all of them are taken for a ride, and all of them are suffering. What Divorce Court fights really come down to is *who will lose more.* It's war of attrition, and often, the battles don't end until there is literally nothing left to fight over.

The only real winners are the Divorce Court attorneys and all the other professionals who have wiggle wormed their way into the system to take as much of the family's assets they can. What is amazing, though, is how so few can ever see past whatever their complaints are about their spouse to understand how they are both being so taken advantage of and who is doing the taking.

Hopefully, we can take some space here to clear the fog. Let's start by looking at how this system established itself in the first place. Somewhere behind a closed door in a smoke-filled room many years ago, some people got together and decided that the only way they were ever going to allow legally married couples to permanently separate would be through the same adversarial process as that used in criminal proceedings and dubbed it "Family Court." Unfortunately, there's very little associated with this court system that's family friendly.

The key to success for the Divorce Industry was making it easy to get into marriage and very hard to get out. Notice that in spite of all the damning news we hear over and over again about how so many marriages are failing, there is nowhere a movement to do a single thing about the ease of getting a marriage license. It's harder in most places to get a yard sale permit! The relative ease of getting into a marriage (as far as executing the legal device of a marriage license goes) and what it takes to get out later (the requirement of going back to the government for its judicial permission to separate permanently) are like night and day. The requirement of a judge's sanction to separate for good is where the high price of getting married in the first place is felt the most. Of course, wherever there's a high price to pay, there's someone there to collect.

The required divorce process is the perfect venue for those who would profit at the expense of others who cannot get along. The odds so favor a couple fighting over something that the lawyers litigating "on their client's behalf" always win no matter what the final outcome of a divorce settlement. Even when a couple is at first agreed on terms, they are often required to consult with an attorney who is sure to egg them on to insist on getting more, or to frighten them into "taking action to protect themselves from getting less," which often leads to costly litigation.[136]

When a couple is breaking up, it's a ready-made opportunity to inflame mistrust where no trust is left, and to encourage retaliation where a lot of hurting is already going on. It's so easy to fuel anger, add to fear, and of course, tap into the natural instincts of parental protectiveness in order to get parents fighting over child custody. A divorce lawyer can easily take advantage when, for instance, a woman walks into his office saying she's had enough of her husband's infidelity. "Yes, we'll make that low-down, cheating, rat pay for what he did to you!" in many cases, suggesting that the husband will likely end up paying, not only for child support and alimony, but also his exorbitant fees which he gets her to accept—"Now if you'll just sign here, and pay my retainer fee, I'll do everything I can to see that he gets what he deserves!"[137]

It's very rare to find two people who have become so incompatible that they wish no longer be together who can turn right around and negotiate with detached and mature reason for an equitable settlement under such pressure. Their emotions are ripe to be taken advantage of, and legal actions quickly escalate in both their severity and cost. Usually, it's only a year or two later, when both parties are depleted of every dime they have and are emotionally exhausted when the reality begins to sink in that whatever it was that led to their initial separation was nothing to compare with the war that ensued.

There is a move afoot to reform the Divorce Industry, but the battle is bound to be a steep, uphill fight. Early in October of 2004, John Cihon, a father who lost a custody fight for his 6-year-old son, became the lead plaintiff in a federal lawsuit against the State of Pennsylvania in the hope of pressuring states to adopt a presumptive standard of 50-50 physical custody in place of the current standard known as "the best interest of the child." The reason is because the current standard (which is perhaps more accurately described as in "best interest of the divorce attorneys") almost always translates into costly and emotionally traumatic litigation between the parents, which in turn, leads to adverse consequences for the children involved no matter which of the two ultimately prevail as the "winner" in court.[138]

One has to wonder, though, why there has yet to be seen a massive protest against the exploitation of the Divorce Industry over separating families. One would think that those who otherwise speak the loudest and longest about protecting the family and looking out for "the best interest of the children" would be at the forefront, decrying the Industry for the avarice of its attorneys and condemning its judges for being either impotent or unwilling to stop the madness. Instead, the most we hear from so-called family advocates is how the devastation of divorce ought to be a motive for married couples to stay together!

Their unwillingness to take issue with the profiteers of separating couples, while bemoaning the costs of divorce, especially for women and children, is really very telling. Rather than to stand together against those who take the greatest advantage of families at their weakest moment, it's plain that they would much rather place all the guilt they can on those who divorce, for whatever cause, in the hope of striking as much fear as they can in the hearts and minds of those who have as yet to divorce.

One of the common themes one hears from these people is how terrible it was that our society began to allow No Fault Divorce, and "now look at what has happened as so many families suffer from its costs." For any who struggle interpreting this code, let me translate: "Now that the State can no longer legally force people to stay together who otherwise wish not to be, at least we can brandish divorce's heavy costs and lengthy, emotional trauma as a deterrence."

How can they reason this way? Or rather, how can they suspend their reason in this manner? How is it that they can be so oblivious? Well, for most of the "Marriage Protection" crusaders, it boils down to a willingness to sacrifice the men, women and children of separating families on the altar of a deity whom they have named "Stability." Trouble is, this god is nothing more than a dumb idol.

In the Name of "Stability"

Quite a number of so-called "Pro-Family" or "Pro-Marriage" organizations, as noted already, have used the statistics on the devastating effects of divorce to argue for a return to Fault Divorce and to automatically constrain all cohabiting couples to be married by common law. Their repeated argument against No Fault Divorce and free cohabitation is that they lead to "family instability."

While there is some evidence to show that cohabiting couples don't usually stay together as long as married couples do, it's very deceptive to make a direct link between the length of time a couple lives together, married or not, and "stability." This term doesn't necessarily mean "better," "more to be desired," and most certainly not "in the best interest of any children that might be involved."

For one thing, these "pro-family" crusaders completely neglect the far lower financial cost and greatly reduced degree of emotional trauma that a cohabiting couple experiences should they separate. There are normally no heavy court costs prompted by emotions of revenge. If there are disputes over separation of property, they're usually settled in a small claims court, quickly and cheaply. There are no divorce attorneys to pay, and consequently, no one constantly provoking them to fight over every little issue. There's no government holding them in a state of legal limbo for months or years, where one is neither in a relationship, nor single. Instead, the amount of time to complete the separation is far shorter, so all the parties can have closure and move on with their lives. The resulting reduction in stress, both financial and emotional, has great benefits for everyone involved—for both of the cohabitants and their children. Of course, there is one party that does lose out a great deal when cohabitant couples separate—the lawyers and other profiteers of the Family Court System who don't get to take everything they can get their hands on from these families if they were legally married.

There's another benefit that often goes unnoticed when cohabiting couples break up. Since they are not immediately thrust into the adversarial climate of a divorce proceeding, they are no where near as provoked into doing things that only serve to escalate their disagreements. For example, some divorce lawyers will urge a woman to charge up all of her and her spouse's joint credit cards, so her husband might have so much more to pay later. Men who never before laid a hand on a woman, are sometimes pushed to the edge and resort to violence. Abuse of alcohol and drugs goes up. The lengthy divorce period so stresses and promotes such anger between parents that sometimes it spills over into mistreatment of their children. On and on and on the long list goes, as each litigating party is subject to more and more duress before the final court date arrives, many months or even years—and usually, many more escalations—later.

The cohabiting couple is much less likely to fall prey to such stress and escalations. A separation—that often leads to a no-holds-barred divorce court war for a typical married couple—serves to give the two cohabiting partners time to cool off and re-evaluate what they really want to do, sometimes even leading to a successful reconciliation. On the other hand, if they should decide to part, they can do so much more quickly, with much less stress, at much less the cost, and with much cooler heads prevailing in all the associated decisions.

Because of the horrendous damage, both financially and emotionally, that usually occurs as a direct result of the divorce process, some family experts are pushing for changes in state laws that would move divorce further away from adversarial confrontation to mediation and counseling.[139] But the one thing no one seems to be suggesting is that the best way to avoid going through all the horrors and costs of divorce is to not get married in the first place!

The problem is there is so much money at stake—as divorce attorneys, court-appointed therapists and counselors are laughing all the way to the bank—the prospect of privatizing Marriage any time soon is not very likely. Though religious conservatives would likely represent the shrillest opposition to privatization, there's little doubt that divorce lawyers all across the country, seeing their exorbitant profits so threatened, would also line up in droves to testify in every state capitol against such a measure.

That said, one would like to believe that there are at least a few ethical people in the Family Court System who can see how criminal it is to make a profit at the expense of separating couples, especially when it comes at the expense of children. Hopefully, the day will eventually come when no one is ever forced by the State to either become part of or remain in a legally binding relationship. Those who can agree to terms of separation on their own ought to be allowed to do so without being compelled to come before a court where people who have no other interest than a profit motive will have the final say as to which terms are acceptable and which are not. If a couple who wishes to separate permanently has a dispute over division of property that they just can't resolve on their own, they could still turn to an impartial venue, such as the relatively faster moving and inexpensive small claims courts. If there are disputes over child custody and support, family courts might still be needed, but without holding a couple in a state of legal limbo on all other issues in the interim. The level of State involvement should be the same when a couple parts as when it had no business deciding on how a couple got together; it should not be automatically involved in their separation! Unless there is a compelling reason to intervene (such as a child who is unsupported by a parent) the State needs to stand clear.

Clinging to Straws of Control

It almost goes without saying that the Church is one of the major social powers perpetuating the Marriage Institution. We're told repeatedly by men and women of the cloth that having sex with anyone except a lawfully, wedded spouse is subject to God's disapproval (if not his wrath) even if one is in a monogamous relationship. But why? Why do preachers and priests all across the country pound out this message over and over again, decade after decade, century after century?

Of course, they would claim that they are merely delivering the "Word of God" from Heaven who tells us how we ought to conduct our earthly lives. As it turns out, though, a little investigation into the earthly doings of Church leadership reveals some very down-to-earth reasons why they try so hard to limit sex to marriage. Let's start with the most general reason, ecclesiastical control, beginning with a look at the reasons why some social control, whether from the Church or elsewhere, is necessary in the first place.

In one sense, having some institution preside over a society to administer some limitations over the behavior of its members, is not necessarily a bad thing. One could almost define the word "society" in terms of control. Any time you have two or more people living together or near each other, there's always the potential for some conflict between them. When conflicts arise, and the conflicting parties can't resolve their differences peaceably among themselves, there are really only two basic options: 1) allow for both to have their own way all the time by no longer dwelling together or 2) requiring the will of at least one of the two parties to be restricted.

We've already alluded to the fact that human societies normally turn to the second option, which means surrendering some degree of personal liberty, in order to gain the benefits of social cohesiveness. By learning to sacrifice a modicum of our individual wants for the greater good was and still is necessary for our survival. Our kind and the many social hominids who preceded us gained a lot of advantages over species characterized by loner lifestyles.

When *Homo sapiens* first appeared, a solitary male could have, for instance, struck out on his own to hunt for food, and perhaps, had some initial success. He could perhaps track down a beast, kill it, and eat what he could on the spot. But such a prehistoric "rugged individual" would not have done as well as the more "socially conformist" *Homo sapiens* that worked in groups.

They were more likely to succeed in the hunt by teaming up. For example, a team of prehistoric hunters could divide up and coordinate their efforts, agreeing that some should make loud noises to drive a herd of animals into a narrow ravine while others atop a cliff might hurl huge stones to cripple and kill their prey. They would have also been able to carry more food back to their base camp than what one person could manage. Moreover, the societal *Homo sapiens* benefited from the staple foods the women of their band gathered while they were out hunting.

A prehistoric, "rugged individual" would have had to make extra time to gather vegetable foods when he wasn't hunting. If for any reason he got hurt or wounded (which happened a lot in prehistoric hunting), there would have been no one to nurse him to health. Certainly, he would have been doomed to perish no sooner than when he reached his mid to late 30s, since their would be no younger generation around to exchange their care of the elderly for the wisdom of their life's lessons. Were there any anti-social *Homo sapiens* around back then, they didn't survive long enough to pass on their highly individualistic bent to later generations.

Some degree of control, then, was needed. Someone had to decide who's going to noise the herd, and who's to throw the rocks. Whenever this power over others was first negotiated, whether consciously or by instinct, is when society first began.

This is where it gets really sticky. To what extent should societal control go? Who should decide how far the control goes? And perhaps most importantly, who will enforce such control if any should decide to revolt against it? Although, the means by which the rules of a society are determined and enforced has varied greatly from the dawn of human consciousness to the present—from the consensus building "big man" of ancient hunting and gathering kinsmen, to the complete subjugation of all members to one, all-powerful ruler (Caesar, Hitler, etc.), to the direct vote legislative democracies such as in modern Switzerland—humans have always dwelled in some kind of society, with at least some limitations on their individual freedom.

Before the Agricultural Revolution, the principle institution that wielded societal control was the Family. Afterwards, two new institutions were added which took over many of the tasks of social regulation. One, as you might have guessed, was Government and the other was Religion. Others, like the Military or Big Business came later. Religion, though, was a one of the first institutions after the Family to preside over the rules of a given society, usually hand-in-hand with or as an extension of the Government.

We should keep in mind that the separation of Church and State is a relatively recent innovation. For most of the history of civilization, there were really only two major groups in any society, 1) the Church/State, who did the controlling, and 2) those they controlled! The hay day of religious influence in regulating society is long gone, but most church institutions today still play a role in shaping the laws of society in order to get everybody to behave a certain way, as they've done for thousands of years.

We've already discussed the original expediency of Marriage to promote the orderly trade of women as sex slaves and to have a clearly understood system of designating who had sexual access to which females.[140] But the reason for instituting this control has changed greatly from that time to the present. The plain and practical, original power once surrendered to village elders and later on to priests and bishops is now rather vague and fleeting. There's not the practical need, as there once was to insist on female virginity to assure paternity. Though the Church of today can try to lay historical claim to having the ultimate say so as to which sexual union can be sanctified and which cannot, in reality, that power has long been lost with only a very few exceptions—such as the marriage of same sex partners. Even there, a number of countries (Holland, Belgium and Canada to name a few) have legalized them.

Still, the major controlling institutions of modern society lumber along with as much determination as ever to preserve Marriage at all costs—perhaps with individual agendas as shall be addressed next—but largely because they have simply gotten addicted to having control itself, and desperately cling to however much or little they have left.

Weakness of Conviction and Sinner Envy

We're pretty familiar with the pressure that the Church puts on single people or even couples living together to put off sex until they are married. The question is, "Why?" To be certain, preachers usually get a nice contribution each time they perform a wedding, but there seems to be an even greater motivation than money that inspires so many men of the cloth to preach so forcefully against non marital sex.

What is the principle motivation for priests insisting on teens being celibate? Why do ministers expect adults who are already in relationships to delay intimacy and wait for months, even years? Is it really just because they believe this is the way God meant for it to be? Do church people really think anyone can be happy at all—much less happier—by "saving oneself until marriage"? Or could it be that the real reason they pressure single people into abstinence and couples into getting married has much more to do with their own issues?

The answer becomes very clear once we understand what goes on within the minds of people who've become convinced that they are "supposed to" give up something that *they really don't want to*, not really. I call this attitude *Weakness of Conviction*, the opposite of having a strong conviction or as some would say, a true belief.

Weakness of conviction is behind most all hypocritical behavior. A strong conviction results in changes of behavior with no regrets. For example, one might decide that eating a high fat diet is bad for one's heart. If one's conviction is strong, one will curtail eating foods high in fat, and be happy with the choice. End of story. When he sees other people eating high fat foods, he might become concerned for their health, he might even try to convince others of the benefits of a low fat diet. But because he has such a strong conviction on this matter, the last thing he'd feel is jealousy at the mere sight of those who are happily gobbling down triple-decker cheeseburgers!

However, the person whose *stated* conviction to eat healthier food is weak, succeeds only in renouncing high fat foods for a while. He might make quite an argument in any discussion about how terrible and unhealthy such foods are. And he may even be 100% correct in all of his assertions. Nevertheless, somewhere deep inside, he secretly wishes that he could get his hands on some big, fat, juicy burger, and somehow "get away" with it. Usually, it's just a matter of time before such hidden desires overwhelm him, and he begins to "cheat," clandestinely slipping into the nearest McDonalds every chance he gets. Secrecy often plays a major role in this behavior because of the inconsistency between what the weak person professes to have given up and what he actually has not.

Now, most convictions are not a matter of absolute right and wrong. Most often, any conviction in question depends on one's personal opinion and choice—what one is willing to risk in order to gain something else. Parachutists, for example, are willing to risk their lives each time they jump out of an airplane for the thrill of the jump. To a lot of other people, taking such a risk for such a brief pleasure is sheer madness. But to the parachutist, it's a risk worth taking. Some people are fully aware that eating high-fat foods increases their risk of heart failure, but they would rather take such a risk than to give up the joy of eating foods they really like. As long as they aren't hurting anyone else or placing others at risk (parachuting over grade school playgrounds or ramming burgers down others' throats against their will), one can at least admire their consistency. The point here is not that all people who have a weak conviction have made a bad choice as to what it is they say they've given up. The conviction, by itself, may be a very good one. The difference is whether or not the person who claims to hold to such convictions, has really done so with all his heart.

We all know there are true alcoholics, for example, who say with very good reason that they shouldn't drink alcoholic beverages any more. They were ruining their lives and making their families miserable because of their prior drinking to excess … but some can't just stop there. No, now that they've finally figured out how very bad it was for them to drink alcohol, all of the sudden, they now have to stop everyone every one else from drinking too! Or how about those former tobacco smokers who, after years of blowing smoke in the faces of others and tossing their butts on the ground for others to pick up, who suddenly become crusaders against restaurant smoking sections? Vegetarians who want to ban the sale of meat, and so on. While it's great to hear about people who've improved their life in some way, there's still something a little haywire when someone says—even though it took years for them to get to the place where they could change on their own—they now crusade to *compel* everyone else to follow suit!

What is going on here? Why can't those who say they've quit doing this or that bad habit simply be content to let the arguments which convinced them to change on their own time table speak for themselves, and allow other people to make up their own minds to decide what's best for them?

The answer is that they really didn't. They stopped short of being fully convinced by all the facts. They changed only for fear. Fear of going to Hell, fear of losing social status, or fear of any number of things that got them to capitulate to the wishes of others. But for whatever reason, their stated conviction is not really coming from their heart. If they have any conviction at all, it's a very weak one.[141] And it is just such a weakness in the soul of those who lay claim to chastity which results in their angry condemnation of the sexually promiscuous.

You can just about measure the extent of their weakness by the strength of their rhetoric against those who indulge. The degree to which one insists that others follow the sexual prohibitions of one's religion, is about the same degree to which one secretly wishes one could get away with participating in the very same sexual behaviors!

It's this weakness of conviction on matters of sexual behavior that makes Fundamentalists get so angry at others who don't abide by what they call "morality." But were they truly OK within themselves about their beliefs on sex and Marriage, they would not be bothered by what others do, and would not feel the need to compel them to act as if they were converted already. And yet so many are so bothered, not in the empathetic sense of having concern for others, but bothered in the sense that they themselves feel pain inside. Why?

The answer is envy. Envy of the "sinner" who gets to do so many of the fun things that the poor, believer has to give up. They are angered every time they see someone enjoying their sexuality without guilt, shame or fear. Seeing or hearing about those who are "getting away with something" they aren't, forces them to become aware of their own sexual misery, an awareness they try so hard to suppress.

If what they were feeling was not due to envy, then they would be happy. They'd feel good. At the worst, they'd only feel sorry for those who were so "unfortunate," missing out on a chaste lifestyle that was so much better and rewarding. Certainly, the last thing that would come to their minds, would be to threaten those who engage in sexual sins with punishments, either in a life beyond or with exaggerated statistics about STDs.

They would think only about the suffering that such sinners are going through already. They would pity those who felt the need to have sex before marriage. They would shake their heads and feel very sorry for all the guys who are getting intimate with scores of young, attractive women. They'd be trying so hard to help the presumably miserable young women who like to wear little to nothing to set them free from having so many guys admiring their exposed figures.

They would try to help them understand that once the Holy Spirit is in their hearts, they would automatically discover the joy of wearing modest clothing and from then on they'd only want to have sex with a lawfully wedded husband. Right? Certainly, they wouldn't expect anyone who hadn't already accepted Christ to have the strength or the desire to give up carnal pleasures. They would know that sin has too much of a hold on the sinner, and that it would be ludicrous to expect an unbeliever to stop sinning without first having the Holy Spirit come into and change their heart. Wouldn't they?

Besides, even if they could persuade some lost soul to start dressing and acting more like a sexually chaste Christian, what good would that do for their soul? Such outward conformity would only serve to delude them into thinking that they are already saved … when they are not. Isn't this what they say they believe, that it is faith, not works, that gets one into Heaven?

Sadly, very few Fundamentalists do any of these things. Instead of preaching their gospel—which by the way, means "good news"—they spend a great deal of their time and energy angrily condemning all those, Christian or not, saved or not, in church or not, who engage in sex prior to marriage. Many also support political organizations that would make it a crime to have premarital sex. How is it that they can claim to have compassion for the sinner, while threatening to put them in jail and plunge them into felony record status, preventing them from getting work or finding a decent apartment when they finally get out? For that matter, why even condemn their own church members who are having non-marital sex, for shouldn't that just be a sign that such people aren't as saved as they claim to be?

The fact is, the Religious Right's efforts to impose their version of chastity on everyone outside their church walls has nothing to do with compassion for the poor sinner. The harder a preacher pounds the pulpit to condemn young women for wearing mini skirts and mid drift tops has nothing to do with concern for their souls ... but everything to do with their secret envy which thrives deep inside their dirty hearts and whispers—"If only I could have my way with these hot, young women!" Their real problem is that it is *they* who are so miserable—either because they are single and believe they have to wait and wait and wait for years before they can have sex or because they're married and aren't satisfied with the partner they have chosen to the exclusion of all others. The only way, therefore, that they can cope with their inner discontent is to try to make everyone else miserable too!

One good example of how weakness of conviction leads to sinner envy and crusading to force change on others was the rise and fall of television evangelist Jimmy Swaggart. On February 21, 1988, the very popular Pentecostal preacher confessed that he had been consorting with a prostitute. The confession was a huge scandal, but what made it so scandalous was not that he had committed a sexual sin, but that he had been doing so at the same time he had been going on rampages during his TV preaching against "sexual sin." He had, for example, unleashed fire and brimstone against his rival televangelist Jim Bakker for "having committed adultery" with his secretary Jessica Hahn, which had gotten Rev. Bakker defrocked and fired from the multi-million dollar PTL Club only a few months before.[142] Obviously, Swaggart's vehement anti-sexualism was the direct result of his own indulgence in the very sin he so condemned.

Much of the pressure Fundamentalists put upon people to be sexually abstinent until they marry is due to their own state of sexual discontent.

Somewhere in the back of their minds, they've got the idea that the only way to tolerate such sexual frustration is to do all they can to keep others from enjoying what they're missing. Better to pressure all the young people in one's church to make a pledge to celibacy, so one can at least have the satisfaction of knowing that no one else is getting to have sex with all those attractive young girls in their church. Better to heap so much guilt on a couple living together, that they can no longer enjoy the love they've found, and get them to join their proverbial miserable company.

The Pressure and The Path of Least Resistance

Unfortunately, society, family and friends in general put a lot of pressure on unmarried couples to conform to the institution of Marriage. It's very commonplace for the friends and family of those who've been in relationships even for only a few months to start asking "When are you gonna get married?" over and over and over and over. Should a couple "fail to commit" after a year or more, the pressure to get married gets worse, especially for women.

There's a constant refrain that is played to them which usually calls into question the motives of the male in the relationship and which seeks to take advantage of any insecurities the woman might have—"If he really loves you, he'll commit." "What? He still hasn't popped the question?" "Are you sure he really loves you?"

Sometimes, it can get real ugly, "Well of course he's never going to buy the cow, as long as he's getting the milk for free!" If one would listen carefully, though, a question like this is very telling, for the message comes down to this—a man should have to pay for getting to have sex with you. The "payment" is the contract to obligate him to stay with a woman for life, the unspoken rationale being that he must do so now, while he still fancies her, because eventually he won't desire her anymore.

In one way or another, these people will do all they can to apply The Pressure. They'll use religious arguments, "God doesn't approve." They'll threaten, "you don't respect us." If there's a child, they'll claim that, by not marrying, "the child will suffer," and some will even go so far as to label the child a "bastard." They'll withhold "their blessing," and in some cases, threaten to remove a relative from their will.

No matter how happy a couple is, and no matter how long they've lived together in harmony, one can hardly underestimate the willingness of certain family and so-called friends to keep pounding away, until most couples finally relent, if for no other reason, just to get them off their backs.

The Pressure can also come in a more subtle form. When a couple is living together, and content to do so without getting married, they can find themselves growing weary of answering the same questions, constantly having to explain why they're not engaged, and almost running out of breath from correcting those who presume to refer to their partner as "your husband" or "your wife." Without a firm and clear set of convictions to stand firm, there are a good number who marry simply because it is the path of least resistance.

Attention and the Miracle of Giving Birth

The day a woman gets married is the day she will get more personal attention than on any other … or at least, that's the promise. The bridal gown which is the visual centerpiece, the long and slow procession where all turn their heads to watch the bride being led in by her father and preceded by a young girl spreading flower petals, and before all this, the months of preparations which are supposed to reflect every wish of the bride's desires for the "biggest day of her life"—all holds out the hope of collecting a very compelling reward—attention.

There's certainly a lot of talk about "My Day," a common euphemism for a woman's wedding. What is it that happens on this day—though the ceremony really only lasts one, maybe two hours at the most—that so captures a woman's imagination and tries to match the "happily ever after" fairy tale ending?

Let's recall how Marriage has evolved and changed since the crude rites attending the female sex trade when Marriage was first instituted by and for the benefit of male land owners. The ancient origins of the ceremony had only a little in the way of anything that could be considered "rewarding" for a bride. But as the millennia passed, and the institution evolved, little by little, the wedding day became less and less "his" and more and more "her day."

In the midst of the social upheaval of the Agricultural Revolution that reduced the status of women to mere livestock, there did remain something of the prehistoric awe of the creative power of Woman in the otherwise dehumanizing marketplace exchanges of women. Nevertheless, a virgin to be sold would often be dressed up and bedecked with fine clothing and jewelry—admittedly in the same vein as a cow is prettied up for a county fair competition in order to get the blue ribbon—and the procession to the gates of the town or village where the trade would be formally acknowledged was, admittedly, the one day when she could expect to draw the most positive public attention she could ever hope for. It was a remnant from a much better time that said, however faintly, "You're special."

No doubt, there is something special about the unique combination of a ceremony which is designed to bring everyone's focus onto one person for at least an hour or two and the promise of a pivotal rite of passage that summarizes one's reason for being. Up until Great Grandma's early days, what used to be the defining moment of a woman's life was when she had a baby. And this was even more so during humanity's earliest era of hunting and gathering. A woman who gave a healthy birth was honored. A sense of reverence and mystery was bestowed upon the fertile woman, as birth was regarded as a supernatural event.[143]

In many ancient belief systems, it was commonly thought that a woman who gave birth was the medium by which The Creative Force bestowed life anew. She was on that very special day "one with the Mother Goddess," and was venerated accordingly. Surely, a deep void was created in the female psyche when this veneration was so severely diminished.

Such veneration is all but now gone from the birth process. Even with the modern movement to have fathers present during labor, the use of midwives, and relying more on special breathing techniques instead of heavy pain killers, most

Western child births occur in a sterile, hospital room, attended by strangers, and looked upon as a medical procedure, not a sacred experience.[144] Instead of receiving veneration as mothers had received for thousands of years, moms are pumped full of drugs, and the child is placed in a ward behind a glass window, where maybe the father and a handful of relatives get a distanced view.

What, if any thing, could possibly restore the virtual worship mothers received as far back as we can trace our origins? How might such an empty place within the Female Collective Unconscious express itself if it can't be fulfilled in the same manner it had been for tens of thousands of years? The answer may be found in women's special need for attention in general, and most especially in relation to the day which has become the de facto replacement for what used to be her most defining moment—the day she first gave birth, and replaced by the wedding rite itself.

We may all be familiar with the tendency of women to want and need attention (Yes, yes, yes, men desire attention too, but we're not talking about men right now). Many relationship troubles can be traced to situations where a woman feels like she is not getting enough attention from her mate, and if need be, she'll do whatever it takes to get it. Why?

Perhaps, deep in the female mind, the yearning for veneration could explain why women, especially once they're in a sexual relationship, never grow weary of getting a new dress, a new pair of shoes, a vase of flowers, a pedicure, a new hair do, and so on and so forth, no matter how many dresses or shoes she already has, no matter if she has a garden full of blooming plants in the backyard, no matter how nice her toes already look and no matter that she just had her hair done a week ago! It could be that the reason she instinctively and unendingly craves (what are to men extraneous) these gestures, gifts or pampering are the symbolic means of affirming her ultimate, female "self-sacrifice." Having laid herself out to be penetrated, having offered her body up, she ever needs to feel that whatever sacrifices or pains are connected to it (like giving birth) are well worth it.

Modern society no longer provides this affirmation directly. We no longer worship a Mother Goddess. As already noted above, giving birth is attended with nothing of the wonder and awe and sense of oneness with the Creative Female Power that was a regular feature of the birth of a child in the ancient traveling bands of prehistoric times. (The closest we come to such a rite nowadays is an infant baptism—the least attended of church rites.) However, the Marriage Rite has evolved into an indirect replacement, and in roughly the same context.

No matter how rich or poor, how pretty or unattractive, how great or bad a personality or how high or low her sense of self-esteem, a woman gets to be a

Goddess and is worshipped, at least for a day.[145] It's hardly a wonder that most all women, even atheists, will get married in a place of worship, or at least, a place that is made to resemble one, not so much to be pleasing to God, but to fill this void.

Glorified Prostitution

It's often been said there are three ways to get rich. One, is to be born into wealth. Two, is to start a successful business, and the third is to marry a rich guy. The 1994 wedding of then 27-year-old former Playboy model Anna Nicole Smith to 89-year-old oil tycoon J. Howard Marshall is probably the best example in living memory proving that gold digging has by no means gone out of style, and for good reason. Marshall died within a year of his wedding to Smith, and in 2002, federal judge David Carter awarded $88.5 million to the "grieving" widow as her share of Marshall's estate. (Unfortunately for Mrs. Nicole Smith, family members are still challenging the judgment.) Ms. Smith/Mrs. Marshall benefited from a law that most states still uphold, the concept of *community property,* where everything a married couple has is jointly owned by both spouses.

When there is a significant disparity between the lifestyle a woman had prior to getting married, and the elevated socio-economic status she enjoyed after marrying, she can often appeal to a divorce court that she has a right to remain in the same elevated lifestyle and receive large awards of alimony to do so. The Women's Movement, along with social, governmental and educational efforts to liberate women from dependency on men for their financial well-being, has helped to modify alimony laws to better reflect compensation for actual work done (such as keeping a home so a spouse can be free to pursue a higher education) and community property laws to exclude wealth that was amassed prior to being wed. Nevertheless, gold digging continues to motivate many women to see Marriage as a way to significantly improve their status of living.

What is perhaps the most ironic aspect to this motivation is the manner in which the Church has done virtually nothing to discourage women from marrying to obtain wealth even though the New Testament clearly prohibits the exchange of sex for money. Though it's widely believed the Bible clearly says so, there is actually not a single verse that specifically condemns pre-marital sex (at least, not for men)! Instead, there are only two forms of sex that are condemned, adultery and prostitution.

Some of the more recent attempts to translate the Bible into a more readable form of English have translated the Greek word PORNEIA, which means prostitution, into much broader term such as "sexual immorality" or "pre-marital sex." However, PORNEIA specifically refers to the exchange of sex for money.

That said, PORNEIA is not limited to exchanging sex for money with many persons. If one is trading one's body for some form of material payment, then even if one is prostituting oneself with only one other, it's prostitution all the same! If the people who claim to take the Bible literally were to actually follow what it says, they would be strongly opposed, not only to traditional street side prostitution, but to the actions of women to lure men to marry them in order to get into their bank accounts! The same intent, regardless of legal sanction (let's recall that prostitution is legal in some countries), ought to be equally condemned if it is to be condemned at all.[146]

The Fear of Abandonment

Perhaps the most compelling force weighing on young couples to marry is the fear of abandonment. The following portion of a counseling session—which is representative of discussions I've had with scores of couples who were contemplating marriage—illustrates how this institution has come to be regarded as a kind of "love insurance," a rite that holds out the promise of assuaging the fear that, sooner or later, a lover will depart:

Young Couple: "We wanna get married."

Me: "OK. So why do you want to get married?"

Young Couple: "Well … because we love each other."

Me: "Do you feel that you have to get married because you love each other?"

Young Couple: (looking somewhat puzzled) "No."

Me: "Do you feel that if you don't get married, that you won't be able to love each other any more?"

Young Couple: (Now starting to look a little dumbfounded) "Well, no."

Me: "Is there anything about your present relationship that you're unhappy with, that you feel getting married will resolve?"

Young Couple: (the young man says) "No!" (the young woman starts looking down at the floor)

Me: "Are you sure?"

Young Woman: "Well, not exactly."

Me: "Try your best. What specifically do you want to get from being married that you don't already have as a couple living together very happily?"

Young Woman: (stuttering) "I, I know David [not his real name] loves me. I know he does. It's just that…."

Me: "Go on. It's just what?"

Young Woman: (finally blurting out) "I just want him to promise me he'll never leave me for anyone else."
Me: "You mean, 'while he still loves you.'"
Young Woman: "Well, yeah." "(After a long pause) I'm not always gonna be young, ya know."

Sad to say, so many people are in such a state of insecurity, so many have such a poor image of themselves, and so many feel so unworthy of love, that when they finally do meet someone who comes to love them, somewhere deep inside, they just can't fully accept that this person loves them for who they are. Though the example above came from a young woman, this problem applies to men as well. A man who manages to get an attractive girlfriend may propose to her because deep down he feels that if he doesn't persuade her to marry him, and thus, "lock her in," she may eventually dump him for a richer, stronger or "cooler" guy.

In a very real sense, Marriage serves as the ultimate form of mate guarding, not at all an uncommon behavior for many species besides *Homo sapiens*. Unfortunately, the more a male feels the need to guard his female mate, the more likely it is that he either is or will signal he is a male of low status, a Beta. Sadly for him, the cooler Alpha Male he's so worried about is likely to circumvent his efforts anyway, and to a good degree, precisely because of his insecure attitude! More about this phenomenon is a later chapter.

For women, the promise of a strong impediment to eventual abandonment also has to do with insecurities. Even those who do feel good about themselves for the present, are constantly getting the message that their time of being in demand is limited. As noted before, our modern culture goes to considerable lengths to offer women an endless supply of products and procedures that might extend or even restore youthful appearance because aging is held out as a woman's worst enemy. Myriad businesses have figured out how to exaggerate the fear—that the natural instinct in men to prefer and to find most attractive the markers of youthfulness also means that men are only attracted to young women. As a result, many a young woman has a deep fear of aging, and if she has found a man that loves her and finds her attractive at the present time, she can readily succumb to the temptation to think that by "getting him to commit" to stay with her for the rest of her life *while he still likes her* will prevent him from leaving later on after she loses her youthful beauty.

Commitment is an Effect, Not a Cause

In any other context this logic would be regarded as a sad expression of very low self-esteem. Yet for some reason, it's the most common logic operating in the minds of people when they first consider Marriage. No one, who has a healthy sense of self worth, would ever consider trying to coerce a friend or a relative to make some kind of a vow or a legal contract or a promise to never stop being a friend! To make such a suggestion would immediately alert the person being asked that something must be wrong. Either friendship is there or not, and if one continues in the friendship, great. If not, so be it. To constrain someone to be one's friend is to admit there's a serious problem in the friendship already.

We all understand that friendship is something that cannot be forced upon people against their will. We accept that, sometimes, a friend stops being a friend, but other friendships last a life time. For however long a friendship lasts, the point is whether it brings happiness to both persons for however long it lasts. We understand with good reason that "brotherly" love is a matter of the free will only. And yet, when it comes to *romantic* love, reason is very often cast aside in the face of fear.

Worse, putting someone in a place where one's free choice to love is effectively removed, no matter how much one really does love someone, has the effect of turning such love off! That which is often hoped for in marriage—security in love—is actually undermined by it, creating the very problem it was supposed to prevent. When someone is constrained to do something, even if one liked doing it before, the constraint itself is enough to take away the enjoyment that was there in the beginning.

Think about it for a moment. Would one feel the same sense of warmth about donating to a favorite charity, if one later learned that the same charity had begun to draft money out of one's checking account without permission?

It's worth repeating, outside of Marriage, we seem to understand how foolish it would be to ask anyone who loves anything or anybody else to make a life-long commitment to the objects of our passion. In every other context, we understand that *commitment is an effect, not a cause.*

Musicians play their music because they love to, not because they have to. There's no such thing as making a life long vow to "The Music Institution." Yet, we often see musicians who so naturally love music in their hearts that they play or sing or write music right up until their dying day. If we love our parents or our children or our siblings or our friends, we may do so until we draw our last breath, but at no point would anyone say to one's dear mother, "Hey Mom, now that we've been together for all these years, don't you think it's high time we make this official before the Church and the State, and put in writing that you're never gonna stop being my mother?" Of course not!

Unfortunately, many, many people today place themselves and the ones they love romantically in just such a bind. Little do they realize that by trying to alleviate their deep fears of eventual abandonment by means of the man-made institution of Marriage, they in fact undermine the natural bond of love that Nature had created between them. They precipitate the very love loss they had so hoped to head off.

I suppose that whoever it was that first got the idea to reframe and repackage Marriage as "making a commitment" could be commended for having come up with one of the best euphemisms of our time. But like so many other terms created by propagandists to replace precise words in order to make them seem less offensive or more palatable, we must understand that "commitment" is a word of disguise and deception.

When the word "commitment" is used to describe a cause, it is in every other case besides Marriage understood to connote something bad! When we hear of a man who "had himself committed," it means that he realizes he has a serious mental problem or a chemical addiction. He realizes he can no longer trust himself for his own good. So he must surrender his liberty and check into an institution where others will govern his life, at least for a time. We normally understand that coming to a point of committing oneself or a family member is not a desirable thing. The idea of commitment here is as a last resort, a measure of desperation, and hopefully, only to be endured until the one so committed is healed or reformed. We normally wish no one to be committed, and if we do, only for as long as necessary! What we all want for the committed, is to be freed, and removed from the institution as soon as possible, if at all possible.

Then again, perhaps this was the point after all. Whoever first got the idea to re-label this otherwise terrible choice into a virtue may very well have had our imprisonment in mind, perhaps, precisely because he or she was 100% convinced it was necessary for our own good.

7

It's Not Just a Piece of Paper

o o o o o o o o o o o o o o o o o o o o o o o o o o o o o o o o o o o o o o

"Did you know," a Venetian who claimed to be an associate of the infamous Marco Polo said to a doubtful pub patron, "Polo has a piece of paper worth a pound of gold in Cathay?" "Sure, sure," lamented the patron, "and next I suppose you'll tell me the Mongols have a great wall that stretches for hundreds of miles across their northern border!"

'Til Death Do You Part

The notion that a marriage is "successful" if a couple stays together until one of them dies is deeply embedded in our culture, even though we know a lot of those who who've been together for decades, who are at best, just putting up with each other. We tend to automatically compliment them every anniversary—"Oh, you've been together all this time; that's so wonderful." But as we give these cheers, somewhere in the back of our minds we're likening their "success" to those barely staggering to the end of a Marathon race!

We'll cheer any who seem like they might "go the distance," that is, to stay together until death, even if they are visibly agonized and exhausted of one another. We've accepted in one form or another the idea that "success in marriage" is not about being generally happy with each other, but meeting an obligation no matter how much misery it brings. Similarly, breaking up is almost always labeled a "relationship failure" even if the couple in question was very happy for many years prior to the time of the relationship's demise. If a couple is together, let's say, five years, and four of those years were happy ones, then why not regard those four years as a success?

There's a story about the famous anthropologist, Margaret Mead worth repeating here: Toward the end of her long career, she was being interviewed by a young reporter for a story about her life, and he touched on this very issue. "… Dr. Mead, do you feel that your dedication to your work contributed to your three failed marriages?" Mead, who had a reputation for blunt-to-the-point speech and for not suffering fools lightly, stood up straight and looked directly into the eyes of the relatively innocent young man. "What failed marriages?" she asked quizzically. "I have had three perfectly successful marriages, each appropriate for its time!"

To remain with someone, after love has gone sour and after all reasonable efforts have been made to regain the happiness a couple once had is the true definition of relationship failure. The difference between this concept and the one that is generally accepted is that of placing more value on the two individuals' happiness instead of on the longevity of their togetherness. The generally accepted low expectation for marital happiness is perhaps the clearest indication that this institution doesn't really exist for the benefit of people directly involved.

The Church, the State and our culture continue to advance the agenda that people in marital relationships exist for the institution. It's thought to be only a matter of good fortune if a married couple just happens to be happy with each other, but if it should come down to a choice between personal happiness and preserving the institution, then one is obligated to sacrifice one's own needs, wants and desires, and must endure to the end, to preserve the institution at all costs.[147]

Many try to justify this "sacrificial attitude" by claiming it's necessary for the stability of any children involved. But there is a great amount of testimony from people who've grown up in homes where parents were clearly unhappy with each other that such leads only to greater suffering for all involved. Staying together for a lifetime is certainly OK, but only if that togetherness is providing satisfaction to both partners, which in turn, is the key factor in determining the happiness of any children they might have.

Another argument which is often put forward to justify holding unhappy couples together for life is the great amount of devastation that accompanies divorce. However, the multitude of problems associated with divorce speak only to the very bad way our society constrains people to break up, not that breaking up is by itself so bad. As noted earlier, once we factor out the necessity of getting divorced to end a relationship—the attorney fees, the court costs, the adversarial nature of the divorce proceedings, and the elimination of the lengthy limbo period of being "separated but not yet divorced," a very stressful state that can last for many months, even years—we get a much different picture.

Cohabiting couples that break up are immediately single. There's not the prolonged agony of waiting, and the higher likelihood of other disputes arising in the interim. Instead of losing most, if not all, of the couples' savings and disposable income to lawyers, they get to keep these funds to help make whatever adjustments are necessary after a break up (finding a new home, buying another refrigerator, etc.). In the situations where there are disputes over property, these are settled in small claims courts, usually in a matter of weeks, instead of months or years. If there are any child custody issues, they are not prolonged in family courts because custody and visitation can be settled without the need to resolve every other issue first (such as property division) before the couple can be finally divorced. Closure comes so much more quickly, as does the healing.

There are a number of Fundamentalist parachurch organizations who advocate reinstating "fault" into divorce law, who base their arguments largely on the confusion between the devastation families suffer at the hands of the Divorce Industry with the separations of couples themselves. Of course, they assume that forcing people to stay in bad relationships will somehow make all their problems go away. They fail to understand that the answer to how to end relationships that are beyond repair is finding better venues for settling disputes over custody and property division rather than pushing them into the minefields of the divorce court room, and the wars of attrition that so often take place there.

You Can't Just Leave

Remember the old Eagles' song "Hotel California"? There's one line in the song that serves as a useful metaphor of what happens when a couple who had skipped down to the county court house to get a marriage license in a matter of minutes, finds out later that their divorce is going to take over a year—"You can check out [of the Hotel California] any time you like, but you can never leave."

In most states, getting married is a very simple process. With a little proof of identification, a few signatures, and a couple of sawbucks, two people can quickly and cheaply become a permanent couple that the State recognizes as a family. The process is so quick and easy that one is almost tempted to think that being legally married is just a matter of registration.

In other words, one could make a pretty good argument for a simple registration process that is more or less uniform all across the country so a single database could be maintained for the purposes of making sure that whatever benefits, such as tax breaks, that the government gives to families are going to the right people, or so that people aren't getting more than what they should by fraudulently being registered with more than one partner—or bigamy.

Unfortunately, the system that let's people jump into legal marriage so easily, often makes it pure Hell to get out! Instead of allowing couples who conclude that they can no longer live together happily go down to the same courthouse office, and for a similar modest fee, be allowed to remove their names from such a registration database, they are forced to go to court. Even couples who agree on all issues—such as custody of children, visitation, division of property, and so on—are still constrained to go through a long, costly and arduous process of filing a petition, being forced to counseling in some states, and then having to wait, wait, wait and wait for a court date. (In some states, like North Carolina, couples who separate are forced to wait an entire year before they can even petition for a divorce!) As noted above, the system is ideally suited to encourage couples to get into fights, which of course, leads to costly and emotionally traumatizing court litigation—the bread and butter of divorce court attorneys' profit.

There's another aspect to this institution, though, that is nothing less than a complete hoax—"to support families." Why? For one reason, because so many family structures are completely left out of the process!

For instance, this book was being written at the same time as public debate was raging over legalizing same sex marriages. Many gay couples have children, not by each other of course, but from previous heterosexual relationships or adoptions. These people and their children have no fewer needs than do any other heterosexual couples who have children (which, by the way, are not always the biological children of both persons in the relationship either). And yet, our government doesn't offer the same support to them.

There are many other family structures that have nothing to do with a sexual union at all. There are adult siblings who are single parents and who sometimes live together to help each other. There are grandparents who live with a son or daughter, helping them to raise a grandchild.

Why is it that there is so much discrimination against all these other variations of family, even though the children of these families have no less need for support than what is liberally offered to the so-called "traditional family"? The answer, of course, is that bigotry has been written into our laws, stemming from social and religious traditions that are completely out of step with the modern world and the diversity of our social structures.

The time is long overdue for a complete overhaul of this system. Either we need to get rid of it altogether, or if we must have some form of keeping track of who is legitimately living in a permanent, domestic partnership—whether they are straight or not, in a sexual union or not—so all should be able to unregister as well as register without being subject to the anti-family abuses of the so-called "Family" Court System.

Thou Shalt Not Make Vows

For all the pressure that the Church has brought to bear on society to "uphold the sanctity of Marriage," a close examination of the holy book upon which they base their authority to create and sustain this pressure reveals some surprises. For one thing, Adam and Eve, the so-called "first married couple," never got married! According to the Genesis narrative, God simply brought Eve (who was naked) to Adam (who was also naked). Adam said he liked what he saw, and the next thing ya know, Eve had conceived! No ceremony, no license, no vows to the death … no purchase price. We're not even sure that they had any time to get to know each other first, much less to fall in love.

And what about those wedding vows that are supposed to be "so integral to keeping a couple together through the worst of times" and providing for the "stability" that would allegedly be lost if such "commitments" weren't required? Perhaps another way of putting it is, "What would Jesus do?" with regard to making wedding vows.

It's particularly ironic that Christian Fundamentalists, who pride themselves in taking the entire Bible as the written and inspired "Word of God," ignore one of the most basic (and best attested to) teachings of Jesus of Nazareth when it comes to making vows: "Again, ye have heard that it hath been said by them of old time, 'Thou shalt not forswear thyself, but shalt perform unto the Lord thine oaths.' But I say unto you, swear not at all; neither by heaven, for it is God's throne, nor by the earth, for it is his footstool, neither by Jerusalem, for it is the city of the great King. Neither shalt thou swear by thy head, because thou canst not make one hair white or black. But let your communication be, Yea, yea; nay, nay, for whatsoever is more than these cometh of evil."[148]

In case the King James English was a little rough to follow, Jesus made it very clear that making vows as a way of ensuring one's subsequent behavior was a very bad idea. In fact, he said that it only results in "evil." Some have tried to split hairs over this Scripture, trying to make some subtle distinction between a "vow" and an "oath." Others, have tried to implant a further hair follicle by claiming that Jesus didn't forbid making "promises." But anyone who can lay their hands on a dictionary will quickly grasp the folly of such rationalizations. The same process is at work no matter what one likes to call it—if you have to add some oath, some vow or some promise to your "yes" or "no," there's already a problem, a problem of mistrust!

Promises Are Made to be Broken

What's going on when Person A asks Person B to do something, and B says, "Sure," (or as the King James Jesus put it, "Yea,") and then Person A feels the need to say, "Do you promise?" (Person A could have just as easily said, "Do you swear?" or "Will you vow that you will do yada, yada?") What's going on when "yes" or "no" isn't good enough? What's happening is, on some level, Person A just doesn't trust Person B.

Now here's where the evil comes in that Jesus spoke about. If one is going to enter into some kind of agreement with someone else whom he or she already feels is untrustworthy, there is no amount of promises or vows or oaths in the world that can change the fact that there already exists a lack of trust. And if that trust isn't there in the first place, then one is a fool to ask that person to agree to any thing. Whoever first said that promises were made to be broken was very wise indeed.

To be sure, a vow/promise/oath was and continues to be a commonly used form of a contractual guarantee. Back in Jesus' day, people actually believed making an oath upon something or someone was backed up by supernatural forces. And even today, one might still hear someone say, "I swear on the life of my children ..." as a way of convincing the person he's trying to reassure with the implied logic that the oath maker's children would be struck dead by some assumed, supernatural power if he is not telling the truth. As long as both parties believe that such forces exist and that these powers would follow through with whatever punishments the oath maker accepts in the event he violates his oath, it surely would act as an effective deterrent to lying. The problem, though, back in ancient times as well as now, is when the oath maker is insincere, while the other party is convinced he is. The falsely assured by the oath/promise/vow will eventually be disappointed, because the person who made the oath (took a vow or make a promise) doesn't believe for a moment that his words of assurance would ever result in harm coming to him or his loved ones.

Jesus of Nazareth (or whoever originated the idea that was eventually attributed to him) came down against the use of oaths altogether, essentially saying that no agreements should be made with anyone about anything unless it was on the basis of complete trust. One would think that those who claim to follow Jesus and take the Bible as the literal "Word of God" would be the first to shun the notion that any good can come of people binding themselves to any oaths, much less by oaths to stay together until death![149] Nevertheless, this is exactly what many Christians and their leaders do. The Church ardently insists that a man and a woman cannot have a legitimate sexual relationship unless they exchange marriage vows even though their own Lord and Savior taught against vow making.

The operating principle behind any contract or commitment is mistrust. In any other context, a "promise" is only necessary between people who doubt each other. A bank, for instance, asks you to sign a contract before they give you a car loan, because they don't trust you to repay them on your word alone. The bank doesn't really know you. There's no natural bond between you, so the bank has reason to doubt you'd follow through without some form of a tangible guarantee that is backed up by the law. In situations like a vehicle purchase—basically an exchange between strangers who are in no other way expected to be loyal or empathetic toward one another—a guarantee like this is understandable. But when this very same principle is applied to a love relationship where empathy and devotion are expected to thrive as much as with any other close family member, the effect is devastating. Once a couple that had a relationship based on trust agrees to the idea, "I have to get this written guarantee because I don't believe our love is going to be enough," it's usually only a matter of time before their trust for one another is gone, and the piece of paper is all they have left.

Water Seeks The Lowest Level

Unfortunately, replacing the "wanting-to-be together" with a "having-to-be together" for the purpose of gaining some kind of relationship security usually results in just the opposite taking place. High divorce rates and an even higher percentage of marriage relationships characterized by cold resignation are solid proof of this. After a marriage contract is signed, many soon wake up to feeling trapped, and all too typically, both persons begin to treat each other very differently.

To be sure, there are cohabiting couples who eventually become incompatible for a host of reasons. Upon moving in together, many annoying habits and attitudes that might not have been so obvious before, tend to emerge. Sometimes, a cohabiting couple will not succeed in working through their differences, and will part company. No one is saying that remaining unmarried is a guarantee of lasting love.

However, when we factor out the conflicts that arise purely from living together (which can result in break ups whether the partners are married or not) by examining those couples who cohabited happily and successfully for long periods of time before they got married, we see a more fundamental problem. When a very substantial percentage of these relationships begins to deteriorate after marriage, we need to seriously consider that it's the Marriage contract itself which is the root cause of the deterioration. It's no coincidence that the main theme of almost every book that offers advice to married couples on how to rekindle their first love centers on adopting attitudes and behaviors that mimic those they engaged in while they were still dating.

So what exactly is it that changes? Why should that little piece of paper have the power to remove the joy that a couple deeply in love had before, even in cases where they cohabited happily for years before getting married? What is it about Marriage that expedites the process of relationship obsolescence? The answer is that upon marriage, the very foundation of the relationship is removed and replaced.

The typical marriage serves as the venue where the substitution is made. This exchange is popularly framed as the epitome of virtue, and we've grown accustomed to think of expressions like "making a commitment" as some act of nobility. However, what's really happening is far from noble or virtuous. The natural bond, or what we call "love"—that very deep sense of empathy, loyalty and sense of pleasure just to be near to each other—is tossed to the wayside! In its place, is an artificial, man-made contract, something that holds together alright but only as good as Velcro ... only until a modicum of pressure is applied, and then, rip, the two sides fly apart! Why does this happen?

In most cases, it becomes impossible after marrying for either partner to set aside the human tendency to take the path of least resistance. Just as water will settle to the lowest point of any foundation due to gravitational pull, so also do most people find it nearly impossible to avoid changing the way they treat their married partner once they buy into the concept that he or she can't leave, at least not without suffering severe punishments in this life, the next, or both.

On the one hand, cohabiting couples who are together on the natural basis of their love bond, tend to treat each other more kindly, have more patience with each other's faults, are more forgiving when mistreated, and hold their tongues from saying cruel things that are hard to take back. They tend to be more aware that what's holding them together is their mutual desire for each other, so they tend also to do those things that reinforce this desire. Married people, on the other hand, are prone to set aside such considerations. A new mind set takes over which, if given voice, would sound something like this. "Now that we're married, I don't have to use the nicest words I can think of to address my irritation with my mate when he forgets to wipe his dirty shoes before coming in the house. He can't go anywhere, so I don't have to be concerned about the way I speak to him." How many times do we hear the story of a "wife who let herself go" or "a husband who quit doing all the nice little thoughtful things he used to do." It's so very, very, very easy to slip into the habit of doing only what we think is the absolute minimum required. Laziness in love sets in fast.

Are there exceptions? Sure. There are some cohabitants who get lazy in their love too, and who begin to take each other for granted just like most married people do. Similarly, there are some married couples who were fortunate enough to have no idea what they were doing when they got married and who still treat each other in all the nice and thoughtful ways they did before, and they make every effort to keep alive the fire they began with, if not at full blaze, at least pretty warm. But one thing is for sure, in the few cases where a cohabiting couple falls into the trap of lazy love, it's not because their relationship was founded only on a natural love bond, it's in spite of it. Likewise, in the few cases where a married couple is happy, it's not because they are married, it's also in spite of it.

The Cart Before the Horse

We need to make a distinction between the uses of the word "commitment" as it applies to relationships. Long term, cohabiting couples, indeed, make all kinds of commitments (please note the small "c" and plurality)—signing leases together on apartments or joint mortgages, buying furniture on the same credit account and probably the biggest commitment of all, having a child together. Even though they don't feel the need to make "The Commitment" before the law or some religious institution to be together, somehow they still manage to make and follow through on all the other practical, every day commitments that married couples typically make. If, as some suggest, a principle commitment to be in a permanent sexual relationship is an absolute necessity for two people to successfully live together, then it would follow that subsequent commitments would be impossible without it. However, we observe that not only do cohabiting couples indeed have no problem making and living up to the same kind of practical commitments that married couples do, but they tend to be much more happy with each other while they do.

Why then is it that so much is made of this thing we call "Commitment" to be in a permanent relationship, and what, if any, connection does this principle commitment have with all the practical commitments that any two people living together will have? First, it should be obvious that it's not at all necessary to make a commitment to be with someone for a lifetime in order to make all the practical commitments of every day life. Those who think this is so unusual confuse the cause and effect roles of commitment. According to what we've been told a million times in a million ways, commitment is a cause, and that all the everyday, practical commitments follow as the effects. If this were true, though, then what explains the fact that cohabiting couples who do not found their relationship on Commitment as a cause, still follow through with the same practical commitments which we might say are the effects of whatever it is that principally binds them together? There must be something else which is causing these effects. That which results in their everyday commitments, is not the same thing that caused them.

That thing, that cause, that force which is at work to inspire cohabiting couples to embrace the every day commitments is the natural bond between them. What holds them together is not an artificial, causal commitment recorded on a legal document or performed as a religious rite in which they vowed to stay with someone for a lifetime. But is, instead, a very deep emotional connection, a bond that is reinforced every time they are with each other, and especially during sexual intimacy. It is this bond of love that is the root cause of all these other practical commitments as the effects.

Does it still seem strange to say that not only is it unnecessary to commit oneself to be with someone permanently, but that doing so is very often a detriment to making and keeping subsequent, practical commitments? Yes, this sounds odd to us at first. It's hard to get past an idea after having heard it over and over again, from almost everyone you know, in tones of perfect presumption. Would you, for example, be likely to jump up and declare the color of the sky to be blue, if everyone you ever heard mention the topic, asserted with beaming confidence that the sky was red? Long after Christopher Columbus made his famous voyage and discovery of the "New World" in 1492, a lot of people still believed the earth was flat. It's understandable that it's "hard on the ears" at first, but the facts tell us that "making a commitment" to a person with whom one is supposed to already have a deep and empathetic relationship of trust is, indeed, anything but helpful.

At the risk of sounding redundant, let's return to our musician illustration. The musician, who has a deep love for music within himself will, out of that love, naturally go on to make the practical commitments typical of musicians—to purchase an instrument, to take lessons, to practice every day and to show up for performances. At no point does he go to the government, the Church or some other authoritative body to vow that he will be a musician until his dying day. He just knows what he wants to do, and he just goes out to do it. Even though no one is making him, he may very well play or sing or write music for the rest of his life, because he loves it so much, but not due to any vow or obligation.

Of course, there are those musicians who do end up playing their instruments out of obligation, not out of love. Often, they do so because the music in their hearts is not popular, and in order to make a living, they have to play what will sell. One can almost see it in their faces, and hear it in their song, a sadness, and emptiness that says, "I'm only here to pay the rent, not because this is what I love to do."

Weighing down anyone with an obligation that was once a free desire, no matter how similar it might appear on the surface, changes everything. That which was previously carried on with joy, becomes a drudgery! Oddly, we seem to understand what happens to people in any other context besides love, were they to exchange the very foundation from which all their efforts sprang for a duty. Common sense and experience tell us that natural passion from deep within is the best motivator for any endeavor, and the very idea of strapping oneself into a causal commitment to any life long cause strikes us as imprisonment, and for good reason. Because it is!

Binding oneself to a sexual relationship, therefore, with the thought that making an obligation to it will in any way help one follow through with all the other practical commitments characteristic of good relationships, flies in the face of all good reason. To do so is putting the cart before the proverbial horse. Unfortunately, this is exactly what most people do when they enter into marriage contracts.

8

Is Marriage Under Attack?

o o o o o o o o o o o o o o o o o o o o o o o o o o o o o o

"Here's the greatest heartbreak of all, 88% of the students who are growing up in our evangelical churches are leaving by age 18 and not coming back."

—From an ad for a church seminar, in which a local Fundamentalist pastor lamented the legalization of gay weddings as an "attack on Marriage" and it's feared consequences for the underage members of church roles

What the Crusaders Are Really Worried About

Fundamentalists have been arguing for decades that "Marriage is under attack." As a case in point, examine the following quotes from a letter-styled pamphlet that was mailed out to a suburban community in the Dallas, Texas area in October of 2003. The letter is basically an appeal by the pastor of a local church to get people to attend a special weekend seminar called "Successful Family Weekend," but it's presented here because it is so telling in its details as to what is really motivating such "grave concern" for the institution of Marriage and for the alleged well being of young people.[150] The pastor begins: "These are strange times in which we live because the very institution of Marriage is under attack. Bride's Magazine is devoting a full-page article to same-sex 'weddings' in its September-October issue – a first in the publication's 70-year history. In March, the Massachusetts Judicial Court heard arguments in a case seeking to allow homosexual couples the same right to marry that historically has been allowed only to one man and one woman. Divorce is affecting one out of every two marriages! What are we to do as followers of Jesus Christ to stand and withstand in a culture where our faith is mocked and immorality is exalted? It's not only a challenge for husbands and wives, it's also a growing problem to parent our kids effectively in this mixed up world! We must remember that God has a plan and it still works even in this mad world in which we live."[151]

From here the letter goes on to promote the seminar (apparently part of "God's plan"), but take note of exactly what this minister equates to an "attack" on Marriage—a popular woman's magazine doing a story on same-sex wedding ceremonies and a state court that (at that time) was considering the legality of same-sex marriages. Nothing more. For this pastor (and a lot of other Fundamentalists), merely allowing people who don't even belong to their church to get legally married somewhere besides in their church (where it wouldn't be allowed), translates into, "We're being attacked!"

They obviously feel threatened, but for what real reason? Were Marriage truly "under attack," then it would follow that somewhere someone would be advocating that Churches be prohibited by the force of law to perform any ceremony wherein couples of any sexual orientation, make vows to God, Jesus or any deity, to stay together permanently. But no such move is afoot.

Clearly, what this pastor and the militant Fundamentalists he exemplifies really mean when they say "Marriage is under attack," is any indication that their Church is losing its influence on people outside of their memberships, particularly in the area of limiting their sexual behavior to the beliefs and mores that they claim for themselves. One could understand their alarm if, indeed, they and their members were being prohibited, by the force of law, from following their own beliefs as to how, when, why and whom one marries, and when you can or cannot have sex. But why should they be so concerned about what other people do who don't subscribe to their particular religious views? The answer lies on the second page of the pamphlet.

After enumerating several social ills that plague today's teens, from alcoholism to suicide, the pastor goes on to say: "Here is the greatest heartbreak of all, 88% of the students who are growing up in our evangelical churches are leaving by age 18 and not coming back [sic]. The current picture is bleak, but there is hope if future parents, parents of children, and parents of teenagers accept their role in molding the values of their children."

Ah ha! Here we find out what is really bothering the leadership of the Fundamentalist hierarchy—that within a generation, they might have to close down their churches and denominational headquarters and lay off countless pastors because there won't be enough people on their roles to pay the tithes and offerings which support them! Clearly, since not coming to church is, in this pastor's words, "the greatest heartbreak of all," then it must not be as bad for teens to die from suicide or get someone else killed by drinking and driving! But the last time I checked, no one ever got hurt from missing church.

It's little wonder, then, that they should be using every fear tactic they can think of—like taking advantage of the prejudices people have toward gays and lesbians—in order to frighten people into corralling their young into church.

Should Stability Trump Happiness?

One of the most frequently heard arguments against cohabitation is that it leads to family "instability." Of course, "instability," as it is used here, carries the presumption that children automatically suffer from changes in family structure, even if the structure they're changing from is a very bad one! They confuse the adverse effects of severe parental incompatibility with the effects of the subsequent parental separation! They omit all evidence showing that separation under such circumstances reduces the stress in those cases (those who manage to set aside their differences to agree on terms without litigation) where the typical divorce process is avoided. Instead, they erroneously conclude, "Since couples who did not cohabit before marriage tend to stay together longer, and cohabiting parents separate at a bit higher percentage than do married parents, children are automatically better off with married parents."[152]

Of course, they also fail to factor in what differences might result were society not to discriminate against families consisting of cohabiting parents in terms of the benefits (or perhaps we should say "bribes") readily offered to married couples with children. The presumption that it's somehow virtuous to set aside individual happiness for the sake of stability—stability for children in particular and for society in general—is very common … and equally unfounded.

Perhaps equally common is the false presumption that, without the external forces of Church and State forcing people to stay together, couples would naturally fly apart at the first sign of trouble in their relationships. Here's what David Blankenhorn, founder and president of the Institute for American Values and author of *Fatherless America* has to say along these same lines. "It's socially risky when marriages depend on a day-to-day temperature-taking of 'Am I happy in this relationship?'"[153] For conservatives like Paul Akers, editorial writer for Scripps Howard News, "No Fault" divorces are the worse thing since Adam's apple, citing in his article *Walk Away Wives*, how divorce results in "a million US children growing up fatherless, divorced fathers losing access to their children, loss of disposable income and divorced women become poorer and seldom finding Mr. Right thereafter."[154] He goes on to advocate the reintroduction of the concept of "fault" back into divorce law. "Then, any spouse who unilaterally abrogated the marital contract without just cause—ennui and a yen to self-actualize don't count—could expect little favor from the court."[155]

Mr. Blankenhorn and Mr. Akers are just a couple of the numerous voices from the Marriage Defense movement, which is made up of mostly conservative Christians but with a more secular façade. These advocates love to tout statistics that, at first glance, may seem to make a good argument that one's relationship happiness is worth sacrificing. They've resurrected the notion that forcing people to stay together who don't really want to be is somehow "good for kids."[156]

Do these "family advocates"—who by the way are predominantly male—really believe that forcing women to stay married to them is somehow going to benefit children? It's always difficult to measure the motives of people, but somewhere in between the lines of Fatherless America or Walk Away Wives, the real message seems to be that there are a lot of guys out there who are such losers that that the only way they can conceive of a woman staying with them permanently is if she's forced to do so! Why?

Why would anyone in their right mind, whether it's the guy or the gal in the relationship, want to force someone to live with them if they really don't want to? What kind of control freaks are we talking about here?

Instead of taking out their frustration with their own weaknesses by trying to change the laws back to the abusive days of Fault Divorce, they ought to be getting some help in figuring out how they can better attract a compatible mate, and keep her attracted enough to want to stick around. If someone feels the need to force other people to be with them in an intimate relationship, then in all likelihood, *they* are the ones with the problem, a problem with their self-esteem and how they interact with the opposite sex.

In another example of how the logic of the Defense of Marriage crusaders goes, Maggie Gallagher of the Institute for Marriage and Public Policy says, "people in *long-term* [emphasis mine] marriages live longer, healthier lives, with higher levels of emotional well-being and lower rates of mental illness and emotional distress. They make more money than otherwise similar singles and build more wealth and experience … than do single or cohabiting couples with similar income levels." Sounds fantastic, doesn't it? Married people are content, not stressed out and have more money than single people or cohabitants. Well, who would be against benefits as great as all these? Marriage must be the source of happiness and prosperity, right? Sorry, not quite.

Notice that Ms. Gallagher is not talking about *all* people who get married. In fact, she's only referring to a very small percentage of those who marry—those few who stay together for the long term. The logic that Marriage must be what makes relationships good because there are some people who've been married for substantial periods of time who seem healthy, happy and financially better off is faulted. Let's illustrate by applying Ms. Gallagher's same logic to another situation: "Because there are a few people who (belong to some Pentecostal sects in the Ozarks) who drink poison and handle snakes who've lived to be 80 and 90 years old, therefore, drinking poison and handling snakes is the key to longevity!"

Something just doesn't sound right, does it? And for good reason. Clearly, just because there are a few elderly Pentecostals who've survived drinking poison and handling venomous snakes for a number of decades is of no comfort to the vast majority of those who did the same thing when they were younger ... and died as a result! Likewise, if a study is to give us some realistic idea of whether Marriage, in and of itself, is beneficial to people, then we can't just simply exclude everyone who has gotten married but failed to stay with it for ten years or more. One must include the majority of those who marry, but end up being unhappy with their relationships, and who then have to face the costly obstacles of getting out. But before we do, let's indulge, and for the sake of argument, take a closer look at Ms. Gallagher's select group for a moment to see if there's any validity to the argument that even those few who do somehow stay married for long periods of time are better off than other people.

People who nowadays marry and stay married fall into two categories. 1) Those who are happy with each other, mostly because they lucked out and avoided the change that typically occurs at marriage, and 2) those who are not happy in their relationships, but stay married anyway. Many of the people in the second category came to marriage with low expectations to begin with, so when they begin to feel trapped and when they each become slothful in the manner they treat each other, they're not surprised. What Ms. Gallagher presents is not a good measurement of how better off married people are, but a calibration of how little happiness most long-term married couples hope to get in the first place, even if they retain a relatively higher degree of wealth compared to divorcées who've suffered huge financial losses thanks to the abuses of the Divorce Industry. *The greater degree of distress, mental illness and loss of wealth she mentions regarding separating couples only tells us what a very bad job our society does to help those who divorce, not how great it is to be married!* By virtue of the fact that long term married couples have avoided divorce, they certainly avoid many of the emotional and financial woes that most all other married people encounter when they just can't take the relationship any more. But the answer is not to force unhappy people to stay together for fear of what horrible abuses they'll suffer at the hands of the ravenous wolves in divorce court, but to begin doing away with the Divorce Industry abuses themselves.

Why Don't More Men File For Divorce?

We're all rather familiar with the reality that most men don't get too excited about the prospect of getting married. Sure, there are those men who will enthusiastically propose to a woman, but usually this only happens when the male perceives himself to be lower on the Alpha-Beta Scale relative to the woman he's proposing to. In these instances, he is merely employing the Beta male's secondary strategy—"I'd really like to have many women like Alphas do, but it's all I can do to attract and keep one. If, therefore, I can't have what I most want, then I'll settle for the next best thing. If I should be so fortunate as to find one female who is attractive, and who is willing to mate with me, then I had better latch on to her and do all I can to keep her from later wanting someone better."

It's interesting to note that even many of these males "get cold feet" or lose enthusiasm for getting married as the "big day" approaches. On one level or another, they all sense that they are resigning themselves, giving up on the hope of ever becoming successful with women, and they'll spend a lot of time trying to convince themselves that they can live with this secondary choice since their one and only mate is more attractive than most, has a better personality, comes from a good family, etc.

Of course, we're talking about those who've found a "quality woman." Unfortunately, many men don't even get this far. In many cases, they are so desperate, they've been trapped for so long in the downward spiral, they will propose to a "fixer upper," only to find that she not only won't be improved, but is likely to get worse.

With the prospects so grim for many men, and at best, a compromise for the few who have "married well," one would logically assume that the percentage of men filing for divorce would greatly exceed that of women. But alas, the opposite is true, by a margin of 2/3 to 1/3! How can this be?

The answer is to regain what is is lost by men on their wedding day. For most men, getting married means they've abandoned the primary mating strategy for their gender—to spread their seed as far and wide as possible. Once they allow themselves to be so "locked in" to one mate, they have put themselves in a position where going back becomes very difficult. The more fortunate are those who succeed in the secondary mating strategy for men—getting and keeping one female, and guarding her well enough to make sure all her children are genetically his. But if the secondary strategy fails, there is usually no where else to go but down. Divorce for most men, usually means, that he is not even getting to keep *one* female, and prevent her from being taken by another. Worse, he is no longer (except in those cases where the male wins custody of his children) able to closely monitor the well being of his children.

In other words, by marrying, a male already gives up a lot, and divorcing later on usually only means that he is going to lose even more! Though there are some exceptions, men usually pay more child support, end up having less time with their children, will sometimes be required to pay alimony, will get to keep less of the marital estate, and all these losses are in addition to the biggest loss of all—no longer getting to keep at least one mate, to keep her from having sex with other males, and to be close enough to ensure their children will survive. As much as men don't really like getting married, they like getting divorced even less!

This explains why men who've become dissatisfied with their wives are much more likely to remain married and cheat, rather than to divorce first before they seek out other sex partners.[157] Most of the men who petition for divorce are those who've had no children. For these men, not even the secondary, Beta strategy is working.

Yes, there's much made of divorced men who are "deadbeat dads," living it up as bachelors once again, getting the sports car their ex-wives wouldn't let them have, and so on. The reality for most divorced men, though, is a huge turn for the worse. They dutifully pay child support, miss their children whom they see only on occasion, and are weighed down with the sense of rejection and failure that often follows divorce. They're generally not very successful at meeting other women and getting to "score" with them, as women tend not to be attracted to men who come off as failures at keeping even one partner. For most, being divorced means anything but getting to enjoy the wine, women and song of Alpha legend, but going from Beta status to Omega!

9

The Love Celebration

o o o o o o o o o o o o o o o o o o o o o o o o o o o o o o

"We are gathered here today to celebrate a union which has already taken place, to recognize those whom Nature has already joined together, to lend our support to this couple who've already formed a bond ... not by man-made obligation, but by Natural Love."

—*From the Celebration of Love*

Reenacting A Past Event

In stark contrast to the Marriage Rite that originated with the crude formalities associated with the Agricultural Era female sex slave trade agreements, the Love Celebration harkens back to the celebrations of thanksgiving during the Hunting and Gathering Era whenever the miracle of love was "bestowed by the gods."

Whereas Marriage is a conscious attempt to change the very foundation of a relationship, the Love Celebration makes no change at all.[158] It doesn't try to fix anything, because it presumes nothing is broken. It doesn't presume, as Marriage does, that prior sexual activity between a loving couple is a sin or something bad or shameful, but instead honors the couples' physical union as the natural culmination of their courtship.

Just as ancient peoples in their small, traveling communities would often set aside some time to give thanks to their deities when a couple in their midst had fallen in love, the purpose of a Love Celebration is to set aside a special day in order for lovers to "come out" as a couple, to celebrate in a public way something that has already occurred privately. Friends and family are invited to offer their support for the relationship, and in order to assist this community of support to feel they are a real part of this new family, some form of a ritual reenactment of the day the couple fell in love is performed.

In some traditions, a ritual dance serves this purpose. The two lovers begin on either side of a circle, and while music is played or the attendees chant, the male begins to "chase" the female around and around—stopping here and there to exchange flirtatious glances, and perhaps other facial or bodily expressions—that give the attendees some idea of what their courtship was like. For instance, a woman who at first wasn't interested in her suitor, might reenact her initial coyness in the dance, by looking the other way at first. Then, at a later point, the man may symbolically produce a flower or food item or anything that might represent what it was that he did or offered to first get her interest.

These rituals are customized, so they tell the love story unique to each couple. They can be very entertaining, and thus, quite memorable.

The point to remember here is that this kind of celebration is not to make any kind of change to the status of the couple in any way, legally or spiritually. Instead, it's a reenactment of a change in their lives that's already taken place, a way to include those who weren't there at the beginning when the relationship first formed.

As a matter of fact, the oldest known form of religious rite is the ritual reenactment. Tribal peoples around the world had a wonderful variety of sacred dances, plays, and rites that might replay a creation myth, or some other explanation for why the world is the way it is. A shaman might, for example, dress up as an Eagle, and dance about a large fire, while all else look on, as he acts out one of his tribe's favorite stories of how the first Great Bird couldn't find a mate, and having fashioned an egg out of mud, screeched to the Thunder God to make them alive, and out hatched the first human beings. Ritual reenactment continues to play a role in modern religions.

The Eucharist celebrated by Christians is a ritual reenactment of the death of Jesus. In fact, the Seder from which the Christian ritual originated was and continues to be a Jewish symbolic reenactment of the miraculous delivery of Moses and the Israelites from Egyptian slavery.

In one way or another, the reenactment rite serves to include people into some event of the past believed to be very important to the present day participants. Reenactments provide a symbolic means for them to participate in these sacred events, to show their faith and support in what came as a result.

The more senses involved in these rites, the more emotional connections the attendees may feel. In a Love Celebration, incorporating all the senses assists the attending friends and family to feel connected to the lovers in a new way, as a couple.

This is why so many rites—religious, social, civic, you name it—involve food and drink for taste, incense or other aromatics for smell, song, music and sound effects for hearing, and elaborate garb for sight. Even the stylized speaking style of preachers—which vary from one denomination to another (the shouting of Pentecostals or quivering tones of Presbyterians) is a way of grabbing the ears of the adherents.

Likewise, a well prepared Love Celebration can serve as a very effective means to capture the imagination and create many an emotional connection through the various senses invoked in order to take friends and family—who've come to offer their support for a new relationship—back in time and make them a part of the day the couple fell in love.

Unlike a wedding day, the day a Love Celebration is held is *not* the "special day." It's not as if the couple *now* has legal recognition, religious sanction or social permission to be intimate. There is no sense at all, implied or otherwise stated, that the couple needed, needs or will every need the State, the Church or Society to do anything! On the contrary, it is more like a birthday party, which looks to the *past*, to an event which they, and only they, experienced for themselves.

The real special day has already happened, and instead of downplaying it or pretending it didn't happen at all, the point of this rite is to relive it with pride and joy, just so others can have a share in the already established relationship.

As noted earlier, in many ancient religions, whenever a couple fell in love, it was often taken as an earthly expression of a cosmic event between their deities. The reenactment of the couple's love story was often thought to be the direct result of the activity of the principle Male and Female gods who had also fallen in love, and were soon to create new life. The celebration of two new lovers was often combined with this cosmic vision, and in some traditions is referred to as "The Great Rite." Neo Pagan religions still practice such rituals to this day.

Pretense Not Allowed

The Love Celebration makes so much more sense than the modern Marriage rites. How very different is the invitation to celebrate "that which Nature hath already brought together" from the mental gymnastics the attendees of modern weddings are subjected to. For instance, how often during a wedding between a couple which has lived together for years do we hear expressions like "as you begin your new life together …"? Does no one bother to tell the presiding minister that the bride and groom are not only living together, but they have a two-year old? Or is this common denial evidence of a much deeper unwillingness by our society to let go of an outdated, religious relic?

In a recent MTV program, the famous swimsuit model Carmen Electra and her rock star fiancée Dave Navarro (from the band Jane's Addiction) allowed cameras to follow them around as they prepared for their wedding. Though the couple had lived together for 3 years, no sense of reality could keep one of the bridesmaids from waxing very emotional a few minutes before the final ceremony about how Ms. Electra was soon to be "entering a new life together" with Mr. Navarro. Of course, what the bridesmaid and almost everyone in attendance were really doing was suspending their reason and pretending that they were only just then beginning a life together! Why?

If you think about it, a lot of what goes on in a modern wedding involves a lot of suspension of reason in order to make everyone involved *feel*, especially the bride, like this ritual is just like the one Great Grandma had. The bride still wears a white dress and a veil, as if to say that she is still a virgin. The many words of the minister or priest and others are time warped, and if they were taken literally, one would conclude that the happy couple had never had any prior intimacy and were only just starting to dwell under the same roof.

What's really happened to the modern wedding, is that it has become a symbolic means by which a woman's "spiritual virginity," can be, however briefly, reinstated (as long as she's wearing the "pure white" wedding gown), as a precursor to being granted a license to have intimacy "the way God intended." As noted above, the pretension to a "new beginning" and "now, you are Mrs. So-and-so" are just symbolic ways of saying, "we looked the other way when you were having sex before, and living with a guy before, and even when you had a baby already, but *now*, we're saying it's OK. (Talk about forgiving and forgetting!) Now (and only now) are you legitimately sexually active. And seeing as how you have finally made your relationship OK in the eyes of God, the Government's and ours, we'll just pretend that you were both virgins up until now."

Just as when Great Grandma's sexual activity after marriage was "kinda sorta accepted" as an unavoidable reality but was never truly embraced until she had her first child, so now a couple's pre-marital intimacy is virtually denied and forgotten once they marry.

What Nature Has Brought Together

Unlike the Marriage Rite, which either denigrates natural love as "sinful lust," or at best, characterizes it as a shallow and temporary emotion that is bound to fade, the Love Celebration gives it full recognition and honor. It expresses confidence that love is an integral part of the human condition, and in no way something to be ashamed of. It affirms that having love is success for however long it lasts, whether for a few years or for a lifetime. It's a rite that says Nature knew what She was doing all along, and that trying to improve on natural love's "wanting-to-be together" is foolhardy. It's a rite that affirms the unity of the human mind and body in contrast to the Marriage Rite which dichotomizes human love, esteeming "spiritual love" and denigrating "fleshly lust." It's an exultation of the natural trust that grows out of the deep emotional empathy that regular sexual intimacy promotes and reinforces.

The notion of "making a commitment" is shunned entirely, and regarded no more desirable than (actually, quite as ridiculous as) "making a commitment" to stay friends with one's best friend, or to ask one's mother to make a legal contract to perform the duties of motherhood until she dies!

Depending on which state one lives in, and if it's even possible to cohabit at all without being automatically pressed into a legally binding marriage contract by virtue of common law provisions, the Love Celebration is very good way to provide a special time of recognition for the happy couple, perhaps just as they are about to move into their home together … without doing any damage to it.

In this sense, the Love Celebration can much better take its rightful place alongside other rites of passage as a way for one's family and friends and community to offer their support after a major change in life has taken place. This is why we have birthdays, funerals or coming of age rites such as the Latino quinsierra (or what is faintly seen in Christian confirmation ceremonies).

For those who are struggling to understand what a Love Celebration accomplishes, perhaps it might be helpful to compare it to the one rite of passage which is still practiced in some communities which is the feint remnant of the Pre-Marriage Era love celebrations—housewarmings. In many respects, the housewarming (which is usually a week or so after a couple moves into a new home) conveys many of the ideas behind the true Love Celebration, only with more emphasis on the couple's new house as opposed to their relationship. Still, it's a good time for friends, neighbors and family to come and officially welcome a new family to a community, bring a gift, bestow compliments and offer to be of service if there is ever any need for help.

10

The Benefits of Privatizing Marriage

o o o o o o o o o o o o o o o o o o o o o o o o o o o o o o o o

"But I don't need your protection!" said the small business owner to the mobster who had come to collect his 'monthly payment.' "Oh, is that right?" said the gangster, who then proceeded to smash every item in the front display window. "Alright, alright! No more. I'll pay. I'll … pay," said the small business man, trembling, as he handed over all that was in his register.

The Protection of All Protections

If you've ever seen a gangster movie, then you might be familiar with the term "protection racketeering." However, for those of you who've maybe heard the expression, but still don't quite get it, I'll try to briefly explain what it is.

"Protection" as it's used in the context of organized crime are the "dues," if you will, that small business owners are compelled to pay to a criminal organization that controls the area where the business is located. In return, the business receives protection (in theory anyway) from anyone who might try to burglarize, vandalize or defraud the owner … with the exception of the mobsters who are "protecting" them, of course. To a small degree, the arrangement is like the insurance contracts many businesses take out in the event of a fire or flood. Of course, there is a difference between taking out a legal insurance policy and paying the kind of "insurance money" that the local gangster collects from his "clients." Should you ever decide you want to switch to another legal insurance company or to do without legal insurance, you don't get your legs broken!

Fortunately, things have changed a lot since the mid-1800s when almost every business in large cities was compelled to join and support one gang or another as was dramatized in the Martin Scorsese film *Gangs of New York*. While organized criminal mobs still operate, they don't have quite as much influence as they used to thanks to many crack downs by state and federal authorities.

One of the federal laws which is often invoked to stop protection racketeering is called the RICO law, which stands for Racketeer Influenced and Corrupt Organizations, enacted in 1970. Nowadays, if some thug comes into your place of business without your solicitation, and claims that you are now subject to the "rights and responsibilities" of his turf, you have some recourse to get help … unless of course, that "thug" is your spouse's divorce attorney.

Now some may find it inappropriate to make an analogy between an organized criminal gang and the Marriage and Divorce Industries, but think about it. In both cases, we have people who are engaging in their own affairs—some more, some less, successfully than others—who are nevertheless compelled or pressured to submit to an organization of powerful people who, for all their words to the contrary, have no real concern for the people they are supposedly there to protect. In fact, in both cases, we find that the people who make up these systems of "protection" profit tremendously off of those who, in one way or another, only join because they are made to feel they have no other choice. Just like the criminally "protected" business, a couple in love who merely wishes to live together is compelled by some states to be legally married according to their common law provisions.

Common Law Racketeering

State laws change, and before we go on to try to summarize which states do what, let the reader understand, that one should always, always, always consult with a licensed family law attorney in the state where one abides, before cohabiting with someone in a sexual relationship. The reason is to make sure what one must avoid doing in order not to inadvertently fall under that state's common law provisions should they have any. The following, therefore, should in no way be regarded as legal or expert advice, but merely a lay person's best understanding of the Law.

There are about nine states (Alabama, Colorado, Kansas, Rhode Island, South Carolina, Iowa, Montana, Oklahoma, Texas and the District of Columbia) which recognize common-law marriages contracted within their borders.[159] We could make that ten if we count New Hampshire which has a limited form of common law marriage effective only at death, and eleven if we include Tennessee that has a doctrine of "estoppel to deny marriage."

Texas calls it "informal marriage," rather than Common Law Marriage. Under the Texas Family Code, an informal marriage can be established either by declaration (registering at the county courthouse without having a ceremony), or by meeting a 3-prong test showing evidence of (1) an agreement to be married; (2) cohabitation in Texas; and (3) representation to others that the parties are married. In 1995, a revision to the Texas law, added an evidentiary presumption that there was no marriage if no suit for proof of marriage is filed within two years of the date the parties separated and ceased living together.

In Utah, a marriage which is not conventionally solemnized is valid if a court or administrative order establishes that it arises out of a contract between two consenting parties who: (a) are capable of giving consent; (b) are legally capable of entering a solemnized marriage; (c) have cohabited; (d) mutually assume marital rights, duties, and obligations; and (e) who hold themselves out as and have acquired a uniform and general reputation as husband and wife. The determination or establishment of such a marriage must occur during the relationship or within one year following the termination of that relationship.

Otherwise, most states have abolished Common Law Marriage by statute because they recognized the similarity between forcing people into a legal agreement without their active consent as no less an abuse of power as racketeering. Common Law Marriage in these states is seen as encouraging fraud and condoning vice, debasing conventional Marriage, and as no longer necessary with increased access to clergy and justices of the peace.[160]

Cohabiting couples in the common law states have to be careful. Generally speaking, what gets them in trouble, i.e., "married," are two things: (1) cohabitation together with (2) "holding out." "Holding out" means that the parties tell the world that they are husband and wife through their conduct, such as the woman's assumption of the man's surname, filing a joint federal income tax return, etc. This means that mere cohabitation should never, by itself, rise to the level of constituting a marriage, but many disputes arise when facts (such as intentions of the parties or statements made to third parties) are in controversy.

Getting the Government Out of Our Bedrooms

In 1997, David Boaz, the Executive Vice President of a libertarian think tank called the Cato Institute, submitted a paper to an internet magazine called *Slate*, in which he made an eloquent case for privatizing marriage.[161] Shortly after the US Supreme Court ruled against the Constitutionality of anti-sodomy laws on November 13, 2003 in Lawrence and Garner v. Texas, the founding editor of Slate, Michael Kinsley, reiterated several of Boaz' original arguments for privatizing marriage, asking why not once and for all, "get the government out of our bedrooms."[162] The following year, in a statement to the US Senate in opposition to President Bush's Constitutional Amendment proposal to ban same sex marriage, Senator Mark Dayton said, "If my colleagues really do want to save marriage for now and posterity, turn it over to the authority of established religions."[163]

Whether or not Congress will ever seriously take up Mr. Boaz', Mr. Kinsley's, or Senator Dayton's proposals, the idea really makes sense. Privatization of Marriage would get the government out of the business of licensing intimate relationships. It would bring an end to the government deciding which unions are considered a "marriage," and which are not, and simply allow people to decide this question for themselves. Couples could proceed to get or not get whatever church or other private institution they choose to confer upon them whatever sanction they seek, be it "marriage" or a "sacred blessing of the universal Soul." Religious institutions could continue to be as broad or narrow as they see fit as far as whom they wish to marry in their churches, synagogues or temples. The state would no longer be involved, except only to provide that all people are treated equally before the Law.

To be sure, this would mean making some big adjustments. Many federal and state laws would have to be rewritten or reinterpreted in order to clarify whether a cohabitant of a sexual union might or might not be qualified to receive a break in taxes, have the right to visit a lover in a hospital, pick up a sick child belonging to a partner from day care or receive an inheritance. Some have argued that these changes would be so difficult to adjust to that it's not worth rocking the boat. However, society has had to adjust to many big changes in the past, that were anything but easy, but we did so anyway because it was for the better in the long run.

Think of what occurred after the Emancipation Proclamation which was the first legal attempt to end slavery in the Confederacy, the 19th Amendment which granted suffrage to all adult women, or the Civil Rights Act of 1964 which banned segregation in public places and institutions. Even today, our society continues to struggle with the many ripples these great stones of change caused after they landed on the pond of our society. The adjustment periods following these changes are always long and difficult for many to accept. Yet people of good reason accept that these changes were still the right thing to do.

Those who say that privatizing Marriage shouldn't be done because it too would have many far reaching effects fail to see that these changes are necessary if we are going to have a just society. When it comes to deciding which mutually consenting adults ought or ought not to have a sexual relationship and to make a home together, the only thing the Law should do is ensure that no institution, such as a business, school or hospital, discriminates against anyone on the basis of one's choice of a domestic, sexual partner, gay or straight.

In fact, what would be so bad if the whole concept of sexuality were excluded altogether? For example, were Marriage completely privatized, a company that previously provided insurance coverage only for "the legal spouse" of their employee could then extend its coverage to "one other adult that lives with the employee." It wouldn't matter if that person is a sexual partner of the same or different gender, an adult sibling or even a parent. If the other partner is in fact a part of the family, then why shouldn't they receive the same coverage as anyone else? What difference, for example, should it make to a corporation, if one of its employees is a single male who has one child and, instead of a female lover, it's his mother who lives with him and who helps care for the child and the home?

This is just one possible combination of what can, and what in millions of homes already does, constitute a family. Just because it doesn't represent a "traditional" family of one man and one woman in a sexual union who live together with their biological, minor children, they should not be discriminated against. The same principle should apply to an employee who has established a home with a cohabitant sexual partner. One should be able to designate whomever one pleases as the beneficiary of one's insurance coverage. The point being that not only one or two family structures should be supported and all others left out, but that *all* families be supported equally.

Domestic Discrimination

There are a number of situations where unmarried cohabitants (as well as gay/lesbian couples) are discriminated against. Unmarried partners are often excluded from rights to hospital visitation, tax breaks or exemptions from subpoena to testify against one's partner in a court of law, all of which are accorded to those who can and do play ball by legally marrying.[164] In essence, when a local government offers a marriage license, it is saying, "If you will procure this license, giving us, the State, the right to determine how long you shall have a recognized sexual relationship, you will receive in exchange the benefit of no longer being discriminated against ... when you pay your taxes, take out a loan, visit your mate in the hospital or apply for insurance coverage." Not too unlike the language used by the gangster who "offers protection" to a small business owner who is made to understand that there are severe consequences for not going along. It's really not a matter of the legally married getting a lot of nice benefits, but exemption from mistreatment when the State in particular and society in general shouldn't be mistreating anyone in the first place

When it comes to organized crime, we recognize how wrong it is for people who could not care less about those under their "protection," force them to accept it and pay for it … or else! By the same reasoning, the State should not be permitted to act in the same way toward people who love each other and wish to make a home together.

The Sky Won't Fall

If the idea of privatizing marriage seems like opening Pandora's Box, why not sit down for a moment to consider just what would be the consequences of our government finally opting out of the marriage business by envisioning the following future scenario.

You wake up one morning to hear some breaking news. The US Supreme Court has made a landmark ruling against the federal and state governments defining, licensing and regulating the institution of Marriage as violations of the Separation of Church and State and the Right to Privacy. The ruling effectively now requires that the government treat all domestic partnerships equally, regardless of their previous status. For the purposes of prohibiting discrimination before the Law, a domestic partnership will continue to include sexual unions, but will now be expanded to all family structures (like a grandparent living with her adult daughter who is helping to rear her minor child). Adults who wish to live together to share domestic responsibilities may do so at will. They may also separate at will, without any need to go to court, unless one or both parties choose to in the event of an unresolved dispute over child custody or division of property. Separating parents will still have access to family courts if they cannot agree on child custody issues (terms of support, visitation, etc.), and they may also file complaints in civil or small claims courts if there are disputes over separation of property. Otherwise, all rights and responsibilities previously extended only to legally recognized married partners will apply to any domestic partnership, without discrimination.

For example, a company that previously offered health insurance benefits only to an employee's spouse would be required to offer similar coverage to one domestic partner. Marriage would become a private matter, defined and entered into only as individuals see fit. Religious institutions would continue to expand, maintain or restrict their beliefs and rites about Marriage as they wish, but the unions they recognize or don't recognize as "married" would have no bearing on how they are viewed and treated before the Law.

As with so many other emancipations, a ruling like this one would probably frighten a lot of people, especially those who've been told over and over again that if any changes were made to the status quo, the sky would surely fall. But as the following days, weeks and months would pass, no doubt, most people would simply go on about their business and nothing bad at all would happen. Instead, they'd come to learn in time that tens of thousands of American families who came in many other shapes and sizes than the *Leave It To Beaver* version, were benefiting greatly.

In fact, the only group of people who would suffer at all from the change would be those who could no longer profit at the expense of separating partners, especially the avaricious predators of the Divorce Industry, who would suddenly find themselves looking for other means of employment! Perhaps Congress would appropriate a special education fund for unemployed divorce attorneys to pay for special training to help them switch to other specializations. As the $40 billion dollar a year Divorce Industry is effectively outlawed, perhaps our government would be able to ask taxpayers to help pay for the modest costs of this re-education fund because families who were previously plagued by the devastating costs of divorce proceedings could then afford it.

Something tells me, though, that the unemployed of the Divorce Industry wouldn't be getting much sympathy, and that they'd simply have to resign to getting a good, long taste of their own medicine.

11

Higamous Vs. Hogamous

o o o o o o o o o o o o o o o o o o o o o o o o o o o o o o o o o o o

"Hogamous higamous, man is polygamous, Higamous, hogamous, woman monogamous"

—Oft' quoted comment by William James on the fundamental difference between each gender's sexual nature

The Three Competing Sexual Instincts

Nature has endowed humans (and most other sexually reproducing species) with three sexual instincts. Each one works somewhat differently depending on one's gender and whether one is an Alpha or a Beta, but they are otherwise very well defined.

We might be tempted to think that under some natural circumstance they would all three be readily compatible with each other ... if only we knew what circumstance that might be. But alas, they're not. Instead, they tend to compete with each other, resulting in never ending sexual contests.

Nature had good reason, though, to create this competition. For the benefit of our species' survival and evolutionary advance, sexual contest was and continues to be a good thing.[165]

Of course, this "win" for the many comes at a cost to some individuals. For wherever there are winners, there are losers; success and survival are only possible alongside failure and extinction!

Before we examine these instinctive, sexual behaviors, let's first talk about the term "survival." We generally think of this term in reference to individual organisms or a species as a whole. But the term can also refer to the ongoing replication of certain genes. This may not sound very flattering to our proud human ears, but our genes are not so much the vehicle by which *we* evolved into a better surviving species, but it is we the individual organisms who are the vehicle *for the better survival of our genes*! In a very real sense, our brains, our bodies, our instincts, and our abilities were all designed by our genes in order to ensure that *they* replicate and carry on, one generation after another.

This principle of Nature becomes clear when we take notice of the many instances in which the survival of an organism is sacrificed in the interest of the genes of that organism. In fact, it's not at all unusual for an individual organism's life to be cut short for the sake of successfully reproducing the genes it carries. For example, a brightly colored male bird, by virtue of his brightly colored feathers, may attract more females, have more sex, and therefore, have more offspring. As far as the survival of his genes go, he's a big winner. That said, he might also die a lot sooner than a less brightly colored male who is not as easy to be seen by predators!

In the tree next door, there's a lonely male bird with pastel colored feathers. He just can't seem to get anywhere with the girl birds; they don't take notice of him. Ironically, neither do predators spot him so easily. So he ends up living a longer, if more solitary life. One might say he's the better survivor, but only in terms of his individual longevity. In the game of Reproductive Success, though, what matters is who leaves behind the greater number of genes in succeeding generations. If it comes down to a choice between living longer or spreading one's seed farther, the latter objective is preferred.

The winners in the game, then, are those who pass their genes on, "losers" are those who don't. To be a "good gene" in this game, means being the kind that produces or contributes to traits that lead to better adaptation to the environment in which the organism carrying them lives, at least long enough and well enough to pass his or her genes on. And what better way to sort out the better or more adaptive genes from the mediocre than through competition.

Had there been no Natural Selection, had there been no "Survival of the Fittest," had no "Genetic Olympics" ever been staged, our most ancient, pre-hominid ancestors would have never evolved and adapted to become who we are. In fact, life as we know it, in any form, may have never lasted longer than the first living cells. As we keep this primary directive of our genes in mind for the rest of this study, the overall purpose of the sexual behaviors our genes drive us to—much as they often seem to be at odds with one another—begin to make more sense.

So just what are these three competing sexual instincts? I answer this question in the following pages, first in capsulated form with breakdowns for the differences and similarities of each gender. Then, I go on into more detail. The first one is often referred to as a biological drive in that it so directly moves us to the act of intercourse. The second is also a drive in the broader sense of the term, but because it isn't as immediately compelling as having sex, we tend to think of it more as a "longing." The third instinct is a bit different in that it is a *reaction*, but no less instinctively compelling than the first two. Before we start, I ask the reader to be patient in coming to grips with what is likely, at first, to look like a jumbled mess of explanations for human sexual behavior, almost like a pile of jigsaw puzzle pieces. As we slowly fit them together, though, hopefully a clear picture will emerge.

For males:

Instinct One is the desire to copulate with as many females as are available, preferring the most attractive, but with the emphasis on quantity. The goal—to spread one's seed as far and wide as possible.

Instinct Two is to find love; the desire to form relationships with the most attractive female(s) available that he can accommodate (in terms of resources, time, etc.).

Instinct Three is to be jealous; to be intolerant of any other males copulating with his (current or candidate) relationship partner(s)if he has one (or more).

Next, notice the similarity, as well as the differences.

For females:

Instinct One is the desire to copulate with the most attractive male available.[166] She may have sex with many males, but only for the purpose of sorting out who is of the best quality.[167] The goal—become pregnant by the best male available.

Instinct Two is to find love; to desire to form a relationship with the best male available who can accommodate her (in terms of resources, time, etc.).

Instinct Three is to be jealous; to be intolerant of any extra-relationship female(s) copulating with her (current or candidate) relationship partner.

Those things that make a female attractive to a male tend to be conspicuous characteristics that signal a greater likelihood of reproductive success for him. That which most "turns a man on" are the easily visible traits most common to a healthy, young, Alpha Woman who is best suited to give birth—an hourglass figure, firm breasts, symmetrical facial features, etc.

The male investment in reproduction is relatively low (sperm is metabolically cheap to make, and a man's direct role in fathering takes only a few minutes). Therefore, he doesn't need to be very discriminating and take a lot of time evaluating his potential partner—he has plenty (of sperm) to spend, so a quick glance will do. As long as a woman appears to have the basic requirements—signs she is healthy and young enough to get pregnant, give live birth and care for a child—his Sexual Attraction Switch will instantly flip to the "on" position almost as soon as he sees her.[168]

Those things that make a male attractive to a female, on the other hand, tend to be *in*conspicuous characteristics that signal a greater likelihood of reproductive success for her. That which most "turns a woman on" are the less visible, inward traits most common to a healthy, strong, Alpha Male—dominance, confidence, self-sufficiency, etc.

Since the female investment in reproduction is relatively high (eggs are metabolically expensive to make, and her direct role in mothering takes about four years—the world average time between pregnancy and weaning), she needs to be discriminating and to take time to evaluate her potential partner. She's on a "limited budget," and therefore, she needs to interact with a potential partner first. During this interaction, the more she perceives he has the traits of an Alpha—the signs indicating he has genetically superior sperm and is healthy, dominant and strong enough to successfully protect and provide for her and the child—the more her Sexual Attraction Dial is gradually turned to the "on" position.[169]

After first copulating with a female, regardless of how attractive she is, males can find other females attractive. If a relationship doesn't form, this attraction to others can begin almost immediately after having sex. However, if they form a relationship, attraction to others wanes considerably … for at least a few weeks. Why?

Well, it's no accident that when a man falls "madly in love"—resulting in his desire focusing solely on one woman—it happens to last only long enough to get her pregnant, for about a month or so on average.[170] For a brief time, no other woman gets his attention. As far as his direct role in reproductive success is concerned, his job is short, which explains why a man is monogamous—in mind and heart, as well as in deed—only for a short while.

After first copulating with a male, depending on how attractive he is (once again, we're not just talking about looks here), females can also soon find other males attractive. If she perceives that a relationship is not possible, or that she can find a better partner with whom to copulate, she can also move on, just as males can.[171] However, if there appears to be no better partner available and a relationship is formed, attraction to others wanes considerably … but in her case, for at least a few *years*! Why?

Well, it's no accident that when a woman falls in love—resulting in her desire focusing solely on one man—it happens to last, on average, long enough for her to get pregnant, give birth and wean a child. Her direct involvement in reproductive success is lengthy, which explains why it takes much longer before other guys become a temptation. A woman, therefore, is truly monogamous—in mind and heart, as well as in deed—for a quite a while, but not for a lifetime.

Males don't tolerate other males copulating with their female relationship partner(s). But the more attractive Alpha Males don't have to worry about it, because their females are unlikely to find other males attractive. Beta males, though, must actively mate guard to prevent other males from copulating with their partners. Even so, Alpha Males will often succeed in getting past their defenses.

Females tend not to tolerate other extra-relationship females copulating with their male mate. But the more attractive Alpha Females in a bond with a Beta male don't have to worry about it very much, because he is unlikely to be attractive to other females. In the rare situations where a Beta female pair bonds with an Alpha Male, she must actively mate guard to prevent other females from copulating with her relationship partner.[172] Even so, Alpha Males will often gallivant outside of her defenses to copulate with other females.

Needless to say, the more Beta one is, male or female, the less likely one is to pair bond with an Alpha in the first place. And even when Betas do succeed in starting a relationship with an Alpha, they are more likely to be cuckolded as well as to eventually be replaced by someone better, that is to say, more Alpha.

Males will generally tolerate other males copulating with those females with whom they've already copulated if afterwards they don't form (or are unlikely to form) a relationship. However, the level of toleration males have for each other while seeking casual copulations is in proportion to the number and quality of females available, the time the males have to share between them, and where they individually fall on the Alpha-Beta Scale.

Gallivanting Alphas will naturally be more successful than their Beta counterparts in seducing females, especially the more attractive ones. Beta males might wish they were "getting as many of the pretty girls" that an Alpha does, but they'll humbly step aside and watch Alphas "work" with admiration. They may envy Alphas, but their envy is kept in check as long as they are getting their "minimum requirement" of getting one partner out of whomever is left, usually by pairing with a Beta female.

Females in a harem will generally tolerate each other copulating with their harem keeper as long as each one has the clear perception that she's reached a maximum place in her relationship with him.[173] Given that the Alpha Male never signals to her that she can have more, i.e., to have him (and all he does and provides for her) all to herself, she'll be more focused on how high a level she's already achieved rather than on what more might be had. As far as her instincts are concerned, her toleration for sharing will remain in effect indefinitely, because it's a small price to pay in exchange for what she and her children are getting in return—an adequate share of his resources (which is likely a lot more than the most any one Beta male could provide), along with his superior DNA, status and protection.

Whatever an "adequate" share among the females within a harem (or for a female candidate to join a harem) consists of, doesn't mean they will all get equal amounts. Their sense of what they "deserve" to get is also in proportion to where they individually fall on the Alpha-Beta Scale. Alpha harem members will naturally get more attention and resources than her Alpha Minus or Beta counterparts. Beta harem members might wish they were getting as much of the resources and attention the "favorites" do, but they humbly step aside and watch with admiration as the Alpha Female(s) receive greater proportions. They may envy the Alpha Females, but their envy is kept in check as long as they feel they are getting their "minimum requirements" from what is left of the Alpha's resources and attention.[174]

The very idea that there was little to no natural jealousy among the women of a harem strikes us moderns as inconceivable. But this is probably because our understanding of polygyny is limited. Harem keeping has not been tolerated in Western society for hundreds of years, and is generally fathomed only to the depth of its role in the oppression following the Agricultural Revolution. However, polygyny operated in a much different way before the time when women were bought and sold to whomever could afford them.

Before the plow, women joined harems of their own free will, and harem keepers took only a handful of them, so the remaining males and females could at least find one person to pair bond with. We will address this distinction in detail later on. For now, let's just try to get a glimpse of how voluntary polygyny is actually more than possible, in spite of what we might think are natural obstacles to it, by observing a very telling sexual behavior among modern, single women.

After copulating with an Alpha Male, even modern women will tolerate his other dalliances, as long as it's very clear that a relationship with him is out of the question. This happens more frequently than we might think because most men will indeed do things that "send a woman into relationship mode" even on or before their first date. Some however, know not to do this if they are single and want to stay that way. Others, usually because of their fame or powerful status, are in a position where it's already unlikely a woman will expect to get him all to herself, as is normal for the "groupies" who solicit sex from rock stars, sports figures, or political leaders.

In rare cases—such as with the famous founder of Playboy magazine, Hugh Hefner, who always seems to have six or seven girlfriends at a time living with him—a prominent male can defy the modern social norm of having only one "wife" and manage to have a de facto harem … as long as he calls them all his "girlfriends."

But again, even a sex king like Hefner has to make it very plain to each woman he invites to live with him in his mansion that she can never have him all to herself. If so, the same, primitive instinct remains at work—the female is not going to become jealous of her "sister girlfriends" because she's moved ahead by having gotten the superior genes and resources of an Alpha Male, and also because she perceives she's gone as far as she can.

For a male, "having it all" means having sex with a variety of Alpha Females on an ongoing basis, both inside and outside of a harem. Normally, only an Alpha Male has any chance at succeeding at this because he can both attract and keep Alpha Female partners while naturally suppressing their (Instinct Three) "Jealousy Gene."

At this point, some might justifiably ask, "Why should Nature have inclined Alpha Males to bother at all with relationships if it was so relatively easy for them to get all the sex they wanted from as many females as they wanted? Why not just let Beta males do the entirety of the relationship thing, pay all the bills, baby-sit and drive the kids to the soccer games, freeing up the Alphas to get what they want … and leave?"

The fact is many Alphas do steer clear of relationships and refrain from "getting tied down." They'll react with ambivalence to one woman after another whom the average Beta male would only die to get a chance to get and keep if only he could get any one to give him the time of day. When a Beta male hears an Alpha mention he quit calling a certain, attractive woman after sleeping with her a few times, he's likely to react saying, "What? You quit calling her! She is such a babe! I would do anything to go out with a girl like that. If I ever had her, I'd do anything to keep her." Little does the Beta male know, though, that it's his very I'd-do-anything-to-keep-her attitude that runs all the "babes" off to begin with!

Even more mysterious to the Beta male is how the Alpha Male's I-could-not-care-less attitude has a way of attracting so many women to him. Alphas can spend many years of their life span going from one bed to another. They can also accrue a number of women into a harem, but they can rarely "settle down" with one mate without jeopardizing their Alpha status.

Yes, it would seem that Alpha Males are only temporarily inclined to have sex with one woman, even those who, to most other men, would be their dream, pair-bond mate. But the Alpha will quickly lose interest in one "dream girl" after another and move on. That said, every now and then, even Alphas will take a special interest in certain females, usually the "cream of the crop," the Alpha Females, and invite them into a relationship. How can this make sense if the male's primary directive is to spread his seed as far and wide as possible? Why slow down?

Perhaps another illustration will help. This one is rather imperfect in that I'm not trying to imply anything villainous about Alpha men (though certainly some might judge them so). So here goes: In just about every action movie where a hero is warring against some evil genius heading a crime organization, the head villain sends numerous henchmen to do away with the hero, only to see one after another fail. Finally, he exclaims, "I see I'm going to have to take care of this myself." After which, the climax of the story comes down to a duel.

Somewhat similarly, an Alpha Male normally expends a lot of his sperm upon a lot of women with little worry that the outcome might be jeopardized. (Remember now, to set aside modern concerns for contracting sexually transmitted diseases or having children out of wedlock, as we're talking about instincts that developed millions of years ago when disease served to eradicate the weak and the more children conceived, the better). If he has sex with a girl that was "Alpha enough," his moderate investment of a little bit of time and a squirt of semen, is adequate. She might produce an Alpha Minus child, so he's getting what he "paid for."

But it's a whole different story when a female comes along who is a "slam dunk" Alpha—at least, one who is very Alpha to him. He is then piqued by a different kind of desire; he suddenly begins to think of her as "a keeper."

This is the Alpha Male's version of selectivity. Most of the women he will seduce are, to him, worth only the relatively small effort and expense of a casual sexual encounter or a brief fling at the most. But when a truly Alpha Female comes along, he's no longer content to leave things to chance, even if she has a dedicated Beta male pair bonded to her who would gladly help her raise their Alpha love child (if only unwittingly). The Alpha Male, like the head villain who's finally met his match, is going to "see to things himself this time."

Diverting from his usual strategy of "loving and leaving," to keep, well, a keeper, would especially be true when Alpha Females are relatively hard to come by. Why chance letting only a Beta male be her protector and provider, and take the chance that their Alpha child might perish? When the odds are pretty good that any children fathered and mothered by Alphas will also be Alphas, then it makes sense to go the extra mile and directly help care for them. The next thing ya know, the Alpha Male's told her she can move into the harem, and the poor Beta male who'd been trying to make her happy for years is left all alone.

From the Alpha Male's perspective, inviting a woman into his home means he is making a larger investment in his reproductive success. In blunt (and yes, not very romantic) terms, when an Alpha Male finds certain females to be the very best available, it becomes worth his while to take a more personal interest in assuring the outcome of having deposited his seed in them.

During most of his copulations, if he perceives the lady he's seduced is not quite an Alpha, he's already invested as much of his time, energy and metabolic produce to match the best possible outcome—a child who is somewhere between an Alpha and a Beta. However, if he happens upon a very special Alpha Female, it behooves him to "add some insurance" to the deal. Evolutionary pressure, then, has favored those Alpha Males who were inclined to develop a deep, emotional attachment with Alpha Females, to not only desire them for sex, but to fall in love with them.

Though we tend to equate "true love" with monogamy, we need to remind ourselves that this equation is man made. Nature's priority was not to make sure all men and all women had fair and equal sized numbers of lovers. The reason was so those who have the most favorable genetic combination would be more likely to copulate and achieve pregnancies, and have children who would survive birth, be better protected through infancy, and grow up to pass their more adaptive genes to succeeding generations.

We also have to keep in mind that we're not talking about a modern situation where even "super stud guys" have essentially adopted the *Alpha Female Strategy*, and will suddenly forsake all others because he's finally found "The One." Not so oddly, once we understand what's really going on, even when modern Alpha Males try as they might to submit to the cultural norms of modern society to be monogamous, they often end up breaking the rules. This is because the natural instinct for the Alpha Male is to take and keep an Alpha Female and make her a permanent mate … but *only in addition to other mates in a harem*, and on top of any other dalliances he may continue to engage in on the side.

Beta males, on the other hand, are fortunate if they can get even one female to pair bond with them, and even then, only by costly compensation. To have more than one sex partner, usually requires wealth, deceit or both. For example, there are some societies (as in certain Moslem countries) where well-to-do men can buy their way into polygyny—but at the expense of all the other not-so-wealthy males and all the other females. In societies that insist on ostensible monogamy (as in the US), well-to-do Beta men might have a variety of extra-marital sex partners if they're willing to share their wealth (with call girls or girlfriends "kept on the side"), all the while keeping their wives in the dark. However, take away the compensation, or reveal that the Beta male has no intention of ever replacing his wife with his girlfriend (though Alpha Males get away with this all the time), and such de facto polygyny falls apart.

For a female, it would seem that "having it all" means having an exclusive, sexual relationship with an Alpha Male. Normally, only Alpha Females succeed at this because they can so attract an Alpha Male, he is willing to not only have sex with her, but invite her into a relationship. That's two out of three, but how to get him to be exclusively hers? Ah. Now we come to the proverbial $64,000.00 question!

The Test of the Quest

She may try to advance to an exclusive relationship if there appears to be an opportunity, but then comes the great irony of the Alpha-Beta Paradox—whenever she achieves this exclusivity, it signal's a Beta tendency on the part of the hitherto perceived Alpha Male! Counter-intuitive as it may seem (and such a mystery to the minds of so many men), the female's quest for a monogamous relationship with "The One," turns out to be as illusive as finding the Holy Grail or reaching a water mirage in the desert. Just as she seems to have it in her grasp ... it slips away and disappears. If he does abandon all other women just for her, he begins to appear very differently to her. The strong, dominating and elevated Alpha she was after so eagerly before, now that she has him, has become like so many other Beta men.

On the other hand, if he remains steadfast and keeps his harem and other love interests, is she therefore denied having it all? Is this some cruel trick of Mother Nature to punish women, on the order of the legendary Sisyphus (who had to spend all eternity in Hades rolling a huge rock up a hill, only to get almost to the top and then fall back down to the bottom and have to start again) by making them ever loyal to men who are always one step away from being entirely theirs?

As it turns out, there actually is a good reason behind the contradiction of a woman either 1) being very attracted to a man she can never get "to commit" and 2) the sudden loss of interest she begins to feel should she finally succeed in getting him all to herself. The problem lies in the confusion between that which is sought for but never found in a quest (the elusive Grail), and the attainable value of the quest itself (a means of proving one's valor). Here again, we see Nature pulling a fast one, but for a purpose.

The Quest for The One (just like the Quest for the Grail) actually serves a practical function all on its own—*as a test*! The purpose of the test is to find out if the male she perceives to be an Alpha, really is. Whenever there is any question as to the Alpha Male's status, the Alpha Female joined to him is at the ready to test him. And one of the best ways to make him prove his worth, is to see if she can get him all to herself.

This is a classic case where instinct and reason collide head on. In the front of her mind, perhaps she wants him to capitulate, but somewhere deep in the back of her brain, where her powerful instinctive desires are at work, she "hopes" he won't! Sounds pretty convoluted, doesn't it? Not to Mother Nature, though.

The woman who, after testing a man, finds that he holds his position, becomes more desirable to her than ever before. The man who proves to be "in demand" by other females, who is a "pro" at seduction and who remains a "sexual conqueror" will actually be all the more appealing to her. The fact that other women remain in direct competition with her for his affections, makes her more, not less, attracted to him.

Should she, however, ever manage to "reel him in," it only means that he's failed the test. He is no longer such a "stud," no longer the one to be competed for. To the degree he begins to restrict his affections only to her, she finds herself losing attraction for him.

So, what does "getting it all" really mean for women? Odd as it may seem, for the female, it's the *anticipation* of her man's undivided affection that is far more appealing than actually getting it.

Wow, that was such an important point, I think it's well worth repeating. For a woman, her anticipation of getting what she's after is what makes her feel so good.

Ironically, on the other side of the Alpha-Beta Paradox coin, it is Beta male and female couples who are much more likely to have and maintain a monogamous relationship, especially if they each perceive the other to be an Alpha! Even then, this usually happens only in societies that heavily enforce monogamy.

The Paradox comes down to this—the kind of partner who is most likely to naturally inspire the fidelity of a mate, an Alpha, is also the kind of partner most likely to attract other partners, making it more likely for the Alpha to stray. "Getting it all," therefore, is rare, for either gender, and when it does happen, it's usually a one-sided affair.[175]

It's nearly impossible for males and females to get all they want at the same time, within the same society. More frequent is the experience of suppressing at least one of the three main sexual instincts, even though suppressing any one of these instincts is also very hard to do.

Unionizing for a Better Share ... of Women

It's no surprise that women would favor monogamy, at least in the form of ostensible pair bonds for a few years at a time. They've little to gain from having more than one male cohabitant at a time in terms of their potential for reproductive success. They can only become pregnant by one man's sperm. Regardless of how many men they've been with sexually, once they're carrying a child, and as long as the father was the best male available, to go for more male partners after that makes no sense at all, at least until the child is weaned.

For men, it's a different story. We've alluded to it a number of times, but let's take some space to figure out why *men* would rally around the cause of monogamy. At first glance, it makes no sense that they would, not in terms of their primitive instinct to spread their seed as far and wide as possible.

Men are bound to lose when it comes to restricting themselves to one female as far as their individual reproductive success goes. Their investment is low, as has been noted, and so restricting themselves to only one woman only means less children. Males who do so are contradicting their most powerful urges. Nevertheless, we see many, perhaps most men, bringing as much pressure to bear as possible on other men to prevent them from spreading their seed beyond one womb (regardless of how effective or ineffective that pressure is). Why?

The answer is found when we consider that this pressure is not really coming from *all men*. The fact is that when men are found calling on other men to be faithful to only one woman, it is a charge leveled specifically at Alpha Males, or at least, those men who are today's version of the Alpha, by virtue of their position, status and wealth in society. Even more telling is that it is almost always Beta males who advocate for monogamy!

It's easier for us to understand why Beta females might object to harem keeping and philandering for their being so often left out of the Alpha Male's league. But why in the world should Beta males be so insistent on imposing or pressuring Alpha Males into monogamy, especially when we consider that they are just as desirous of getting more than one female as are Alphas?

To help us understand what's going on here, let's look once more at the union labor movement for a helpful analogy. About 200 years ago, poorly paid workers began to organize for the purpose of extracting some concessions from the wealthy who owned almost all companies, and who kept almost all the wealth those companies produced. Much as they might have personally wished and wanted and fantasized about themselves being wealthy, the workers understood that, in the real world, they were not likely to ever have the kind of wealth that the business owners they worked for had. But they had had enough of those few bourgeoisie keeping almost all the wealth to themselves, and leaving only a pittance for the many who had done the work in the first place. By banning together and striking when necessary, they did in time, pressure big business owners into allowing for a greater share of their companies' success if, admittedly, they continue to this day to keep most of their businesses' profits. The unions were formed, not because workers had no desire to ever be wealthy, but to keep the wealthy from keeping *all* the wealth for themselves.

Likewise, long before any labor union movement came along, there was another movement of a similar nature made up of the men who had been denied all but the "leftover females," because the Alpha-like princes, kings and sultans were taking all the desirable women available in terms of youth and beauty. Men of lower sexual status had finally had enough, and banned together to insist that they at least get a better share of better women.

Before this, it wasn't at all uncommon for elite men to keep taking as many of the youngest and prettiest women they could afford, even well into their old age. There's a very interesting example of this practice in the first chapter of the Old Testament book of First Kings. We read that King David, the same king who had already years before taken the beautiful Bathsheba, the wife of one of his most loyal military leaders, has now grown so old and frail that his body can no longer stay warm at night. So what to do? His servants get the idea to find a beautiful, young virgin to sleep with him, supposedly, "just to keep him warm." Why none of the many wives he already had couldn't have kept him warm, or a bigger fireplace or more blankets for that matter, is not explained. Most likely, the reason is because this was a mere cover story.

The servants made sure to find, not the woman who had the highest bodily metabolism, but the most "fair damsel … throughout the coasts of Israel" (verse 3). Translation? They got one of the hottest, young babes in the land, a certain Abishag. Oddly though, the short mention of this last young woman to come into King David's life ends with the disclaimer, "And the damsel was very fair, and cherished the king, and ministered to him: but the king knew her not" (verse 4). In other words, he never had intercourse with her.

In reality, King David's problem was impotence, and his servants thought to blame the problem on his aging wives' inability to get him aroused. Unfortunately, not even the young and beautiful Abishag, who was apparently very fond of the old king, and did what she could, was not enough. Rather than let the word get out that the king had what is today known as "erectile disfunction"—a very bad omen in times when the king's virility, or lack thereof, was taken as a symbol for how happy God or the gods were with the nation as a whole—they cooked up an explanation (and a rather lame one at that) for why the wedding of Abishag to David was never intended to be consummated.

What really makes this story interesting, though, is what it doesn't say, for at no point is there any question as to why an old king needed to marry such a young, beautiful girl, and add her onto all the other wives he already had. But the day finally came when even powerful rulers could no longer freely exercise unlimited power and have unlimited sexual access to all the quality women.

We can go back to the days of the Roman Republic to see how limiting powerful men from taking all the desirable women ran side-by-side with the slow progress toward the kind of government which put other limits on otherwise all powerful rulers. By the time of Rome's founding, most nations were ruled by kings who took full advantage of their power, meaning among other things, acquiring large harems, often numbering in the hundreds, sometimes even the thousands. Harems were a status symbol as well as the ultimate privilege of a king. But as we'll see in a moment, they served a very practical function in terms of securing their control over everyone else.

Though by no means a monogamous society, the Roman Republic was different. Instead of having one, great king, their government was organized around a Senate where political power was more spread out. Sure enough, one way Roman Law kept any one man from ever ascending to a king-like status, was the restriction that a citizen have no more than one, legitimate heir-producing wife at a time.

Let's be clear. The reason why Roman Law, at least nominally, barred polygamy, wasn't to elevate the status of women or to clamp down on sexual promiscuity. The ban was part of a larger effort to prevent men of wealth and influence from expanding their political power over everyone else by means of a large posterity. Kings got a real nice extra benefit from having hundreds of beautiful, young wives ... besides the obvious recreational one—hundreds of children who could be married off to others *in exchange for their loyalty!*

Roman men were not at all adverse to getting a lot of sex, from a lot of women. A free man could have all the sex he wished with concubines, prostitutes (assuming he could afford it) and even with the wives of other men on certain occasions. But they were very concerned about any one man using formal sexual unions as a means to taking power! By limiting marriage (i.e., the purchase of a woman for breeding a recognized heir) to one woman, the Romans made sure no one man would ever take *all* the desirable women for himself, and even more importantly, ensured they would not end up with a king who would undermine their republic. Even when the Republic finally gave way to imperial rule by the Caesars, they too were required by the sheer force of hundreds of years of tradition—if only a façade as far as the actual number of their sex partners—to have just one wife.

It was, therefore, largely in the context of a power struggle between patricians and aspiring rulers that Beta men later on joined forces with the Church to insist on monogamy. In a very real sense, they had formed a sexual mating union. This union has never really leveled the playing field completely, as we know that even today, wealthy, powerful and famous men, still get a disproportionately higher percentage of beautiful women … and more of them. Still, the "UBA" (Union of Beta Males) has made it so that Alphas can't get them all.

Take a close look at the men who rally the most behind the cause of imposing monogamy and we see that these are the kind of men who find it all they can do just to get one woman—Betas. So they have nothing to lose and relatively more to gain by doing all they can to bring pressures upon those who would otherwise "take all the good ones," and leave them either with none to choose from, or at best, only what's left—those who aren't young, healthy and attractive. In a society like the US, where there is also particular social and religious pressure brought upon Alphas to restrict them to one, or a few sexual partners at the most, a Beta has a much better chance, or so he might perceive, of at least getting a higher quality woman; maybe he can even aspire to swaying an Alpha Female to form a pair bond with him.

Why "Sluts" Are Not Really Promiscuous

While many might agree that most women are looking for a relationship with only one man, or "Mr. Right," some object to the idea that all women do so. It would, at first, seem logical that if there's any truth to the idea that men cheat more than women, that they must be committing their adulteries with a minority of women who are so promiscuous, that they can make up for the larger percentage of women who don't cheat. Take actress Kim Catrell's character Samantha from the popular HBO television series *Sex and the City*. Like any male playboy, she gave every indication, at least until the final few episodes, that she was only interested in sex for its recreational value. She was going from one bed to another, sometimes more than one, on every episode. Do such women truly exist? If not, then the character might not have had much entertainment appeal.

Certainly, we all know about certain girls that have "a reputation" for being "loose," or who are thought to be, to use the more vulgar aspersion, "sluts." Assuming for a moment, then, that there are at least some women who have a lot of sexual partners, and who at least appear to be very promiscuous, is it really accurate to say that they behave this way for the same reason men would? The answer I propose is "No."

I believe the longing within all females to form a relationship with an Alpha Male is so strong, that even when some women engage in what appears, on the surface, to be "headlong abandon to physical lust," they are, in fact, only engaging in the same general competitive process that most women use, consciously or unconsciously, to find The One. The only difference is that, rather than "screen testing" most men *before* having sex with them, they will test them in bed! So called sluts, are just as selective as the "chaste;" both are setting up male competition to determine an eventual winner. The only difference is the location of the contest arena—inside her vagina.

As a matter of fact, it's really not quite correct to call these women "promiscuous," which implies no sexual discrimination, because even they are still attempting to discriminate whether one man is more Alpha than another ... if only *after* they've entered her vagina. Those women who seem more prone to "fool all around" are still applying the same principle female mating strategy that other women, who seem more "chaste," are using.

The problem for both "chaste" and "unchaste" women, who are all trying to find The One, is when there is no clear answer who he might be. There might, for instance, appear to be a number of men within a given woman's social circles who all seem to be Alphas, at first. She might even find herself feeling irresistibly attracted to one of them, long enough to bed with him, only to watch him morph afterwards into a major Beta! Many women who seem to be "screwing every guy in town," are merely those who, time and again, have found a man who seems to have the qualities she's really looking for, only to wake up with him a day, a week or a month later, wondering how she could have fallen for such a Beta in Alpha's clothing.[176]

This is not to deny that there are some women who have given up on finding Mr. Right, and though they might wish to find him, have concluded "all the good ones are taken," and settle for casual sex only. Just because their deepest want is thwarted, though, doesn't mean it isn't there. It's very similar to the resignation of the many men who, deep within themselves, envy the Alpha Male who can walk into any bar on any day of the week, and be confident of leaving with a woman on his arm. They, too, fantasize about being such a "macho man," but settle for the modicum of sexual fulfillment they get from their wives. In both cases, their outward behavior suggests they've embraced the primary strategies of the opposite sex, but somewhere deep inside, they still long for the same thing anyone else of their gender wants.

Sometimes, even after years of suppression, that inner longing manifests itself. Once in a while, a man who's been in an unhappy marriage for years, will find a way to break out and rediscover his "Mojo," and become quite the "stud" after years of being sexually faithful to one woman, but unhappy. Likewise, every now and then, one hears about a woman who was the "tramp of the town" who one day finally meets "the right man," settles down, and never strays again.

These exceptions are evidence that, even in those cases where the principle sexual goal (for that person's gender) is all but a feint memory of a long ago dream, it can be revived. The problem, of course, is that each gender's idea of "living the dream" conflicts with the other's. How in the world, for example, would the former tramp and the former, unhappy husband ever find a way to meet up and both be happy at the same time? It would seem that William James was pretty close to being right after all.

But there have been attempts by human societies in the past to find some kind of middle ground that may not have been perfect, but did to some degree satisfy the primary, sexual objective of both men and women simultaneously. Believe it or not, I refer here to polygyny or to use the more common term—polygamy.

Harem Scarem!

While writing this book, I wondered whether including a discussion on polygyny was worth the risk of upsetting certain people at the mere mention of the subject apart from condemning it as a dastardly evil. "Some might misconstrue my intentions," I thought. But in the end, I felt that it was absolutely necessary.

The fact is, our modern notion of monogamous unions as the "model" sexual behavior is the exception, not the rule, of human history. For most of that history, the ideal sexual arrangement—and I mean ideal for *both* genders—was for men to have or women to join a polygynous family if at all possible![177]

If we modern men and women are ever going to have happy, enduring sexual relationships, it behooves us to at least understand why this mating strategy endured as long as it did, whom it worked for (Don't jump to conclusions just yet!) and why.

In early agricultural times, most societies favored polygyny as the ideal family structure, but not in a natural way. Women couldn't normally choose whom they wanted to have a relationship with. They were bought and sold to whomever could afford them, and it didn't matter if she found her male owner attractive or not, nor if she loved him or not. It was almost certain that she would have to contend with suppressing the female version of Instinct One, as well as Two. Unless a woman was fortunate enough to have been purchased by an Alpha, she was likely discontent, even if she and her children were well provided for. She would naturally, therefore, be predisposed to committing adultery. This instinct was so powerful that it often didn't matter that she knew what severe punishments awaited if her adultery were to be discovered. She couldn't help but throw herself at any Alpha that might come along.[178]

And it wasn't just the women who usually got a raw deal out of polygamy at this time. Though the involuntary sexual servitude in harems benefited wealthy men, most men could barely afford to purchase one wife. And even then, they could only choose from among those not already snapped up by the rich and powerful.

It shouldn't be surprising then, to learn that involuntary polygyny, the sexual slave trade and severe social punishments for purchased women who strayed, went hand-in-hand with the institution of prostitution. Since the male's primary sexual directive was the same for the rich, poor and in between, men who couldn't afford to "buy a whole cow" often resorted to "paying for one cup of milk at a time." For the Beta males who were not themselves enslaved, occasional dalliances with a prostitute were as close as he could ever come (pardon the pun) to fulfilling the male's natural primary directive.

In start contrast, Pre-Agricultural societies dealt with our three conflicting sexual instincts very differently. They were less intolerant of extra-relationship sex, and had developed a sexual balancing act that maintained community cohesion. And voluntary polygyny played an important role in achieving it.

Most adults of the Hunting and Gathering Era had socially monogamous relationships, and only a minority belonged to polygynous families. At the same time, though, both men and women would venture outside of their relationships for sex with others, but with relatively less serious, adverse consequences. For example, indulgences of Instinct One by males were largely tolerated as long as they were discreet about it in the case of extra-pair copulations. Or if a man had more than one female mate, he could philander all he wanted as long as no one in the harem was being denied an adequate amount of resources, time and attention for themselves and their children. When females went outside of their relationships for sex, they were not punished as severely when discovered by their ostensible male partner. In fact, they were chastened more for having been discovered than for committing the act itself. Though not all men could attract women enough to have them volunteer to share his affections simultaneously, those who did were far from being understood as cruel oppressors. The most attractive women wanted to be with the most attractive men, and that normally meant a man who already had others at his side.

Today, this seems hard to believe. One reason many find non-monogamy so difficult to accept is the influence of Christianity in the last millennia upon so many societies around the world. However, once we look beyond the influence of the Church, we find that most other cultures regarded polygyny and pre-marital and extra-marital sex quite differently.

Studies of societies around the world reveal that only a minority held out monogamy as the only socially acceptable sexual behavior. Anthropologist C.S. Ford and psychologist Frank Beach studied 185 societies and found that only 29, or 16%, formally restricted their members to monogamy. Of that 16%, only a third, just over 5%, wholly disapproved of premarital or extramarital sex. The same study also showed that 154 societies, 83%, socially approved of men having two or more simultaneous relationships or polygyny. This confirmed the results of an earlier study by G.P. Murdock who found that, of 238 societies around the world, only 43, or 18%, regarded monogamy as the only acceptable mating system.[179]

Moreover, even a brief examination of certain human, physical characteristics reveals a high correlation with the same characteristics of other species which are known to be polygynous. The fact that men are, on average, larger and stronger than women (a phenomenon known as "dimorphism"), the fact that women enter puberty earlier than men (a phenomenon known as "sexual bimaturism"), the fact that human males have large testes relative to their size and weight, and the fact that men tend to be much more aggressive than women point directly to a male reproductive strategy of striving with each other for the greatest quantity of female mates possible![180] Alpha Males of animal species, mammals especially, who are known to be harem keepers all have the exact same physical traits and behavior.

Of the very few animal species that tend toward monogamy, the opposite is true. Males and females tend to be the same size, the different genders enter puberty at the same time, the males' testes are small relative to their size and weight, and the males are no more aggressive than the females of their kind.

Obviously, these studies lend weight to the argument that there should be a natural inequity between those human males who get most of the girls, and those who are fortunate enough just to get one, respectively, the Alphas and the Betas.

Odd as it may seem to us now, females in Pre-Agricultural times who belonged to harems were rather content … as long as their shared mate was an Alpha and there were adequate resources and time for all.[181] Actually, it would have been rare that they would be so deprived because a Hunting and Gathering Era harem consisted of only a few women, two to five at the most, not the hundreds of wives as was the case in later agricultural times for kings and sultans. A harem-keeper would never take on so many women so as not to have adequate food, shelter and time for intimacy with them all.[182]

Unfortunately, we tend to think of polygyny strictly in terms of the abuses that followed the invention of the plow. During that era, polygyny, indeed, represented one of the worst expressions of female oppression and sexism. Women had no choice as to whether they would become the mate of a Beta or an Alpha, whether by herself or as part of a harem. The natural attraction women have for Alpha Males—which in the previous era led them to willingly join harems—had given way to an unnatural mating system based strictly on wealth. A male who had all the markers of an Alpha wouldn't necessarily have been a land owner who could afford to purchase two or more wives.[183] Conversely, many a male who, in every other way displayed Beta characteristics (submissiveness, lack of confidence, neediness), could be a great land owner, and could, therefore, purchase scores of women … and yet not be at all sexually appealing to them.

Sexual Capitalism

It took a number of millennia, but thanks to a confluence of religious, social and political forces, the socially acceptable ideal family made up of plural wives gave way to ostensible monogamy. While most of us can understand why Alpha Males would find polygyny a socially acceptable family model in the Pre Agricultural Era, we might have trouble understanding why the majority of men who were Betas put up with it for as long as they did.

To help us understand, we turn again to analogy. I once heard someone summarize the difference between the way workers in socialist countries view the rich and the way workers here in the capitalist US do. The socialist workers had seen centuries of abuse by the well-to-do. In their societies, the elite never moved from their position, and neither did the working class. There was no such thing as social mobility, and thus, no hope whatsoever that a poor worker could ever have wealth. For this reason, the workers finally rose up to demand that the wealth of the rich be taken from them. Now, whenever they see a rich foreigner traveling in their country, they say, "One of these days, you'll be down here with us."

On the contrary, in nations like the US, where now and then, one will hear about a rags to riches story, where there does seem to be the possibility, and thus, the hope that even a poor worker could one day be rich, a worker views the rich very differently. These workers see the rich pass by and say, "One of these days, I'm gonna be just like him." Even if the odds are against the poor worker of ever rising that much above his current state, as long as he doesn't see his position as hopeless, he'll not only tolerate those who are well above him, but reward them with his admiration.

It may very well be that the reason polygyny did so well for so long in human history is because Beta men could at least hope for better and more women. It was only after the Agricultural Revolution made the situation for Beta males so hopeless, that the seeds of revolution against the Alphas were planted and began to grow. Had the great, new, landowners not been so selfish, taking scores, hundreds, and sometimes, thousands of the women for themselves alone, they might have been able to keep the masses of Beta men pacified. Had they not taken all the attractive females, and left enough so every Beta man could at least think he had a shot at getting one, the call for universal monogamy may have never been sounded.

Mormon Polygyny

The last time polygyny made any real headway in a modern, Western nation began in 1830, when a former Congregationalist minister named Joseph Smith founded the Church of Jesus Christ of the Latter Day Saints, more commonly known as the Mormon Church.

Smith privately advocated polygyny as part of his new revelation, drawing from the many examples of the practice in the Old Testament. He was rather successful in gathering followers, but as the word leaked out of his "barbarian" practice, persecution of the new American faith quickly followed.

Even before his advocacy of polygamy came to light, though, Smith and his followers were not well received. Traditional Protestants found his other claims (that Jesus Christ had imparted to him a new set of inspired scripture, for example) to be heretical enough, and were quick to condemn the sect. Several attempts to establish Mormon communities in Ohio, Missouri and Illinois all failed one after the other as their neighboring "Gentiles" became increasingly uneasy with their growing presence. Then, as information about the group's "lascivious practices" leaked out, people found the sect completely intolerable. Smith was finally shot and killed by a mob in 1844 after reports were published of his having secretly taken a number of wives. It seemed for a moment the movement had met its end.

However, Smith's martyrdom actually united the Mormons, and made them even more determined to find some place where they could practice their faith uninhibited. Continued opposition to the sect, mainly for their practice of polygyny but also for their insistence on temporal control of their communities, resulted in an exodus to the West. They finally settled in the Great Salt Lake basin of Utah.

Leading the move was Brigham Young, Smith's successor, who at first, similarly practiced and advocated polygyny with as much discretion as possible. Then, in 1852, the Mormon leadership decided to openly announce that plural marriage was not only acceptable, but "ordained and commanded by God for every Saint [male Mormon Church member] to acquire." Verbal and written opposition to the Mormons for sanctifying "a relic of barbarism" was heard and read all the way to the East Coast. But after the majority of the Saints had moved and established themselves in the West, they found sanctuary from legal impediments and active persecution. The distance between the United States border and the Salt Lake basin, in addition to preoccupation with the Civil War and the Reconstruction, distracted the US government from interfering with the Mormon Church. It appeared that the Mormons had finally found their "Canaan Land," and for several decades, they thrived, winning a lot of converts, many of them, single women.

Eventually, though, the westward expansion of the US caught up to the Mormon settlements in Utah and the surrounding territories as traditional Protestants began to move in around them. Conflicts intensified as the federal government came under increasing pressure to intervene and crush the sect. A US Supreme Court ruling in 1879, upholding a federal law banning polygyny in its territories, spelled eventual doom for the practice, at least out in the open.

Mormon Church lobbying efforts and other tactics were used to buy more time, but the writing was on the wall. The leadership had hoped they might regain legality for polygyny when Utah's statehood petition was accepted. "Then," they reasoned, "the federal, anti-polygamy laws would no longer apply (or at least could be severely curtailed in their enforcement)." However, statehood petitions were repeatedly denied, and when federal authorities began to imprison "bigamists" in large numbers and, perhaps more threateningly, to seize Mormon church property and assets, the leadership finally conceded defeat.[184]

In 1890, Mormon Church President Wilford Woodruff declared in a "Manifesto" the Church would no longer continue the practice. Though some Mormons, even a number of church leaders, continued to take on plural wives, especially in Canada and Mexico, the practice dwindled considerably. By 1910, only a minority of "Mormon Fundamentalists" continued to take more than one wife, and even then, only with considerable discretion.

I mention this portion of Mormon history for a reason. Although, there are questions about the tendency of at least some Mormon harem keepers to have been tyrannical in the manner they ran their households, this is not to say that the only women who joined Mormon harems were so destitute, unattractive or so religiously brain-washed, they'd put up with any man who would take them, even men who had other wives. The fact is, so many women voluntarily signed on to polygyny—once a social and religious context was provided that validated the practice—and this is very telling! These weren't women who had been captured by foreign raiders and sold into slavery. They weren't drug addicts pressed into "white slavery" by their pimp/boyfriend/drug dealer. They weren't all obese, ugly, destitute or suffering from poor self-esteem either. Many of those who had converted to Mormonism had previously been faithful adherents to traditional Protestantism, educated, raised in loving homes, and schooled very much on the importance of chastity.

Once given a chance, though, to partake of a family order where the male head was perceived both as a strong, dominant figure (if for no other reason than because he had or was able to accrue multiple wives without constraint) as well as "godly," they came in droves and wasted no time in finding harems to join! The fact that they even did so in the face of severe persecution also suggests that, deep within the female psyche', there is a place where she equates male sexual success (as manifest by having many other women who *choose* to mate with him) with Alpha status.[185]

Likewise, in Pre-Agricultural times, women faced neither religious/social opposition to joining harems, nor were they compelled to do so, as was the case later on, by the wealthy after the onset of the Agricultural Era. Instead, they were generally free to choose whether they would become part of a harem or not, assuming they were appealing enough for an Alpha Male to invite them in. As long as the male could accommodate her in terms of resources, attention and time, the female version of Instincts One and Two—to find an Alpha Male nearly irresistibly attractive and to have a relationship with him if possible—resulted in her being very pleased to have gotten his love and care in addition to his good genes. With no expectation that she might get him all to herself, sharing him with other harem mates was not only not a problem, but a big part of what attracted her to him in the first place.

If she were to become jealous at all, it would have likely only occurred if she had perceived that her keeper would not seek sex outside the harem. In other words, the competitiveness we moderns normally associate with female jealousy for any other woman trying to approach her man would have been limited to those females who might threaten to pull her back from the maximum place she had achieved, even if that place was short of what most modern women have come to take for granted as the only acceptable form of sexual union—monogamy.

There are several reasons why this presumption is now so broadly accepted that suggesting otherwise is almost always taken as a joke. One, we live in a culture that has insisted on monogamy for a very long time—even though it is in serial fashion. Another is the great deal of latitude given to jealousy in general, almost to the point of making it a virtue![186]

Though men are universally inclined to want a variety of women, their natural jealousy under any circumstance for other men having sex with a relationship partner so mirrors the common experience of most modern females, that it makes it that much more difficult to question whether women would ever react differently under other circumstances.

Finally, the modern expectation of monogamy is also shored up by the popular antipathy for polygyny as it was practiced during the Agricultural Era or in contemporary nations where women have very few liberties. With such an overwhelming prejudice prevailing, it's so easy to assume that no woman would ever, of her own free will, enter into a sexual arrangement where she would be sharing a bed with other wives.

However, we need to make a special note of exception here. It bears repeating that much of the reason why a voluntary polygynous family seems impossible to us has to do with possessive expectation. Just as we don't get upset when we have no expectation of exclusive access to a certain place—i.e., spatial possession—when others enter upon it, that under a different circumstance, we would feel a trespass has occurred, the same holds true with sexual possession. For instance, when one is lodging at a hotel apartment suite, one is not outraged to learn that others have been there before and more will follow. However, if the very same hotel were converted into a condominium, and a former traveler were to purchase and become the owner of the very same place he stayed in before, he'd feel very differently about anyone else barging in the door and making themselves at home.

If this idea seems far-fetched and more a fantasy of male lust than a conclusion of scientific inquiry, think again. Neuroscientists have actually determined the specific areas of the brain set aside for processing "reward expectation." In certain centers of the prefrontal cortex, humans calculate and store information on what kind of rewards they might get from a given circumstance, and not surprisingly, this very same area of the brain is also closely connected to the "circuitry" involved with the emotions of anger, particularly as they are prompted by jealousy.[187] In other words, once a certain reward "brain file" is labeled as an *expectation*, then it automatically triggers the jealousy-anger response when it is not fulfilled.

Perhaps, we need to turn once again to a modern phenomenon of unconventional, sexual behavior to help us understand what was going on in the Pre-Agricultural era when roughly ten percent of the men had small harems of three women on average (or thirty percent of the women) who not only tolerated it, but felt like it was the model family arrangement! Think again for a moment about the young women whom we sometimes refer to as "groupies," those—generally quite attractive—women who do all they can to have sex with the rock stars (or sports stars, movie stars, etc.) they're enamored with. These women are quite aware of the fact that they have no exclusive sexual access to these men they want so badly. In some cases, they are more than happy to share intimacy—even simultaneously—with other women, as long as they are getting to be with these particular men.

How is it that the otherwise pervasive gene of jealousy seems so inoperative under such circumstances? Why would females who, in most every other situation tend to be very intolerant of others coming near their sexual partner, behave so differently in the company of certain guys?

I believe the answer is that, for women, jealousy kicks in only when they *perceive* they have lost or are about to lose ground in their reproductive advancement according to their gender's strategy—obtain as much of the best quality male as possible. Unlike the male strategy to get the greatest quantity of women possible, either with or without a relationship, women are driven to obtain the genes of the best male possible, if not with, then without a relationship. Only once a relationship seems possible, is sex alone no longer good enough. This explains why women will, if it's with a certain kind of man (an Alpha), knowingly participate in one night stands. Satisfying Instinct One is good enough, if Two is out of reach.

But when a relationship is possible, we're mistaken to think there is no tolerable, middle between them. In spite of the myriad infractions that occur each day, our modern culture continues to hold out only two, socially acceptable reasons for two adults to have sex—purely for the sake of recreation or within a monogamous love relationship. In other cultures, however, as well as in the earlier history of Western Civilization, there was another level in between. Even though it is currently suppressed in our society, the fact that this "middle ground" emerges rather predictably under the right circumstances tells us something important about our sexuality: For women, sex *and love* with an Alpha, ranks higher than *just sex*, but if that love is not perceived as attainable within an exclusive relationship, then an inclusive one will do! It would still represent an upward advance from casual sex alone.

The female reproductive strategy proceeds, therefore, in a definite, prioritized order: 1) find an Alpha Male and have sex with him. Then, if possible, 2) have a relationship with him, even if it means sharing him with others. And then, if possible, 3) *try* to have him all to herself.

Here is where it gets real tricky, though. As it was pointed out in our earlier discussion of the Alpha-Beta paradox, Alphas are, by definition, so attractive to females, that advancing to the highest level—to have him exclusively—was rare (usually only because there are few other women available). As long as there were other women around, if a harem member, even an Alpha Female, were to issue an ultimatum to her keeper to restrict his affections to her and her alone "or else," she would likely only succeed in getting herself kicked out. The Alpha would simply move on to find others more "appreciative" and less demanding. Natural Selection would not have favored women who were so determined to be monogamous that they would have preferred it to membership in an Alpha's harem.

Besides, one of the clearest signs that a guy is indeed an Alpha is the fact that he has many female sex partners. We've already noted that when females are under the impression that a male has no other woman interested in him, this fact alone tends to influence them to write him off as an undesirable "Beta." Well, the converse is also true. It may seem counterintuitive, at first, but rather than turning women off, the more a male appears to have women interested in him sexually (Stay with me here! Notice, I said "women showing interest in him," not him constantly checking out all the other babes walking by while his tongue is hanging out!), the more other women—observing this—will find him attractive also. This phenomenon, which is also very common among animals, is sometimes called "mate copying." It's a kind of sexual bandwagon effect—"So many other women want him, he must be an Alpha, and so I want him too."[188] As the old saying goes, "Nothing succeeds like success."

The Polygyny Threshold Vs. "Relationship Mode"

Rather than feeling "used," "not really loved," or "slighted," the amazing reality is that voluntary harem members are generally quite happy with their situation. And no wonder. They've achieved all of their reproductive directives—getting to have the genes (sex), a relationship (love) and care (access to his resources) of an Alpha.

Does this still sound like some kind of unrealistic, male fantasy? Perhaps stemming only from his selfish desires, with nothing really in it for women. Guess again! The following is a direct quote from an article publish by Polygamy.com on the benefits of polygamy for women, the first written by none other than modern polygamist wife and career journalist, Elizabeth Joseph:

"I've often said that if polygamy didn't exist, the modern American career woman would have invented it. Because, despite its reputation, polygamy is the one lifestyle that offers an independent woman a real chance to "have it all".

One of my heroes is Dr. Martha Hughes Cannon, a physician and a plural wife who in 1896 became the first woman legislator in any U.S. state or territory. Dr. Cannon once said, 'You show me a woman who thinks about something besides cook stoves and washtubs and baby flannels, and I will show you nine times out of ten a successful mother.' With all due respect, Gloria Steinem has nothing on Dr. Cannon.

As a journalist, I work many unpredictable hours in a fast-paced environment. The news determines my schedule. But am I calling home, asking my husband to please pick up the kids and pop something in the microwave and get them to bed on time just in case I'm really late? Because of my plural marriage arrangement, I don't have to worry. I know that when I have to work late my daughter will be at home surrounded by loving adults with whom she is comfortable and who know her schedule without my telling them. My eight-year-old has never seen the inside of a day-care center, and my husband has never eaten a TV dinner. And I know that when I get home from work, if I'm dog-tired and stressed-out, I can be alone and guilt-free. It's a rare day when all eight of my husband's wives are tired and stressed at the same time.

It's helpful to think of polygamy in terms of a free-market approach to marriage. Why shouldn't you or your daughters have the opportunity to marry the best man available, regardless of his marital status?

I married the best man I ever met. The fact that he already had five wives did not prevent me from doing that. For twenty-three years I have observed how Alex's marriage to Margaret, Bo, Joanna, Diana, Leslie, Dawn, and Delinda has enhanced his marriage to me. The guy has hundreds of years of marital experience; as a result, he is a very skilled husband.

It's no mystery to me why Alex loves his other wives. I'd worry about him if he didn't. I did worry in the case of Delinda, whom I hired as my secretary when I was practicing law in Salt Lake City. Alex was in and out of my office a lot over the course of several months, and he never said a word about her. Finally, late one night on our way home from work, I said, "Why haven't you said anything about Delinda?"

He said, "Why should I?"

I said, "She's smart, she's beautiful. What, have you gone stupid on me?"

They were married a few months later.

Polygamy is an empowering lifestyle for women. It provides me the environment and opportunity to maximize my female potential without all the tradeoffs and compromises that attend monogamy. The women in my family are friends. You don't share two decades of experience, and a man, without those friendships becoming very special.

I imagine that across America there are groups of young women preparing to launch careers. They sit around tables, talking about the ideal lifestyle to them in their aspirations for work, motherhood, and personal fulfillment. 'A man might be nice,' they might muse. 'A man on our own terms,' they might add. What they don't realize is that there is an alternative that would allow their dreams to come true. That alternative is polygamy, the ultimate feminist lifestyle."[189]

The appeal to women of these benefits is so strong it leads them willingly join a harem if they can. The combined circumstances which lead females not only to willingly join, but even to compete for admittance to a harem, are called the *polygyny threshold.* It's actually a very common phenomenon that biologists talk a lot about when they're studying *animal* mating behavior.

If you've never heard a lot about the science behind the possibility that *human* females might actually want to join a harem, there are probably good reasons why. For one thing, a lot of biologists are married and have long been quietly conforming to many other of society's institutions while pursuing their interests in science. This can make things a little intense when scientific observation begins to reveal a major contradiction between human behavioral expectation and actual behavior, so much so that it might rock the very boat one's been standing in for a long time. It's a tough thing to talk about openly about the truths of human, sexual nature, such as the polygyny threshold, even for scientists, while our society clings to such a strong taboo against the very idea of it.

But since we've basically crossed the rubric of what moves women to join either a literal or de facto harem, let's also consider what might make a women feel the need at a later point to kick all the other girls out. To put it another way, the polygyny threshold, is indeed like the plank or stone at the bottom of the one and only door to a home, as was once common before fire codes insisted on back doors. It swings both ways. So it is quite possible to go back over the threshold to leave a harem.

Now, while we all seem to readily grasp why a woman might want to leave a harem, and it's all we can do to imagine what might induce her to voluntarily join one to begin with, what on earth could possibly entice her to stay?

This "place" is very much like the highest point a climber can camp before reaching the peak of a mountain. A mountain climber strives hard to get to the top. But once he finally gets there, he can't stay for very long. There's not much to do, except to take a snapshot or two, and then all that's left … is to start *going down*. Once off of that mountain, all they can think about is climbing up another one, because the real joy for a mountain climber is the climb itself!

Similarly, women greatly enjoy the process of meeting, being seduced by, and eventually being invited to live with an Alpha. They might even enjoy doing all they can to out perform and ascend in rank among their harem sisters to become "the favorite." After that, they may try to get him all to themselves, if they sense (notice I didn't say "think" because the instinctive sense usually long precedes any conscious thought) there's even the remotest chance, to exclude all the others. Until they reach that point where there is no where higher to go, they are generally quite happy.

But a very strange thing happens when a woman, who even for the longest time was actively and physically competing with other women to have a man all to herself. Once she finally does get him, the satisfaction is very temporary! Soon, she's whining, complaining, bored, dissatisfied … feeling a vacuum within that she might try to fill with getting things, things and more things, sometimes, even with wanting a baby to care for. Nevertheless, it's clear that something has changed, and no matter how much she loved every second of struggling to make her way to the top, now that she's there, she can only look forward to going downhill!

Biologists have determined that the polygyny threshold really comes down to a cost:benefit ratio calculation for the female in question. If the "costs" for her to join the harem of an Alpha Male (such as only getting a part of his time, attention and resources) are less than the benefits she gains in terms of breeding-situation quality (such as his protection, his status in the community, and most of all, his superior DNA) then she won't mind sharing. In fact, she might even fiercely compete with other women just for a chance to get admitted!

What's not discussed is what happens, if the male, either purposely or inadvertently, conveys to a female that she's got a clear shot at seemingly getting an even better cost:benefit ratio by getting to have him all to herself, and thus, getting all of his time, attention, resources and his superior DNA to boot! But when this happens, a woman has actually stepped over and back across the polygyny threshold before she or the unwitting guy even knows what's happened.

In our modern culture, women cross the threshold only in the early stages of dating. They may have suddenly found a really hot guy that just does something for them that they can't explain. Oddly, they may be very aware of the fact that he's seeing a lot of other women. In fact, they are drawn to him all the more because he's in such demand. The same holds true when a woman begins an affair with a married man. She knows he's sleeping with someone else, but that doesn't deter her, at least not initially.

What most often happens next, though, is that the male has only to give this girl the slightest indication she's got a chance of having an exclusive relationship with him, and then, from that point on, she's starts acting very differently. Among male dating aficionados, this is often referred to as sending a woman into "relationship mode." This term is really only about half right, though. Sure, the woman is feeling her relationship instincts kick in, but there's more going on inside of her than a simple choice between having or not having an exclusive, sexual relationship with a man. Were it not for our current societal restriction that the only way to have a relationship is exclusively with only one person, then other in-between steps, like a stage in which a woman is sharing a man sexually, would be more common, or perhaps more accurately, more commonly practiced out in the open.

At the risk of sounding very repetitive, let me say it once more (because I know how hard it is to swallow this idea): the only time the jealousy gene kicks in for women who have begun a relationship is when they have done so *with the expectation that they would not have to share.*

Perhaps the reader has wondered (as often as I used to) how it is that whenever a man is cheating on his wife with a another woman, the "other woman" is often much more tolerant of his going home to bed with his wife on the nights they can't be together than the wife is when she first learns that her husband has been intimate with another woman, even if it was only once!

This is not to say that the other woman wouldn't prefer to replace the wife if she perceives she can. But here is where we see the threshold clearly. If the other woman should start to become jealous, it's usually because she's come under the impression that she has a clear shot at getting the cheating husband to herself and ousting the wife.

Otherwise, the other woman will show remarkable toleration for the wife she's cuckolding, sometimes for years, if its clear that she has gone as far as she can! She might have a dozen friends or family members who have tried countless times to persuade her to get out, that surely, "he must not really love her," that "he's not going to buy the cow while he's getting the milk for free," or that "if he really loved her, he'd divorce his wife," and she'll seemingly have no trouble accepting any kind of rationalization for maintaining the status quo, such as (and this is my personal favorite) "Oh, I know he really loves me, but his wife is ill, and he just can't leave her right now."

We might be tempted to think "only bimbos fall for this kind of philanderer" who seems to be able "to string women along" so easily, but the reality is that they have simply achieved that special place where a woman is getting the best deal possible, best in terms of her female mating strategy is concerned.

The perception of getting the man all to herself is not always because the male in question has intentionally and specifically promised her his fidelity. Often, she's gotten this raised expectation from something the male has done (even if he didn't mean to) to signal his willingness to forgo other women for her (calling often, giving her lots of gifts, introducing her to his mother, etc.). Once she feels she has come thus far, going backward is just out of the question. Ironically, his (intentional or inadvertent) signal that he's willing to be faithful is also an indication that he might not be as much of an Alpha as she thought. She may proceed to accept his fidelity, but only with some hesitation.

This is the point many "macking experts" advise their disciples to avoid at all costs. They usually say it's because doing or saying things that indicate an offer of exclusivity sends an otherwise casual sex partner into "relationship mode," characterized by behaviors such as withholding sex, playing hard to get, asking lots of "relationship" questions and so on. They may not know why this happens, but they're right.

Offering sexual exclusivity to a woman often prompts her *instincts* to say, "Ah oh! I thought this was an Alpha, but now, maybe he's only a Beta. I still like him, but maybe I could do better than this guy if only someone better were around. Now, I have to see what he can throw in to make up for the difference."

"Relationship mode" behaviors are often the result of the woman's now confusing loss of attraction and her attempts to rationalize her initial, all-cares-to-the-wind, sexual feelings. This doesn't mean she won't eventually partner with him, but to the degree he is now signaling to her how Beta he is, she'll want more than just his genes. In other words, an obstacle has been thrown in between a human female's primary directive—getting the genes of an Alpha Male, and the second one—getting to have a relationship *with an Alpha.* Had the guy who was being so cool—doing all the right things; showing that he was interested, but not too interested; calling her, but not every day; giving her some of his attention, but not *all* of his attention—not suddenly become such a clingy wimp, she would have been more than happy just to be around him. Going Beta on her, though, only serves to disappoint, and the best she can hope for now is to be reimbursed in other ways. She was happily ascending, competing and winning, and then all of the sudden, she was thrust to the top of the mountain, which might have felt good for a little while, but then that weird, other feeling began to gnaw at her saying, "OK, now what?"

There's another mistake, even an Alpha can make. As bad as it is to unwittingly signal to a woman that she can now have a relationship, whether it's exclusive or not, intentional or not, it's nothing at all compared to what happens when a male tries to undo the relationship signal and send her backward. Though we normally think of the hellish fury following a woman being scorned as only when a woman is dumped out of an exclusive relationship, the same fury is to be expected at the time of any other "demotion."

As we've noted already, a woman is usually very pleased when she gets the opportunity to "ratchet up" her reproductive success by having sex with an Alpha Male, even though he gives her no indication that he's inclined to have a relationship with her. In fact, she may be perfectly aware that he has one or more other girlfriends. Since she has made an advance toward greater quality of reproductive success, she's not jealous of the other women in the Alpha's life. However, should the Alpha be so impressed with her that he begins to signal to her that she's a candidate for a relationship, even if it's shared with others, then things become different. Once she understands that she has advanced beyond a one-night stand or intermittent "booty calls," the jealousy gene is at the ready to kick in at any sign of regression. Should the Alpha send that message, and then change his tune and begin backpedaling, "Hey, baby, I know I said I could see you on a regular basis, but things are kinda complicated right now," she's gonna be anything but a happy camper!

The reason for her displeasure? Not because she was going to have to share him, she knew that up front. But because she is *losing ground* she felt she had made already—from occasional sex to shared love. Had the male whom she was previously so happy with—just by getting "some" of his "affections"—been consistent enough not to lead her on into thinking there was more in store, she would have remained fine. But having once allowed her to perceive she had advanced, taking her backwards was only asking for trouble.

Sure, in our modern culture where monogamy is so expected (even if it is rarely practiced faithfully), it is extremely difficult for women to accept the idea of sharing a man with others in a polygynous arrangement. The middle ground arrangement—a shared relationship—has been effectively removed for most modern women in Western societies. Nevertheless, we do find that in other societies where monogamy is not automatically presumed (or in underground subcultures such as the clandestine polygynists of the Morman faith who to this day secretly have more than one wife), women give every indication that they are not normally threatened by their "sisters" who share their man's bed! On the contrary, they boast about their lifestyle's numerous advantages—how they can have such a higher standard of living because they're able to pool their resources. Never having to worry about finding child care. Relief from having to do all the sexual pleasing, and so on.[190]

Open polygyny, though, is rare in Western society, and while it might be technically legal as long as the parties are careful not to claim multiple "wife" status, things can get sticky when the neighbors become aware of so many women living under one roof. Unless you're a Hugh Hefner, the biggest chance for a man to *openly* have more than one woman in his life at the same time is to remain single, and try to schedule his girlfriends' visits on different nights (yes, there are more guys who do this than you might think).

Once again, allow me to reiterate that the reason women seem to be so readily poised to get a man all to himself is not because they, instinctively, want to succeed. This may be taken as a Chauvinist comment, but time and again, we see that when women do succeed in this endeavor, they're soon disappointed with the outcome, and there is, indeed, a solid biological reason why. Let me it again. I propose that the answer has to do with an instinctive testing mechanism, a genetically induced behavior which Nature wired deep in the female psyche' as a way to ever ensure that, whenever a woman is fortunate enough to find and be invited into a relationship with an Alpha Male, that she can be certain he never loses his Alpha status.

To be sure, this hypothesis flies in the face of conventional wisdom and all that we think of as "normal." Then again, take a good look around, and try to assess which women seem to be the most content, the most in love, the ones who just want to be with their man, the most happy in love. Those who perceive that they have gotten everything they can from a man, those who have a man who is at their beck and call for his utter devotion to her, ironically, seem to be the most discontent. On the other hand, those who seem to always be at least one step from getting it all, are the most pleased! They are at the threshold, way up above, *near* the top of the mountain peak, but not quite there. The anticipation of sexual exclusivity is far better than exclusivity itself.

Why in the world, then, would Nature do such thing? How many men are crying in a room somewhere, all alone, wondering why it was that at the moment they professed their eternal and undying love to a girl is when things began to all go downhill? How often does a women, time and again, think she's found Mr. Right, but once the thrill of his profession to choose her above all others has come and gone, finds herself waking up one day no longer feeling anything for the man in her bed whom she once adored? As unfair as it seems—and probably is—getting to an exclusive sexual relationship with a man who is first perceived as an Alpha, serves as proof positive that he is a Beta male after all.

Nature had good reason, then, to endow Alpha Females with a way to test men—to ensure they would ever seek out the "best man for the job" of reproducing with them. No matter how much a particular guy seems like the most Alpha in town, the Paradox ensures that any Alpha Female who succeeds in "hooking him" will sooner or later be on the lookout for someone—to borrow from Orwell's *Animal Farm*—"more Alpha." Also, the Paradox ensures a man who really is the Alpha of Alphas, will always have the best women available chasing after him. In a very real sense, the only way to give a woman what she really wants, is "to always leave her wanting more." It was the Alpha-Beta Paradox, perhaps more than any other factor, that made polygyny, and the threshold contentment which followed, as successful as it was, and for as long as it lasted.

None of this is to say that other realities may have made it difficult at times, even for Alpha Males, to have sex with a constant variety of women. In an era when the population of *Homo sapiens* was still very sparse, there may have been many "dry periods," when there just wasn't anyone else around for Alphas to have extra-harem trysts with. Another factor that may have limited their sexploits would have been other Alphas. If there were enough Alphas around, all the desirable, Alpha women would quickly join one harem or another. At such times, even Alphas had to be content with either the variety that trysts with lesser quality Beta females could provide or that which could be had from rotating between the members of one's own small harem.

Perhaps limitations like these are what made the overwhelming feelings of desire women have for Alphas all the more necessary. If occasions to meet a new girl were infrequent—for instance, when two traveling bands happened upon the same fresh water source at the same time—Natural Selection would have favored those males who could, relatively quickly, arouse the interest of a passing female, as a way of efficiently getting those with the best genes together when the opportunities to do so were far and few between.

The limited number of females, especially Alpha women, may have also been another contributing factor to predisposing our species to the abuses of the Agricultural Era. If even the Neolithic Alpha Males could only find and support a limited number of women in their harems, and the Betas were envious of them enough as it was, the invention of the plow, together with land and female ownership, made expanding the size of harems quite a temptation. It may very well be that one of the principle motivations for men to acquire as much land as they could—once they figured out how to own land at all—was to acquire large harems. For Beta men especially, land and female ownership meant they could finally make up for their prior deprivation. Since Beta males could never attract and seduce the quality and number of women they really wanted, once some of them acquired large areas of farm land and the wealth it produced, they could simply purchase them.

How Could Less Be More?

Since polygyny was a critical part of *Homo sapiens*' sexual lifestyle for most of our existence and, by definition, resulted in a small percentage of men getting a disproportionately larger number of the women, how could this have played well at a time when humans lived in small, traveling bands that necessitated the cooperation of all, even the lowliest of Beta men? It would seem that there would have been a significant number of men completely left out as there wouldn't have been enough women to go around for every man to have at least one sex partner. If that were the case, then how would those who were so sexually deprived get along with those who were "hogging all the babes"?

In the modern world, society can still function with a considerable number of discontents, and still have plenty of people available to do all the jobs required, from trash collection to chairing executive business offices. However, lack of full cooperation from even one member of a small, hunting and gathering band can only lead to disaster! Would, for example, a group of men who had not had any sex for months be all that happy to follow and work together with their Alpha leader in the hunt, knowing he was "getting all the girls" upon their return? It's one thing for Beta men to admire the Alpha for doing so much better than they—getting more women of better quality. But for the Betas not to be getting any sex at all would make for plenty of frustration, enough to break the band's chances of survival.

This question assumes, however, an even number of males to females. Even though the percentages of males and females born are roughly 50-50, we need to factor in another reality of early *Homo sapiens*' lifestyle that helps make more sense of this apparent disparity—higher male mortality. Even before the Agricultural Revolution brought about the marching armies of young men who perished by the thousands in every bloody battle that followed to control land ownership, men were subject to many dangers that often resulted in their dismemberment and death—Stone Age hunting. It's fair to say that in the harsh world of the Pleistocene, there was always a good chance that one or more of them would never return from any given hunt. To be sure, other dangers like disease, took their toll on women as well as men, but hunting was a dangerous profession, and it's not too much of a stretch to think that polygyny was also a way for Nature to make up for the number of eligible men needed to mate with the higher number of eligible women left alive. Add to this the shorter, natural life span of men, and we can easily arrive at an average male population difference of about 75% to that of women.

On average, then, this would have allowed the Alpha Males to get a larger share of the more quality females, and at the same time, leave an even number of Beta males and females to form pair bonds. Polygyny, then, was not only rewarded by Natural Selection for helping Alpha men and women to reproduce more successfully, but it also served as a balancing strategy for everyone else to have at least one mate. These social units made up of both polygynous and monogamous family units would have had more cohesiveness, better cooperation, and would have been more likely to survive than a group which might have insisted on monogamy for all. A strictly monogamous society would not have had the advantage of the genetically best members reproducing the most children, and they would have also been weighed down by a significant number of the least desirable, single females having no mates at all.

12

Fooling Mother Nature

Dressed in a gown of white and adorned with a crown of daisies, Mother Nature tastes a creamy substance and smiles. Then, an unseen narrator informs her "That's Chiffon Margarine, not butter." A perplexed Mother Nature replies "Margarine, oh, no, it's too sweet, too creamy." When the narrator tells her "Chiffon's so delicious, I guess it fooled even you, Mother Nature," the perturbed woodland goddess lets loose lightning and thunder to express her anger, and protests, "It's not nice to fool Mother Nature!"

—Chiffon Margarine Commercial from 1971-79

Is There No Where To Turn?

Whatever forms of sexual relations were socially acceptable or unacceptable in Pre-Agricultural or Post-Agricultural times, the situation is much different now. In our modern society, the pressure is on both men and women to suppress their desire for multiple partners (Instinct One) in order to compel us to be monogamous. Instinct Two, the desire for a relationship is exalted, and Instinct Three, jealousy, is not only tolerated but expected, even though it's a very negative impulse that often leads to violence.

What to do, then, if one finds the modern societal demand for monogamy by external pressure too much to ask? There are a few who refuse conformity by actively swinging or who openly have multiple relationships—polyamory. But most of those engaged in swinging or polyamorous relationships have to go far out of their way to distance themselves from the Agricultural Era's abusive polygyny which was founded on wealth-based, male domination over women. And on top of that, they still have to work very hard to subdue natural jealousy. More commonplace are those who sooner or later cheat on their partner or who look the other way when they strongly suspect their mate is cheating. Even so, most can only get away with or tolerate clandestine affairs for a limited time, with break ups resulting more often than not. Also common are men who won't have love affairs, but they'll turn to prostitutes to appease their appetite for sexual variety.

For most people, none of these alternatives are desirable or practical, so what's left other than to grin and bear monogamy, all the while longing for more?

Of course, one could opt to suppress Instinct Two—to just be single—but by no means abstinent. It's a strategy that works very well for Alphas, in that they can readily satisfy Instinct One, as they have little trouble attracting sexual partners for "one night stands" or having intermittent trysts with "a fuck buddy." As long as they avoid "getting in too deep" with anyone, Instinct Three is rendered inoperative because they have no relationships to be jealous over.

Beta males, though, have difficulty with being single because they often find themselves unable to satisfy Instinct One. They are just not attractive enough to succeed very often in soliciting casual sex. Betas usually give up on really satisfying Instinct One, and settle for persuading one female (usually herself a Beta) to pair bond with them. Even then, they have to compensate the female for settling for a Beta male—with everything from buying her dinners to building her dream home. The female will go along and grant a minimum amount of sex in order to obtain these other benefits, but she's not really getting that turned on. It's only when an Alpha comes along that she feels the same level of desire (if not more than) a male has when he sees a "really hot babe," in which case she will be very inclined to copulate with him at the first opportunity.

Beta males therefore, must spend much of their time and energy guarding their females for fear of an Alpha cuckolding them. And of course, while they're mate guarding, they have little to no opportunity to get anything else on the side (not that there'd be many other females willing to have them). Their best hope for reproductive success is to "stay home with the kids," hoping those kids are, in fact, theirs!

Consequently, Beta males are two-time losers—paying more (in terms of time, attention and sharing of their resources) and getting less in return, as far as reproductive success is concerned. They serve their purpose, though, as far as the overall benefit of the species is concerned. Indeed, they often end up helping to care for children biologically fathered by Alphas, freeing up the Alphas to spread their superior genes even further.

Alpha men of ancient times could have it all. The fact that hunting and gathering societies allowed them more than one relationship partner, plus others on the side, meant that he had even more advantages than a modern, single "stud" who enjoys all the casual sex he wants, but at the expense of making sure he never gets "hung up" on any one woman.

This was not a problem in those earlier times. An Alpha could fall in love with a woman, and keep right on enjoying the company of others as well. He got to personally oversee the care of his children born to the best of the women he seduced, without having to sacrifice casual sex with extra-harem females.[191] The fact that he was so "in demand" only affirmed his Alpha status making his relationship partners all the more unlikely to want anyone else (so their Instinct One and his Instinct Three were rendered inactive) even though it meant they had to share him. Thus, he didn't have to mate guard, so he had both the time and the opportunity to go gallivanting for sex outside the home with other women who, because he was an Alpha, found him very attractive.

The only time he might have had trouble with his mates' Instinct Three jealousy kicking in was when his time and resources were spread too thinly or if he ever signaled to them he was willing to limit himself to intra-harem sex. If his harem members ever got the impression they had advanced to the level of having the Alpha all to themselves, then if any of them became aware of his extra-harem indulgences, they would quite naturally respond with jealousy toward his casual sex partners. We might think of the male in this situation as being an Alpha-Minus. The extent, then, of his partners' unwillingness to share was directly linked to the extent that he became less than a pure Alpha.

Of course, most modern men can hardly imagine what it's like to have the advantages that even an Alpha Minus would enjoy. They struggle to get even one woman to bed with them. Sadly, many will enter a monogamous relationship largely just to find some relief for their daily sexual frustration. If while they were single their sex lives were especially unsuccessful, they'll often settle down with a Beta female who is a far from whom they'd really like to have. However, even in cases where they do get "the girl of their dreams," their feeling of sexual success is short-lived. As time goes on, they sense somewhere deep inside that they are still not getting what they really want. On some level, they understand that entering an exclusive relationship means forgoing, however hypothetical, their primary directive to spread their seed to multiple female partners. At best, they might content themselves that they got the better end of a compromise … at least until they find one day that what made their compromise tolerable, the fact they had pair-bonded with an Alpha Female, is exactly what set them up to eventually be dumped by her in that she would find them increasingly unattractive!

It would seem, then, that no matter one's gender or status, there are serious challenges ahead of getting what we really want. What to do, even if you're an Alpha Male, but wish not to suppress Instinct Two to find love? Should you suppress Instinct One though women everywhere find you so irresistible? What if you're an Alpha Female who may be so attractive that you've managed to "hook" an Alpha Male, but on some level you know it's only a matter of time before the temptation for him to stray will be too much to resist (as women are constantly throwing themselves at him)? Sure, you could try with all your might to make him unattractive to other females, but in the process, he also becomes unattractive to you! What if you're a Beta male or female, and you're maintaining an ostensible or even an actual monogamous relationship, but you no longer find your partner attractive, because, he or she too is a Beta?

I believe the only way to have a satisfying, long-term, monogamous relationship comes down to two things—one, is for men and women to do whatever they can to "become" an Alpha, and two, is to make every reasonable effort to mimic those behaviors and circumstances which otherwise satisfy all three of the fundamental sexual instincts. In other words, men and women have got to fool Mother Nature into thinking they're each giving their partner what they really want, and they each have to be willing to allow for their own instincts to be similarly decieved.

What's a Woman to Do?

Let's begin with those things women can do to help their man since he is the least naturally inclined toward true monogamy. What can possibly be done to get around a male's incessant desire to want 1) a variety of women, and 2) prefer the most attractive? We've already taken a long, hard look at the failure of societies, religious institutions and even personal fortitude to suppress this drive by will power alone. The more one tries to resist—as President Jimmy Carter once confessed to—the temptation to "lust after a woman in one's heart," the more difficult it becomes to get such thoughts out of one's mind. "Hunger" tends to increase the more one resists "eating." Fortunately, there's a much better way.

I've noted in my research that the women who belong to that small handful of monogamous couples in long-term relationships who are actually happy with each other practice what I have dubbed Extra Pair Copulation Mimicry (EPCM for short). To put it another way, they've learned how to act as a virtual harem of Alpha girls. If a female can succeed in tricking her mate's biological Instinct One into "thinking" that it is being indulged, when in fact, the male is still copulating only with her, then not only is he sexually satisfied, but her Instinct Three jealousy is also rendered inoperative. Granted, fooling Mother Nature is a daunting task, but with a certain amount of creativity and willingness to put forward some effort, it can be done.

In practical terms, the woman must do whatever she can to satisfy the two aspects of the male's principle drive. To review, let's recall that the male's sexual directive works as a two-edged sword: 1) he wants to be with attractive women, and 2) he desires to have as many of these attractive females as possible.

Looks Do Matter

As politically incorrect as it may be to say so, I have concluded that it would be a disservice to both men and women to cloud the importance of outward, physical appearance to attracting men. Unfortunately, our duplicitous culture has made such frank discussion difficult.

On the one hand, the Beauty Industry has never been so prosperous. Women are bombarded every day with a myriad number of products and services offering the promise of improved looks and the greater success in attracting men that goes with it. Attractive women are by far preferred in all we see in ads, shows, even when just selecting a new tool at the hardware store. On the other hand, we are also constantly getting the message that it's so bad to openly talk about how important beauty is to a relationship. Sometimes, the very same woman's magazine loaded with ads for beauty products and splashed with air brushed faces and the athletic bodies of very attractive and young women, will carry articles criticizing men for their "superficiality" due to their "obsessions" with—you guessed it—young, slender and pretty women!

But I am betting on the reader's willingness to confront reality no matter what it is. I wish I could say that women who are just plain, physically ugly can fare as well as those who are physically pretty. The truth is that they are going to be limited in the kind of men they can attract, just as men who are not tall, rich, powerful and hold a high status in society are likewise limited in the kind of women they can attract.

Telling women who are "butt ugly" that "beauty is only skin deep," may seem like a kind thing to do, but in the end, it only does more damage than good. Unattractive women know only too well where they actually stand. Dishing out platitudes about "inner beauty being more important," or "there's someone out there who will see you as the most beautiful woman in the world," is actually quite cruel and condescending. They are no more fooled by this rhetoric than are attractive women by men who try to impress them by saying they first found them attractive for their personality.

I hope it's clear to the reader that I am in no way suggesting that it's OK to be mean or insensitive toward unattractive women. I merely point out that telling those at the lower end of the "One to Ten Scale" that they are beautiful "in their own way," or attractive "in their soul," or perfect "for someone out there," is no better than saying, "you're ugly"!

Rather than pretending that looks don't matter, it's better to be real. Think about it for a moment. No matter how challenged she is in the "looks department," what woman really wants to date a man who is only trying to like her for her personality, humor and intelligence, but doesn't find her physically appealing? On some level, she's going to figure this out, and not be very happy about it.

A similar process occurs when a very pretty woman who's tired of dating one abusive guy after another, goes out with a man whom she's always thought of as a really nice guy and therefore "she ought to like him." She may even try really hard to find him attractive, but it's to no avail. She might think there's something terribly wrong with herself, because there's nothing she can do to make herself feel attraction for even the nicest guy in the world.

Being honest with oneself if one has not been blessed with a lot of natural good looks can be tough, but there's a worse phenomenon at work in our culture. In spite of so many promises from so many sources to aid women in improving their appearance, many fail to make the best of what they have. Just as it does no good to delude oneself into thinking looks don't matter, it is even more unhelpful to be so distraught over not being a natural "10," that one makes no reasonable effort to do what she can to look her best. We'll address this point in more detail in just a few paragraphs, but let's first review and expand upon the reasons why outward beauty is so critical to stimulate attraction within men.

What is "attractive" to a male in his conscious mind are those outward features which indicate to his primitive, unconscious nature the greatest likelihood that a woman would be reproductively successful. What men think of as all that goes into a women being "hot," are signs—flags, if you will—calling attention to the hidden, inward reality of a healthy body, together with her youth and strength, the key factors in successfully giving birth and raising a child.

Of course, males are not consciously thinking, "Why, there's a woman who appears to be healthy, young and strong enough to bear me a child and take good care of him" when they see a "hot babe." As noted above, Nature had to endow males with this instinct eons before any species even had a chance to evolve the ability to think consciously. Though the ability to reason can, on occasion, help a man to take into consideration factors like health and strength, men are still almost exclusively driven to focus almost entirely on the "flags" of these factors instead.

What men find attractive—a trim waist, curvy thighs, firm breasts, smooth skin, symmetrical facial and body features, healthy hair, all that figures into a "10"—are the features that a healthy, young woman of child bearing age typically has. Eons ago, Natural Selection rewarded those males who were attracted to these features with reproductive success, resulting in these preferences being passed on from generation to generation. Those females most likely to reproduce successfully, the "fertile, young and healthy," were the first and most likely to mate; they got "first dibs" of the stronger males who, in turn, better protected them and their young. Conversely, what we think of as "unattractive" features are outward signs of aging, weakness and ill health, signs indicating a likelihood of reproductive failure … or at least, they used to.

Now though, the world has changed so dramatically and in such a relatively short period of time (from an evolutionary perspective), these deep-down, hard-wired, "triggers" have had no chance to catch up, and are no longer necessarily accurate. Sure, a healthy, shapely, 18-year old with a "pretty face," will instantly trigger sexual attraction within a male, and normally, these outward signs will match their original purpose of pointing men to those women who will most likely reproduce successfully. However, after eons of Nature "hard wiring" men to respond this way, even an older woman who has had a hysterectomy (in other words, who cannot reproduce), but who nevertheless has these same, basic features will still trigger a similar, primitive response from men.

Our deep down, primitive responses can also work in direct contradiction to reproductive success. A very fertile, healthy and young woman who nevertheless lacks outward beauty will communicate (quite against her wishes) to the primitive portion of the male brain, "I may be sickly, unable to give a successful birth, and not healthy enough to lactate and care for an infant." As a result, she gets passed up by many a guy, quite unfairly in terms of what a successful mother she would make.

When it comes to sexual attraction, it's so important to understand that conscious reason has nothing to do with it, neither for men, nor women. No one can ever be *rationally convinced* to be attracted to someone. Attraction just happens. In spite of all our great learning and scientific advances, human sexual behavior is still governed almost 100% by instincts.

It seems so unfair to the logical, reasonable part of our minds … and it is! But let's remember that these "automatic responses" to certain qualities of the opposite sex were actually pretty good indicators of likely reproductive success long ago. If they hadn't been, they wouldn't have been rewarded by Nature with, well, reproductive success.

Sure, it would be great if we could simply set aside our most gut-level feelings, and select our mates on purely rational criteria. Men would faithfully devote themselves to those women who were smart, witty and responsible, no matter what they looked like! (Women might then choose more ultra-nice, Beta guys for their knowledge of good wines, their education and their manners instead of falling for "bad boys.") Topless night clubs and adult Vegas shows would close down for lack of interest. Playboy and Penthouse magazines would rot on their shelves, and mechanical parts magazines would actually display mechanical parts on their covers instead of scantily clad women.

Don't hold your breath, though. If we simplified the amount of time it took our instinctive sexual desires to be forged by Natural Selection to a one-hour clock and then compared it with how long it took to our rational abilities to evolve, the latter would have occurred only in the final minute of that hour! In other words, the result of millions of years of evolution isn't going away for a very long time. Our sexual instincts are as formidable as ever, and human reason can only do so much to restrain them.

Consequently, no matter how much one rationally knows that beauty is only "skin deep," irrational desire is so overwhelming that, sooner or later, men and women will dive into having sex (paradoxically with the body part they're using the least) head first, especially with an Alpha. True, there are a disciplined few who manage to act in contradiction to these desires for years on end. However, they do so at a terrible price—constantly hungering for what they refuse themselves and often becoming obsessed by these hungers.

In many cases, those who are constantly battling not to do what they want to so badly, become resentful and angry. Their negative emotions become especially acute whenever they rub shoulders with others who are guiltlessly indulging in the very thing they feel they can't. More often than not, they will take out their frustrations on those whom they view as "getting away cleanly" with behavior they believe they'd be seriously punished for. Some, for example, will attempt to influence governments and other institutions to impose on everyone else the same restrictions they can only barely hold themselves to, and sometimes they do worse, lashing out against those whom they secretly wish they could bed.[192]

Given, then, the enormous forces acting within a male, driving him (thus the term "drive") to want a variety of attractive women, a woman who is practical and hopeful of keeping her mate happily faithful to her will do all she can to mimic those preferred characteristics and circumstances that naturally trigger these same instincts so they can be redirected toward her. Females who insist that their husband simply "love them the way they are,"—who make no effort to stay in shape and use what means are available to them (within reason, of course) to preserve beauty—only increase the likelihood of their mate cheating on them. Those who "let themselves go" are just asking for trouble, no matter how "committed" their man may be to the idea of monogamy and no matter how much he might wish he could live up to his marriage vows to "forsake all others."

We can either spend all our time and effort being upset at the cards Nature has dealt to us or we can take the advice of St. Francis of Assisi, "… to accept the things we cannot change." The good news is that we can take this knowledge and make it work for us. With the help of modern medicine, health care, a broad array of beauty products, work-out videos, and a multitude of other ways to preserve youthful appearance, these instincts can be fooled in a way that helps us have better and more satisfying love lives.

Even modest investments in looking one's best have big payoffs. The closer a woman can come to looking like an Alpha Female, the more responsive her mate will be to her. Even after getting older, there are many practical ways of "tricking" the male libido into greater arousal (low lighting at bedtime for example, can do wonders to make one's wrinkles "fade") even if one is not in a position to spend tens of thousands of dollars on cosmetic surgery. For the female, mimicking an Alpha really comes down to doing the best with what she has.

Of course, it helps when one is "naturally" attractive, a "10," young, or if not, well off enough to afford the latest makeover procedures to preserve youth. The more she has and retains the Alpha look (youthful, healthy, symmetrical), the better. But even if she is a "wall flower," or even if she could use—but can't afford—to get breast implants, a lipo-suction or a "tummy tuck," or even when she gets older and age begins to take its toll, these are not her greatest hindrances. Most of the time, the main reason most women are not having success in attracting men and keeping men attracted is not so much because they have such a limited "number of cards" to work with, as far as their physical looks go, but a much larger limitation *in their minds*!

How often do we see a woman who seems to be doing all she can to make herself unattractive! Sure, it might be unrealistic for a woman who is a "4" to ever come off as a "10," no matter what kind of help is available to her. But so very, very often, the "4" will have such a poor attitude about herself, or will be so overcome with anger and jealousy toward younger women who don't have to do anything to look good, they will make themselves look worse, and come off as a "1," or even a "0." The sad part of this phenomenon is that most of the things these women do that make them unattractive are things that they *could* change, but choose not to.

Conversely, there are some women who get it. They may not have been naturally blessed with a great deal of beauty, but they waste no time worrying about what they don't have, and focus on making the best use of what they do. They eat right, exercise, pay attention to how they walk and talk. They dress as well as they can within their budget. They cultivate a personality that is attractive and charming, instead of feeding into an ugly and bitter one. They carry themselves in a way that says, "I'm beautiful," and like the proverbial, self-fulfilling prophesy, they project beauty wherever they go. They may never come close to being a model, but they often raise their "appearance rating" by several points, and consequently, have much more success in attracting men.

Perhaps, we can all think of some woman who was a "late bloomer," someone who, back in high school, had a lot of poor self-esteem issues, but who showed up a few years later at a reunion with a whole new attitude about herself, and now has a look that reflects the positive change.[193]

And if we think about it for a moment, we've probably all witnessed the opposite of this phenomenon. How about the girl who, at one time, was endowed with every natural advantage as far as looks go, and then after only a few years, seems to have done all she could to ruin them. Usually, this happens because somewhere deep inside, a person has developed a very bad view of herself. In time, her outward appearance begins to match her inner state.

Another fact that should give hope to those who have to work harder to look attractive is the relative nature of the Alpha-Beta Scale. A woman who would seem quite average in a room full of top models and Alpha Male studs, could appear very much an Alpha to an average guy in a small town cafe. Also, while there are certain physical characteristics that all attractive women share, the degree to which any one will appeal to a man depends a lot on where he is on the male version of the scale. It's no wonder that people tend to form relationships with those who are either in the same or close to their "league." In other words (at the risk of batting this baseball analogy into the ground), it's not as if only those who can match the appearance of the "major leaguers" are attractive, and everyone else is doomed to utter loneliness. Rather, there's a very good chance of attracting men at the top end of one's league as long as a woman is playing like she belongs there too. Sure, if a woman begins in the "sandlot," it's not likely that she'll ever be playing the major leagues (dating Brad Pitt?), much less going to the World Series (getting to live with Brad Pitt?). On the other hand, those who apply themselves, can often graduate to a higher league, and then, get to date the best men there.

In the end, there will always be someone who looks better, objectively speaking. But most men in a long-term relationship, who would like to be sexually faithful, are not struggling so much with the disparity between their mate and top models, but with her lack of doing what she can to look her best. Unfortunately, especially after getting married, a woman will often allow herself to descend to the bottom of her rank, while thinking that she can insist on her husband's marital commitment alone to keep him faithful. No matter how much will power a man has, the frustration of having a wife who could be so much more appealing, and yet, cares not to even make the effort, is what most often finally pushes him into the arms of another!

This is one of the main reasons why Marriage tends to damage most relationships, because the temptation to rely on such unnatural constraint leads directly to forgoing that which would otherwise naturally reinforce the relationship bond the most! On the contrary, the woman who understands this reality and is willing to do what she can to look her best will greatly increase the odds that her mate will be faithful to her … because he'll continue to find her, not perfect, but still attractive.

One more word to the wise. Even the hottest women—and I'm talking about the hottest models in the world—can still turn off a guy by doing other things like nagging, whining and complaining about every little problem, and acting like a spoiled brat. Alpha men, who have so many other options, need not remain involved with a woman just because of her looks. True, Beta males are much more susceptible to putting up with behavior they really don't like, but even many of them will eventually get the picture, and as difficult as it may be, will stop seeing or living with a woman who demonstrates to be ugly enough on the inside.

Yes ladies, work on looking your best, and use your creativity to be a "virtual harem." But don't sabotage all your good efforts by turning right around and doing all you can to see just how much he'll put up with in terms of "ugly" behavior!

"Wait a minute," some will no doubt protest. "I know lots of women who are beautiful, who even in their later years, looked great, and their hubbys cheated on them anyway!" Yes, there are men who will cheat even if they have the most beautiful wives in the world, even those who have every means at their disposal to preserve their beauty. But this phenomenon doesn't mean their efforts are all in vain. It only means that looking good is just half of the equation. Again, the male's version of Instinct One comes in two parts, and his preference for youth and beauty is important, but the other aspect is even more so. A man is also driven from deep within to seek out variety, and he can only truly be satisfied if he can keep getting someone new … or at least, to make it seem that way.

Variety is the Spice

There's a story about President Coolidge who, while visiting a model farm and inspecting the chicken house, was told by his guide that Mrs. Coolidge, who had completed the tour separately, wanted him to take note of the rooster's frequent copulations (as a way of registering a complaint about the infrequency of their lovemaking). The President then asked, "Does the rooster copulate so frequently with the same hen?" "Oh no, sir," he replied. "Then please inform Mrs. Coolidge of that," he ordered.

This story has often been used to describe a phenomenon that biologists and zoologists have known about for a very long time, the "Coolidge Effect"—that variety plays a large role in sexual attraction, especially for males. Much as men will strive to bed the prettiest girl they can find, not even physical beauty can trump the male's deeper instinct for variety. This is so true that even a "wall flower" has a good chance of arousing a male more than an attractive female if he has been partnered with the more attractive one for a long time.

From the standpoint of how Evolution has shaped the human male reproductive strategy, the Coolidge Effect makes good sense—it encourages men to spread their seed as far and wide as possible. Perhaps this tendency is one of the oldest genetically-induced male sexual behaviors, because it simply says, "Hey, here's someone new, so you should go get her!"

Sure, for most Beta guys who can only, at best, persuade a "5" to go out with them, it would seem that if they could ever convince a "10," to be their mate, they would be so happy, they'd never think of cheating on her. But the reality is that guys who do get "10s" often end up straying anyway … and it's not always because their "10" had an awful personality. Time and again, we learn about super models, movie stars and beautiful princesses that were "dumped" for someone else who didn't seem all that pretty or elegant. Think of Prince Charles' affair with Camilla Parker Bowles who, by any account, was a far cry from matching the late Princess' Diana in terms of her physical appearance.

Therefore, if a woman is serious and wise about wanting to have a happy, lasting, monogamous relationship, then she must be willing to accept this deeply ingrained biological reality. She must be prepared to do whatever she can to "fool" this primitive desire which unceasingly craves for a variety of women into "thinking" it's getting what it wants. And the best way to do this is actually quite simple in concept, though perhaps challenging to implement—include as much variety as possible in your love life.

Such "deceit" is not as uncommon as one might at first be tempted to think. The fact is many couples engage in this EPCM behavior in one way or another. How many, for example—if they were asked to really ponder the question and answered honestly—would agree that their mate probably fantasizes about being with other people, even while they are copulating? (How many would have to agree that they do it themselves?)

There are, however, many less "mentally unfaithful" ways to mimic EPCs. Simply wearing different, tantalizing night gowns each evening can help tremendously (maybe we now know what Victoria's Secret really is.).

We've all probably heard (in whispered tones perhaps) of "weird couples" who like to "dress up." This may sound "weird," but it's not really. What is so bad about taking one night a week, for example, to dress up as different people, maybe even call each other different names, make love in different positions, play different music, use different scents of perfume, wearing wigs even?

Even very conservative couples report how taking a trip somewhere they'd never been to before seemed to reinvigorate their love lives.

Some couples will purposely arrange to meet "by accident" at a bar, and go through all the motions of a pick up, sometimes leaving some room for spontaneous decisions as to where they will go from there.

Others try to see how many different kinds of places they can make love (occasionally getting into trouble when it's in a public place!)

All of these measures are varying ways of fooling the male's sexual instincts into "thinking" he's found someone new without actually straying, and thereby, averting the arousal of the monster of jealousy, all the while deceiving the female's sexual instincts into "thinking" she's crossed the polygyny threshold and been invited into the "harem" of an Alpha Male.

Some, of course, will object to such overt measures to "pretend they're committing adultery," but again, we are not in a position, biologically speaking, to subdue the instinct to want others by sheer will power. Yes, a couple may choose to go along with the rhetoric of religious prudes and try to call up all that is within them to suppress this desire by determination alone. They might even succeed in never committing the act of adultery. But it is highly likely that the more they rely on a sense of obligation to subdue the desire to stray, the more they'll become obsessed by it!

Far better, then, is it to just accept that wanting others is simply a natural desire, a longing that, at one time, served an important purpose in our evolutionary development. Facing up to the truth about our sexuality is winning half the battle. Rather than denying our desires, which only serves to intensify them, it's so much easier to accommodate them in practical ways.

Suppressing a powerful desire like the sex drive is like climbing up a very steep hill ... while wearing roller skates! The threat of punishments (going to Hell, losing custody of children, physical abuse, etc.) for straying is a very difficult strategy that not only makes "going the distance" a drudgery, but often precipitates the very behavior it seeks to prevent.

However, when a couple realizes what's in play here, and instead of getting mad at their partner every time they look at someone else, they use this knowledge to their advantage, they'll find themselves happier than ever before. This is one of the secrets that the handful of really happy couples out there have discovered. The more variety couples have in their love life, the more they are working in concert with (instead of futilely resisting) the Coolidge Effect.

Kissing Lots of Frogs

Variety is not only a stimulus for men, but for women also (not to worry, we will soon be delving into what a man can do to keep his woman attracted to him). Though higher quality is the far greater force of female attraction, they are also stimulated by change. Part of the female's mixed reproductive strategy involves seeking out men who are different, those not found in their usual social circles or even in their same tribe. At first, this sounds no different than the male's principle strategy to spread his seed as far and wide as he can. But for women, the purpose is more complex. They're not just out to get as many guys as they can. Variety, for women, is not an end in itself. Instead, when women seek out a diversity of men, it's only a means to an end.

That "end," of course, is finding the best male possible. Dating, even if it should result in having intimacy with a large number of men, is still just a sorting process. While many men are easily ruled out before they can even get to "first base," a woman can still end up with two or more "final candidates" who all seem to have what it takes to be an Alpha. What to do, then, if a woman can't decide by interacting with them *outside* of the bedroom, which one is the most Alpha? Natural Selection came up with an answer—be attracted to each new candidate if he seems to be at least as Alpha as the one you already have, and if need be, let them compete one-on-one to determine the winner *inside* the bedroom.

It probably bears repeating that, a woman (especially an Alpha Female) will pass up a lot of guys for every one she even considers to test further. But out of those who get past "the screen test," it might not be so easy for her to determine if he is the best she can get. Many times, she can only find this out by actually having sex with him.

Granted, the better she perceives herself to be, and the more men she has to choose from, the more likely she is going to reserve intimacy for a special, few "finalists." But the more Alpha she perceives a man to be, the more likely she is going to acquiesce to intimacy. In those cases where the man is giving every indication to her that he is the most Alpha guy she's ever met, then she not only acquiesces but is likely to actively solicit sex from him!

Unfortunately, there are many guys who do a pretty good job coming off as an Alpha ... until after they get a girl to bed. Then, they quickly reveal themselves to be needy "wimps" after all. They rush to profess their undying love, and sometimes, they propose marriage after only a few dates. Sure, their intentions are great, and many times they are just so happy to have found such a wonderful, beautiful woman, that they are just trying to express their gratitude by giving her anything she might ask for. But as we've already noted, this seemingly logical, gallant and romantic behavior only serves to trigger a negative reaction somewhere deep inside the female brain.

If we could supply words to this illogical feeling, it might go something like this—"I was so attracted to you at first. I thought you were The One. You were so strong, dominant and secure. I wanted nothing other than to be with you and to be intimate with you. Now, though, you're acting differently. You seem weak, submissive and needy. I've lost that strong desire I had only a few days ago. Looks like I made a mistake."

For women, this process can be very frustrating. Sometimes, they get so tired of thinking they've found their Alpha at last, only for him to turn into yet another Beta; they'll give up. Some give up on ever finding a real Alpha man who would truly satisfy their deepest longing. Many of them subsequently settle for less than what they really want. They will finally accept a proposal from a Beta just because of everything else he can offer—money, prestige, a large home, travel, security. But the more Alpha she is, the more likely she is to become discontent in such a relationship.

Perhaps what is most unfortunate about this phenomenon is that our society is still much more tolerant of those women who settle for a Beta, then of those who hold out for an Alpha. Fortunately, it's nowadays no where near as difficult for those women who don't want to settle, as it was for Great Grandma. The more men they date, the more they might be subjected to ridicule by some for being such "sluts," but with more emphasis being placed on personal happiness than religious or social obligation, women are better able in today's society to select a better partner from a better number of men.

We might compare the female reproductive strategy to a boxing tournament. Hundreds of men might "come to the try outs," only to be disqualified and never get anywhere close to the ring. But out of all those who never get close, a percentage do. It's a mistake to think of a woman as an indiscriminant, promiscuous "slut" if she allows ten or a hundred men "into the ring" as it were, because in all likelihood, there were many more thousands she'd weeded out first!

The big question, though, is, "Who is The Champ?" In many cases, the only way is to let them get in the ring, and duke it out. The winner, as far as she is concerned, will be the one that not only gets her to bed, but who continues to be just as strong, just as elevated, just as Alpha afterwards. Once a woman is convinced she's found Mr. Right, she'll forgo all the other "Mr. Right Nows."

Yes, this conflicts with much of what we've been taught by our culture, by society, by our families and by the church. But when direct experience and scientific observation tell us something different from what has been alleged but not proven in the real world, I for one have decided to go with science. If any still doubt that Nature has purposely inclined women to engage in setting up such competition between men, note the following. Laboratory tests have confirmed that when sperm from two men are introduced into a woman's vaginal tract, the spermatozoa themselves will actually combat with each other to prevent the sperm of the other male from moving further up the tract toward the woman's egg!

We see, then, that while females have a different purpose for doing so (though it's not a purpose "in mind"), they too are stimulated by variety. There's more than a little truth to the proverb, "you have to kiss a lot of frogs to find a prince."

Combating Habituation

So just what is it that we're up against? If for both men and women, there exists some deeply entrenched, emotional mechanism that drives us to seek out others, what is it? If at times, it should become necessary to fight with our instincts, it behooves any of us who wishes to combat our very nature, in a smart way, to know what it is we're fighting. The "enemy" here actually has a name—habituation. It's a phenomenon very familiar to biologists, and under most circumstances, is a force for good. However, when it comes to keeping the fires of passion alive, habituation can be the biggest "passion extinguisher" of all.

Habituation is actually a learning phenomenon, and it's very common in all living things. Habituation happens when our senses are subjected to the same stimuli over and over again … until they get used to them. The more we get the same stimuli, the less stimulating they become.

Normally, habituation helps us focus on things that are more important, and to not get too preoccupied with the familiar. This is good if we're talking about tuning out all the different scenery on the route we take everyday to work, leaving our minds free to spot that one vehicle that's weaving in and out of traffic lanes. But it's very bad news in terms of "no longer being stimulated" by a lover we hope to be faithful to on a long term basis.

For the purposes of our species' evolution, it was a good thing that what first really got us attracted to someone—whether a shapely, young babe, or a strong, masculine hunk—that as time went by, our ancestors were not as "turned on" as they were at first. In time, a reduction in stimulation would naturally occur by virtue of seeing, hearing, feeling, touching, smelling and experiencing the same things from the same person day after day. This gradual process would eventually help lead to the obsolescence of relationships.

Bad as that sounds to us now, though, relationship obsolescence encouraged genetic variety. Each time our ancient forebears would strike out and find someone new, the odds of their children's (by different partners) survival improved. (Recall our earlier discussion about the advantages in preventing the intrusion of parasitic diseases by virtue of each child having a different, genetic "combination lock.") But for those of us who now live in a very different world and who would like to remain with a sexual partner permanently, habituation can really make things difficult.

Cohabiting couples often report that their passion for each other is not as strong as it was years before when they were first dating. But married couples seem to lose their passion much faster, and many of these report not only a reduction, but a complete loss. One of the big reasons for this is because getting married tends to expedite the process of habituation! When a couple chooses to change the very foundation of their relationship from wanting-to-be together to havng-to-be together, they actually precipitate the end of sexual stimulation. They will often ignore the signs of habituation when they first appear, and then keep ignoring them! As you may have guessed, habituation is not something that will go away if you ignore it long enough. Instead, it only gets worse.

Resentment

Now, before we go on to discuss other things couples can do to outwit habituation and use other natural forces to their advantage, we need to confront a common, but not very helpful, attitude. As we've been discussing the advantages which Alpha men and women have over all others, it's very easy for those who've not had much success in the past with the opposite sex to feel like they can never be like Alphas. There are many people, in fact, who've resigned themselves to unhappy marriages because somewhere inside themselves they not only believe they "are not worthy," but they've developed a very unhealthy emotional condition state that only serves to seal the coffin of their dead love lives—resentment! Some cannot even bring themselves to believe it's worth their while to even try to overcome the obstacles that are keeping them from having a happy love life.

For instance, there are women who are constantly putting down men for finding Alpha women attractive. Their complaints often go as follows, "Men! All they care about are these young girls who don't have the experience or intelligence or maturity that I can offer." The more they sense that they are "lower on the totem pole," the more they spend their time and energy finding faults with "those skinny, stupid, immature" girls, and the men who "leer" at them. Their frustration might be understandable, especially if Nature hadn't given them much to work with in the first place as far as looks go. That said, getting angry at men for only doing that which is normal is not going to help.

Not to be outdone, though, men also fall into the same trap, though the reason why differs. Since women are not so much attracted to "nice guys" as much as to inner strength, confidence and dominance, many a nice—even a good-looking—guy will become very frustrated with women in general, after so many encounters with girls who will agree that they are so nice, but take no further interest in them (except as a friend). Guys can complain all day long that women must be crazy for only going after "bad boys." Some get just as resentful as the aforementioned unattractive women, as they cannot to save their life understand why girls seem to run from them instead of appreciating their nice qualities. What's going on here?

Well, let's recall once more that attraction is not a choice, but a reaction to some very specific characteristics of the opposite sex. In both of these examples, neither gender can ever logically convince members of the opposite sex to be attracted to them. In both cases, they're mistaking qualities about themselves (that, yes, are really good) that would cause the opposite sex to be very attracted to them … were human sexual attraction based on *reason*. But it's not!

Sure, all these other qualities can make for some good, added extras. It's not that men wouldn't like to have a relationship with a giving, intelligent and mature-minded woman, nor is it that women wouldn't like to have a relationship with a nice, caring and sensitive man. But these qualities are not what trigger attraction in the opposite sex. Attraction is not a rational choice made in the frontal lobe of the brain, but a deep, emotional response which emanates from the base of the brain, the instinctive "lizard" area. Whine about it all you want, but if you'd rather be successful in attracting a mate and keeping them attracted, you have to accept the reality that whatever you can do to make yourself more Alpha like, the more attractive you will be.

Also, let's not lose sight of the good news here—that women don't have to be selfish, stupid and immature bitches to be attractive to men, and neither do men have to be abusive, violent and insensitive jerks to be attractive to women. The fact that people like these manage to attract the opposite sex so much is only a coincidence.

What If We Didn't Have All Three Sexual Instincts?

If there's any chance of ever having a satisfying, monogamous relationship, the odds are much more in favor of those couples who are willing to accept our sexual nature for what it is, and then to do whatever they can practically to accommodate it. And acceptance begins with understanding. It helps to understand that Mother Nature gave us all three conflicting sexual instincts for a reason—mainly, to "create" competition. As far as the survival of our species goes, it was a good thing that She did. However, it's difficult sometimes for individual members of the species, living in the here and now, to appreciate why such conflict was necessary. That said, let's give it a try, beginning with a short review.

One, we humans have a natural drive to copulate with more than one partner. It's no surprise that men are especially driven to have sex with as many different women as possible, preferring Alpha Females first. The less well known fact, though, is that women are also driven to seek out multiple sex partners too. Yes, they'll remain content with one partner if he is an Alpha. But until then, they may copulate with many other men first. They may attempt relationships along the way, but if all they could do is settle for a Beta male, they will find any Alpha that comes along later almost irresistible.

Two, both men and women also have a natural longing to form pair-bonds, i.e., to fall in love and start a relationship. However, these bonds tend to last only about four years on average, especially during a woman's best reproductive years (the late teens to the early thirties. It's not unusual for people to have several relationships during this period, even if they intended each one to be permanent. Some call this behavior "serial monogamy," but it's very likely that the kind of monogamy meant here is only in a social sense. Instinct Two doesn't prevent humans from straying sexually, especially after several years have gone by.

Three, we have an instinct to become jealous when we believe our mate is or might be copulating with anyone else. The most typical behavior associated with jealousy is mate guarding, especially for males. Jealousy is particularly acute during our reproductive years, after which, the instinct tends to wane somewhat.

Were at least one of these three instincts missing from our nature, it would seemingly make things much easier for us today. For example, if we only had Instincts Two and Three, we would be content with a single mate (in accordance with Instinct Two), and Instinct Three would never be stimulated as there would be no desire to stray (thanks to the absence of Instinct One). If we only had One and Three, we would never find ourselves falling in love and dealing with all the entanglements of relationships. We could be single all our lives, copulating with as many partners as we desire. Again, jealousy would not come into play because we'd have no mate to be jealous over. If we had only One and Two, we would be capable of falling in love and having a mate, and at the same time, copulate as much as we'd like with others ... and it would be OK, because we wouldn't mind our mate copulating with others, nor would they mind us doing the same. There would be no instinct to become jealous or sexually possessive of our mates.

However, such wishful thinking is just that. For one thing, such "simpler combinations" would have some immediate, negative repercussions. Combination One and Three, for example, would likely result in removing fathers from the family, leaving all children to be raised by single mothers, or perhaps, by institutions run by the State. But more to the point is that our species would never have even evolved—much less survived for very long if it had—with only two of these three instincts, regardless of the combination. Instinct Two, or the "love" instinct made possible the lengthy period of human infancy, long enough for our advanced brains to grow.

Two:Three would have resulted in genetic mediocrity. Our forebears would have just kept the same old genes and passed them on again and again with no improvement. Had those with the best genes not been instinctively inclined to spread them farther and wider, we would've never gotten the genetic upper hand to evolve and adapt into who we are. The "sin of lust" that so many religious ascetics attribute to Adam's Fall was actually a critical necessity to our evolution, and probably still is.

One:Two would also have resulted in genetic mediocrity, but for a different reason. With Instinct One in place our ancestors would have spread their genes to many mates, but there would not have been a higher proportion of the better genes being spread. In other words, just as many mediocre genes as superior ones would have been spread far and wide, which is no better than keeping the same ratio of mediocre genes to superior ones as with Two:Three. Jealousy was—and continues to be—one of Nature's best ways to "sift out the chaff from the wheat." Only those with superior genetic quality, the Alphas, can overcome the barrier of jealous, mate-guarding Betas, to sweep their mates off their feet regardless. Other Betas may try to seduce women "already taken," but they would not only be discouraged by the in-pair males, but also by the disinterest of the females themselves.

One:Three would not have worked either, even though it would have helped the better genes prevail. Without Instinct Two, there would not have existed the extra support that young children and their lactating mothers get from a special male socially bonded to her in an empathetic relationship. Whatever gains made in genetically superior infants is lost to not enough help to get them through their high maintenance infancy. Sure, many mothers of other species—like lizards who have small, mostly reactive brains—get along just fine without pair-bonding, because their young are ready to go it alone the minute they hatch. But to have the kind of intelligence we and other "higher thinking" animals evolved, means a prolonged period of infancy and dependency to allow our superior brains time to grow. Our kind, not only survived, but rose to the top of the food chain, ultimately because of our ability to form pair bonds making it possible to protect and nurture our young while they're so vulnerable for so long.

There's no getting around it, then. We have all three instincts thanks to the evolutionary benefits they provided. We have to live with them in the context of our modern world, even though "the rules" have changed so much in a relatively short period of time (that is, "short" compared to the millions of years it took evolution to forge them). It's perfectly understandable how Natural Selection would have favored us with these conflicting instincts in order to promote the reproduction of the fittest at the highest rate possible, and shut out the least fit. But now, the world is over populated. We're much more concerned about things like fairness and helping everyone live a decent life, even if it means allowing for the weak to be as reproductively successful as the strong. Most of us—in the developed countries anyway—live in non-agrarian societies where each child represents an economic liability instead of an asset. And a lady-killing, successful Alpha Male today who isn't careful to use condoms every time he "scores" can end up paying a lot of child support. What to do, now, that the rewards which shaped our nature over millions of years virtually disappeared overnight, though our nature remains the same?

The Uphill Strategies

The traditional (Judeo-Christian) answer to this dilemma is to label Instinct One as an evil, to claim that it was not a part of our original biology (in the Garden of Eden before The Fall), and to resist it at all costs, even if it means being personally miserable. In exchange for resisting the drive to gratify sexual desire here on earth, there is offered the hope of being rewarded with even greater gratification of other sorts in the next life.

Easier said than done, though. And only to the extent that one truly believes such a next life exists. More effective in swaying people to suppress their desires was the fear of horrific, eternal punishments awaiting those who cave in to "immediate gratification." And even then, the vast majority of humans, even the most devote, fail to be chaste. What this means in practical terms, though, is choosing a very negative strategy to constantly resist this drive, all the while doing much to stimulate it (not eating has a way of making one *more*, not less hungry).

Instinct One is not accommodated in any way, making it most difficult to suppress. All that keeps one from doing what one really wants to (aside from lack of opportunity) is negative reinforcement—fear of punishment by God, fear of adverse legal repercussions in Divorce court (more applicable to men than women), and to a degree, fear of social rejection (more applicable to women than men). Those who succeed in being "faithful" are usually only doing so outwardly, often at the expense of being quite miserable inwardly. Either way, they end up "giving in to temptation," and feeling very guilty, ashamed and afraid. Whether they commit adultery in deed or in the heart, both lead directly to dishonesty, since they must constantly deceive their mates while they fantasize or act in contradiction to their own fundamental beliefs.

Nevertheless, the Suppression of Instinct One continues to be the most widely attempted strategy for reconciling the three conflicting instincts, in large part because organized religion and many other institutions—such as the Divorce/Marriage Industry—benefit so much from it. The Church, for instance, benefits because they are guaranteed a non-stop, steady stream of easy-to-control, guilt-ridden supplicants who are always in need of absolution. Feeling poorly about one's self (because one is always "committing adultery in one's heart," if not in deed) always makes one more susceptible to the control of others.

There are, however, other strategies. A small number of people choose to suppress Instinct Three and accommodate Instincts One and Two instead. These folks are either swingers or polyamorous.[194] Swingers and the polyamorous (or "polys" for short) are couples who believe that they are better off allowing their drive to copulate with others to prevail, at least every now and then. They must, however, be willing to deal with the intense emotion of jealousy that is almost certain to arise as a natural response.

Swingers counter jealousy by engaging only in recreational sex, only for short periods of time (maybe one weekend out of the month, for example), only with people they don't know, and whom they are unlikely to meet again (which is why they favor having these encounters out of town). They do this in order to avoid any emotional attachments from forming. By adhering to these rules, they hope to head off jealousy by making it as unlikely as possible for these encounters to lead to love.

The polyamorous, on the other hand, use a different strategy to placate the desire for sexual variety and still fend off jealousy. They do not engage in recreational sex. Instead, they actively form relationships with others, and attempt to thwart jealousy by encouraging all partners to get to know and trust each other. Each one must be, at least rationally convinced, that no one in their "circle" of three or more partners will try to move in on the others' relationships to keep someone for themselves.[195]

Both polys and swingers have to restrain urges of jealousy, but they believe it's the lesser of evils, easier than restraining Instinct One. Moreover, they have the advantage of being much more honest with each other, in that they've already acknowledged that their relationships don't stand or fall on absolute sexual monogamy or the desire to have sex with others. Even so, very few people pull off this strategy successfully for any length of time. Those who do are almost always past the age of active reproduction (in their 40s or older, after the jealousy instinct wanes), and they have to be very discreet about it since society in general is not very supportive of their lifestyle.

A third strategy, which is becoming more and more popular, is to suppress Instinct Two in favor of accommodating One and Three—being single and sexually free.[196] Unlike swinging or polyamory, society has become much more tolerant of this strategy, particularly for the young. For Alphas who find it relatively easy to find a partner for a "one night stand," this strategy is even more appealing, because there's no worry about being alone, unless one wishes to be. The challenge comes mostly in communicating clearly enough so none of these partners get the impression they are in the running to have the Alpha all to themselves.

Even so, the older we become, the more difficult it is to set aside Instinct Two. Women speak of their "biological clock ticking down," and even the most (sexually) successful Alpha bachelors will begin to complain about the "hassles" of scheduling different women into their date books (yes, difficult as this is for Beta Males to grasp).

Might this simply be Nature's way of encouraging Alpha men to slow down their pace as they mature, once they've spent a good number of years spreading their superior DNA far and wide? It makes sense from the perspective of Natural Selection, that as a male matures, becomes wiser, and if nothing else, more knowledgeable about how to survive longer, that these gifts should translate into more relationships with women (so his children might benefit directly from them).

Work With, Not Against Nature

So many people waste so much time—often, their entire lives—wishing that others do all the work of change. Many complain that they just can't find a mate who will accept them "for who they are."

Men get frustrated and angry when they find themselves again and again being dropped into the "friend category" by the women they wish they could be with, who at the same time, complain to them about their abusive, jerk boyfriend who mistreats them! They may try doing more of the same old things to try to convince these women that they would be a much better partner because they are nice, romantic and gentlemanly. Unfortunately, they fail to come to grips with the reality that a woman is so overwhelmed by her deep down feelings of attraction for any male who has the characteristics of Alpha strength and dominance that she will helplessly throw herself at him, even if he is a mean jerk. Sure, guys can try all day long to find a woman who will discount the deepest longings she has within her, and base her choice of sexual partner strictly on what makes logical sense, and decide to date a "nice guy." But they might as well be waiting for the proverbial freezing over of Hell.

It just makes much more sense to—and will save men decades of frustration—to acknowledge that Nature has women so deeply programmed to respond to the strong, Alpha Male, to just go ahead and begin making changes to one's self in order to become the kind of man a woman will naturally want—work with Nature instead of against it. One need not become an abusive jerk—who is very attractive to women, not for his abusiveness, but for other characteristics that accompany it as a matter of coincidence.

A very selfish and self-centered male might coincidentally "beam" with self assurance. He is anything but submissive, but not because he has good leadership qualities. Instead, it's only because he cares for no one but himself. Still, it's close enough to trigger the feeling deep down inside the female brain which says, "You've found a leader, a real man!"

But a nice guy can also acquire the same "trigger." He can actually de-wimpify himself of acting submissively and needy, he can get the same reaction from women … without having to become a selfish, abusive jerk in the process.

Likewise, woman could avoid much frustration by learning a similar lesson. Though many women seem to understand that looking good can first attract a man, once they get a guy "hooked," many tend to stop doing what worked in the first place. So many bang their heads against a wall by insisting that men change their motive for being with them from natural attraction to unnatural obligation and then wonder, "Why doesn't he look at me the way he used to?" "After all," they reason, he said "I do."

Obligation, or the more popular term "making a commitment," doesn't hold a couple together very well, and often, not for very long. In fact, it serves to undermine what really does work. No wonder, so many women are frustrated with their relationships, because they've abandoned the one thing that was actually working to give them what they really wanted.

Then there are those who think that once a man loves them, he'll put up with anything, for any length of time. Sure, love does endure many things, and this is true of both the love of men and of women. However, no matter how much a woman is convinced she's found the truest of true love, it's a pure fantasy to think that she can do everything humanly possible to extinguish the fire of love and still expect it to be there. Clinging onto a partner's commitment only serves to drown the love for both persons.

Let's remember that love is the result, not the cause, of attraction. This point is so important, and yet so widely misunderstood, that it bears repetition—love, not even if someone is "totally committed" to it, is neither an eternal force, nor a magic power that has no limits. Love is an emotional attachment, that is either being reinforced or being broken down. Each day, the things that happen, or which don't happen, have the effect of either fueling the "fire" of love or putting it out. Those who subscribe to the philosophy which elevates what they call "love" above "carnal passion" only serves to leave people alone and miserable. The knowledge we have about our sexual nature ought to encourage us, as a responsible society, to accommodate our natural, sexual drives just as we do most every other biological drive.

Let's compare our sex drive to a river and the traditional means of restraining it with a water dam. The common wisdom to dealing with our desires to have sex with more than one person is to forcibly oppose it. All the religious injunctions, the legal restrictions, the social antipathies directed against those who stray could be compared to building a dam to hold back a great river. But unlike real world dams which allow for the same amount of water to flow as before, but only in a redirected manner, the conventional approach tries with all its might to reduce the flow to a mere trickle—no sex until you marry, marry for life, and no sex outside of Marriage ... or else! Even those who want very badly to abide by these restrictions most often break down and give in to the enormous pressure that builds. The "river flow" of sexual desire just doesn't stop moving. It continues to flow up against the "dam," and as it does it begins to rise higher and higher. The pressure against it becomes overwhelming. Sooner or later, the water either flows over it or breaks through it, but one thing is for sure, the dam cannot hold out indefinitely.

There's another strategy, however, to deal with the powerful flow of the human sex drive ... *redirecting it instead of trying to dam it up altogether!* Real life dams don't actually stop the water from flowing. They merely hold it back temporarily until it can flow through underground channels and move through giant turbines which generate electricity. In fact, real dams are very flexible, built to allow for water to flow though at greater rates, sometimes circumventing the turbines altogether, when there are heavy rains or snow melts, and there's more water coming down the river than normal.

In like manner, having sex within a monogamous union that is intended to be permanent is a good thing, and perhaps a wonderful goal to strive for. Unfortunately, striving for this ideal by means of "damming" the sex drive is foolish, just as damming a river to completely stop the flow of water would be. But what if we were to provide for some ingenious ways to re-channel the sex drive, so that it could flow relatively unimpeded, but in a way that provides for greater benefits? What if we were to recognize that, sometimes, due to times in our life when the pressure of the sex drive builds up, there just needs to be some forms of release in order to prevent the entire "dam" from breaking apart. Instead of acting to destroy the dam, releasing the flow actually serve to preserves it.

Fight for Your Right to Poddy

What we're really talking about here is accommodating instead of suppressing the sex drive. Look at how we accommodate the natural drive of elimination (that very strong urge deep within us that says, "Hey, you've got only a few minutes to find a restroom.") by placing restrooms almost everywhere ... at no small expense either![197] We don't beat people up emotionally or try to make them feel they're bad or sinful ... just because they regularly get the "urge to go." Employees who might otherwise get in trouble for taking personal phone calls are allowed to use the restroom if need be ... even on company time. School children are allowed to leave their desks during class, and we even put toilets in prison cells! We go to considerable trouble to educate our children about the importance of good hygiene and sanitation—flush, wash hands with anti-bacterial soap, etc. We provide for privacy in most places, and we try to reduce any unpleasant side effects with regular cleaning and air fresheners. To be certain, we expect that everyone (except infants and those who've not the physical or mental capacity to do so) restrain themselves from just relieving themselves anywhere and everywhere. Nevertheless, we rather matter-of-factly accept that "going to the restroom" is just a natural function, and as long as people agree to abide by a few practical limitations (like making every effort to use the proper facilities), no one is made to feel ashamed or guilty or fearful about it.

Why then, don't we do the same with the sex drive? Knowing that the younger one is, the stronger the drive is to seek out multiple partners, knowing that even when we get a little older and begin to form relationships, that built-in obsolescence will tend to prevent a couple from staying together for a lifetime, and knowing that the longer we live past the ideal age for having children, the more likely we are to naturally form a lasting pair bond ... ought to make us much more tolerant and pragmatic in the way our society responds to these stages. We ought to accommodate our sexuality by helping teens prevent unwanted pregnancies through better education about contraceptives and disease prevention, rather than to delude ourselves into thinking that they can and will practice abstinence.[198] We ought to encourage our young adults to delay having children. We ought to be more tolerant of those who might go through several relationships while in their 20s or early 30s before having a family. And we ought to be much more helpful toward those couples who do break up by moving the process out of adversarial divorce courts to mediatorial venues, and not treat them as if they've committed the Unpardonable Sin, simply because their relationships ended.

Sexual Tacking

Perhaps, one more metaphor is in order. Much of this thesis has been about the futility of unnecessarily going head-to-head with Mother Nature, and yet, I've also spoken about how we can accommodate our natural drives in our modern society. The difference between the two may seem only a matter of semantics. But in reality, they are worlds apart.

If I may borrow from my limited knowledge of sailing, maybe the distinction will become more plain. I'm told by sailboat aficionados that, with a little knowledge and practice, one can adjust sails to accommodate almost any wind direction in order to sail where one wishes. For example, if the wind just happens to be going in the exact direction you wish to go, the sails need only be set, more or less perpendicular to the wind in order to take full advantage of its power, and away you go. This is called "running," and even a "land lubber" like myself was able to grasp the logic of this sailing skill right away.

But what do you do if the wind is blowing in the opposite direction? In ancient times, before sailing was perfected, you either had to wait or do as the Iliad's King Agamemnon in order to launch the thousand ships against Troy—have your daughter sacrificed to sway the gods to grant favorable winds!

Then as now, if you're just absolutely determined to go only in one, straight direction, and you fix your sails 90 degrees to the winds blowing just the opposite way … you're not likely to get very far. In fact, your boat is likely to blow over were you to try. Of course, you could take the sail down, and begin rowing, but even this would be very difficult, very strenuous, and very, very slow at best.

The good news for those who would become modern sailing enthusiasts is that they need not wait for winds to blow in the exact direction they wish to go. Sails are now very adjustable, and the science of manipulating wind directions has come a long ways. By adjusting sails in just the right way, a sail boat can go in almost any direction. Even when heading to some point that lies exactly opposite a headwind, a clever maneuver called *tacking* can be used to get there all the same, essentially by zigzagging.

The sail is set to go just to the left or right side (port or starboard tack) of the headwind, almost in the same direction as straight ahead. By going just a bit to one side—"close hauled"—and then to the other side, in zigzag fashion, the boat can go generally in the same direction as where the wind is coming from. True, it does take longer than if the wind were coming from the other way, but the point is that you can still use the wind to get you there, and the only sacrifice necessary is the little extra mileage (or knotage?) thanks to the zigzagging.

I find this metaphor very helpful for our discussion. There are a few people who are fortunate enough to be able to live their love lives in complete harmony with Mother Nature's urges, the Alphas. They are not likely to become exhausted and frustrated in their love lives, much like sailors who are always "running" with the wind at their backs. There is little to no conflict between the direction they want to go and the course which their fundamental, sexual nature is taking them. For Alpha men, this means dating and having sex with many, attractive women. For women, it means getting a relationship with a man she perceives to be at the top or even out of her league, and even though she never gets a clear sense that she's "hooked him," she's always happy to keep trying.

Most of us, though, even if we have the ability to live Alpha life style for a while, might at some point choose to go another direction, one where the "wind" isn't going to readily take us without some special knowledge and skill. Unfortunately, most folks don't know that there are ways to take advantage of Nature's "wind direction," and use it to their advantage, to learn and apply a kind of sexual tacking. No, most feel that their only option is to "paddle as hard as they can," in complete contradiction to the direction Nature is trying so hard to move them.

When they find themselves about to go backwards, the common wisdom remedy is, "You better start rowing harder!" It really shouldn't be surprising that they are constantly frustrated, exhausted, and how often their "boats" (relationships) capsize! After one, two or three lost boats, many give up, take their sails down, throw down the anchor, and sit there helplessly. If they're lucky, they won't be blown too far off course, but it's clear that they are not in control, and they're not going where they wish.

The experiences of these poor sailors, who either can't keep their boats afloat or if they do, can't sail them to where they want to go, sadly, are what most marriages are like—relationships of exhaustion, going nowhere at best, and often sinking.

It doesn't have to be this way. Like sailing experts do, there's a way to interact with Nature in such a way so you can still get to where you want to go and enjoy the trip. As with the tacking method, it does take some knowledge, skill and practice, but it can be done.

Much of what we've already discussed is the way in which women can "adjust their sails" so that they don't find themselves going against the "wind" of Nature, and therefore, "dead in the water" as far as their love lives are concerned.

But what can men do for their women? I've chosen to specifically deal with this issue in the last chapter of this book, because a man tends to begin making big mistakes as soon as he starts going out with a woman, and it gets even worse after Marriage. Perhaps this will seem a bit unfair in that I didn't devote an entire chapter to what women can do to attract, and keep attracting men. But I did so for good reason, and I hope that women won't feel slighted because it is in fact a compliment to their gender's greater perception when it comes to things sexual.

After all, learning how to attract women, and to keep their interest, is a far greater mystery to most men, then the converse is to most women.

First, we need to come back to Marriage itself. Though the unmarried have a clear advantage in getting and keeping a happy relationship, there is still a lot that can be done to help the already married to make love thrive in their admittedly disadvantaged situation.

13

What Can the Already Married Do?

o o o o o o o o o o o o o o o o o o o o o o o o o o o o o o o

"Where's the Marriage book section?" asked the woman who was desperate to find some help for her crumbling relationship. "Can you be a little more specific?" replied the bookstore employee. "I mean, the section on how to be happily married … or how to save an unhappy marriage," the unhappy wife explained. Pointing to an entire aisle of books, "Here, ya go. Take your pick." The woman's jaw dropped, and she exclaimed, "Where do I begin?" "That's easy," said the store employee. "Pick any one you can afford … they all say the same thing!"

The Epiphany

It was over a decade ago when I first began to question why Marriage is such an unhappy experience for most people. I knew there was something wrong. My own experience and the state of almost every married person I knew all told the same story—getting married wounds and often kills love. I had little idea at the time what was wrong and why, but I was determined to find out.

I made up my mind that I was going to get to the bottom of this problem no matter what. And if I may, I want to pause to address that first step, because there was something very critical about it—the "no matter what" part. I didn't want to merely look for information that would support what I already thought was true. I knew if I did, my research would very likely be flawed. Instead, I came to this quest with a willingness to throw out years of presumptions, conditioning and ideas that I might have accepted along the way without ever having looked to see for myself if they had any validity. (By the way, this is where all true learning begins—making the decision to be completely open to new ideas, and being willing to toss out anything, and I mean *anything* that doesn't stand the acid test of working in reality.)

I started with the Marriage Repair gurus. I read book after book. Yes, some of them had a few good ideas about how to "spice up" relationships, but they would never explain how "the flavor" gets lost in the first place. Sure, they had all kinds of suggestions for how to put a splint on a broken marriage, but no one, and I mean no one, dared try to explain how to stop the fractures from happening.

It was as if there was some unspoken, but universally understood law which said, "Never question the Marriage Institution itself!" Not a one was willing even to suggest that the reason behind the phenomenon of "bad marriages" might be because there was something about Marriage itself that was bad. Instead, they were all focused on convincing unhappily married people that if their marriages were unhappy, then the only explanation is that they, and they alone, must be at fault. They all agreed that Marriage gave benefits to relationships, but none could explain what those benefits were. I could find aisle upon aisle of books, audio and video recordings offering temporary fixes, but no real solution; band aids, but no cure. Like the proverbial rabbit chasing the carrot on a stick tied to its back, they were all holding out the reward of a "good marriage," but I could never find anyone who had any lasting success following their advice.

After much disappointment and frustration, I finally decided to start from scratch. I started researching what history had to say, and it was there that the clouds surrounding this mystery first began to clear. I learned where Marriage came from, and when I did, I realized that there was a huge gap between the truth and where most people think the Institution originated. Instead of finding that Marriage was first designed to bring some equity or fairness or something good to human sexual relationships, the truth was quite the contrary. Marriage began as an institution of sexual slavery. Right there, I thought, is at least part of the explanation for why getting married wrecks the havoc it does for most couples.

But as is the case with so many other discoveries, I quickly began to have more questions than answers. For example, if Marriage began as such an evil, "How then," I wondered, "do a few people manage to avoid its damning effects?" Could it be that this institution, which started off so badly, may have along the way been converted into something good, at least, for a few? Might there be some benefit that Marriage, as we now know it, confers if only we could find out what it is, and how to make it happen?

To find the answer, I next began to take a real close look at the small handful of married people I knew who really seemed to be happy with each other. At first, I thought the key was "compatibility." Perhaps these people had just "gotten lucky," and had each found a rare, but near-perfect match. "Maybe, Marriage does benefit those who come into it with this thing called compatibility" I hypothesized.

This theory goes at least as far back as Plato's Symposium in which a certain character named Aristophanes tells of a time when humans were made of only a single gender, complete and perfect. Then, the gods became envious of man's completeness, and decided to split humans into man and woman. From then on, everybody spends their lifetime looking for their perfect match or "split-apart."[199]

Though I never thought there was such a thing as a "soul mate," I had to consider that if certain couples were compatible enough, they could overcome all the other strikes which are against those who are incompatible. Though this hypothesis seemed reasonable, the results of my research proved it false.

A closer look revealed that many of these happy couples were *very different* from each other. In fact, more than a few of them had all kinds of issues that actually led to frequent conflict—from differences in how to spend money to hygiene habits. Some had personalities that were as contrary as night and day, and yet their differences didn't lead to serious or prolonged trouble between them. I had to abandon my first hypothesis, but in favor of what? What was their common denominator? What was helping them stay together *and* be happy?

I struggled with this question for years while I gathered as much information as I could from other disciplines like biology, anthropology and sociology. I was learning a lot about what was going on in human sexual behavior, but nothing seemed to explain how so many were so frustrated and yet some were not. I felt like the scientists in the Sci-Fi movie *The Andromeda Strain*, who were trying to figure out why all but two people in a town had been killed by an alien virus. I'd hit a brick wall in my research, and for a while I contemplated giving up.

Then one evening, during a party at the home of one of these happy couples, the answer finally came. I recall sitting on a couch, watching how all the couples were interacting with each other. I noted much of the usual behavior—partners avoiding each other, some getting upset with each other, others giving each other dirty looks, and quite a number flirting with others behind their partners' backs. Sure, there were those who were quite adept at putting up a good front of togetherness, but even they lacked the body language to match. I'd seen this behavior countless times before. But what was it about that one couple, the happy one.

Why were they so different from everyone else at this gathering? And then it hit me!

It suddenly occurred to me that at no time during the party had either one referred to the other as "husband" or "wife"! I could hardly believe I hadn't noticed this before, but as I began to watch and listen even more carefully, sure enough, scores of details that had previously seemed like a random pile of jigsaw puzzle pieces, all started to fit together. In almost every manner—the way they touched each other, addressed each other, and joked with each other—*this couple was not acting like a married couple*! In fact, they could have easily been mistaken for a couple that had just fallen in love a week ago. The answer why was so simple, I nearly slapped the side of head. The reason they were acting like they did when they were first dating was because *they honestly didn't see themselves as being married.*

After years of painstaking research, hundreds of interviews, and countless hours of contemplation, asking the questions no one else was asking, and pounding away at the walls of ignorance and double speak, I finally received what I like to call "The Epiphany." No, I didn't see angels. No, I didn't hear the audible voice of God. No, I didn't discover some glowing crystal, nor had I climbed to the summit of a mountain to confer with a great guru. I didn't even take a red pill. Well, maybe.

The answer had been right there in front of me the entire time. Just like the little kid in the movie, The Matrix, who was bending a spoon with his mind and trying to explain to the character Neo (played by Keanu Reeves) that the "trick" was understanding "there is no spoon," so too, did I finally wake up that evening and got the message—"There is no benefit" from Marriage.

OK. Now if you are reading this, and wondering how I can say such a thing after I just got through telling you about this sweet, married couple who were as happy as clams with each other, it probably sounds a bit contradictory. I know. Please, bear with me, the answers are coming (sorry Morpheus, I couldn't help it).

Also, if it just so happens that you are already married, I suppose the idea that "there's not a single benefit to come from Marriage" doesn't sound too good, does it? Well, you're in luck. Because, assuming you're willing to hear me out on this one, the situation is not as hopeless as it might seem.

As much as I would prefer that everyone who is in a relationship but not yet married, stay that way, this doesn't mean that the already-married are doomed. They certainly have a far greater challenge ahead of them, but I'm also convinced that it's possible to be happy with one's marital relationship *in spite of* being married.

What we're talking about here is making a major change to the way you think and the way you feel about your most intimate relationship, first, in your frontal lobe and then, more importantly, deep inside the "lizard" part of your brain. You have got to change in the most fundamental way. You have to change the way you relate to your significant other. You've got to find a way to turn back the clock, and *you must begin once again to interact, on every level except the legal one, as if you are not married.*

If I may once more invoke The Matrix again, this complete change of what you really believe about yourself and your intimate relationship is not too unlike the way Neo had to completely change the way he looked at what he previously thought was the only reality. It was pretty hard for him. Morpheus (played by Lawrence Fishburne) had to tell him, "Don't think you can, know you can." He had to shake out of his head all the preconceived notions of what was possible and what wasn't. But in the end, he finally began to do it, as Morpheus finally said, "he's starting to believe."

Hopefully, we're not all literally sitting in bathtubs of goo in a giant Machine City with tubes stuck in our bodies and wires in our heads constantly stringing us along into thinking we're living a real life when, in fact, we're all just prisoners. Notwithstanding, most people are imprisoned in much the same way when it comes to permanent relationships. They've been duped into thinking that there is no other way to make a home with a mate, and so they just keep trudging on, many of them for their whole lives, in quiet desperation. But just like in The Matrix, there is something just like "the red pill" that you can take, if you're willing to see "just how far down the rabbit hole goes."

If you're married, and if you want to be happy with the person you're married to, you've got to get yourself into a totally new frame of mind. You've got to become completely convinced within yourself, that you are—one more time, in every way except the technical, legal one—no longer married. You and your significant other (notice I avoided saying "wife" or "husband") have got to make your way back to that place where you were when you were still dating or living together freely. You've got to undo that exchange you made (hopefully in ignorance) when you gave up on your natural bond—the "wanting to" be together—for that artificial contract where, ever since then, you've "had to" be together.

Bliss of Ignorance

As hard as I try to explain it, I bet there are still some who are reading this right now saying, "Wait a second! I know some people who are happily married!" Sure. Of course you know one, two or maybe even ten married couples that honestly seem to be very happy with each other. But if you were to look closely at these very blessed people—assuming of course that it's not just a front that they're putting on—and compare them with other couples, you'd likely notice a very high correlation between the degree to which they *act like* an unmarried couple and the degree to which they're happy. I wish I didn't have to whip this horse so often, but from my many discussions with people, I believe it to be warranted, one more time—any couple who is married and happy with each other, did not achieve that marital happiness from being married, but have only found a way to avoid the adverse effect Marriage normally has on most people.

How, then, did they become so fortunate? Good question. In most cases, when these fortunate couples get married, they walk right over the real meaning of Marriage … and (thankfully) miss it entirely! Yes, they went and got some document from the courthouse, but didn't even bother to read it. They may have had a wedding ceremony of some sort, but they weren't really paying attention to the purpose. They rattled off some words, but all those vows and the "death 'til you part" stuff just didn't register. Maybe, there was a reception party that they enjoyed, and they got some nice presents, but other than that, they were blissfully ignorant of where these traditions originated. Apart from the presents and a promise from the government not to deny them a few rights and tax benefits (which ought to be extended to every family), they otherwise didn't really expect anything to change. They weren't looking to the vows as a way to prevent their lover from ever abandoning them. They weren't getting a marriage license as a way to (however unlikely) ensure themselves of some financial compensation in the event of a divorce. They were simply not looking for Marriage to do anything for them, and because they basically skipped through the entire process in such a cavalier way, relatively little harm was done to their relationship.

They avoided disaster because, deep inside, in the way they think and feel and interact with each other, they managed not to change. They probably didn't even know why they got married. It was just some, little, social formality they went through, without any anticipation that it was supposed to do anything. As far as they're both concerned, they could have just as easily not even bothered with it. In every way except for a legal one, they are still together *only because they wish to be.*

Crazy sounding? I know. But think for a moment about the people you know who are married and truly happy with each other. You might have been tempted to believe that they just happen to share the exact same values, or that they are both so attractive neither could ever find someone better looking, or that both persons were just real easy going people who could tolerate anything from anybody. You may even have thought—though you didn't know why or how—that getting married somehow contributed to their happiness with each other.

Well, it's certainly an advantage to find a mate with whom one shares a lot of common values, is very physically attractive, and is easy going. However, none of these things is anywhere near as important as having a strong, natural bond of love. Marriage itself, only acts as an emulsifier, like those strong chemicals used to weaken a strong cement or glue. In most cases, Marriage does just that, and relationships tend to fall apart as soon as the honeymoon is over. Only in rare cases, does the adverse effect of Marriage fail to erode the natural force that brought the couple together in the first place.

If you are like most married people, you only know too much about what happened after you got married. You may have thought up until now, that the reason why things went so badly was because of something you did or because you chose the wrong person. If you or your spouse cheated, according the advice of the typical Marriage gurus, it could only have been because "one or both of you failed to live up to your commitment," or "because you weren't spending enough time together," or (the worst one I've ever seen) "you didn't have enough faith in God."

But as was discussed previously, these gurus have it all backwards—commitment is an effect, not a cause; wanting to spend time together will naturally follow doing those things that make you long to be in your partner's company; and while believing for God's help doesn't usually hurt, let's just say that God is not about to give you any more help if you aren't making use of the many good gifts he's already given you!

So now what? What to do if you are in between that "rock" of wanting your relationship to work and "the hard place" of realizing that since you've been married, you've not really been happy with the results? It's too late for you to go back in time, and change what you did, and as I keep saying over and over, getting divorced is just too risky a way to undo the damage of getting married.

Nevertheless, if you and your partner are willing to make the effort—and I'm talking about some real work here—there is hope of getting back that same "Super Glue" that held you and your mate together before you traded it away for the man-made Velcro of a marriage contract. Ready? Good!

And while it might seem unfair, let me put most of the burden of changing on the *guys* (OK Ladies, you can stop clapping and cheering now)! But seriously, it is the guys who need to take charge here (hint: this is what the women *really* want from you). Once a guy gets his Mojo back, his woman is very likely to respond in the same way she did when she was first in love.

14

How Men Can Get Their Mojo Back

o o o o o o o o o o o o o o o o o o o o o o o o o o o o o o o o o

As cavemen were first learning how to fish, Grog said to Ugh, "Hey, see those fish in the pond, I'm going to catch one." Ugh watched Grog for nearly an arm's length of the Great Fire's movement across the blue skin above as he futilely tried again and again to smash a fish with his club. "So," said Ugh, "how much longer are you going to chase those fish through the water? They know what you're up too before you even move." "Hey, I've caught fish this way before!" Grog protested. "Right." explained Ugh, "The old, sick ones who couldn't swim anymore!" Angrily, "OK, so how do you do it?" Grog finally asked. Ugh patiently demonstrated, "Well, I used to do it your way, and I hardly ever had any success." As Ugh lowered a grub in the water, "Then, I got this idea to do something different. I quit chasing them." A few seconds later, several fish swam up to Ugh's hand to get the grub, and he readily swept them up onto the shore, "ya see, now I just show them something they really find appetizing … and they come to me."

Making Women Come To You

Let's say that you're someone who's been unhappily married for a number of years, but you have just gotten The Epiphany. Sure, you probably just spent the last hour kicking yourself for not having figured this out years ago. Maybe you even cried with grief for all the years of your life that you wasted trying over and over to "renew your commitment to your marriage vows," or trying in various other ways to follow the advice of others which never did your relationship a bit of good. You love your partner, but for a very long time now you've not been happy together. Before, you only knew your relationship wasn't fulfilling, but you had no idea why and you felt so helpless. Maybe you'd even resigned to the idea that Marriage and unhappiness go hand in hand. Now though, you're determined to fix things, especially since it's starting to become clear to you where you messed up.

Now that you've got a grip on yourself, there's something else going on. There's a glimmer of hope. There is hope because, if you have taken that first step—realizing that Marriage itself never did, doesn't now, and never will ever do you any good, no matter who you're with, how smart they are, nice they are, attractive they are, compatible they are, etc. You have already accomplished the hardest part of all. So congratulate yourself. You are on your way to an enjoyable love life.

So let's get down to some nitty gritty. How can you actually make this change? What can you do ... or rather ... how can you *undo* that very bad trade you made for a having-to-be together, in order to get back the wanting-to-be together?

Basically, it's a two-fold process. The first part is not as important as the second, but it's probably the easiest to understand. I'm talking about some practical behavioral changes or what has been called by dating advisor and author David D'Angelo, changing your *Outer Game.*[200]

For reasons that go as far back as the origin of sexual reproduction, what works for guys and what works for gals to get attraction going, and keep it going, are very different. So please, don't shoot the messenger once I begin to explain what works to attract the ladies, and what keeps working once you've found one so special that you're willing to leave all the others behind to have a relationship with her. I'm just relaying what Nature has done with no intention to be sexist, if that's how it might sound to some. So with that disclaimer out of the way....

If you're a guy, do you remember how you behaved when you and your mate were dating? Did you used to have a life? Were you always surprising her? Did you lead the way. If for any reason, she tested you by acting immaturely or demanding that you make unreasonable concessions just to please her, did you refuse to cave in? In other words, did you act like a man?

If you were anything at all close to being attractive to her, then you may have been a nice guy, but you didn't act *too* nice. If you were an Alpha, or at least close to it, you never allowed your feelings for a woman get such control of you, that you gave up your soul. You may or may not have been physically attractive, but what most attracted this special woman into your life was what you had going on in your innermost being—a sure sense of yourself, a special kind of confidence, a deep-down feeling of being complete, a thing which I like to call "Mojo."

One of the biggest ironies about what causes a woman to be attracted to a man is how little it has to do with how much a man shows her how much he care's for her! In fact, if you show that you care for her *too much*, her attraction to you will disappear. If you fall so head over heels in love with a girl that you begin to compromise your own best interests, the object of your affections will only begin to see you as a weak wimp. If you, even out of true love, go too far in sacrificing yourself to indulge her every whim, instead of appreciating the sacrifices you're willing to make to have her, by getting turned on, she'll at best only feel about you the way she does her best gay friend. She'll interpret all your offers, no matter how good and well intended they are, as manipulative bribes … and not without some justification. And this dissipation will occur even faster if she is an Alpha Female.

While, in your mind, you're just trying to be a good boyfriend (or husband if this began after you married her), by offering to support her, take her on trips, buy her a dream house, have children with her, take her to fine restaurants, get her jewelry, and on and on and on the list goes, you very likely signaled to her that you must be a Beta! Deep inside of her brain, the part where her "gut feelings" emanate from, she's interpreting your nice offers as compensations, payments in exchange for going with or staying with a "wussy."

Seems crazy doesn't it? Wouldn't a woman who had a man that was "willing to do anything" just to win her heart and convince her of his devotion be so overwhelmed with his gallantry that she'd be thrilled? Doesn't every fairy tale Prince Charming get the beautiful princess once he offers to provide her with all she could every ask for?

Yeah, in fairy tales, but not in reality! Unless you're prepared to believe there's a real Santa Claus, the stories you've heard about Prince Charming (and its million other variations depicted in movies, TV shows and novels) are just as phony. Instead, women are drawn—and they continue to be drawn—to guys who do *not* signal how badly they need them, and therefore, who don't need to compensate them for their time, attention and sticking around! Truly attractive guys, who may or may not be physically handsome or "buffed out" muscular hunks, are those who act quite content all on their own. They are guys who, when they meet an attractive woman, act like they could not care less if she liked him or not. They are guys who would never consider offering anything they owned or doing anything within their means *for the purpose of convincing a woman to like them or to continue liking them.* They are guys who give every evidence that they *know* they have something within themselves that all women want, and that it's up to them to decide if any particular woman is worth their time and attention, not the other way around.

This brings us to the second part of what a man has to do to "get his Mojo back"—having the right attitude, or perfecting his Inner Game.[201] Men that attract women are confident, secure and cool. They are convinced within themselves, and thus, they carry themselves, in a way that says, "I'm in charge of my life." They are real men, and women can just tell when they are around one. While women are not turned off by good looks, athletic figures, fame, lots of money, and so on, these are just added extras. (Much like a man is not turned off when a woman is smart, witty and educated, but what really attracts him is her appearance.) What really counts from the female perspective … what really causes them to be attracted is his *inner strength.* He doesn't have to chase after women; his inner strength makes them come to him.

A real man just naturally attracts women, by having the right disposition within himself, and by not acting like a wimp. Unlike wimps, he doesn't have to do what really amounts to being manipulative—bribing a woman for her attention and affection. What we often think of as "romantic gestures," flowers, gifts, dinners, trips, jewelry, are often nothing more than attempts at bribery. Even if a man is very attractive physically, tall, muscular, and has a "macho" way about him, he can easily send the wrong message to a woman's fundamental instincts by trying to offer her such gestures, particularly when they first meet. For many women, doing so only signals, "there must be something about this guy that's weak, otherwise, why would he be trying to buy my attention and interest."

The Invisible Traffic Signal

Perhaps it will help us to discern the difference between attractive and unattractive behaviors and attitudes by looking at a phenomenon that most guys can relate to. Many single men complain about women "putting their shields up" whenever they just try to talk to them. Then, a few months later, after they get a girlfriend and they're no longer available, the very same girls—who would always run away before—now suddenly walk up to them with a look of interest in their eye!

I recall talking to a friend of mine who had a name for this behavior. He called it the Invisible Traffic Signal. For many men, their experience in attracting or repelling women can be likened to having a traffic light on top of their head which they can't see, but every woman can spot from a mile away. If they're single and out and about looking for women, it's as if the light is flashing RED to every woman they meet, especially if she seems attractive to him! Then, whenever a guy gets a girlfriend or gets married and is unavailable, it's as if the traffic light on his head has turned to GREEN. Now, the girls are all over him.

Why couldn't they have acted this way before, when he was free? It's as if the only time the light goes to green is when he is behaving as if he is completely uninterested in women other than in just a platonic way. What is going on here?

What's happening is that most guys unwittingly behave way too interested in a woman they are, well, interested in. The "red light" telling attractive women, "Stop! Stay away from this guy," is a good metaphor for how this behavior affects them. So many single men behave in ways that only serve to tip off women that he is needy, that he is willing to pay for a girl's attention, that he is weak ... that he is a Beta. Any little clue he gives which indicates how eager he is to get with her is taken as bad news. So naturally, women who pick up on these signals (and they have been equipped by Nature with a built-in, special kind of long range Beta detector) will head for the hills before he even gets close.

The reason for this kind of reaction is actually quite logical if men would look at it from the attractive female's perspective. A female who is an Alpha begins to learn from the time she is a baby that she has power over men. Once she enters puberty, she soon finds out that everywhere she goes men cannot help but take an interest in her. In many cases, she finds that she's being offered all kinds of gifts, favors and attention from guys that she has only just met. When this sort of thing happens day after day, month after month, and year after year, she comes to take it for granted. In fact, if she's very attractive, she probably had to learn very early on not to indulge males with any reaction such as eye contact, a smile or being friendly. She's learned already that by doing so, boys whom she thought were not at all attractive mistook her honest niceness as an indication she liked them. So it's usually not too long before she just figures any guy who is gawking at her, offering to do things for her, or to buy things for her is just like all the other 100 losers she's encountered that same day.

On the other hand, when a guy is not trying to "hit on" other women, or when a man is around a woman he doesn't find attractive, he, equally unwittingly, behaves very differently. He acts disinterested, sexually speaking. He's aloof. He might even make fun and tease a woman in a good-natured way, and treat her as if she were his bratty kid sister. He is now coming off in a totally different way, and his actions are telling the woman, "I'm a confident man. I don't need you. I already have all I want. I'm relaxed. I'm strong." In other words, his subtle behaviors are proclaiming he's an Alpha. Unlike all the other guys who were falling all over her all day long, she finds herself in the presence of someone who stands out, a guy who is transmitting an entirely different signal that all the other guys are oblivious to, but to the woman who's come within range are loud and clear—"Here's who you've been looking for, a real man."

It's quite an irony, but as we've seen already, women are hard-wired to find most desirable those men who are, among other things, the most sexually successful. But how does she normally figure this out when she's first encountered a man? Under rare circumstances, she might have the chance to meet an Alpha whose reputation goes way ahead of him. (Remember, we mean sexual, not financial success, though having lots of money doesn't hurt!) Rock, rap and movies stars, and major league athletes may have a throng of attractive women all around them, which naturally tells her she's come into the presence of a man in demand. But under normal circumstances, all she has to go by is the man himself. What, then, tells her instincts that a man she's only for a brief time begun to interact with must be an Alpha Male?

Well, one way is to see how sexually satisfied or unsatisfied he comes off. The guy who acts like he's not "gotten any" in ten years, is going to signal what a loser he is. But the man who *acts like* (whether or not this is indeed the case) he's got so many women at his beck and call, that he could use a break, is going to send a super sonic message in big, bold letters right to the base of her brain, saying, "here's a sexy Alpha Male that you want really bad!"

What separates Alphas from Betas is behaving in a self-satisfied and confident way when they're in the company of a female who is very attractive. The longer a Beta goes without "getting laid," the more desperate he becomes, and it shows! He often gets anxious and nervous when he's around attractive women. Before he even opens his mouth, he's already telling her he's in a way inferior league, unworthy of her time. But an Alpha is so strong within, that he is not overwhelmed by an attractive woman, regardless of how many or few dates he's had recently. He can even go for long periods of time without any sex at all, and still, he acts like getting a woman to bed is something he can get around to whenever!

An Alpha Male is confident that he can get what he wants, when he wants it. In ancient, pre-agricultural times, he likely had a voluntary harem of women, and oddly enough, the fact that he had other women already, had two great advantages. One, it made him all the less likely to feel sexually needy, and two, it made other women see him as successful, strong and therefore, desirable.

An Alpha is very consistent. It's hard to tell whether he's got a girlfriend or not. He may have just bedded ten different women in the last three days, or he may not have been with anyone for months (which usually happens only because he's too busy with other things he likes to do, not because he can't get a date)! It's not that he doesn't like to have sex; he's still like every other man in this respect. But the difference is that he doesn't let his sexual desires run his life. He keeps them tamed and under control. Only when a woman meets his standards, and only after he's naturally seduced her, and only at just the right time, when she has become putty in his hands, does he then unleash his desires upon her. (And by the way fellas, this is exactly what women really want from a man!)

Don't Take Your Mojo For Granted

Unfortunately, even guys who were true Alphas at one time in their life will often lose this seemingly magical quality, not all unlike the movie character Austin Powers (Mike Myers) who also for a time thought he had "lost his Mojo."[202] This occurs most often after they settle down into a pair bond, and then due to a break up, find themselves single again.

Before, they were getting all the girls. They came off as strong, confident and cool. They had confidence and plenty of healthy self-esteem. They put out the Alpha "vibrations." Then one day, they got involved with a special woman who "got them hooked." They fell in love and got married. They went on a great honeymoon, and for a while it seemed they'd live happily ever after. But then something strange happened. Somewhere along the way, they began to lose their "Alpha projector." Not all, but more than a few Alpha guys who say "I do," eventually turn into clingy, predictable, approval-seeking wimps. Just because they once had plenty of Mojo, doesn't mean they can't ever lose it.

Now let's make sure that there's no confusion here. Once more, I'm not saying a guy has to be an inconsiderate, selfish "prick" in order to attract, and keep attracting a woman. Nor am I saying that one should never do nice things for a woman. You can do a lot of nice things for a woman you like or have come to love. You can keep doing plenty of great things for your partner in a relationship if one should develop. The key is to make sure they're done in the right way, and for the right reason.

The problem with most nice guys is *not* that they are nice. *It's the way they do nice things and the motive behind them* that so often has quite the opposite effect they hope to achieve. Many times, a guy will do something nice like taking a woman out to an expensive dinner ... but with the thought that this gift will convince her to like him. And no, I'm not just talking about the jerk who thinks if he wines and dines a woman enough, he can break down her defenses enough to where she'll have sex with him.

Unfortunately, even if a guy is just trying to impress a girl into liking him, and he has no intention of taking her to bed on the first, second or third date, because he wants her to know that he's not just interested in her body, the fact that he is trying to convince her to like him is bad enough, and will be all too plain to see. Most women will immediately "pick up on the vibe" that you're trying to buy her attention, that you hope to *persuade* her into liking you, and that because you think you have to essentially bribe her into liking you, there must be something wrong with you! The same principle continues to apply in a relationship. No matter how long you've lived with a woman, the day you start doing things for her *just to appease her* is the day her feelings for you will begin to deteriorate.

Confusing to be sure. However, the Alpha Male knows well the art—and it is an art—of doing wonderful, nice, creative and special things for his woman, but does so in a way that clearly communicates he's doing so *just because he wants to.* For many, perhaps most men, this may seem an almost indistinguishable fine line, but to women, it's a glaring florescent boundary as wide as a highway! Oh but once a man figures where this line is, and how to stay on the right side of it, success in love is bound to follow.

The good news is that most women can easily tell if you're doing something nice for her just because you want to, as opposed to trying to buy her affection when first meeting or just to get her off your back after being in a relationship for a while. Once a man demonstrates that he doesn't need to buy her attention, or manipulate her just to get her to like him, then he can do all these very nice things that we've been talking about (like taking her to dinner, buying her flowers or giving her gifts).

Alpha men usually don't do these things right after they meet a woman. They know not to give her the false impression that he needs to pay for her interest. They wait until later on, after they've gotten to know her, and they've had time to decide if *she* meets *their approval.* And even then, he's careful not to do nice things in a predictable way, and most attentive never to do something nice in response to demands, or other immature behavior.

Even after dating for a while, a guy has to be careful not to fall into the trap of doing things for a woman so it comes off like he is paying for her continued affection. For example, he's not likely to catch his lady off guard by giving her things she likes *when it's expected*, like on her birthday, Valentine's Day, anniversaries, and so on. Instead, it's always better to avoid any appearance of caving in to expectations.

I know one guy who has a woman that practically worships the ground he walks on. He's a very giving, caring and generous person, but that's not what causes her to worship him so. Much as he likes to give her gifts, especially if she's hinted or openly asked him to get her something, he wisely makes it a point to never, ever give her anything … *right away*. He always waits until later. He even goes so far as to pretend not to hear her when she's dropping hints for what she'd like him to get for her, or makes a joke of it, "Is that what I have to do to buy your love?" Then a day or two later, he shows up with it! Even then, if she says, "Oh you got me just what I asked for," he stops and teases her, "No, I didn't. I got you exactly what *I* wanted." Not in a mean way, but with a little, sly smile.

We need to pause here for a moment to address what I believe is a common problem, especially for guys who've gotten into a relationship with an attractive woman. As I pointed out earlier, it's not unusual for attractive women to become spoiled. Their beauty gives them power over most men. And sad to say, a lot of women take full advantage of it. Some will take, take and take, and give blessed little in return.

Maybe some of you male readers are nodding your heads because you've been on expensive dates with this kind of gal. You might have asked her out a bunch of times, and finally she agreed. You spent a huge chunk of money on her, and she might have said thanks, but the more you did for her, the more she began to talk about how great it is to have a "friend" like you.

Oh, and then it gets worse. A week or two later, she calls you to tell you all about this other guy she went out with, who treated her like garbage. She's going on and on and on about how inconsiderate he is, and there you are listening and wondering, "Why doesn't she stop seeing that ratfink and go out with me?" After an hour of listening and understanding and feeling her pain, she suddenly has to hang up … because guess who's on the other line, Mr. Ratfink, and now she's gotta go!

Yes, brother, I feel your pain, but now it's time to turn the tables around … without having to be an abusive, inconsiderate ratfink. Now, it's time to do what that jerk is probably doing without any clue he's doing it … inadvertently sending those signals of inner strength, signals which, in turn, generate a remarkable, primitive response deep inside of her—attraction. The difference is that you're only going to be like him in this one respect.

The kind of behavior that says, "You have The Mojo!" may seem stupid, contrived and even crazy to most men, but to women—who, by the way, are ten times better at "reading between the lines" than men are—the message is loud and clear. "Here's a man that I cannot control. All the other guys do whatever I ask them, when I ask them. But this one, if he does anything for me, it's because he really wants to. He doesn't follow, he leads. He listens to me, but only if I'm not whining. He'll hear me out, not to comply with what I tell him to do for me, but to get information so he can decide what he wants to do for me, *when he's ready*. Here's a real man, that I can follow!"

OK, let me clear up another question, especially for any reader who is sensitive to women's rights. On the surface, advocating that men lead and that women like to follow may seem very sexist; to some, even misogynist.

As a long time advocate of equal rights for women, this was a real tough issue for me. For the longest time, I was convinced that it was just plain wrong for men to expect women to take anything smacking of a submissive role toward them. I was convinced that any woman who would fall for a dominant male was a victim of our Chauvinist, male-dominated culture. "Surely," I thought, "a healthy relationship is one in which neither the man, nor the woman dominate each other, but are equal partners, making decisions together, and never a situation where the man is 'on top.'" It was a noble hypothesis, and I was sure that most women would find my liberal mindedness very appealing.

Well, guess what? I was wrong, at least when it came to understanding what really makes a woman happy with a man. Sure, men have definitely oppressed women, and in many ways still do. There's a lot of inequity yet to be conquered, in the way women are treated in their careers, in educational opportunities, reproductive rights, and so on.

Don't get me wrong, I am *not* at all saying that it was a mistake to liberate women from the sexual slavery that set in soon after the onset of the Agricultural Revolution. No, I'm not for keeping women in the kitchen, barefoot, uneducated, and restricted to only cooking, cleaning and making babies.

What I am saying, though, is that even for us men who are otherwise feminist sympathizers, the reality is that the female's most fundamental, sexual instincts are never going to respond positively (not for another million years anyway) to the kind of male behavior that puts him at her side as an equal, and certainly not behind her like a servant.

Like it or not, fair or not, Evolution didn't reward pre-historic males who were all about equality by making women find them irresistibly attractive. In that harsh and dangerous world, it was the strong who survived, and those who could best ensure their children survived. The women who found the strong, dominant males attractive, had their babies, and they lived. The women who liked "girly men," just didn't reproduce.

Of course, the world has changed a lot since the Cave Man Days, but our instincts have not. So rather than beat our heads against the wall, trying to convince women to be attracted to what they should, why not be smart, and find ways to trigger those same instincts, and still be a good guy who respects women's rights.

Now, just in case you're tempted to think that projecting a dominant, Alpha Male personality is disrespectful or unlikely to really work, stop and think about the *real life* experiences you've had when you tried to give a woman what she wants, when she wanted it. In the real world, when a woman seems to be asking her man for something, she often tends to become unhappy when he just gives it to her right away. The better she succeeds at "training him" to do as she pleases, the less pleased she becomes. In contrast, a man who seems impervious to such asking, has her utter devotion.

This begs the question. Why do women get so aroused, and stay so turned on by a man they have tried so very hard to control … but find that they can't?

The Door Lock Test

The answer is that an Alpha Male is the one who understands that his woman is testing him, and he knows how to pass the test. Women test men the same way a night time security guard tests to see that all the doors in the building are locked—by trying to open them!

So many guys make the mistake of just throwing open every door a woman tries to get into, only to watch her stand there, look at the wide open door and the red carpet rolled through it, with disappointment and getting all upset. They just don't get it. They think that when a woman "grabs the doorknob and jiggles it," that she actually wants the "door to open." So what do Beta Males in their ignorance do? They unlock the door at the first touch, and are time and again, confronted with anything but appreciation. And what's worse, they keep scratching their heads wondering why their repeated attempts to make their woman happy by giving her what she wants, when she asks for it, fails and fails again.

However, the Alpha Male is the guy who understands what a woman really wants. He understands just how relieved his woman will become each time she grabs and shakes and tries with all her might to turn that knob … only to find that it holds strong! The Alpha patiently waits. It might take a little while, especially if she has been spoiled before, but his woman soon responds to his firm stand with incredible appreciation and gratitude.

If she starts acting up, whining, making demands, begins giving him orders, and so on, he sees what's really going on. He realizes that she's just "checking the door to make sure it's locked."

She—most of the time unconsciously—is simply trying to find out if her man really is a man, one who won't put up with bad behavior. Once she sees that "the door is firmly locked," that he won't put up with demanding, immature and unreasonable behavior, she'll calm down and then, somewhere deep inside, a feeling of respect for him will overtake her. Quickly following that respect, is something even better. Soon that sense of respect triggers an even stronger desire shooting up like a geyser—attraction.

Better a Tyrant Than a Wimp

Of course, there are guys out there who take advantage of this Alpha power, just as there are women who use their beauty to take advantage of men. I'm reminded of a declaration made by the Southern Baptist Convention a few years ago, "God has ordained that man should be in authority over woman." To be fair to many Southern Baptists, many interpret this doctrine to mean that a husband should be a leader, not a tyrant. Still, there are a whole bunch of domestic tyrants in that denomination who use this belief to justify many an abuse.

What is noteworthy, though, is how many women in the Southern Baptist Church claim to be content with their submissive roles. How is it possible that women in this age of Feminism could be happy with such "bondage"? Most likely, they don't really enjoy it when a man is abusive or running their lives in a such a way that they are become slaves in their own homes. But compared to having a relationship with a wimpy, Beta male who is not only unattractive, but repulsive, even a guy who takes advantage of a woman's feelings will seem the far better alternative.

On the flip side, I've had the occasion to become personally acquainted with a number of women belonging to the Wiccan religion, which for many, of its adherents, hold that God is female, or more accurately, a Goddess. Many of these women are ardent feminists, who can talk for hours about the abuses of our paternalistic culture. I thought at first that most of these women would be inclined to date men who shared their beliefs and "were in touch with their feminine side." Imagine, then, how surprised I was to discover that many of these women were either married to or in relationships with domineering, Christian men?

I recall one in particular, who even complained regularly about her husband's "Chauvinistic, male god" beliefs, and how she only wished that she had a man who shared her faith in the Goddess. Then, after finally breaking up with this guy, she turned right around and fell in love with yet another, domineering Christian man, even though there were a number of available males in her religious community that had pursued a relationship with her.

This behavior by women who otherwise speak long and loud of the equality—if not the superiority—of The Female made no sense at all to me until I came to understand the Alpha-Beta Scale of Attraction and began to grasp the evolutionary pressures which created it.

It's my hope that the men who read this work are not interested in learning how to be tyrannical jerks. But just in case, maybe I need to say it one more time. The good news is that there doesn't have to be conflict between being a really good guy and a real man who inspires attraction. If a man wants to trigger the "Alpha response" in his woman, he can do a lot of nice things for her. However, his motive for doing so has got to be, "I'm doing this because I want to, not because she expects it." This may seem like a very subtle difference to a man, but to a woman, especially an Alpha Female, it's like night and day.

When I began my research on this issue, I was, and still am, as much for women's rights as any of those who've marched on the streets for equal pay, to ban workplace discrimination and to uphold a woman's reproductive rights. I believed then, and still do, that women are not to be treated as second class citizens, the mere servants of men. So imagine how hard it was for me—and it was very difficult—to accept the evidence I found which told me over and over again that women really do want men to be strong.

It's not that they want to be mistreated, nor do they want men to be so domineering that they abuse them. They don't want men to *push* them around. However, they do want men to *lead*! The guy who grasps this concept will be well on his way to attracting all the women he wants if he's single, or keeping his woman attracted to and happy with him if he's in a relationship.

Savoring Instead of Gulping

The principle of this Alpha strength applies most acutely in the bedroom. I remember reading the typical dating gurus' advice about the importance of "foreplay" in giving a woman satisfying sex. As far as different ideas about *what to do* go, most any of the "sexperts" out there have plenty of good suggestions. The only problem is that they frequently miss telling their readers what's most important about foreplay—the attitude and feeling behind whatever is being done. In other words, it's really not as important that a guy do a lot of kissing, rubbing, licking, and so on, as long as he is doing things (like kissing, rubbing, and licking) in the right way. To succeed in sexual foreplay, what matters is the frame of mind you have while engaged in it.

It's great to do all kinds of touching, massaging—even "rougher" things—but only if it's in a way that says, "I'm a real man who might be taking you in a little while ... if I want to." A man best conveys his Alpha status when he keeps his desire reigned in, and he "toys" with his woman for a while. Teasing her, easing back, touching her again, then easing back. This kind of foreplay sends the message—"I'm an Alpha that doesn't *need* your body ... though I might enjoy having you at some point." With practice, a man can learn how to "turn up a woman's attraction dial" so much that she'll practically jump on him.

I can't emphasize this point enough. Once a man learns how to project the Alpha attitude and keep it, the rest is a piece of cake. It's this same attitude that allows other men to do everything else wrong and still have a woman cling to him like Super Glue.

I hope no one ever does this on purpose, but it's worthy to note that by projecting the Alpha vibration, even those who are mean, selfish and abusive, those who have poor hygiene, those who do the same things over and over, even those who care only for their own satisfaction, will attract and keep attracting women. Imagine then, what kind of effect a man has on a woman who has this very same power, and on top of all that, is kind, caring, creative and always coming up with surprises ... but only because he wants to?

By itself, foreplay doesn't mean much in terms of triggering female attraction; it can even be an annoying, stumbling block. Light candles, play music, break out toys, give back rubs, do a hundred different things, and yet if the right attitude is lacking, a woman will just wish you'd hurry up and get it over with! But if The Mojo is there, they are great compliments to that fundamental magnetism.

In marriage relationships, it's so tempting for men to believe, "now that we're married, it's my wife's duty to give her body to me." Just like the wife who let's herself go as she relies on her husband's marriage vows to keep him faithful to her, so can a man become similarly lazy. A man who is depending on his wife's marital commitment to keep her faithful tends to think he needs do nothing else. He assumes that what he wants sexually is what she's now "supposed to deliver." Well, there's another name for doing what we're "supposed to do"—a chore! What was before a mutual, magical work of art, becomes a unilateral chore. And a dreaded one at that.

If any of the guys reading this right now are guilty of acting like a Beta and being lazy in love, then, you need to start changing your attitude and actions. What this really boils down to is doing what it takes to break some deeply entrenched bad thought patterns, bad attitudes and bad habits, and then, one by one, replacing them with good ones.

There's no magic formula that will instantly change the way you've been acting for years. However, once you make up your mind that you are going to actively do whatever it takes to change yourself, to root out and replace some very lazy habits, the results will soon be noticeable and will prove far better than any magical spell Harry Potter or Gandolf ever did.

Real "magic" takes time. So don't worry about making this change overnight. Start, for example, by changing some very simple things. You might begin with a very simple thing, like no longer referring to your wife as, "my wife." The next time you're talking to someone, and your mate is within ear shot, say something like, "Well, mah Laydee (saying it in a slow, deliberate way) … and I were doing thus and so.…" (Watch out, be sure to gesture toward her so she won't think you're talking about some other woman!) But once she gets over the shock and realizes that you actually were referring to her, just watch for a twinkle begin to appear in her eye that you haven't seen in a very long time.

Do this for a week, and then add something else, like turning off the damn TV an hour before bedtime, take a quick shower, and sneak up on her and touch the back of her hair. Then walk away, and come back 5 minutes later, and give her a little spank (a playful "love pat") on the bottom. Then go do something else, come back, grab her and kiss her. In other words, don't rely on marital duty to get laid. Instead, do what you did when you were dating—seduce your woman!

"What? Seduction? You don't mean get her drunk, do you?" I can hear some men reacting like this. They have no idea what seduction really is, and many are under the impression that it's something bad. Well, let's take a closer look at this amazing phenomenon and then see if it's something evil, unethical … or perhaps, one of the most important aspects of human courtship and mating.

Seduction and the Spawning Place

We're so conditioned to think of seduction in negative terms. Women are often depicted as victims when they respond very powerfully to the seductive advances of certain men. Afterwards, they themselves might have difficulty explaining why they did things with a man they just met that they would never have otherwise thought they would do until "they had really gotten to know him first."

However, seduction is what women really want! Unless something goes terribly awry afterwards—like waking up to find themselves in bed with a married guy or an escaped prisoner—they will often look back at such experiences with blissful awe. In fact, many times they will recount seductions with dreamy-eyed wonder … even when they do find out the next day the guy was married … and had just gotten out of prison!

What, then, is this thing called "seduction"? Where did it come from? Is it a "work of the devil"? A manipulative skill perfected by lascivious men who know just when to take advantage of a girl who is at a "low point in her life"? Or is it simply a primitive, biological response, something put deep inside women by Nature for a very good reason?

While religious fanatics can only understand seduction in terms of "demonic powers luring women to carnal lusts" and media psychiatrists only in terms of "poor self-esteem," an understanding of our biological evolution, I believe, provides a solid, scientific explanation for this remarkable behavior.

Seduction occurs when a man positions himself near a woman he wants sexually and—rather than pushing himself upon her to try to break down her barriers—interacts with her in such a way that she voluntarily puts down her defenses and comes to him.

A good seducer has a way of communicating with a woman without even speaking. Most other men are deaf to what is going on. To women, though, his body language is speaking loud and clear, saying things on the order of, "Hey there, I've got something you really need. You should get over here while you've got a chance." Soon, the woman "lowers her shields." She is drawn out of her "protective shell." She finds herself being "caught up" and "carried away" by a powerful, super-emotion. Sometimes, she will later try to describe what happened and have difficulty putting it in logical terms—"I was just talking to this guy who was so cool. Then one thing led to another. And the next thing I knew, my clothes were on the floor and we were making wild and passionate love!"

Seduction comes from the Latin word *seducere*, which literally means "to lead away." It seems so odd to the logical mind that a woman would ever want to be led away. How does she know she isn't being led astray? Isn't this dangerous? Shouldn't she get to know him first? Led away from what? And where to? And yet, we often hear women describe their most enjoyable romances with expressions like "he just swept me off my feet!"

A lot of men see certain guys doing this all the time, only wishing they had one of those "magical brooms" themselves. They can't figure out, not even to save their lives, why women are time and again uninterested in them. They might be tempted to think it has to do with their looks. But even a lot of guys who are physically attractive struggle just to get a date. Or they might think, "If only I could tell women how dependable, well-mannered and financially stable I am, then they'd fall right into my arms." Unfortunately, most of these guys never even get a chance to tell a girl about all they have to offer, and when they do, the girl begins to fidget and get uncomfortable. They frequently get a look of rejection even if they're just trying to give a girl a polite smile. The final blow comes when the girl they just tried so hard to impress turns right around and falls head over heels for some guy she bumped into the day before, someone who is average looking, who hasn't even told her where he lives or if he even has a job.

Why do some men have this power to gather women up into their arms and "carry them away" while so many others meet so much resistance, even before they get a chance to say one word?

The answer, again, has to do with the female's selective mating strategy. Women basically put men into two categories when they see them coming. One group is made up of all those who have no clue as to how to go about seducing them, and the other, is for the type of guy who "just has something about him" that makes them "fall into his arms." They assign men to these columns within seconds of encountering them, usually, without even consciously thinking about it. It's like there are two, opposing magnetic forces at work deep inside the base of their brain. One is pushing most men away, and the other, once triggered, pulls her like a Star Trek tractor beam toward that special kind of guy.

These opposing powers are the result of a two-fold, ancient instinct all females carry within their emotional makeup—1) to protect her eggs from bad or mediocre sperm, so she can 2) enthusiastically yield them before the best sperm.

Remember that a woman has more at stake than men do when it comes to sex. Her eggs are metabolically expensive to make—compared to men's sperm anyway—and then there is the "price" of pregnancy and child rearing. The female reproductive strategy hinges on "getting a good return for her investment." Were she to be as indiscriminant as a typical male, she could end up wasting an egg—going through the trauma and pain of childbirth and years of hard work rearing a young child, only for him to turn out to be a genetic dud![203] She can't afford to chance getting some inferior seed that will produce a weak or sickly child.

Her deepest instincts direct her to conserve her eggs until she finds superior seed, i.e., sperm from an Alpha Male. Once she finds her Alpha, she will want to copulate with him in order to satisfy her most important goal—getting his seed. From there, if possible, her instincts will direct her to see if she can get his care and protection as well. Should the Alpha Male, who is high in status, begin to signal to her that he has room for a relationship, all the better.

In contrast, Beta males are those guys that signal to her, often before they even get close, that they are weak, unhealthy, and low in status. They can't give her good genes, and couldn't help much to protect and raise a child, even if they could. She, therefore, automatically keeps an invisible "force field" around her, to keep Beta males away, so that only the best man, hopefully an Alpha, gets to fertilize her.[204]

Generally, the more attractive a woman is, the more she becomes adept at using a variety of body language gestures, postures, and facial expressions, and if need be, actual words, to tell Beta guys, "Stay away!" Attempting to force one's way past these communications, like persisting in "hitting on" an uninterested woman, can feel just like running right into an invisible, but very thick brick wall.

It's equally important to understand that this barrier is also like the lid on a pressure cooker. The reason is because there's something a whole lot worse than allowing mediocre sperm get to her eggs—not getting any sperm at all. Below her superficial rejections of one man after another is a powerful longing to lay out her eggs, to make them accessible, and have them liberally covered in semen![205] This deep desire, if it could speak, might reverberate with the words of the normally reserved character Charlotte (Tristin Davis) in an episode of the already mentioned HBO series *Sex and the City*. Speaking with her friends at a moment where she was being uncharacteristically candid about her deepest sexual longings, she burst out, "I just need a man to fuck me really hard!" Seduction, then, is the process whereby a woman is led out of her usual, strong, protective instinct … toward her even stronger reproductive one.

Seduction is a mystery to many, and maybe, most men. Perhaps, one reason men find this dynamic process so confusing is due to the complexities of mammalian sex. I've already pointed out that internal fertilization—which requires that mates physically join and copulate—was a relatively late development of Evolution favored by it's advantages for stronger and more healthy male sperm to fertilize female eggs. For eons before, however, all sexual reproduction was done the way fish still carry on today, by external fertilization or spawning.

When fish "have sex" it's not very "up close and personal," because the female lays her eggs before they are fertilized. A male fish, then, has to swim over and ejaculate his sperm onto the eggs. The whole process can be completed with neither one ever touching the other (though various fish species do touch each beforehand as a kind of foreplay).

Now, this kind of mating may not seem very pleasurable to us humans, for the apparent lack of physical contact between the genders (but as we shall see, looks can be deceiving). But for whatever it lacks in intimacy is made up for in its simplicity. The male can actually see the eggs he's after, and he has a "clear shot" at fertilizing them. Assuming there aren't any predators or competing males nearby, much of his sperm—whether good, bad or mediocre in quality—can reach the eggs.[206] External fertilization favors the individual male's primary reproductive strategy to spread his seed far and wide, regardless of quality, but it's not necessarily the best thing for his species.

Here then, is one of the big problems with spawning—what is good for the male, as far as getting his sperm on the female's eggs, is what makes it difficult for a female fish to guard her eggs from bad sperm. As noted, once she's laid them, any male in the vicinity, should he be healthy or sickly, strong or weak, can fertilize them. Plus, even when fertilized by a strong and healthy male, she's only getting a net average of his sperm "swim team"—because even the "amateur swimmers" have about as good a chance at getting inside an egg as the "Olympians" among them. For these reasons, female fish compensate by typically laying hundreds of eggs at a time, in the hope that a few might survive to adulthood and themselves reproduce successfully. And there are other dangers to spawning, like strong water currents that might sweep eggs away the moment they're laid and hungry predators nearby who really like caviar.

As a result, male fish had to become adept at luring females away to some relatively private place, away from strong water currents, predators and competitors, just before they lay their eggs, so they alone can hose them down with their sperm. Eventually, though, Natural Selection came up with a better idea, by evolving species like ours, in which females keep their eggs inside their bodies until they can be fertilized first.

Now, no one's ever, to date, gotten a fish to give a description in plain English of how much sexual satisfaction they get from spawning, but based on the intense, and often dangerous risks they take, it's reasonable to assume they are driven by very strong, biological urges to do so. All we need to do is think of the way Salmon swim thousands of miles, and fight their way up streams though hungry bear paws and fishermen's nets, to have some idea as to just how strong the urge is.

When internal fertilization came along, these urges remained strong, but the process got a little more complicated as sexual intercourse evolved. This new way of mating (new in terms of million of years of evolutionary history) keeps eggs hidden, and sperm has to travel along dark and treacherous corridors, where most perish in the effort, and the male is blind to whether any of them are getting through. Nevertheless, it was this complexity that made for passing on better genes, and thus, kicking Evolution into high gear!

By keeping her eggs inside of her, a female doesn't have to worry as much about predators and environmental hazards. Internal fertilization helps a female to better keep Beta males from cutting in on a better choice of mate and ejaculating on her eggs at the last second. Most importantly, though, the need to copulate first translates into the mother getting the best sperm of the male she's mating with since only the "Gold Medal swimmers" can make it all the way to the egg!

Unlike the big "wading pool" of spawning, where one has to constantly be concerned that some interloping sperm can get in, copulation is more like a long and treacherous obstacle course. Not only is the course long (a veritable Marathon as far as the microscopic tadpole like creatures are concerned), but chemically hostile to all but the strongest spermatozoa. From the sperm's point of view, the vaginal tract can easily be compared to a mined, obstacle course.

As noted earlier, the course can also serve as a final battle ground between final male contenders. If a female should be so fortunate as to encounter two or more males that all appear to have really good genes to share, she doesn't have to guess which one is the best of the best, and have sex only with him. Instead, she can have sex with all the final contenders and quite literally let their sperm to "duke it out to determine the winner" within her vagina itself!

Suppose, for a moment, though, that Evolution had done things differently, and we humans reproduced the "old fashioned way," by spawning. An Alpha woman who would, as a rule, have her guard up and who usually had to push most men away whenever they got a little too close, would behave a little more consistently as far as male logic goes. Whenever she did find herself being drawn to an attractive male, she would follow him to as private a location as could be found, and there lay her eggs for him to fertilize. It's easy to follow this kind of mating dance (as long as one can get past the imagery), because it goes in such a nice, logical, straight line: Boy meets girl. Girl likes boy. Boy and girl go off together. Girl gives boy what boy wants, her eggs. Boy sees eggs and deposits his sperm accordingly.

As it is, though, human eggs are deep inside a woman, and human mating is, therefore, a more complex, push-and-pull process. At first, the woman is pushing men away, men who want to penetrate her, but whom she must keep out because they don't match up to her standards. But when she finds herself with just the right kind of male, it is she who is drawn toward him. Then, at some mystical point, they stop, and he handily moves from his cool "I can take it or leave it" manner to begin vigorously copulating with her!

And he does so with just the right timing. She's not only stopped pushing away, lowered her defenses, come out of her shell, and melted in his arms, but is quite actively pulling him in to penetrate her. It's as if he knows some secret code the woman is transmitting that most other guys can't even see or hear, much less read and comprehend.

Internal fertilization is basically the same process as spawning, but with more twists and turns: Boy meets girl. Boy does something that makes girl take interest and want to go with him. Girl follows boy. Boy and girl stop. Boy is doing "all the right things," until girl signals she's ready. Boy seems to know exactly when Girl is "there." Then, Girl gives Boy what he wants, access to her eggs. Boy then places his seed as near to egg(s) as he can get.

There's a reason why we refer to men who are successful in seducing women as "smooth operators." They seem to know how to keep cool, to not behave like clumsy Beta males who are sexually desperate, who are so pushy, who try so hard to convince, bribe or intoxicate a women into "opening up," but with little success. The Alpha, instead, smoothly attracts her out of her shell, takes her and leads her along. Step by step, he gradually amplifies her attraction for him, until at last, she can no longer bear the waiting, and begins doing essentially the same thing as our most ancient sea dwelling mothers did—laying out her eggs for him to fertilize.[207]

That critical moment when the woman who is being "led away," instinctively desires that the male penetrate her "now" is a phenomenon resulting from the special location of her eggs. The "place" he's taking her is no longer a nice clearing on a shallow part of the ocean floor, a coral reef or an upstream pond, but she is "there" nevertheless. The physical locale is different, but *the human female's need to be led away to a special place emotionally is as strong as ever.*[208] Once there, she will just as eagerly lay her body out just as female fish lay out their eggs for the right guy fish to fertilize them.

To the human male, though, the unseen eggs have changed his orientation from a visible place to a special time. For him, successful seduction is all about timing. Assuming he is communicating by his body language, voice tone, and wording that he is an Alpha, he will cause a woman to feel such attraction for him that it will build and build until it draws her out of her normal, protective mode. He'll continue to "lead her away," and he'll be able to tell when she's ready and has entered the Must Reproduce Now Mode.

An Alpha Male is keen to this timing. He knows how to lead (notice I didn't say "push") her "there," and when she is "there." He may be every bit as "horny" as every other Beta male who hasn't had a date in over a decade and has tried and failed miserably to get with the woman he is presently seducing. However, he knows not to unleash his desire until she has reached this critical juncture. Only once her Attraction Dial is turned up high enough, does he then begin to copulate with her as if he hadn't had sex in ten years! By this time, her reproductive instinct takes over from her normal protective mode, and she, quite literally, aches for him to go as deep inside of her (where her eggs are) as possible.

Now, I went into this detailed discussion of these primitive, mating instincts for a reason. By understanding how attraction and seduction work, why they work, and what keeps them working, a man can have the complete and utter fidelity of his woman. This kind of natural fidelity, is so much better than what most people rely on—the negative threat of punishments by God, the State, Society, Family, and so on—because it is so positively reinforced. Rely on the obligations of the marital contract to constrain a woman to please you, and you'll be lucky to get a bare minimum of routine and boring sex. Learn how to seduce a woman, though, and not only will she be happy, but she'll want to, and I mean, really want, to make you happy too.

How often one needs to seduce a woman is a common question, and there's no single answer that applies to all. Some feel like once a week or once a month is enough. The rest of the time, sex might tend to be routine, but if that routine is broken often enough, it makes those special nights, well, all the more special. So I'm not saying that a relationship can't be happy unless a couple has a one to two hour seduction sequence every single night of the week!

A happy couple can actually have a degree of routine sex. There's nothing wrong either, not in principle, with one person doing certain sexual things that only directly benefit one partner on a given night as long as the other person is getting enough in return on other nights. The point, though, is not to see how little seduction you can get away with. The best rule of thumb is to seduce as much as you can, as often as you can.

I know of one couple that makes it a point to make seductive love every night except when it's "that time of the month." However, the guy is so good at seducing and satisfying his lady most of the time that, when she is physically indisposed, she happily provides him "oral satisfaction." She doesn't mind a little "extra giving" because she's still "glowing" from the physical joy she's gotten before. In turn, her overall happiness greatly reinforces the emotional bond she has with her man and lends itself very well to the empathetic good feeling of knowing she can still make him happy.

The problem with most couples, though, is when this kind of one-sided sex becomes the rule, instead of the exception. The key is to make as much time as you can for seduction to take place. Don't leave it to chance. If you do—work, kids, household chores—all the myriad things that can take up your time and energy, will leave you with either no love life, or a boring ten minute ritual at best. Instead, begin each day with the goal of seduction in mind, and start seducing your woman from the moment you awaken. Even if a particular seduction sequence doesn't conclude that same night with lengthy intercourse and both partners having really great orgasms, it can carry over to the next.

Attitude Adjustments

In a sense, it really hardly matters what a man does with a woman on the outside as long as he has the right stuff going on inside. Yes, the way one behaves is critical. However, if you have the right attitude, the right frame of mind—if you stop thinking you can and start knowing you can—you can almost get away with going to bed each night with a beer stained shirt and still drive your partner wild! "How?" you might ask.

Basically, you must begin by thinking of yourself as an Alpha who is dating once again, even if you're already in a relationship. Each day, you have your own life to live, and your own interests. Certainly, you can enjoy being with your mate, but deep inside you've begun to reprogram how you view her. You no longer depend on her to make you happy. Odd as it may seem, you and she will both be much happier, the more you become less dependent on what she can do for you.

Some ridicule this attitude, claiming it's just an excuse to act single (as if "acting single" is bad). They assume, ever so mistakenly, that turning the clock back on a relationship to where it was when you didn't have to be together is threatening to its stability. But the reality is that by getting back to that place as close as possible, you are actually making it much more likely that you'll be happy with each other, and thus, truly stable.

What you are hoping to do is restructure your thinking, your attitudes, and your behavior, for the very purpose of regaining the natural bond you had when you were first dating. By all means, your intention is to think of your mate, no longer as someone who is now obligated to love you, but as someone you are going to seduce tonight ... and you start the seduction sequence even before breakfast is ready.

Instead of thinking that it's your woman's "duty" to satisfy you sexually, you've gotta lose that attitude and begin taking it upon yourself to create attraction within her so she'll want you. Begin carrying your new attitude with you everywhere you go. Remember that you're not just putting on an act whenever you're around your partner. No, you have to actually change who you are. When you do, not only will your woman notice and begin to respond positively (and if she's not, then it's a good sign she's not going to prove worthy of staying with you), but others will see you change from a wimp into a real man.

There are many fringe benefits that you'll soon see. You'll find that your friends, your boss, and even strangers you meet for only a few minutes, begin to treat you in a whole new, positive way. On some level, they will walk away with admiration, saying to themselves, "I sure would like to be more like that guy."

You have to visualize your relationship as a vibrant, dynamic, daily challenge. Instead of just assuming that your partner is just going to be there, and is just going to do what she is "supposed to do." Quit being so lazy, and take it upon yourself to do what will naturally entice your partner to do what you'd like in return. Get it out of your head.... I'll say it again. Get it out, out, out of your head that this person is your "wife," and replace those evil thoughts with things like, "Yeah, that's my Baby Doll."

The man's role in making a relationship successful (happy and enduring, not just enduring) is in direct proportion to the extent he can better become an Alpha—by changing his general outlook, the way he carries himself, by leading and being more assertive. The more one becomes dominant, instead of acting in a submissive manner, the more attractive he will be. With even a modest amount of effort, a man can incline his female companion to be so attracted to him, that she will naturally desire his company, and be far less tempted to stray.

Of course, the way one thinks about one's self internally has much to do with how one is perceived and how one takes care of oneself on the outside. So many men (as the earlier warning was given to resentful women) waste so much time being angry at women for not "liking them as they are." Their resentment and anger leads only to their getting more and more rejection from women. It's a waste of time and energy to blame women for not being attracted to you for the reasons you wish. Instead, work on making yourself attractive to women for the reasons that naturally attract them.

A much more healthy and helpful attitude is to adopt a borderline "devil may care" outlook. When approaching an attractive woman, automatically assume (if need be, tell yourself over and over first) "I'm a great guy, and this gal I've spotted should recognize it. If she doesn't, there must be something wrong with her." Instead of looking to women to approve of you, you do the approving or rejecting.[209] Even in a relationship, it's important to discern the difference between, let's say, hearing out your mate's thoughts and criticisms, weighing them fairly, and considering them for their own merits, as opposed to simply being afraid she might think badly of you unless you agree. The art is to know the difference between being strong without abusing that power, and being weak for fear of becoming abusive.

Beta Males fail within themselves all the time. Long before they've said or done anything to attempt attracting a woman, they've convinced themselves of failure! Those who are in a relationship have great difficulty maintaining their dignity, because they are so fearful that if they should displease their woman, she'll punish them, either by withholding sex or abandoning them.

The Beta male is unsure of himself. If he perceives that his wife is an Alpha (or an Alpha relative to him), he will fear never finding another one like her. On some level, he thinks he doesn't deserve her. He thus empowers her to take advantage of him, for all she needs do is give him a bit of rejection, and he is putty in her hands. Of course, this wimpy behavior is only going to make it even more likely that she will desert him the first chance she gets, because he is showing such unattractive weakness.

This is a very tough one for those who think there is something noble or virtuous about feeling they are with someone they don't deserve. But this attitude is, in fact, based on deception and manipulation. How fair is it to be tricking someone into being with you, if in reality, you are beneath them? It stems from a false kind of humility, and women can normally sense this falsehood a mile away.

The necessity to overcome weakness is also a very tough one for those who can't distinguish between *pigheadedness* in the face of better argument (not being able to admit being wrong or that someone else is right) and *capitulation* in the face of a demanding woman just to pacify her. Knowing where you stand, why you stand there, and being unwilling to capitulate just to please someone can be difficult if you're worried about pleasing a woman at all costs. Some women will do all they can to get a man to change his position just to see if he'll break down. If he holds firm, though, she'll develop and retain a respect for him deep down inside, one that will contribute to her feeling more attracted to him. If he allows himself to be moved, she'll lose both respect and attraction for him.

Now, let's not confuse this with hearing out a woman's ideas and opinions, and being honest enough to admit she's got a better idea when in fact she does. It's worth repeating—changing you view for a good reason is very different from changing just to get her approval. If a man does nothing else but get it out of his head that his measure of himself depends on anything a woman might think of him, he will improve his success in dating and in relationships a hundredfold.

Knowing That You Can

Ironically, once you begin to "get your balls back" and your partner begins to respond very positively to the reacquisition, you may begin to notice that other women will start taking an interest in you as well. Even when they know you're in a relationship (and likely, *because* they know you're making at least one other woman very happy), they'll begin finding you very attractive. Yes, you could use your new found confidence to cheat on your wife (or your steady girlfriend or cohabitant). But if you really don't want to limit yourself to one woman, you're probably better off in the long run by first getting divorced (or breaking off the relationship). After that, you'll be single, and then you can honestly and openly date and have sex with all the women you please.

There are some rare couples who are basically happy with each other except for the fact that they really want to have sex with others every now and then. If they can be honest enough to admit this to each other, and have the determination to restrain their jealousies, they do have a few options. They can join a swingers club (if they're only after occasional recreational sex), or get involved with a polyamory or open relationship network (if they're actually looking to have other lovers), or if we're only talking about the man in the relationship, attempt a polygynous arrangement within a supportive (but likely socially isolated) sub-culture, such as the Fundamentalist Mormons or by moving to a Moslem country that permits polygamy. But let's face it, for most Americans, these options are not feasible, and many of those who try going one of these other routes, however determined, find that they cannot stand the idea of their partner "doing it" with some one else.

Our culture allows few options to married men who find themselves unsatisfied with monogamy, and they usually have to hide their dalliances should they seek sex outside of their marriage. Of course, they can try to "resist all temptations" to cheat, but even those who are faithful in deed, spend much of their internal lives longing for other women. Sooner or later, many will attempt a love affair, but as we have noted, Beta males have a lot of trouble getting other women to be interested in them. So what else does Western Society have to offer to men who—as much as they might believe they are supposed to be faithful to their wife in thought, word and deed—can't escape the powerful, primary directive to spread their seed farther?

Many turn to prostitution. For a fee, they can satisfy their primary desire to spread their seed, at least to some extent. Having sex with prostitutes has some benefits. It's fast, discreet, uncomplicated, and in big towns, full of variety. All of which helps to placate, at least temporarily, the male's number one drive.

On the down side, it can be expensive. Prostitution fees have gone sky high in most parts of the US, thanks to legal restrictions which have added more costs to the business (e.g., bail fees whenever prostitutes are arrested), and which reduces the number of available workers. Fewer women on the street translates only into higher charges from those remaining. The higher profits, in turn, have only served to invite organized crime to take control of "red light" districts as the potential profits outweigh any risks involved. Though Fundamentalists and other conservatives who pushed for these restrictions hoped higher prices would deter men from fornicating, instead, men have only paid more, leaving their families with that much less to live on.

In some cultures, like those of Western Europe, prostitution is tolerated. They figured out long ago that prostitution serves as a kind of sexual/social "release valve" so the pressure of monogamous based societies doesn't become so great that even ostensible fidelity might blow apart, impairing the very functionality of society. In countries (like some predominantly Catholic ones) where divorce is either illegal or very difficult to obtain, even wives who know their husbands go to prostitutes tend to look the other way as long as their home lives remained undisrupted. Nevertheless, even in countries like the US, where the efforts of the major institutions of society to suppress it have only pushed it underground, prostitution continues to thrive as it always has since civilization began.

Then there are those sexually frustrated, married men who stop short of having sex with other women, but they get as close as they can. Men's clubs featuring topless or nude dancers offer the fantasy of getting to be with the kind of women they really desire, but again, only for a fee.

Sex dolls, though expensive—not to mention too big to hide in the closet—have come a long ways from the old, blow-up versions to looking more and more realistic, and they represent a growing product area in the Sex Paraphernalia Industry.

The use of pornography is another form of substituting actual intercourse with many, desirable women, and the technology to have fully interactive, "virtual sex" with contraptions (to imitate a female's anatomy) attached to video goggles providing sexual imagery (which makes the experience seem real) is just on the horizon.

The problem with all of these options, though, is that they can only mimic sex. As the old saying goes, "close only counts in horseshoes and hand grenades." Masturbation—even with a vivid imagination, pornography, the use of dolls or the eventual development of virtual sex machines—never fully satisfies like the real thing. These other avenues serve as effective stop-gap measures at times when real sex is not an option, but Evolution has so fine tuned the primary directive of the male sex drive that it's impossible to arrive at the same level of satiation with anything other than a warm, living and breathing woman.

What to do then, when the one, real live woman a man does have is proving to be quite a disappointment, and he realizes that conventional substitutes aren't enough to make up for it? It's quite a dilemma for hitherto, sexually unsatisfied, married men, when they wake up to what they really can do to change from being an unattractive Beta to a real man in demand. Though most women will respond very positively to this change, it doesn't mean a former Beta male will automatically remain content with his partner. To put it another way, if you got married to someone who wasn't all that pretty and had a lot of issues, but at the time, you felt like she was the best you could get, what to do later on when you realize you can do a whole lot better?

Yes, for a Beta woman who has a partner that has "leaped ahead," this very notion can seem very threatening. Unless she, too, chooses to join with him in an active effort to improve, she may continue to do all the things that make her naturally undesirable. Worst of all, she may be unwilling to abandon the conventional uphill strategy of using force to keep a man bound to her—dependency on the commitment of a marriage contract. In a case like this, a man may have to choose between indefinitely prolonging unhappiness for both himself and his wife or doing something that might hurt for a while, but will eventually leave them both better off.

No one likes being dumped, but then again, why would anyone in their right mind want to be with someone who really isn't happy? (Of course, forcing someone to love you is not acting out of a right mind.) I can't, nor would I ever presume to, tell any married guy what to do if he should find himself in this position. In the end, though, each one must decide for himself how to handle the consequences of previous mistakes.

Thankfully, having to dump a mate is the exception. Normally, getting one's Mojo back, whether one is dating someone exclusively, cohabiting or married, will result in a man's partner responding in a very positive and satisfying way.

Even if a man is in a relationship, there's nothing wrong with improving himself until everywhere he goes, women are finding themselves attracted to him. I'm not talking about cheating or trying to "hit on" other women like so many Beta guys do behind their wives backs. On the contrary, an Alpha, isn't ogling and chasing after other women; it is they who are after him! A single Alpha can accept or reject the solicitations made to him. But choosing to be in a relationship doesn't mean one has to turn all other women off. An Alpha who has chosen to be in a relationship can be just as alluring as when he was available; it's just that he doesn't accept any of the offers he gets on a regular basis. He's just being who he is, and when other women see that he has The Mojo, he lets their smiles—and yes, more stares than you would imagine—contribute to his feeling even better about himself.

I'd like to compare this sexual mind frame to something that was once illustrated in a popular motorcycle TV commercial. The commercial began with a man revving the engine of his "hog" while a voiceover informed the viewers that this model had the capacity to travel at a speed limit far above anything legal. The rider then began to drive off, but only at a legal, speed. The camera then zoomed into his face, depicting a deep sense of satisfaction. At the end of the ad, the voiceover said, "It's just knowing that you can."

I submit that having an Alpha Male frame of mind is, all by itself, so satisfying, that it acts as a liberator from constantly longing for more sex with more women, even if a man is in a monogamous relationship. This frame of mind, and the ability to manipulate a natural force to help you get where Nature would otherwise be working against you, mirrors the knowledge and skill sailing experts use to move against a head wind when they employ the tacking maneuver.

Nature's original intent was for Alphas to actually have sex with a great variety of women, and there's no question that some men will choose to do just this their whole lives long should they ever grab hold of the Alpha attitude and make it their own. However, it is also possible for men to choose not to take full advantage of their ability to attract women everywhere they go. They can take a good deal of satisfaction just from realizing that they could.

Competitive Risk Vs. Sideline Security

The Beta male is very often overwhelmed with a sense of sexual neediness. He constantly longs for other women—the same women who typically show no interest in him. The Beta male is, therefore, also prone to suffer from the discontent reflected by the one mate he does have. The temptation to abuse him with sexual control is so easy to give in to, because on one level or another, she knows just how unlikely it would be for him to successfully get sex elsewhere.

The Alpha, however, experiences just the opposite. He doesn't feel overwhelmed by unfulfilled sexual desire. The knowledge that he could get other women anytime he wants, is fulfilling in itself! Moreover, his one mate is acutely aware of how much in demand he is. This awareness has the effect of tempering her behavior toward him, in that she knows if she were to displease him too much, he could replace her in a heartbeat!

On the surface, this sounds very threatening. We're inclined to see a woman in this situation as living in a state of constant fear! She seems to be just one foot away from being kicked out and replaced by someone new. The scene smacks of brutishness and sexual cruelty. We can hardly imagine why, for example, a woman would ever put up with "uncertainty" even with an Alpha, when she could have such "security" with a Beta? Wouldn't having other women constantly checking a man out generate jealousy within his wife, cohabitant or steady girlfriend? Wouldn't she become angry with him? Wouldn't she grow weary of constantly wondering how many other women are going to compete with her for his attention? Ironically, the answer is "No!"

This is because we're not talking about a man who is always ogling other women (a behavior that's typical only of Beta males) while out and about with his wife. We're not talking about a guy who only wishes he had other women after him, or a guy who is always after other women. We're not talking about a guy who starts to act like an abused puppy whenever his wife so much as hints that he might not be "getting any" unless he does what she says and gives her what she wants right away.

And how does this make the Beta Male's mate feel? Pretty lousy! The price a female pays for having the security of a Beta male is an all too clear sense of being a loser for having him!

In other words, one of the biggest misconceptions in the world about women and relationships is that they want security instead of competition. True, no woman wants to *lose* in the game of love, but this doesn't mean she would rather have the security of not playing at all! Yes, participating in a competition means there is always the possibility of losing; it can and does happen … sometimes, and maybe even most of the time for some players. *But not playing at all is sure fire way of ensuring that one will never win!* This is why the security of not losing is feeble compensation at best.

Women quickly grow weary of sideline security, because *what they really want is to compete and to win!* Maybe I need to repeat this. Never mind all the talk about relationship security and commitment, implying some kind of fair playing field in the game of love. The profound female instinct is not at all interested in playing fair. It's about competing and winning, and "winning" means total victory, not agreeing to some armistice!

If the reader will recall our earlier discussion about mate copying—the sexual bandwagon effect that occurs when women perceive that a particular man is especially desired by other women—her reaction is to become even more attracted toward him! Unless there's a very forward trespass, such as making uninvited physical contact, seeing other women become attracted to her man actually serves only to elevate her attraction for him.

On a sub-conscious level, her instincts are responding, "I must really be with an Alpha Male. Look at how much all these other women want him!" She not only feels like she's a winner for being arm-in-arm with the Alpha, but also because having all the other girls in the vicinity wanting him too instantly elevates her status among them. And this is something that makes women feel really good.

This is so different from what a loser Beta husband and his wife experience. When he's out and about with his mate, and sees an attractive woman, he's virtually compelled to look for an opportunity to stare at her without his wife catching him … or so he thinks. In fact, he advertises how much of a complete slave he is to his sexual desire. All the women involved find him disgusting, the ones he's ogling, any others in the vicinity, and most of all, his incensed wife. Why? Because just the opposite dynamic of Alpha attraction is in effect.

The Beta Male's partner is not so much appalled at his finding other women attractive as she is by the reaction of the women his tongue is dragging after and those who witness his behavior. In that secret, non-verbal code mentioned before (which some crudely refer to as "Chickspeak"), they are all silently screaming, "What a pervert you've got there!" His wife's status is now diminished, she feels like she's the real loser, and as you might have figured, it makes her feel really bad! And you can probably guess whom she's going to take her frustrations out on later.

To be sure, one could argue that appealing to women's fundamental, primitive urges, instead of to their reason, is "unfair." In a sense, it certainly is. But it's also not very fair that women will time and again pass right on by a hundred really nice guys that would treat them like princesses, only to fall madly in love with some jerk. Were Nature "fair," that is to say, if Evolution were given enough time to reward men with more sexual success by virtue of their niceness and good work ethics, and to women for their intelligence and wit, perhaps in a million years or so, we would naturally find those who have these, admittedly very good traits, sexually attractive. But since we don't have the ability to speed up the process of Evolution, it behooves us to be more practical and accept the reality that is before us—attraction is a matter of primitive, non-rational desire.

The good news, though, is that one need not give up good personal qualities in order to inspire attraction in the opposite sex. A man can be nice, gentle and caring and at the same time, behave in a strong, dominant and confident way no matter what his status in the rest of the world. A woman can be mature, witty and intelligent, and at the same time, have a nice figure, dress attractively and carry herself in a sexually appealing manner, no matter her age. We have the ability to accommodate our natural tendencies and make them work to our advantage, if we'll only choose to adjust the way we think and change our behavior accordingly.

It's a State of Mind

Now, there might be someone reading this who is thinking, "This is stupid. You just want me to pretend to be someone I'm not. That's not gonna work." If so, let's clear up the difference between pretending and changing your state of mind.

First, by no means, am I suggesting that anyone "pretend" to be single, as far as legalities are concerned. If you are already married, then there is a real document in a real government records building that says you are legally married. It's too late now to go back and undo that, without getting a divorce.

So no, don't lie on your tax return. Don't try to start a secret affair. Don't do anything that would be dishonest or unethical with regard to you being married. We're not talking about acting single in these regards. However, there are two aspects to modern Marriage. One is the legal side of it, and while it's admittedly a very damaging thing to be stuck with, it's not the part that does most of the damage to relationships. The other aspect of Marriage that *is* the most damaging, and which also happens to be the part that you *can* change is the married state of mind.

Sure, it's a lot easier to retain and reinforce a natural bond when you're not legally married. That said, it's not impossible to overcome the legal reality by focusing on how you relate to your spouse mentally and emotionally. I'm not talking about pretending here. You truly can change the way you think and the way you feel about someone.

Now, it's gonna take a lot of work, a lot more than if you had never gotten married in the first place, but think about it this way. What is there in life that is worth anything which doesn't require a lot of work? How about nothing! The happiest people in the world are not those who've had everything handed to them on a silver platter. In fact, those who do are usually bored and whining all the time. But people who have goals in life and who work hard to achieve them are the ones who feel very good about themselves. They know what the term "rewarding work" is all about it.

You Can Only Change Yourself

Once you've decided that you are willing to do whatever it takes to make your relationship what it ought to be, keep in mind this very important principle—don't focus on trying to get your partner to change. The reality is that you can't change others. You can't *make* someone else do anything differently, no matter how right you may be that they should.

However, you can change yourself! So don't take this material and shovel it all onto your partner, thinking, "Yeah, she (or he) needs to do this and stop that." Instead, you need to focus on what *you* need to do, to change you! Once you start becoming more whom you want to be, then others respond accordingly.

If for any reason, your partner chooses not to change himself or herself to make your relationship a happy one, then it's their loss, and at some point, you may decide to move on and find someone else. Most often, when one person in a relationship makes some big strides in self improvement, the other is inspired to do the same.

Change is never easy, even when you really want to. But take heart that if you're willing to do the work, you can, and you will, change yourself. If your partner joins you, great. If not, then at least you will know that you gave your relationship with that person your best shot, and if you end up moving on, you won't have to regret doing so.

The Road Back

There's a wise old saying that applies here. "No matter how far down the wrong road you've gone, the only thing to do is to turn back." You may be single, and if so, hopefully, you've learned that getting married is a really dumb idea. So if you thought that you might get married some day, you haven't gone too far down the wrong road, so the distance back (to a happy love life) is relatively short.

But what if you're already married? If you want to have a happy relationship with the person who is now your spouse, there is still a way to make it happen, and it all begins by stopping, turning around, and starting in the other direction. Even if it's a longer way to go, it's worth the effort.

Decide today. If the opinions that I've shared in this book make sense to you, take it upon yourself to become responsible for your love life. Stop now, and declare that you are no longer going to rely on the State or the Church or Society or Family or anything or anyone else, not even your sexual partner, to make your love life a happy one. Choose to have a new frame of mind, to accept Nature's gifts of love and desire for variety, and instead of working against them, work with them.

Will there still be problems? Sure. Might you and your lover have a fight now and then? Count on it. Might you or your partner slip back into an old pattern on occasion. It's bound to happen. But don't worry about it. If you catch yourself thinking the wrong way, just be glad you did, and tell yourself, "Wait a minute, that's the old me talking. Not the new me. No more!" That's progress.

Realize that you are now on a new road, a new course, a new life. Think of when you were a baby, and could only crawl. When you first stood up, you were pretty wobbly, and you fell down a lot. But in time, you were not only walking, but running. When you first learned to speak, you could only babble, and it took many months to get to where you could speak intelligibly. It took even longer for you to learn how to read. No matter how long it takes, and no matter how much the effort, if you begin now and stay the course, you will get to where you need to go a lot sooner than if you wait.

So don't wait anymore. Get going! Begin to love freely so you can have a honeymoon that never stops.

APPENDIX A

Privatize Marriage

◆

A simple solution to the gay-marriage debate.

By David Boaz

In the debate over whether to legalize gay marriage, both sides are missing the point. Why should the government be in the business of decreeing who can and cannot be married? Proponents of gay marriage see it as a civil-rights issue. Opponents see it as another example of minority "rights" being imposed on the majority culture. But why should anyone have—or need to have—state sanction for a private relationship? As governments around the world contemplate the privatization of everything from electricity to Social Security, why not privatize that most personal and intimate of institutions, marriage?

"Privatizing" marriage can mean two slightly different things. One is to take the state completely out of it. If couples want to cement their relationship with a ceremony or ritual, they are free to do so. Religious institutions are free to sanction such relationships under any rules they choose. A second meaning of "privatizing" marriage is to treat it like any other contract: The state may be called upon to enforce it, but the parties define the terms. When children or large sums of money are involved, an enforceable contract spelling out the parties' respective rights and obligations is probably advisable. But the existence and details of such an agreement should be up to the parties.

And privatizing marriage would, incidentally, solve the gay-marriage problem. It would put gay relationships on the same footing as straight ones, without implying official government sanction. No one's private life would have official government sanction—which is how it should be.

Andrew Sullivan, one of the leading advocates of gay marriage, writes, "Marriage is a formal, public institution that only the government can grant." But the history of marriage and the state is more complicated than modern debaters imagine, as one of its scholars, Lawrence Stone, writes: "In the early Middle Ages all that marriage implied in the eyes of the laity seems to have been a private contract between two families.... For those without property, it was a private contract between two individuals, enforced by the community sense of what was right." By the 16th century the formally witnessed contract, called the "spousals," was usually followed by the proclamation of the banns three times in church, but the spousals itself was a legally binding contract.

Only with the Earl of Hardwicke's Marriage Act of 1754 did marriage in England come to be regulated by law. In the New England colonies, marriages were performed by justices of the peace or other magistrates from the beginning. But even then common-law unions were valid.

In the 20th century, however, government has intruded upon the marriage contract, among many others. Each state has tended to promulgate a standard, one-size-fits-all formula. Then, in the past generation, legislatures and courts have started unilaterally changing the terms of the marriage contract. Between 1969 and 1985 all the states provided for No Fault Divorce. The new arrangements applied not just to couples embarking on matrimony but also to couples who had married under an earlier set of rules. Many people felt a sense of liberation; the changes allowed them to get out of unpleasant marriages without the often contrived allegations of fault previously required for divorce. But some people were hurt by the new rules, especially women who had understood marriage as a partnership in which one partner would earn money and the other would forsake a career in order to specialize in homemaking.

Privatization of religion—better known as the separation of church and state—was our founders' prescription for avoiding Europe's religious wars. Americans may think each other headed for hell, but we keep our religious views at the level of private proselytizing and don't fight to impose one religion by force of law. Other social conflicts can likewise be de-politicized and somewhat defused if we keep them out of the realm of government. If all arts funding were private (as 99 percent of it already is), for instance, we wouldn't have members of Congress debating Robert Mapplethorpe's photographs or the film The Watermelon Woman.

So why not privatize marriage? Make it a private contract between two individuals. If they wanted to contract for a traditional breadwinner/homemaker setup, with specified rules for property and alimony in the event of divorce, they could do so. Less traditional couples could keep their assets separate and agree to share specified expenses. Those with assets to protect could sign prenuptial agreements that courts would respect. Marriage contracts could be as individually tailored as other contracts are in our diverse capitalist world. For those who wanted a standard one-size-fits-all contract, that would still be easy to obtain. Wal-Mart could sell books of marriage forms next to the standard rental forms. Couples would then be spared the surprise discovery that outsiders had changed their contract without warning. Individual churches, synagogues, and temples could make their own rules about which marriages they would bless.

And what of gay marriage? Privatization of the institution would allow gay people to marry the way other people do: individually, privately, contractually, with whatever ceremony they might choose in the presence of family, friends, or God. Gay people are already holding such ceremonies, of course, but their contracts are not always recognized by the courts and do not qualify them for the 1049 federal laws that the General Accounting Office says recognize marital status. Under a privatized system of marriage, courts and government agencies would recognize any couple's contract—or, better yet, eliminate whatever government-created distinction turned on whether a person was married or not.

Marriage is an important institution. The modern mistake is to think that important things must be planned, sponsored, reviewed, or licensed by the government. The two sides in the debate over gay marriage share an assumption that is essentially collectivist. Instead of accepting either view, let's get the government out of marriage and allow individuals to make their own marriage contracts, as befits a secular, individualist republic at the dawn of the information age.

◆ ◆ ◆

Slate Magazine
Posted Friday, April 25, 1997, at 12:30 AM PT, http://slate.msn.com/id/2440.

APPENDIX B

The Love Celebration

By
Rick Lannoye

At the day and time selected for the Love Celebration, the persons whose union shall be celebrated shall gather with their family, friends and neighbors; and there standing together, the Master of the Ceremony shall say,

Dearly beloved, we are gathered here today to celebrate a union which has already taken place, to recognize those whom Nature has already joined together, to lend our support to this couple who've already formed a bond … not by man-made obligation, but by Natural Love.

A sexual relationship is an honorable estate, and Love, is one of Nature's greatest gifts. Because of this miracle of Nature, our kind, survived, thrived and emerged triumphant from the harshest challenges of our prehistoric past.

Those who have been brought together by Love and who, based on that mutual bond, chose to make a home together, are become part of a long legacy, one that reaches back through eons of time. From Ice Age surges to the daily struggle to find or hunt food, it was the loving bonds of couples like this one before us today, that provided the foundation for our ancient ancestors' communities, where one looked after the other, supported each other, and worked together for the good of all. Human society, therefore, begins, is maintained and has a future, only because of Love, and therefore, it is sacred to us all.

Because these two persons present have entered into this sacred legacy, it is only fitting that we now take time to celebrate this wonderful work of Nature, and with their permission, allow us an opportunity to share in the joy they've found, as well as to offer them our support.

Speaking to the persons whose love is to be celebrated, he shall say,

[Celebrants' names], will you now share with this assembly how it came to be that you met and fell in love with each other, when you realized that Nature had brought you together, that a bond had formed between you, and because of that bond, you wished to make a home together?

The Celebrants shall then say together,

Yes, we wish to share our story, to invite all of you present to relive that special moment in time, when we first fell in love.

The Celebrants then tell their Love Story. This may be done in any number of creative ways, reading a statement in prose or poem, singing a song, or through a ritual dance or some combination of all the above.

After the Love Story is told, then shall the Celebrants symbolically reenact the moment at which they first consummated their love. The Master of the Ceremony, says the following,

Come now and journey back in time to behold the mystery of Love in this Great Rite.

The couple then faces each other, and proceeds to replay the moment when they first came together in the flesh. Again, this moment can be replayed in many different ways, depending on their wishes, and the ages and sensitivities of those in attendance. One ancient tradition, for example, is for the woman to hold out a cup or chalice, as a symbol of her body, and the man, a blade or knife, as a symbol of his body, and saying the following.

(The woman speaks while holding her chalice upright, before the man) Man, I come to you with all my mind and body. I make both bare in perfect love and perfect trust. I give myself to you, to receive you unto myself, to love, to hold, to take shelter, to bring forth fruit, to listen, to comfort, and to stand with you in all things.

(Then the man speaks while holding his blade downward, before the cup) Woman, I come to you with all my mind and body. I make both bare in perfect love and perfect trust. I take you unto myself, to be received, to love, to hold, to shelter, to bring forth fruit, to listen, to comfort, to stand with you in all things.

Then, perhaps while a song is being sung or music played, the woman, slowly and deliberately, turns the open end of her cup toward the man, and the man, slowly and deliberately, lifts and points his blade toward the open end of the cup and inserts it in until it touches the base of it, and while the blade and cup are joined, says,

As it was in the beginning, when the First Two became one, so now, we too have come together.

Then, the woman says,

Our hearts, minds and bodies have joined to carry on the miracle of Love and Life.

Then both the man and woman say together,

We are part of the great Cycle of Life.

Then shall the Master of the Ceremony add,

We who are gathered here are now witnesses to the miracle of Love which you have allowed us to share in. We offer to you our best wishes for happiness, fulfillment and we lend our support to you both.

Then the Master of the Ceremony says to the couple,

Behold now what Nature has done. May you continue to live together in patience, in wisdom and in happiness. May your home be a haven of blessing and of peace, and may you now also be assured that we are happy for you both and rejoice with you for the bond you share.

Notes

Introduction

[1] Spencer Wells, *The Journey of Man, A Genetic Odyssey* (New York: Random House, 2003), p. 128.

Chapter One

[2] While most reasonable people today reject the notion that a child born out of wedlock is "illegitimate," this is a very recent change in attitude as shall be elaborated on further.
[3] Simmons, Tavia and Martin O'Connell, "Married-Couple and Unmarried Partner Households: 2000," US Census Bureau, *Census 2000 Special Reports*, C2kbr01-8.pdf, February 2003.
[4] Dumas, J., and Alain Belanger. "Report on the demographic situation in Canada 1996: Current Demographic analysis," *Statistics Canada, Demography Division*: Ottawa, Ontario (1997). While still a minority in the US, by 1997, the number of permanently cohabiting couples in Canada became the majority of all cohabitants, from 44% in 1986 to 57% ten years later.
[5] Laurie D. Krauth, MA, "The Contentious Debate About No-Fault Divorce: Who is Most at Risk?" *American Association for Marriage and Family Therapy*, http://www.aamft.org/Press_Room/Press_releases/risk.asp (February 2004). Much of the "research" that is touted as "evidence" that divorce is harmful to children is in fact due to the negative effects of their parents' conflicts that *pre*-dated their separation. C. Ahrons, *The Good Divorce* (New York: HarperPerrenial), 1994.
[6] Oblivious to the multitude of abuses that used to be so commonplace for married couples, Colorado Republican and US Representative Marilyn Musgrave—who recently submitted legislation calling for a Constitutional Amendment that would ban same-gender marriages—has argued that passing her bill is necessary because "Look at what a mistake it was for us [the government] to allow for No Fault Divorce. We don't want to make things worse!"
[7] I chose to use the term "Great-Grandma" as a simplifying expression to help show the dramatic changes to marriage just between the time of the oldest living

generation (who now have at least one great-grand child) and those now in their early 20s who are marrying for the first time.

Chapter Two

[8] The following is to be understood as an attempt to get a general grasp on the *prevailing attitudes* of the time period in question, as opposed to making any claim as to what everyone actually did as individuals.

[9] Even today, the term "virgin" is only awkwardly applied to *men* who've not yet had sexual intercourse.

[10] It would have been quite scandalous at this time for a widow or a divorcée to wear a white dress—especially with a veil—to her second or any subsequent wedding ceremony, so deeply ingrained was the tradition that the wedding garments were to signal the virginity—or lack thereof—of the bride to be.

[11] Recall the biblical story of Joseph who after getting engaged to Jesus' mother decided to quietly break off the engagement upon learning that she had become pregnant. The faithful are told that his initial decision was because he had not yet had sex with Mary, but being a nice guy, he didn't want to subject her to the harsh penalties awaiting *women* caught having pre-marital sex. But it is also quite possible *that it was Joseph* who had gotten her pregnant, and that he had seriously contemplated leaving her for fear of what social repercussions there would be *for him* once the word got out that he was willing to be married to a woman who had failed to resist *his own* advances.

[12] The Church did much to perpetuate the belief that mere thoughts of sexual desire were condemned by Christ, often citing the Gospel account of Jesus' hyperbolic criticism of the Pharisee's condescension toward adulterers, "But I say unto you, that whosoever looks on a woman to lust after her hath committed adultery with her already in his heart." Matthew 5:28

[13] Difficult as the Church and society made it for American women to enjoy sex at this time, their dilemma was nothing to compare with that of women in other countries, even until today. Female "circumcision" or more correctly, the mutilation of the female clitoris—usually right after they attain puberty—is still a common practice in northern Africa, in order to physically prevent women from enjoying sex, and therefore "less likely to betray their husbands."

[14] In fact, most all states at this time (and a few remaining ones today) forcibly regarded couples as lawfully married under "common law" provisions after living together for a certain period of time, in some cases, for as little as a few weeks.

Chapter Three

[15] The connection between this term for "farmer" and what is now the most commonplace term for a married man will soon be explained.
[16] There were some exceptions. A few men did some of the gathering and a few women went out to hunt, but as a rule, hunting was primarily a male task, and gathering, a female's.
[17] Wells, pp. 148-150.
[18] Harris, Marvin. *Our Kind* (New York: Harper Perennial, 1989), pp. 324-326.
[19] Harris, pp. 324-326.
[20] It was this very same mindset that allowed early American colonist Peter Minuit to purchase Manhattan Island in 1626 from the Iroquois Indians for about $24 worth of beads!
[21] One of the Old Testament laws specifically prohibits moving a boundary marker in Deuteronomy 19: 17, and in Chapter 27:17, a curse is pronounced on anyone who violates this commandment.
[22] Of course, paternity had always been a big issue from the perspective of the unconscious male reproductive strategy. It was at this point in human history, though, when men became *consciously* focused on passing on their seed.
[23] The concept of a father/owner having complete control over his children, as a master over a slave, survived well into the Common Era as is clear from the apostle Paul's advice to Corinthian father/owners: "… he that standeth stedfast in his heart, having no necessity, but hath power over his own will, and hath so decreed in his heart that he will keep his virgin [daughter], doeth well. So he that giveth her in marriage doeth well; but he that giveth her not in marriage doeth better." I Corinthians 7:37-38. Notice that it was up to what the *father* decreed in *his* heart, not the daughter's, as to whether he *kept* her or sold her off.
[24] Similar but simpler procedures were used to sell other females in the household such as slave girls. But since they were not as valuable, in that they were not to become the mothers of land heirs, their sale prices were lower and the procedures to trade them were accompanied by little to no fanfare.
[25] As with any other domesticated animal, a hole was often bored into the nose of women for a ring to which a leash could be tied and she could be led about by her respective owner. In time, the metal the ring was made of, and the body part to which it was placed has changed, but the meaning of a ring signifying sexual ownership has continued to the present day.
[26] To our modern ears, it may seem strange that certifying virginity was the only sure fire way to insure paternity, but even as this work was being written, a Nige-

rian widow, accused of having committed adultery—by virtue of the fact that she was pregnant outside of marriage—was recently acquitted by the Islamic judges of her village. Why? They reasoned on the basis some passages in the Koran, that there was a possibility she could have become pregnant *years* earlier when she was still with her husband. Likewise, the ancients had no way of being sure that a man's semen could not lie dormant within a woman's womb in the same manner that plant seeds could remain fertile for years before being planted in the ground.

[27] Centuries later, especially in the parts of the British Isles where Celtic peoples had settled, this part of the rite evolved into "fasting" or tying a cord around one hand each of both the woman and the man, as a way of announcing their intention to temporarily cohabit in a sexual union, and which gave rise to the term "hand fasting."

[28] Drunkenness was, as it still happens today, a common part of marriage transactions, and a brand new owner might not later clearly recall what happened when he first had his way with his new purchase. If later, he was tempted to call into question the virginity of his bride, the seller/father could produce the cloth and summon the witnesses, not so much to protect the reputation of the girl's chastity, but *his* reputation as an honest businessman.

[29] Later, however, these restraints morphed into symbolic items designating sexual ownership, down to the modern symbols of gold and silver necklaces, bracelets and rings. Perhaps, even earrings were first conceived as a means of tagging a female's ear with her owner's name, not unlike the way cattle are still ear tagged today.

[30] These practices went on for so long, that deep, emotional conditioning set in, connecting the use of restraints and painful punishments to sex. The connection between restraint and pain with sexual arousal may have worked its way into the human Collective Unconscious, ultimately leading to the modern practice of sadomasochism, which not too surprisingly, includes much use of leather and metal restraints, as well as scourges made of the same.

[31] We will address this phenomenon in detail in a later chapter.

[32] *Myth of Monogamy, p. 136.*

[33] Numbers 5:11-31

[34] Recall the scene in the movie *Braveheart* where an English baron could have his way with the bride of any of his surfs according to the practice of *prima nocte* though certain death would await any surf who might have sex with a baron's wife, regardless of her consent.

[35] Recall the famous New Testament story of the confrontation between Jesus and the angry crowd who had brought a "woman caught in the very act of adul-

tery." The crowd was fully prepared to stone *her* to death, but there's not even a word in the story mentioning the man with whom she was caught, much less whether he was subject to any punishment whatsoever.

[36] Sometimes, a wife who was barren would "have a child by" a concubine or slave, the original surrogate mothering service. In fact, Sarai, the wife of Abraham had her first "son" in just this manner. Genesis 16:2.

[37] Consistent with this trend, the Old Testament proclaimed the cursed state of all illegitimate children in Deuteronomy 23:2: "A bastard shall not enter into the congregation of the LORD; even to his tenth generation shall he not enter into the congregation of the LORD."

[38] Of course, it was no *moral* problem for *Jacob* to have more than one wife. He just didn't have the ready cash to purchase whom he wanted.

[39] Bear in mind that the average age of entering puberty for women has gone down dramatically in the last century or two. Before, girls tended not to have their first period until their middle teens. Most medical experts agree that our modern diet, which is so high in protein and fat, is the root cause for girls—as young as 10, and sometimes even earlier—already entering puberty.

[40] Unlike all other female mammals—whose breasts only enlarge after they become pregnant and while suckling young—the unusual phenomenon of human females having *permanently* protruding breasts may have been encouraged by Natural Selection as a mimicking action designed to fool males into being more attracted to women who appeared to have given birth when they had not necessarily ever gotten pregnant before.

[41] Recall that less than two centuries ago, right here in the good 'ol USA, slavery was still legal, and there were more than a few plantation masters who saw themselves as having a "God-given responsibility to take good care of their Negro slaves who would be completely at a loss without them."

[42] I Samuel 28:15

[43] The recent Stephen Spielberg movie *Saving Private Ryan* demonstrates how a remnant of this concept has survived even into modern times, as so much effort was made to prevent the loss of a last surviving male so he could "carry on the family name" as none of his other brothers were left alive to do so.

[44] It's rather amusing to hear some preachers attempt to equate these passages of the Mesopotamian afterlife with the Hell of Christianity. Many a first time (and intellectually honest) Christian reader of the Old Testament is usually quite baffled by the fact that there's no mention of the faithful getting to go to Heaven after they die, but only "going to rest with their fathers."

[45] Bernhard Lang and Colleen McDannell, *Heaven, a History*, Vintage Books, New York, 1990, pp. 2–7. Even in modern times, a funeral ceremony is often concluded with "may he/she rest in peace," which really makes no sense if one really believes that the soul of the recently departed is actively conscious in a Heaven or a Hell.

[46] Job 1:6-11

[47] Genesis 13:16

[48] Of course, a virgin woman doesn't always bleed the first time she has sex. She might have ruptured her hymen beforehand in some accident or it might be that her hymen is elastic enough that penetration doesn't break it. For women of the Agricultural Era, such a physical irregularity, sadly, often resulted in her being outcast, brutally punished or even put to death.

[49] During a visit to Sicily in 1976, I learned of an ongoing tradition of married women who kept a "nuptial blanket" from their wedding night (usually discreetly stored in a box somewhere in the back of their wardrobe cabinets) just in case their was ever any question about their virginity and a need to prove that on their wedding night they had been *fresca dalla mama,* "fresh out of her mother!"

[50] I Samuel 18:25.

[51] The hiding period after abducting a woman in this manner is thought to be the origin of the "honeymoon" tradition, because it normally lasted for a moon, or a month, long enough for her to ovulate. The "honey" is perhaps a reference to the mead (wine made from honey) which he made her drink in order to make her more receptive to his advances. The Best Man tradition originated with the abductor's best, male friend who assisted him directly or acted as a look out during the abduction and to warn of any search parties while he was in hiding with her. Carrying the bride over the threshold is now a symbol for the abducting male who literally carried a woman away from her home to the hideaway where he would take her virginity.

[52] Deuteronomy 22:29.

[53] Ruth 4:5.

[54] Three of the Gospels (Matthew 22:23-33; Mark 12:18-27; Luke 20:27-38) relate the story of a woman who was married to each of seven brothers as they all died, one by one. The reason each succeeding brother married his sister-in-law was, we're told, to "raise up seed" to his late brother who had died childless.

[55] The only other biblical tradition that suggests Jesus supported the institution of marriage was the story of Jesus turning water into wine at the wedding in Cana. "Why else would Jesus have gone to the wedding if he didn't believe in marriage?" is the typical argument made. Of course, we need only ask ourselves

how many times we ourselves have attended weddings only out of a sense of social obligation to call this logic into question.

[56] "To put away" was just another way of saying "to divorce," not to be confused with the modern slang expressions meaning "to murder" or "to institutionalize."

[57] Of course, none of this is to say that Jesus would advocate the same teaching today. What is today called "marriage" is about as similar to what it was in his day, as slavery is to blue collar labor. Just as southern plantation owners tried to justify African slavery on the basis of Paul's admonition to slaves to obey their masters, so too have some modern Christian sects and a few small denominations tried to teach that Jesus' ban against putting away and replacing a female sex slave be equated to a ban against divorce and remarriage.

[58] Ephesians 5:23, 33

[59] Colossians 3:19

[60] I Peter 3:1, 7

[61] Deuteronomy 6:5

[62] For those who may, with good reason, regard the Bible stories of the patriarchs as mythical tales, the reason for reviewing them here is not to comment on their historical accuracy, but to look for insights into the cultural lessons they were intended to convey. In other words, there may never have been a historical Jacob, but the stories told about him centuries later tell us a great deal about the beliefs and practices of this time period, and for this reason alone, are very helpful to this thesis.

[63] Chapter 28:9 says that Onan "went in unto her [Tamar], but spilled his seed upon the ground." Believe it or not, this is the only place in the Christian Bible that comes anywhere close to the subject of masturbation, and because the text claims that God struck him down for this action, many a Christian teacher has argued that this passage is proof that God regards masturbation a sin. But clearly, the context makes no such case. The point of the story is that God was punishing Onan—*not* for getting a little sexual jolly apart from an honest attempt to conceive a child—but for refusing to help out his not-so-dearly departed brother to have an heir.

[64] It might be difficult on our modern ears to read this without getting stuck on the idea of a young teenager getting an "older woman" (though Tamar was likely only in her late teens at the most) for a wife. But again, had Judah given Tamar to his young son, it would have been for reasons of property and inheritance, not love or sexual compatibility.

[65] Then as now, certain roadsides and cross roads were typical locations for prostitutes to conduct their business.

[66] Again, being the mother of an heir, while still a very subservient position, was relatively much better than being the displaced, non-virgin who'd been returned to her father's house. As property, being sent back like this was somewhat akin to being one of the returned items at a department store customer service desk. You might eventually be re-sold "as is," and at a much lower price, put you're regarded as a "damaged good" (oddly enough, an expression that is still sometimes used to describe a young woman who is not a virgin by her wedding day).
[67] Clearly, land ownership and animal domestication went hand-in-hand with the double standard between men and women for the toleration of infidelity. That said, it should also be noted that humankind was predisposed to such behavior by evolutionary forces long before. The mere fact that women were always certain which children belong to them and that men could never be *absolutely* sure, resulted in Natural Selection favoring any male tendency, like sexual possessiveness, to ensure their paternity. The Agricultural Revolution, therefore, merely took what Barash and Lipton call a "biological molehill" and "exaggerated it into a mountain." *Myth of Monogamy*, p. 153.
[68] A famous Cynical parable relates the story of a teacher who had given up almost all possessions with the exception of a cloak, a staff and a cup. Then one day as he was about to dip his cup in a pool of water to get a drink, he noticed a boy who had come to drink by only cupping his hands. Realizing what a "fool" he'd been for having been "so attached" to the cup, he promptly smashed it on the ground! Seneca, *Epistulae Morales*, 90.14-16; Basore et al. 5.402-405.
[69] John Dominic Crossan, *The Historical Jesus, The Life of a Mediterranean Jewish Peasant*, (New York: HarperCollins, 1992) p. 421.
[70] Of course, we can't be absolutely certain if any of the oldest surviving Greek texts that make up the New Testament are really accurate renditions of Jesus actual teachings. All we now have are copies of copies of copies of the original texts that were first penned long after Jesus and the original disciples were dead—plenty of time to get things turned around. But for the purposes of this study, it doesn't matter whether the Christian Bible contains Jesus' actual words or vignettes originated by someone else that were later attributed to him. We are interested in these texts for the value they represent in having been used to shape Western culture.
[71] 1 Corinthians 7:1-9
[72] Plato had expanded on the philosophy of Cynicism by essentially denying the "reality" of material existence altogether. Only ideas were "real" because they never changed, died or could be destroyed. The often cited metaphor of this teaching was the reflection of the flames of a fire against a wall, which to Pla-

tonists, represented the phenomenal world, and the actual flames, the world of ideas, to which they owed their illusionary existence. By the time of Augustine, the Christian Neo Platonists had substituted the spirit world for the world of ideas, but otherwise agreed with their Pagan cousins, looking upon carnal existence as a prison, during which the soul of man longed to be freed from its passions.

[73] It has been estimated that the Church of the Middle Ages had reduced the number of days during which sex was permissible down to a total of 90 days out of the year! Laura Betzig, *Darwinian Approaches to the Past* (New York: Plenum, 1992).

[74] For example, the fact that it generally takes women much longer to become sexually stimulated is one such factor.

[75] Incidentally, this is precisely the same argument used by marriage advocates to try to get around admitting that marriage is a legal constraint. Just because some can be persuaded to voluntarily enter bondage, whether as a plantation slave or a spouse, doesn't make it morally right to allow for either practice under secular law.

[76] "Privatizing marriage" is not to be confused with prohibiting churches from performing marriage ceremonies in any way they see fit, for whomever they believe is qualified for marriage in their respective churches. On the contrary, privatization refers only to removing the *government's* role in licensing and regulating the choices of sexual partnerships by mutually consenting and informed adults. Marriage would then be limited to a private, religious rite, a choice that would remain entirely the prerogative of any church and its adherents, to carry on in any manner they wish or wish not. More about this topic will be discussed in a later chapter.

[77] In contrast to today, where marriage records are maintained in local government archives, it used to be the Church where all documentation of marriages was kept.

[78] The Church's use of the term "annulment," was for all practical purposes a divorce, but it provided a convenient way of paying lip service to the teaching of Jesus against divorce.

[79] "What Luther Says" CPH 1959, Vol. II, p. 885.

[80] By the time the United States Constitution was ratified in 1789 and State Churches were no more, American marriages had already become a dual process, where a license from the state had to be obtained in addition to arrangements for a ceremony that could either be performed by a civil servant (the proverbial Justice of the Peace, for example) or an ordained minister.

Chapter Four

[81] In fact, forcing couples to stay together—by strong Church pressure "not to break marriage vows" and by the threat of costly divorce attorneys' fees and unpredictable court judgments—has many adverse consequences. These include domestic violence, chemical abuse, sexual abuse, depression, financial irresponsibility and neglect.

[82] National Center for Health Statistics, *Monthly Vital Statistics Report*, Vol. 38, No. 12 (S) 2, May 21, 1991.

[83] Radical Christian Fundamentalists get around answering this question by denying the validity of the wealth of scientific evidence that proves hominid species have existed for millions of years in favor of a belief that the creation myths in the Book of Genesis are to be taken literally—and thus claiming that *Homo sapiens* has existed for little more than 6000 years.

[84] Harris, pp. 174-178.

[85] The very physical construction of the human sexual organs are proof they were not adapted merely for procreation. The large size of the male phallus (compared to the pencil size typical of most apes), and the concentration of nerve endings around the female vagina, particularly by the clitoris, are specifically adapted to facilitate the maximum amount of pleasure sensations during sexual intercourse, and they can be stimulated to orgasm regardless of whether the female has an egg ready to be fertilized or not.

[86] Prostitutes, for example, are often said to put themselves into an "emotional shell" while conducting their business so that they don't become emotionally attached to any of their regular customers. Most will limit the kinds of positions they will perform in, and (unlike what is often falsely portrayed in movies) rarely will they kiss, hug or engage in other forms of physical affection, in order to make it as unlikely as possible to fall in love while having sex.

[87] The common expression "Love 'em, and leave 'em!" is the credo of men who wish only to have sex in the form of one night stands in order to avoid emotional entanglements, which is rather revealing, in that the credo clearly implies that having repeated sexual encounters with the same person is likely to lead to such attachments.

[88] Helen Fisher, *Anatomy of Love: The Mysteries of Mating, Marriage, and Why We Stray* (New York: Fawcett Columbine, 1992) pp. 162-164.

[89] This phenomenon was dramatized in the classic book and movie *A Clockwork Orange* in which a young criminal was subjected to a process of conditioning that made him extremely nauseous any time he even thought about committing an act

of violence rendering him incapable of acting out such thoughts. Ironically though, the violent films he was constrained to watch while he was being injected with nausea-causing drugs by coincidence had Beethoven musical scores. So upon release, the young man also became ill each time he heard the same music as well as when he was tempted to hurt someone.

[90] As this work was being written, a fiery debate raged in the media after President Bush's 2004 re-election campaign aired some TV ads depicting images of the September 11th terrorist attacks. The ads clearly represented an attempt on the part of the campaign to create an emotional association between the sense of unity and loyalty to country that followed the attacks with Bush's presidency in the hopes of winning potential voters.

[91] Helen Fisher, *Why We Love, The Nature and Chemistry of Romantic Love*, (New York: Henry Holt and Co., 2004) pp. 88-93.

[92] Page 78.

[93] Unfortunately, most Hunting and Gathering cultures around the world have been systematically destroyed by the colonizing nations of Europe in the last four centuries.

[94] Again, let's recall that he Bible reinforced the harsh sexual regulations put upon women that followed the Agricultural Revolution by permanently stigmatizing children born out of wedlock—"A bastard shall not enter into the congregation of the LORD—Deuteronomy 23:2.

[95] We're all familiar with the expression "it takes an entire village to raise a child," and such communal child rearing was even more commonplace when "villages" were always on the go.

[96] See also the comprehensive study by David Buss and his colleagues (Buss, D.M. [1989] Differences in mate preferences: Evolutionary hypotheses tested in 37 different cultures. *Behavior and Brain Sciences 12: 1-49)* which provided an overview of human mate preferences from 10,047 individuals between the ages of 14 and 70 living in 37 different modern cultures.

[97] Yu, DW and GH Shepard, *Is Beauty in the Eye of the Beholder?* Nature 1998; 396:321–322. Devendra Singh, Discover Magazine, *In the Eye of the Beholder*, aired March 12, 2005.

[98] We can only hope that the knowledge available to us now from scientific research can at least help all of us to become more understanding of young teenagers' dilemma, and to accommodate their instinctive needs and desires as much as possible in our modern society. If not, we're bound to find ourselves spending an ever increasing amount of time and resources battling in futility to suppress instincts which took millions of years of evolution to develop. Perhaps, at least,

we can be a little more tolerant of teens who are sexually active with each other, and find practical ways to help them adjust to the changes and urges they're experiencing rather than to condemn those who finally engage in sex with others their own age as if they are somehow committing a crime.

[99] An entire new field of science has recently been opened, called *neuraesthetics* by a University of London professor, Scour Zeki, which looks to understand the relationships between human evolution and "hard wired" or innate predispositions to regard certain features "beautiful." Ian Hoffman, "Scientists Ponder Beauty and the Eye of the Beholder," *Oakland Tribune*, March 11, 2004, http://www.sigidaiart.com/Docs/beauty.htm.

[100] In fact, it's been well documented that what we now call "adolescence," the lag time in emotional and mental maturity after the onset of physical adulthood or puberty, was unheard of until about 200 years ago when the Industrial Revolution began to force the need to prolong childhood education and teenagers' dependency on parents. In fact, younger women at this time were thought to be so much more mature that there were some states that permitted girls as young as 12 to legally marry well into the late 1800s.

[101] Those who recoil at the widespread "unnatural" efforts modern women employ to look younger and prettier, might want to reconsider their stance. Even Nature has gone to some trouble to augment women's appearance by adding fat to women's breasts and buttocks that isn't directly related to a greater capacity to breast feed or give birth respectively. Why? Simply because larger breasts and a small waist-to-hip ratio make women *look like* they can better reproduce.

[102] Wells, p. 178.

[103] *Myth of Monogamy*, p. 174.

[104] While living and traveling in southern Italy in the mid 1970s, I learned that many housewives were quite aware that their husbands frequented prostitutes, but were nevertheless unalarmed about it. When I inquired *what would* make them jealous, most answered they would only feel threatened if their husband were to have a love affair with a single woman. In other words, someone whom he might conceivably run off with.

[105] Fisher, pp. 128-131.

[106] P. 169.

[107] Harris, pp. 324-326.

[108] Not all experts agree on this point. Some, in fact, would say that territoriality was the result, not the cause, of sexual possessiveness. Within this view, the notion of generally owning an area where one's mate nested was merely an evolutionary expansion of the genetic tendency to regard a mate as one's own. For the

purposes of this study, it suffices to say that some genetic predetermination, whether territorial to mate possession or vice versa, seems to have laid the groundwork for eventual, full-fledged commoditization of women.

[109] Fisher, pp. 114–117.

[110] For modern mothers, the math here may seem to be a little off, since very few children in modern times are breast fed more than a year. But it's not at all uncommon for children in tribal societies to be breast fed until they are 3, 4 and even 5 years old.

[111] Of course, open approval for a man to lust for one's wife is a very recent development that Fundamentalist Christians have only in the last few decades turned to as a way of responding to the challenges of the Sexual Revolution. Prior to the Sexual Revolution, most Christians defined *all* sexual attraction as "sinful lust" even though the Bible declares that "marriage is honorable in all and the [married couple's] bed is undefiled." Until the 1970s, there was a kind of mass denial among Christians when it came to sexual desire within marriage. Although most everyone knew privately that men and women, even in a sanctioned sexual union sought to fulfill their sexual "lusts," they were compelled, at least superficially, to behave as if no such thing existed. Even men, in polite company, had to pretend that having sex with one's spouse was only for the purpose of bringing a child into the world.

[112] Matt Ridley, *The Red Queen, Sex and the Evolution of Human Nature*, First Perennial Edition (New York: Harper Collins) 2003, pp. 71-79.

[113] Fisher, p. 169.

[114] Actually, many scientists believe we are still in "the" Ice Age, because this period in Earth's history is really composed of a series of many surges toward a colder climate divided by lulls of warmer periods. The present period could very well be just another one of these warm lulls since the last cold surge about 15,000 years ago.

[115] US Census Bureau

[116] Wells, pp. 130-132.

[117] Fisher, pp. 112–114.

Chapter Five

[118] A term commonly used to designate the broad popularity and record breaking sales of albums and singles by British rock-and-roll groups like The Beatles, The Rolling Stones and The Who. Many of these bands were popularized by appearances on a Sunday evening variety TV program that was watched by anywhere

from 30% to 40% of Americans throughout the mid to late 60s—*The Ed Sullivan Show.*

[119] George Marsden, *Understanding Fundamentalism and Evangelicalism* (Grand Rapids, Michigan: Eerdmans, 1991) pp. 26-27.

[120] Not much is left of the original "saved and sanctified" denominations (well known for their very stringent rules against women wearing revealing clothing, make up, cutting their hair, etc.). Except for the Nazarene Church, most of its members left to join the Pentecostal Movement of the early 20th Century, taking their strict codes with them.

[121] Marsden, pp. 51-52.

[122] The notion of a "rapture" was quickly adopted by the Fundamentalists, just a few decades after it had first been promoted by a Brethren evangelist named John Darby in the late 1800s. The new interpretation claimed that Christ would return *two* more times instead of once more. In the second return, Christ would "rapture" or beam up (not unlike the transporter machine of Star Trek fame) all "true believers," and after 7 years of a "tribulation period"—during which God would pour out numerous punishments upon the unbelieving world—Christ would return a third and final time to conquer all evil and begin a thousand year reign on earth.

[123] Marsden, pp. 55-56.

[124] One need only compare the church hymns of the late 19th Century to those more popular in churches today to see a big difference. Songs focused on material relief in the afterlife from hunger and homelessness, like "I've Got a Mansion Over the Hilltop," have given way to a new host of songs holding out the promise of immediate rewards—inner peace, love, friendship, etc.

[125] As many women of the 60s soon found out, they were not as naturally suited to having a variety of sexual partners as men are. Once society began to tolerate women making their own decisions about how many partners they wanted, it slowly but surely became clear that even when they were having sex with one man after another, they were instinctively still looking for The One, and their ostensible promiscuity was but a mere sorting process.

[126] I recall seeing a James Bond movie in the late 60s where 007, clothed only in a towel, gets in a shower stall with a woman and begins making love. The glass walls were translucent, and the camera revealed only Bond's bare back as the towel fell to the shower floor while the two began to embrace. Such a "sex scene" would have been impossible only a year or two before, and though no "private parts" were shown, the far more remarkable aspect was the characters' unabashed and unashamed attitude demonstrated before and afterwards. Sex for pleasure's

sake alone—at least by single people who were not dating steadily, engaged or married—had become tolerable.

[127] We must understand that the terms "conservative" or "liberal," as used here, are relative to the upbringing of the children in question. This phenomenon was exemplified on a popular TV program of the 80s called *Family Ties*, where actor Michael J. Fox played a character who was a hard core, teenage Republican child of an older, liberal-minded ex-hippie couple.

[128] Some evangelicals have even gone so far as to say that the "fiery torment" of Hell is only a metaphor of the "tormenting knowledge" that there's no hope of ever having their relationship with God restored. In any case, the *overt* appeal of a positive gospel—while retaining the *covert* threat of eternal punishment—has proven far more effective than "fire and brimstone" preaching.

[129] Grand Rapids, Michigan: Zondervan.

Chapter Six

[130] One good example is the Lady of Guadalupe, a revered image of Mary, the mother of Jesus, by many Hispanics of the American Southwest. The original pagan deity worshipped by the natives of present day Mexico was named Tonanzin, whose shrine was located in the exact same place where the Christian shrine dedicated to her reinterpretation as Mary, is located.

[131] As will be elaborated on in a later chapter, it is for this very reason that I highly recommend that couples who intend to make a home together, but who wish not to marry, hold if they can some form of a ceremony that affirms their relationship, preferably at or soon after the couple moves into a home of their own. They should, however, first consult with a family law attorney in their state to make sure that they avoid inadvertently becoming married by common law statutes which might regard *any* ceremony affirming or recognizing their union as a civil marriage.

[132] Think of how often we drive our cars, for miles, while our minds are completely preoccupied with other thoughts. Part of our brain can be quite busy with certain active thoughts, while another part of our brain—the one that has learned a habit of driving—is also very busy, keeping the car in its proper lane, stopping at red lights, and hopefully, staying within the speed limits … but with no conscious direction. As long as nothing unusual happens, such as sudden stop by the vehicle ahead, the "auto pilot" part of the mind is perfectly capable of handling the task.

[133] According to The National Association of Certified Wedding Coordinators, the nationwide average was even higher: $22,360.03.

[134] *The Dallas Morning News.* "No Time to Split," August 8, 2005, p. 13A. In 2000, data from the US Census Bureau, National Center for Health Statistics, estimated the average cost of a divorce as $15,000. per divorcee or $30,000 per divorce.
[135] Estimate based on US Census Report of 1,163,000 divorces granted nationwide in 1997.
[136] Unfortunately, those who've never actually been involved in a divorce proceeding are often tempted to think they can come out better. This is evident by the efforts of gay/lesbian rights groups who are battling for the "right to marry." In a recent decision by a Superior Court judge in San Francisco in which registered domestic partners' "rights and responsibilities" were upheld as legal after a radical religious group calling itself "Campaign for California Families" had challenged the provisions, Jon Davidson of Lambda Legal Defense and Education Fund, a Gay rights group, said that beginning next year, gay couples "will [finally] have access to family courts for dividing their assets if they split up …," as if to say that "having access to family courts" is a good thing! Associate Press, *Domestic Partner Law Upheld, Benefits and Responsibilities of Married Spouses,"* Thursday, Sept. 9, 2004.
[137] While there are some rare occasions when one spouse ends up paying the fees of both attorneys, usually each one ends up paying for their own representation. But this doesn't stop many lawyers from over-exaggerating the likelihood of getting such an order in a final decree.
[138] Law Center *Parents Seek Custody Law Reform*, CNN, Friday, October 8, 2004, AP, www.cnn.com/2004/law/10/08/custody.rights.ap/index.html.
[139] Krauth, p. 4.
[140] Such prevented a lot of feuding, but of course, every now and then, they erupted anyway, and sometimes with wars ensuing! Homer's Illiad, the Arthurian Tales and Shakespear's Hamlet are just a few of the many epic stories which dramatized the phenomenon of disputes over women leading to violence and war.
[141] Ironically, the writer of Revelations, the last book of the New Testament, had a vision in which Christ addresses this very issue, using the metaphor of a drinkable beverage—"I know thy works, that thou art neither cold nor hot: I would thou wert cold or hot. So then because thou art lukewarm, and neither cold nor hot, I will spew thee out of my mouth." Revelation 3:15-16. Being "cold" is to not believe at all. Being "hot" is to truly believe, to have a strong conviction. However, being "lukewarm" is not acceptable because it represents having a weak conviction.

[142] British Broadcasting Network, "1988: TV Evangelist Quits Over S Scandal," http://news.bbc.co.uk/onthisday/hi/dates/stories/february/21/newsid_2565000/2565197.stm.

[143] In fact, an excavation in 1961 at one of the oldest known Neolithic villages located in Catal Huyak, in Southern Turkey, recovered 33 statues of female deities shown to be giving birth or having exaggerated vulvas, breasts and hips. Only 8 statues of male deities were found which is thought to be an indication of how much Pre-Agricultural Era humans highly regarded the female's status as life giver.

[144] Of course, the movement to use midwives and to give birth at home has tempered this rather antiseptic interpretation of giving birth, and returned a bit of the sacredness to the experience it had once upon a time.

[145] This brings to mind a story about my grandmother who was very fond of a daytime game show called *Queen for a Day*. Apparently, it was a very popular program for housewives of the early 50s, for what woman—if she can't actually be a princess or queen, wouldn't want to vicariously enjoy the experience through other "everyday" women who were brought on as contestants, and got to wear the crown, at least for one day?

[146] I make this point only to show the hypocrisy of condemning *any* sexual behavior between consenting adults. While I'm not a proponent of prostitution, I believe it should be legalized and regulated for reasons of privacy, health, safety, and fair taxation purposes.

Chapter Seven

[147] Some pro-marriage advocates cite surveys where substantial percentages of married people report "being happy," but these surveys often fail to take into account the lowered expectations many people have about being married. This was particularly the case in the 40s when "having a happy marriage" meant that a husband had a steady job and didn't beat his wife.

[148] Matthew 5:33-37.

[149] Again, some claim that Jesus must have endorsed marriage because the New Testament records that he attended a wedding in a small town called Cana, the same place where he is said to have turned water into wine. But this logic is false. Attending a wedding is not necessarily the same as endorsing the marriage institution, no more than turning water into wine is necessarily an endorsement of drunk driving.

Chapter Eight

[150] Pope, Rocky. Senior Pastor of Mimosa Lane Baptist Church, in Mesquite, Texas, letter-styled pamphlet advertising "Successful Family Weekend", October 22, 2003.
[151] Page 1.
[152] Wu, L.L. (1996). *Effects of family instability, income, and income instability on the risk of premarital birth.* American Sociological Review, 61, 386-406.
[153] Blankenhorn, David, *Fatherless America: Confronting Our Most Urgent Problem*, (1996).
[154] Akers, Paul, "Deadbeat Dads, Meet You Counterpart—Walkaway Wives," *The American Enterprise*, May/June 1996.
[155] Ibid.
[156] *Fatherless America.*
[157] Perhaps, we should look to the male's fundamental, sexual drives and resulting strategies as a better explanation for cheating than a lack of personal morality. Very few enter marriage with the intent of setting aside their vows at a later point in time, but without a clear understanding as to our true, sexual nature, it's quite unnatural for men to, happily, stay faithful.

Chapter Nine

[158] A complete rendition of The Love Celebration is included in Appendix II.

Chapter Ten

[159] See, Piel v. Brown, 361 So. 2d 90, 93 (Ala. 1978); Deter v. Deter, 484 P. 2d 805, 806 (Colo. Ct. App. 1971); Johnson v. Young, 372 A.2d 992, 994 (D.C. 1977); Smith v. Smith, 161 Kan. 1, 3, 165 P. 2d 593, 594 (1946); Sardonis v. Sardonis, 106 R.I. 469, 472, 261 A.2d 22, 23 (1970); Johnson v. Johnson, 235 S.C. 542, 550, 112 S.E.2d 647, 651 (1960); IOWA CODE ANN. §. 595.11 (West 1981); MONT. CODE ANN. § 26-1-602, 40-1-403 (1985); OKLA.STAT. ANN. tit. 43, § 1 (West 1979); TEX. FAM. CODE ANN. § 191 (Vernon 1975).
[160] See, e.g., CAL. CIV. CODE § 4100 (West 1983); N.Y. DOM. REL. LAW § 11 (McKinney 1988 & Supp. 1992); Furth v. Furth, 133 S.W. 1037, 1038-39 (Ark. 1911); Owens v. Bentley, 14 A.2d 391, 393 (Del. Super. 1940); Milford v. Worcester, 7 Mass. 48 (1910); Ira M. Ellman et al., Family Law: Cases, Text, and Problems 21 (1986).
[161] The complete text of Mr. Boaz' article is in Appendix I.

[162] Kinsley, Michael, "Abolish Marriage, Let's Really Get the Government Out of Our Bedrooms," *Slate*, July 2, 2003.
[163] Dayton, US Senator Mark, "Floor Statement on S.J. Res. 40, The Marriage Constitutional Amendment," www.markdayon.org/blog/display-one.html?id=45, (July 13, 2004).
[164] As this book was first being written, a videotaped interview with the lesbian, domestic partner of comedian, show host and former magazine editor, Rosie O'Donnell, was forcibly entered as court evidence by attorneys for magazine publishers Gruner and Jahr who had sued Rosie for allegedly breaching a contract in September of 2002. Had Ms. O'Donnell's lover been a male spouse, her testimony would not have been allowed in as evidence in accordance with centuries of court precedence that married couples should never have to testify one against another, except in divorce court.

Chapter Eleven

[165] Of course, there have been many entire species that have gone extinct for lack of developing more adaptive traits, sexual or otherwise. Competition, then, not only plays an *intra*-species role, which rewards some individuals and punishes others with reproductive success, but an *inter*-species one as well. In this broader sense, we can think of entire species as winners and losers.
[166] Keep in mind that by "attractive," I mean those male qualities which arouse attraction within the female which are characteristics much more complex than merely looking physically attractive.
[167] The apparent inconsistency of having multiple sexual partners and a desire to determine a single best mate is explained in more detail in a later sub chapter. But in a nutshell, I mean to say that rejecting most sexual advances serves only as a screen test. From there, a select few go on to a final "tournament round" where the "arena" of competition is a woman's vagina.
[168] It was Robert Trivers who, in 1972, is credited for having first proposed the idea that the gender which makes the bigger *investment,* in terms of making and caring for offspring, tends to seek out fewer sex partners and the gender which makes the least investment tends to see out more.
[169] *Myth of Monogamy*, p. 174.
[170] Long enough for her to have at least one ovulation no matter where she was in her menstrual cycle when they first began having intercourse.
[171] It's been demonstrated in studies of other primates that females will have more orgasms when they copulate with Alpha males than with Betas—Nature's way of rewarding them for finding a sex partner of *better quality*, pp. 176-177.

[172] We'll address the dynamics behind the defusing of female jealousy and mate guarding within harems in more detail in a later sub chapter.
[173] This point was dramatized in an episode of the HBO series *Big Love*, when the three wives of a polygamous Morman family showed no indication of jealousy until their husband began to sneak off to have extra sexual encounters with one of them. Once the extra sessions terminated, though, the other wives were once again content, no longer feeling threatened that one of their sister wives would get ahead of them, or more to the point, leave them further behind.
[174] A "pecking order" usually occurs among harem members, in which a dominant female will become the organizer of the rest—from what their household duties are to scheduling which nights each gets to sleep with the man of the house.
[175] In societies that tolerate polygyny, the odds of getting it all are tipped more in the favor of, at least, some men. In the modern, Western nations, the odds are tipped more in the favor of certain women.
[176] This phenomenon also explains why there tends to be more "fast women" in larger cities, than in smaller towns and rural areas—a greater population means a greater number of men to choose from, and therefore, a greater likelihood of needing to go to "final rounds" with more men.
[177] Of course, just as modern humans hope for a fulfilling, life-long, monogamous relationship, with only a percentage actually achieving it, likewise, most men of pre-history never had more than one, simultaneous relationship. Though a substantial one, only a minority of women succeeded in being admitted to harems. Nevertheless, harem keeping/membership was the *goal* most everyone hoped for!
[178] Had this not been a common problem for Beta husband/owners of female sex slaves, then the need for severe punishments for women who committed adultery would never have been instituted.
[179] Clellan S. Ford and Frank A. Beach, *Patterns of Sexual Behavior* (New York: Harper & Row, 1951) and George Peter Murdoch, *Social Structure* (London: MacMillan, 1949).
[180] *Myth of Monogamy* pp. 141-142.
[181] Interestingly, no sooner had Mormons begun to openly practice polygyny, did the leadership also begin to offer "annulments" to any married woman who wished to "marry up" in the church hierarchy, as long as all the concerned parties were in agreement. What is most striking about this policy is, not so much the apparent convenience it offered to men of high ecclesiastical rank, but the fact

that Mormon women were so eager to go along with it! *Mormon Polygamy*, pp. 45-48.

[182] One has to wonder if Mohammed had figured this out as well when he decreed that no man may ever have more than 4 wives at a time, and that he had to treat them all equally.

[183] This brings to mind the biblical story of Joseph who, though he was a slave, was so very appealing to his master (Potiphar)'s head wife, she accosted him and demanded, "lie with me!" Genesis 29:7-14.

[184] "Polygamy" is actually a broader term which literally means "many mates." This term could be used to designate a sexual relationship between one woman and two or more men or vice versa, one woman and two or more men. But it is most often used in reference to the former. In recent years, the more specific term to identify the practice of one male taking on two or more female mates, "polygyny," literally meaning "many women," has come to be used more frequently by experts and is the one preferred in this work.

[185] There is documentation—obtained from private letters, diaries and the like—that it was mostly first wives who struggled with jealousy under Mormon polygamy, especially if they had been married prior to their conversion or before the Church began to openly advocate the practice. However, documentation of jealousy or marital discontent from those women who accepted proposals from married men who already had at least one wife are very rare. Their contentment lends weight to the argument that sexual expectation plays a strong role in either arousing or suppressing the female instinct to become jealous. Van Wagoner, Richard S., *Mormon Polygamy, a History*, Second Edition (Salt Lake City: Signature Books, 1989) pp. 89–104.

[186] Take the first of the Ten Commandments which begins with God himself, declaring with no apology, "… thou shalt have no other gods before me … for I the Lord, thy God, am a *jealous* [emphasis by the author] God…." Exodus 20:3-5. Also, at the time this book was nearly finished, a news story prompted national attention when a jury sentenced a man to only six months in jail for having shot his wife to death when he discovered her in bed with another man. One of the jurors was reported to have found the husband's testimony, that he was "overcome with jealous rage," as convincing and that his reaction to his wife's adultery was "understandable."

[187] J. Panksepp, *Affective Neuroscience: The Foundations of Human and Animal Emotions,* (New York: Oxford University Press), 1998.

[188] It's likely no accident that rap stars often depict themselves in their videos surrounded by teams of beautiful women—a very good way to impress upon other women that they are "in demand."

[189] Elizabeth Joseph, "Creating a Dialogue: Women Talking to Women," http://www.polygamy.com/articles/templates/?a=10&z=3, May 3, 1997.

[190] In 1998, a polygynous family from Utah agreed to do a number of talk show appearances. The harem-keeper, a Tom Green, and his 5 wives all appeared. They spoke about their lifestyle in very positive terms, and the women, in spite of constant gasps from audiences, gave every indication they were happy, and felt they were better off. Unfortunately, the publicity resulted in a Utah prosecutor charging Mr. Green with 4 counts of felony charges based on a hundred year old law which defined bigamy as cohabiting with a woman while still married to another. Though Mr. Green was only technically married to the youngest of the women, he was arrested and remains in prison to this day, pending an appeal. Defense lawyers are pointing out that were the same law applied to others—like former New York mayor Rudy Giuliani who began to live with his paramour after separating from his wife—they too would be guilty of the same "crime."

Chapter Twelve

[191] It's difficult for us to detach ourselves long enough from this discussion to clearly understand the biological imperatives at work here. We are so inclined to focus purely on love—longing for love, missing those we love, etc. However unromantic it may seem, though, we must recall that "love" is really just Nature's way of keeping us together with someone for the purposes of long-term reproductive success. Even the secondary benefits of love relationships were selected by Evolution for their survival benefits, such as the way pair-bonds help solidify a community.

[192] Take for instance the priest in Victor Hugo's *Hunchback of Notre Dame* (1831) who succeeds in overtly suppressing his sexual desire for the gypsy girl Esmerelda, but who becomes so pained by the suppression that he conspires to have her falsely accused of witchcraft and attempts to have her put to death as the only means by which he, in his obsession, could be relieved of his suppressed desire.

[193] It will be interesting to see how many of those who get these Extreme Makeovers eventually end up looking poorly again, for lack of making any changes to how they feel about themselves inwardly.

[194] We could throw in the polygynous here, but polygyny is only acceptable in certain parts of the world, and even then it is only rarely the kind of polygyny where women enter and remain in harems of their own free will.
[195] The polys and the polygamous technically cross-section when there is only one male in a relationship with two or more females. However, even polys who meet this criteria tend to dislike the label "polygamous" because they associate it with the abusive practice which followed the Agricultural Revolution.
[196] The 2000 US Census reported a large increase in the number of single adults.
[197] In fact, when pay toilets (stall doors that could only be opened by inserting a dime) began to appear in rest stop facilities in the mid 1960s as a way of offsetting the cost of their upkeep, the public outrage was so loud that they were quickly replaced with plain doors.
[198] The recent movement by Fundamentalists to get teenagers to make pledges to remain abstinent until they are married together with the Bush Administration's large federal funding campaign to teach "abstinence-only sex education" has only resulted in more teens becoming sexually active at an earlier age and, of those teens who do wait longer, being unprepared to use protection from pregnancy and sexually contracted diseases when they finally break down and do have sex. Bearman, Peter S., January 2004, "Pledgers Delay Sex, But Breakers Fail to Use Contraception" *American Journal of Sociology*; Buzz Pruitt, "Sexual Activity Among Teens," *Texas A&M University*, 2005; Harry Wilson, "What's Wrong With Abstinence Education," *American Journal of Health Studies.*

Chapter Thirteen

[199] This was the theme of a charming movie called *The Butchers Wife* (1991), starring Demi Moore and Glen Davis. Moore's character is a psychic who confuses a New York butcher for her "split-apart," only to later discover that her "real" split-apart was living across the street.

Chapter Fourteen

[200] David D'Angelo, *Double Your Dating*, www.doubleyourdating.com, 2001. I *highly* recommend this ebook for men who want to improve their love lives, whether they are single or in a relationship.
[201] *Double Your Dating*, p. 48.
[202] *Austin Powers, The Spy who Shagged Me*, Director Jay Roach, 1999.
[203] I hope no one takes this comment the wrong way. Of course, our modern values look upon every child as valuable and worthy of love and care. However, Nature didn't have the luxury of such high ideals. Had genetically inferior chil-

dren been encouraged by Evolution, our entire species would have perished long before we even had the ability to think of caring for those born with any deficiencies.

[204] While many men might have trouble putting their finger on it exactly, most can tell from experience what it's like to approach a woman they find attractive, only to *feel* some kind of "wall of resistance surrounding her."

[205] Such ancient instincts date all the way back to our egg laying ancestors, long before internal fertilization evolved.

[206] Incidentally, this helps explain why spawning species, like fish, have not evolved larger brains as rapidly as those whose females must be fertilized internally. One need only compare mammal brains to fish brains to see the difference.

[207] Perhaps this accounts for the reason why pornographers often conclude their presentations with a male ejaculating onto the surface of the female's body, usually either near the lips of her vagina or the lips of her mouth. On some primitive level, these images are tapping into a very ancient sexual longing to place sperm, if not actually upon, at least as close to a female's egg(s) as possible, i.e., on the vaginal lips, or symbolically, on the facial lips.

[208] This phenomenon can also account for the fact that most romance novels are set in a foreign location and often a different time period, where the manner of speech and dress is removed from the female readers' everyday life experience.

[209] Yes, the personality of an attractive male does borderline with being arrogant. I don't advocate actually being a mean and cocky person, but it's actually quite OK to come close by being as confident with yourself as one can manage without turning into an abusive jerk.

Bibliography

Ahrons, C. *The Good Divorce*. New York: HarperPerrenial, 1994.

Akers, Paul. *"Deadbeat Dads, Meet You Counterpart—Walkaway Wives,"* The American Enterprise, (May/June 1996).

Associated Press. *"Domestic Partner Law Upheld, Benefits and Responsibilities of Married Spouses,"* (Sept. 9, 2004).

Barash, David P., Ph.D., and Judith Eve Lipton, M.D. *The Myth of Monogamy, Fidelity and Infidelity in Animals and People*. New York: W.H. Freeman and Company, 2001.

Beach, Frank A. and Clellan S. Ford. *Patterns of Sexual Behavior*. New York: Harper & Row, 1951.

Bearman, Peter S. *"Pledgers Delay Sex, But Breakers Fail to Use Contraception,"* American Journal of Sociology, (January 2004).

Betzig, Laura. *Darwinian Approaches to the Past*. New York: Plenum, 1992.

Blankenhorn, David. Fatherless America: Confronting Our Most Urgent Social Problem. New York: HarperCollins, 1996.

Crossan, John Dominic. *The Historical Jesus, The Life of a Mediterranean Jewish Peasant*. New York: HarperCollins, 1992.

Dallas Morning News, The. *No Time to Split*, August 8, 2005.

D'Angelo, David. *Double Your Dating*. www.doubleyourdating.com, (2001).

Dayton, US Senator Mark. *"Floor Statement on S.J. Res. 40, The Marriage Constitutional Amendment,"* www.markdayton.org/blog/displayone.html?id=45, (July 13, 2004).

Dumas, J., and Alain Belanger. *"Report on the demographic situation in Canada 1996: Current Demographic analysis,"* Statistics Canada, Demography Division: Ottawa, Ontario (1997).

Fisher, Helen. *Anatomy of Love: The Mysteries of Mating, Marriage, and Why We Stray.* New York: Fawcett Columbine, 1992.

Fisher, Helen. *Why We Love, The Nature and Chemistry of Romantic Love.* New York: Henry Holt and Co., 2004.

Harris, Marvin. *Our Kind.* New York: Harper Perennial, 1989.

Hoffman, Ian. *"Scientists Ponder Beauty and the Eye of the Beholder,"* Oakland Tribune, www.sigidaiart.com/Docs/beauty.htm (March 11, 2004).

Hugo, Victor. *The Hunchback of Notre Dame.* 1831.

Joseph, Elizabeth, "Creating a Dialogue: Women Talking to Women," http://www.polygamy.com/articles/templates/?a=10&z=3, May 3, 1997.

Kinsley, Michael. *"Abolish Marriage, Let's Really Get the Government Out of Our Bedrooms."* Slate. (July 2, 2003).

Krauth, MA, Laurie D. *"The Contentious Debate About No Fault Divorce: Who is Most at Risk?"* American Association for Marriage and Family Therapy, www.aamft.org/Press_Room/Press_releases/risk.asp (February 2004).

LaHaye, Tim and Beverly. *The Act of Marriage, The Beauty of Sexual Love.* Grand Rapids, Michigan: Zondervan, 1976.

Lang, Bernhard and Colleen McDannell, *Heaven, a History.* New York: Vintage Books, 1990.

Law Center. "*Parents Seek Custody Law Reform,*" CNN, AP: www.cnn.com/2004/law/10/08/custody.rights.ap/index.html, (October 8, 2004).

Lemley, Brad. *"Isn't She Lovely (Humans Tend to be Attracted to Symmetric Beauty)."* Discover, (February 2000).

Luther, Martin. Genesis Commentary. *What Luther Says.* CPH 1959, Vol. II.

Marsden, George. *Understanding Fundamentalism and Evangelicalism.* Grand Rapids, Michigan: Eerdmans, 1991.

Murdoch, George Peter. *Social Structure.* London: MacMillan, 1949.

National Center for Health Statistics, Monthly Vital Statistics Report, Vol. 38, No. 12 (S) 2, (May 21, 1991).

Panksepp, J. *Affective Neuroscience: The Foundations of Human and Animal Emotions.* New York: Oxford University Press, 1998.

Pope, Rocky. Senior Pastor, Mimosa Lane Baptist Church in Mesquite, Texas, letter-styled pamphlet: *Successful Family Weekend*, (October 22, 2003).

Pruitt, Buzz. *"Sexual Activity Among Teens,"* Texas A&M University, (2005).

Ridley, Matt. *The Red Queen, Sex and the Evolution of Human Nature.* First Perennial Edition. New York: Harper Collins, 2003.

Seneca. *Epistulae Morales.* New York: Putnam, 1925.

Shostak, Marjorie. *Nisa: The Life and Words of a!Kung Woman.* London: Penquin Books, 1981.

Simmons, Tavia and O'Connell, Martin. US Census Bureau, Census 2000 Special Reports, "*Married-Couple and Unmarried Partner Households*: 2000," (February 2003).

Singh, Devendra. "*In the Eye of the Beholder*," Discover Magazine. (2005).

Yu D.W and G.H. Shephard. "*Is Beauty in the Eye of the Beholder?*" Nature (1998).

Van Wagoner, Richard S. *Mormon Polygamy, A History.* Second Edition. Salt Lake City: Signature Books, 1989.

Wells, Spencer. *The Journey of Man, A Genetic Odyssey.* Princeton, NJ: Princeton University Press, 2002.

Wilson, Harry. *"What's Wrong With Abstinence Education,"* American Journal of Health Studies, (2004).

Wu, L.L. "Effects of family instability, income, and income instability on the risk of premarital birth." American Sociological Review. 61: 386-406 (1996).

978-0-595-43447-3
0-595-43447-9

Printed in the United States
72762LV00003B/70-114

9 780595 434473